Capitalism's Conscience

'A lively and well-researched history and critique of Britain's best newspaper, exposing the ideological contradictions and editorial tensions which generally keep the *Guardian* allied to a soft liberalism but shies away from radical or socialist answers to capitalism's recurring crises.'

—Jonathan Steele, former Chief Foreign Correspondent for the *Guardian*

'Fascinating and timely.'

—Angela McRobbie, Professor of Communications at Goldsmiths, University of London

'A page turner – reveals the liberal establishment in all its ingloriousness, sprinkled with a few moments of integrity.'

—Beverley Skeggs, Professor, Sociology, Lancaster University

Capitalism's Conscience

200 Years of the *Guardian*

Edited by Des Freedman

First published 2021 by Pluto Press
345 Archway Road, London N6 5AA

www.plutobooks.com

British Library Cataloguing in Publication Data
A catalogue record for this book is available from the British Library

ISBN 978 0 7453 4335 8 Hardback
ISBN 978 0 7453 4334 1 Paperback
ISBN 978 0 7453 4338 9 PDF
ISBN 978 0 7453 4336 5 EPUB
ISBN 978 0 7453 4337 2 Kindle

This book is printed on paper suitable for recycling and made from fully managed and sustained forest sources. Logging, pulping and manufacturing processes are expected to conform to the environmental standards of the country of origin.

Typeset by Stanford DTP Services, Northampton, England

Simultaneously printed in the United Kingdom and United States of America

Contents

Figures and Tables

FIGURES

TABLES

Introduction: 'Just the Establishment'?

Des Freedman

The *Guardian* is not a left-wing newspaper. It publishes left-wing columnists, is read by people on the left and has a reputation for identifying with left-wing positions. But it is not a title *of* the left; it is not affiliated to nor was it borne out of left-wing movements. It has never been a consistent ally of socialist or anti-imperialist voices and has failed to perform for the left what titles like the *Mail* and the *Telegraph* have done for their constituencies on the right.

Instead it is the home of a vigorous liberalism that consistently outrages voices to its right and, equally regularly, disappoints its critics on the left. If the *Economist* can be described as the 'lodestar'[1] of a certain type of laissez-faire liberalism, then the *Guardian* can be seen as the harbinger of a more progressive, socially conscious form of liberalism that combines support for existing social relations with appeals to 'enlightened' views and a 'moral conviction', in the words of its current editor Katharine Viner, that 'we are all of equal worth'.[2] This is a liberalism that can pursue equality, celebrate diversity and extol emancipation whilst simultaneously defending the institutions that give rise to inequality, discrimination and militarism. It is a liberalism that is based on a commitment to liberty that 'has provided an ideological bulwark against authoritarianism [but that] has also always been connected to the configurations of the liberal democratic capitalist state'.[3] That is why we describe it here as 'capitalism's conscience'.

In May 2021, the *Guardian* turned 200. From its inception in Manchester in 1821 as a response to the murder of ordinary people by soldiers in the 1819 Peterloo Massacre to its historic identification with centrist and centre-left politics, the *Guardian* has remained a key institution for the definition and development of liberalism. The stereotype of the 'Guardianista', an environmentally conscious,

Labour-voting, progressively minded public sector worker remains part of the popular mythology of British press history.

Yet the title has a complex lineage.

The *Guardian* advocated the abolition of slavery in the US, favoured Home Rule for Ireland, stood virtually alone in the national press in criticising the Boer War and exposing the existence of British concentration camps, backed women's suffrage, supported the Republican cause in the Spanish Civil War and opposed UK military intervention during the Suez crisis. While Friedrich Engels described it as the 'organ of the middle-class' in his *Conditions of the Working-Class in England*, he was nevertheless heavily reliant on it as a source of data for his study of poverty in nineteenth-century Manchester.[4] The *Guardian* has since published some of the most celebrated examples of investigative journalism, which in recent years include the breaking of the phone hacking story, Edward Snowden's revelations of US and UK surveillance programmes and the uncovering of the Windrush scandal in 2018.

On the other hand, the *Guardian* owes its existence to a cotton merchant determined to head off more radical ideas at the start of the Industrial Revolution. Some 40 years after its founding, it criticised Abraham Lincoln's Emancipation Proclamation and refused to back Manchester cotton workers who, following Lincoln's plea, were boycotting the raw cotton picked by US slaves. It condemned direct action taken by the suffragette movement, opposed the creation of the National Health Service, has at various times called for a vote for the Conservatives, Social Democrats and Liberal Democrats (rather than Labour), supported the First Gulf War and the NATO bombing of Yugoslavia and consistently denigrated Jeremy Corbyn's leadership of the Labour Party between 2015 and 2020. It has both fiercely defended the need for fearless, independent journalism and handed over documents and hard drives to the authorities; it has carved out a niche for itself in the UK press market as an occasionally bold and angry voice but has also consistently diminished more radical projects to the left.

Its business model shows signs of some of the same contradictions. Following its origins in the Manchester business community, it was then controlled by a trust after 1936, and has therefore been partially protected from the proprietorial interference that its counterparts have always faced. It has led the way in innovative design and formats, was the first British title to set up a reader's editor, established editions in the US and Australia and now champions a membership model with some one million people who have either signed up to the scheme or made a one-off contribution. The *Guardian* now proclaims on every page that it is '[a]vailable for everyone, funded by readers' and its editor insists that its 'ownership structure means we are entirely independent and free from political and commercial influence'.[5]

At the same time, it has ramped up its commercial orientation: the Scott Trust was wound up in 2008 and replaced by a private company, Scott Trust Ltd, with a mandate to secure its financial future in a much tougher marketplace. This has led to a series of commercial partnerships, rarely acknowledged openly, including 346 such relationships in 2014 alone and the creation of branded content opportunities through the *Guardian* Labs team together with extensive philanthropic partnerships with a range of individuals and foundations.[6] Of course it is by no means the only news organisation pursuing these commercial opportunities, however its online partnerships with, companies such as BT, Unilever and Philips in its 'Sustainable Business' section, are bound to test its claim that it is a unique and wholly independent voice in global journalism.[7]

The current editor is aware of this complex history and acknowledges some of the 'missteps', as she describes them, in the paper's record. Indeed, she admits that the newspaper 'began to drift from the political ideals that had inspired its founding' after the death of its founder John Edward Taylor in 1844 and suggests that its support for the Confederates in the US Civil War marked a 'period of complacency' that was out of kilter with its liberal origins. It has, she argues, not always lived up to its own values and its newsroom still falls short of the diversity necessary to truly serve a multicultural public. She has, however, promised that the title will now 'challenge the economic assumptions of the last three decades', 'challenge the powerful' and 'use clarity and imagination to build hope'.[8]

This collection seeks to examine these claims and to contest the notion that the *Guardian* has ever been a reliable ally for the left. It is by no means a comprehensive overview of the *Guardian*'s history, journalism, business model or newsroom culture. It does not seek to emulate the official biographies that already exist: William Haslam

Mills' centenary book on *The Manchester Guardian* (with an introduction by the then editor C.P. Scott) and the subsequent volume by former *Guardian* journalist David Ayerst that was published on its 150th anniversary in 1971 (with copyright held by *Guardian* Newspapers Ltd). A third official biography is due to be published to coincide with the bicentenary but, in any case, our book is designed not to provide an impartial or disinterested overview of the *Guardian*'s record but to propose an analysis from the left of some prominent controversies in which the paper has been involved.

The book opens with a challenge to the widely promoted view that the *Guardian* was founded as a direct response to the Peterloo Massacre of 1819 in order to extend the mass movement for democracy and workers' rights. Instead, we provide a radical narrative that argues that the title was intimately connected to the interests and emerging liberal orientations of a section of the Manchester business community that sought not radical change but social stability. Aaron Ackerley then provides an analysis of the *Guardian*'s political economy: its business model, its emergence as a Trust, its plans for the future and the endless conflict between commercial and editorial priorities.

Former editor-at-large, Gary Younge, reflects on life as a working-class black journalist at the *Guardian* and considers how its liberalism permeated its newsroom culture and editorial agendas. Victoria Brittain explores the rise and fall of *Third World Review*, the weekly section of the newspaper she edited in the 1980s that was dedicated to providing first-hand reports from marginalised voices in parts of the world, notably the Global South, that were then undergoing major social transformations. The Palestinian author and activist Ghada Karmi tackles the *Guardian*'s record in reporting on Israel and Palestine, which she argues is more favourable than the rest of the UK press but nevertheless shaped by a liberal conception that this is a 'conflict' involving two equivalent sides rather than an 'old-style settler colonialist project'. Alan MacLeod examines how the title has covered the 'pink tide' in South America and condemns the paper's reporting on developments in Bolivia, Brazil, Colombia and Venezuela before concluding that it has 'attacked progressive movements . . . while failing to hold the region's right-wing rulers to the same standard'.

Hannah Hamad acknowledges the contribution of the *Guardian* women's page to twentieth century liberal feminism and highlights the role of Mary Stott, its editor from 1957 to 1972, in paving the way for 'second wave' feminist movements and beyond. Jilly Boyce Kay and Mareile Pfannebecker then identify how a 'centrist feminism' came to dominate the *Guardian*'s coverage of trans issues after 2014, which provided a 'progressive feminist gloss' for its broader criticisms of Corbynism and the rise of the left inside the Labour Party.

Investigative journalists Matt Kennard and Mark Curtis of Declassified UK consider how the *Guardian* went from the title that published Edward Snowden's revelations about comprehensive state surveillance to a 'platform trusted by the security state to amplify its information operations'. Informed by interviews with current and former *Guardian* journalists, they suggest there is an increasingly risk-averse environment, in part caused by the departure of some of its most experienced investigative reporters. Natalie Fenton reflects on a similar trajectory: how the *Guardian* at once broke the story of phone-hacking in 2009, paving the way for the Leveson Inquiry that later recommended the creation of a more robust form of independent press self-regulation, and then refused to support Leveson's recommendations. She concludes that 'if the *Guardian* saved itself, it did so at the expense of other casualties'.

Justin Schlosberg focuses on the political and economic contexts of the *Guardian*'s negative framing of the leadership of Jeremy Corbyn and the broader movement of 'Corbynism'. In particular, his chapter identifies inaccuracies and distortions in its coverage of the antisemitism crisis within the Labour Party. While defending liberal values against a populist insurgency, Schlosberg concludes that the paper eventually came to undermine its own core commitment to 'the sanctity of facts'. Tom Mills then provides a detailed analysis of the Twitter networks of key *Guardian* columnists which reveals that they are ensconced in insular networks that are largely oriented towards other journalists and centrist politicians. The *Guardian*'s commentariat, it appears, is locked inside its own liberal echo chamber.

Mike Berry uses the 2008 financial crisis to explore how the press narrated both the crisis and subsequent developments concerning the UK's deficit and austerity programme. He argues that, particularly thanks to the tenacity of its economics editor, Larry Elliott, the *Guardian* was better prepared than most papers to critique mainstream economic thinking but was nevertheless hamstrung by the paucity at that time of radical alternatives to austerity. He suggests that the paper's coverage of the economic proposals that emerged under Corbynism was more positive than any of its other policies but doubts whether this approach will survive under the leadership of Keir Starmer. Mike Wayne then considers the significance of what he describes as 'liberal neoliberalism' in achieving hegemony in the conjunctural moment of Brexit:

> The *Guardian*, as a leading organ of 'progressive' neo-liberalism, played a key role in discrediting Corbyn (for whom Brexit was his 'Achilles heel'), fracturing Labour support along class lines and orchestrating this 'game of thrones'.

Finally, Katy Brown, Aurelien Mondon and Aaron Winter evaluate the *Guardian*'s series on 'The New Populism' to identify ways in which mainstream media run the risk of 'euphemising' and 'amplifying' illiberal speech even at the same time as condemning it. While they welcome some of the *Guardian*'s comment pieces, the authors nevertheless warn how certain tropes around populism and 'free speech' have been used to legitimise a 'false equivalence' that helps to 'mainstream' far right ideas.

In the end, should we simply be disappointed or angered by the *Guardian*'s social liberalism and dismissal of radical left politics or should we value the space that it continues to provide to voices on the left? Should we reserve our ire for the most pernicious proponents of market fundamentalism and right-wing politics or does it matter even more that liberal voices have been used to condemn movements to their left? Media Lens writers David Cromwell and David Edwards argue that the *Guardian*, along with the BBC, forms a crucial part of 'a propaganda system for elite interests'[9] while others, including Gary Younge in his chapter for this collection, suggest that we should never have invested our hopes in a title that has an historic relationship to liberal, rather than socialist, values.

Tony Benn put this dilemma very well back in 2008 when reflecting, in his diary, on the *Guardian*'s affiliation with elite interests and its attraction to power:

> The *Guardian* represents a whole batch of journalists, from moderate right to moderate left – i.e. centre journalists – who, broadly speaking like the status quo. They like the two-party system with no real change. They're quite happy to live under the aegis of the Americans and NATO; they are very keen on the European Union because the Commissioners control everything. They are very critical of the left, but would also be critical of a wild right-wing movement. They are just the Establishment. It is a society that suits them well. I should think that probably most of them send their kids to private schools. I should think a lot of them don't use the National Health Service, but they tolerate it as the price you have to pay in order to keep the populace content. They're not interested in me any more because they don't think I have any power, and I can't say I'm very interested in them, except as exhibits in a zoo.[10]

Yet liberalism is far from a mere sideshow or spectacle and instead constitutes a powerful brake on any radical political project from the left. For all its occasional and welcome forays into investigative journalism, the *Guardian* – with its huge international audience of some 160 million global monthly browsers[11] – plays a key role in marking out a space for liberal politics that is explicitly hostile to transformative social change. In these circumstances, disappointment is surely not a sufficient response. It is essential to build an independent media that tells the story of the left and that more consistently holds power to account, and that is precisely what this collection aims to do: to scrutinise an institution that, in the final instance, is intimately connected to existing relations of power. The *Guardian* is read by many people on the left but, as with liberal democracy more generally, it does not serve them consistently or adequately in the pursuit of radical social change. This book is an expression not simply of disappointment but of the conviction that we need a very different sort of media if we are to pursue a very different sort of society.

NOTES

1. Alexander Zevin, *Liberalism at Large: The World According to the Economist* (London: Verso, 2019), p. 7.

2. Katharine Viner, 'A Mission for Journalism in a Time of Crisis', *Guardian*, 16 November 2017, www.theguardian.com/news/2017/nov/16/a-mission-for-journalism-in-a-time-of-crisis (accessed 17 October 2020).
3. Gholam Khiabany, 'Introduction' in Alejandro Abraham-Hamanoiel et al. (eds) *Liberalism in Neoliberal Times* (London: Goldsmiths Press, 2017), p. 4. See also Domenico Losurdo, *Liberalism: A Counter-History* (London: Verso, 2014).
4. Friedrich Engels, *The Condition of the Working-Class in England* (London: George Allen & Unwin, 1943), p. 69.
5. Viner, 'A Mission for Journalism'.
6. Arif Durrani, 'Why HSBC's Relationship with the *Telegraph* and the *Guardian* is the Press Story of Our Time', *Campaign*, 26 February 2015, www.campaignlive.co.uk/article/why-hsbcs-relationship-telegraph-guardian-press-story-time/1335446; 'Philanthropic Partnerships at the Guardian', 2 October, 2018, www.theguardian.com/info/2018/oct/02/philanthropic-partnerships-at-the-guardian (both accessed 17 October 2020).
7. See www.theguardian.com/sustainable-business/partnership-opportunities (accessed 17 October 2020).
8. Viner, 'A Mission for Journalism'.
9. David Edwards and David Cromwell, *Guardians of Power: The Myth of the Liberal Media* (London: Pluto, 2005), p. 2.
10. Tony Benn, *A Blaze of Autumn Sunshine: The Last Diaries* (London: Arrow Books, 2014), p. 153.
11. See www.advertising.theguardian.com/advertising/media-kit (accessed 17 October 2020).

1

In the Wake of Peterloo? A Radical Account of the Founding of the *Guardian*

Des Freedman

INTRODUCTION

The *Guardian* regularly, and proudly, declares that it was born in the aftermath of the Peterloo massacre of August 1819, one of the turning-points in British working-class history. Some 50,000 people attended a mass rally in St Peter's Fields in Manchester to press for electoral reform and trade union rights and were met with a brutal assault by local yeomanry that led to the deaths of 18 people and widespread outrage against the authorities. Peterloo, argues one historian, 'was no accident; it was a political earthquake in the northern powerhouse of the industrial revolution'[1] that ultimately weakened the grip of the old aristocratic forces and emboldened the movement for reform.

In the crowd that day was John Edward Taylor, a cotton merchant and part-time journalist who wrote up his account of the massacre for *The Times*, helping to make what might have been contained as a local event into a national sensation. According to the current editor of the *Guardian*, Katharine Viner, 'Taylor exposed the facts, without hysteria. By reporting what he had witnessed, he told the stories of the powerless, and held the powerful to account.'[2] Peterloo radicalised Taylor and prompted him, in the words of a *Guardian* feature in 2018, 'to start his own paper, two years later, to campaign for reform'[3] and to pursue a democratic agenda based on truth-telling and a commitment to progressive, liberal values. This paper was the *Manchester Guardian*, and its supporters argue that it has continued ever since to devote itself to the pursuit of 'enlightenment values, liberty, reform and justice'.[4]

This chapter argues that this account of the *Guardian*'s birth conceals far more than it reveals and glosses over a central fact: that the liberal values espoused by Taylor served to contain, rather than to promote, demands for more fundamental democratic change. Taylor had a far more ambivalent reaction to the events at Peterloo than is widely credited, and launched the *Guardian* in order to foster a constitutional alternative to radical social forces and to cater to the needs of an increasingly politically confident business community in Manchester. The chapter challenges some of the myths surrounding the founding of the newspaper (not least that it was designed to serve as a fearless advocate of progressive social change and working-class representation), explores the objectives of the group of businessmen who sponsored it and examines its coverage of key reform issues in its first few years.

PETERLOO IN CONTEXT

There is little doubt that the second decade of the nineteenth century was an insurrectionary period in English history. With the French Revolution a recent memory and with basic democratic rights to vote and to organise denied to the vast majority of the population, there was a rebellious mood amongst a growing working-class movement characterised by the smashing up of machinery, huge radical meetings, hunger marches and food riots.[5] As Viner notes: 'The combination of economic depression, political repression and the politicisation of workers with economic need was combustible.'[6]

This presented a threat not simply to the landed gentry still in power but also to an emerging professional class who were terrified about the prospects of a powerful labour movement. According to John Saville, the middle class at this time 'never forgot the history of revolutionary France and they were constantly reminded of the problems and the dangers of too rapid change when they listened to the ultra-radical doctrines of their own working people'.[7] The choice for the old order in this context was either continued repression or else accommodation to the demands for change. However, in 1819 the latter approach, as E.P. Thompson argues, 'would have meant concession to a largely working class reform movement; the middle-class reformers were not yet strong enough . . . to offer a moderate line of advance.'[8]

The violence meted out at Peterloo helped to transform the balance of forces amongst proponents of reform. It exposed the barbarism of the authorities to a national audience and opened the door to liberal reformers to make a case for piecemeal change and thus to pre-empt the need to cave in to radical demands for universal suffrage. Indeed, while the 'constitutionalist' wing of the movement gained in confidence following Peterloo, the 'revolutionary' wing, facing sustained repression and internal division, temporarily lost its momentum. According to Thompson, once the 'clamour of 1819 had died down, the middle-class reform movement assumed a more determined aspect' and the industrial militancy that had characterised that decade died down, at least for a few years.[9]

In Manchester, this paved the way for liberal-minded business leaders to agitate for parliamentary reform, religious freedom and, above all, free trade. People like Taylor, his good friend and fellow journalist Archibald Prentice, his then business partner John Shuttleworth and his future publisher Jeremiah Garnett were part of what was known as the 'Little Circle', a group of Manchester merchants that opposed both the rule of the 'old order' and the extension of the franchise to all working people. According to David Knott, the Circle believed that, 'it was preferable to have a small bourgeois public such as themselves exercising political rights, as they alone would approach this role with objectivity and rationality.'[10] Many of its members were connected to the cotton trade, an industry that was intimately linked to and dependent on the profits yielded by slave labour in the Caribbean and US, even though, as individuals, many of them were also active as abolitionists, an apparent contradiction to which we will return later in this chapter.

Peterloo played a key role in the development of the Circle, convincing its members of the need for a new, constitutionally focused political strategy. Knott argues that while Circle members were outraged by the violence they witnessed at Peterloo, 'they also wanted to distance themselves from the event' and to channel radical political dissent into 'deliberative assemblies' that took the form of 'rational debate within legally sanctioned indoor local political forums'.[11] What they lacked at the time was a vehicle that could articulate their values and promote these assemblies – such as a regular newspaper – and the fallout from Peterloo provided precisely this opportunity.

TAYLOR AND THE LIBERAL RESPONSE TO PETERLOO

The two most recent editors of the *Guardian*, Alan Rusbridger and Katharine Viner, both identify Peterloo as the main inspiration for the birth of the title. For Viner, the 'history of the *Guardian* begins on 16 August 1819'.[12] Yet one of the *Guardian*'s official biographers, David Ayerst, suggests that, far from emerging spontaneously from the battleground of St Peter's Fields, the idea actually emerged a few months earlier, following Taylor's victory in a libel case in March 1819 that was brought against him by a Tory politician who accused him of inciting vandalism. 'It is now plain you have the elements of public work in you,' remarked a friend of his on the way home from the trial. 'Why don't you start a newspaper?'[13] Taylor was aggrieved, according to another *Guardian* biographer, Haslam Mills, not simply that he had been wrongly accused of criminal behaviour but that his Tory opponents had claimed that he was not a 'moderate reformer' but a more incendiary one.[14] Taylor was already contributing to the liberal *Manchester Gazette*, but events would propel him to seek a more reliable outlet for his worldview.

Peterloo and its aftermath however, provided Taylor with a further incentive to imprint his values on a volatile political landscape. This was necessary largely because he was uncomfortable with the orientation of the radical leaders whose voices were dominant up to and including the day of the massacre, and who were demanding universal suffrage, annual parliaments and the immediate repeal of the Corn Laws. For Ayerst, Taylor 'was out of sympathy with the extreme radical leaders' and penned an article two weeks before Peterloo criticising them for appealing 'not to the reason but the passions and sufferings of their abused and credulous fellow-countrymen.'[15] Taylor certainly had little time for Henry Hunt, the radical leader who was the main speaker on 16 August, even if he was horrified by the violence meted out by the yeomanry against innocent people in St Peter's Fields.

Taylor threw himself into a committee aiming to raise funds for the victims of the attack and then wrote a lengthy report, *Notes and Observations*, in response to the government's own account of the events. *N&O* attacks with some passion the abuses of power that he witnessed, exonerates the ordinary people who attended the meeting and challenges official 'misrepresentations', for example that 'clubs' allegedly used as weapons by ordinary people were in fact walking sticks held by a small minority of the crowd. Referring sarcastically to the '*glorious* victory of the 16th of August', he excoriates the authorities for losing control: 'I know of no law, which authorizes a yeoman to sabre me, because I may not give way to him quite so soon as he wishes I would.'[16]

Yet the report is also determined to be even-handed about where the blame should lie and suggests that the revolutionaries are just as bad as what he calls the 'plebeian aristocracy'.

> I have not a word to say in defence of the presumption, vulgarity and violence of some self-styled reformers on the one hand; but I certainly do think the inhumanity, the ignorance and the rancorous bitterness of many anti-reformers, equally inexcusable on the other.[17]

Notes and Observations demonstrates Taylor's reluctance to lay responsibility at the door of the state, insisting that the 'yeomanary are incapable of acting with deliberate cruelty' and blaming instead a handful of wayward individuals 'whose political rancour approaches to absolute insanity'.[18] The key lesson for Taylor was not that Peterloo demonstrated the need for thoroughgoing political change and the extension of democracy to the poor but the need to build social harmony and to restore faith in the law – a law that had just permitted the slaughter of more than a dozen citizens. There will be no peace, he argues, 'until the poor have regained that perfect confidence in the impartiality of the law.'[19]

Taylor sought deliberately to distinguish his political programme from that of the radicals who had organised the meeting in St Peter's Fields. Indeed, he chose never to refer to 'Peterloo' – a phrase first coined by the left-wing *Manchester Observer* shortly after 16 August and which caught on straight away – confining himself in *N&O* to a single reference to the 'tragedy' and the 'atrocities' of that day. Meanwhile, as he and his friends devoted a lot of time to organising relief for the victims of the violence and led demands for a public inquiry, the 'middle-class radicals' (as the Peterloo historian Donald Read calls them) exploited the gap left by a divided working class movement and extended their influence over the campaign for reform.[20] Faced with a wave of protest following Peterloo, the government passed the 'Six Acts', that criminalised large public meetings, increased stamp duty on newspapers and launched a major assault against the working-class and unlicensed press, all of which resulted in a 'temporary diminution of Radical agitation'.[21] The brutality of Peterloo, combined with the blunt nature of the government's response,

> convinced many of the middle class that Reform was the only alternative to a policy of repression that would lead inevitably to civil war. From this time parliamentary Reforms began to be 'respectable' and to appear prominently on the programme of the [liberal opposition] Whigs.[22]

Whereas a militant working-class movement had dominated demands for reform in the run-up to Peterloo, middle-class reformers – with a far more limited programme of social change – were able to consolidate their grip in the years that followed. The *Manchester Guardian*, therefore, was born not from an industrial and political upturn powered by a mass movement – let alone in a flowering of radical journalism – but, as E.P. Thompson describes the period, in a 'mildly prosperous plateau of social peace'.[23]

THE FOUNDING OF THE *MANCHESTER GUARDIAN*

The official narrative is that the *Guardian* was launched, above all, as a vehicle to campaign for parliamentary reform. According to Katharine Viner, Taylor was 'determined to agitate for fair representation in parliament. He decided to start his own newspaper, the *Manchester Guardian*, with the financial backing of other middle-class radicals.'[24] Taylor's great-great-great granddaughter argues that Taylor was motivated by 'what he witnessed at Peterloo, and in its aftermath, galvanised in him a belief that education in the form of balanced, honest, well-researched reporting could be the spark for renewed hope.'[25] The full story is a little more complicated than this and involves a range of commercial, ideological *and* political considerations.

The first point to note is this was far from an individual venture. As has already been noted, the group of cotton traders organised in the 'Little Circle' were seeking an outlet to articulate their brand of liberalism. Attempting to provide the reform movement with a more 'respectable' leadership that would also champion their commitment to free trade, 'a vigorous reform newspaper was the top priority' for the Circle as it entered the 1820s.[26] Their first instinct was to buy out the liberal *Manchester Gazette*, to which Taylor, Prentice and Garnett were already contributing. According to Michael Turner:

> The wealthier members of the band and some of their prosperous friends and business partners . . . agreed to advance the sums that would be needed and Taylor was spoken of as prospective editor. According to Prentice, Taylor was chosen because he was the only member of the band not fully occupied with business concerns and because he seemed to have the qualities required in a spirited advocate of reform.[27]

It was only when negotiations with the owner, William Cowdroy, failed that Taylor then approached his friends for financial support to set up a new title. Less than a year later, the *Gazette*'s owner died leading Turner to note that had Cowdroy died just a little earlier, 'the *Guardian* might never have been started because his widow would probably have sold up' as she did shortly afterwards.[28]

Nevertheless, Taylor secured the necessary capital from his friends in the Manchester business community to launch the newspaper and immediately produced a prospectus designed to publicise its imminent arrival and, more significantly, to secure advertising. Viner describes it as a 'powerful document, and one whose ideals still shape the *Guardian* – a celebration of more people getting educated, of more people engaging in politics, from different walks of life, from poorer communities.'[29] Yet the prospectus is actually quite cautious in its political orientation, noticeably failing to mention the events in St Peter's Fields nor the government's ongoing repression. Instead, it promises that the newspaper will be committed to 'the promotion of public happiness and the security of popular rights' and that 'it will warmly advocate the cause of reform' without being tied to any particular political party (despite the Whiggish outlook of its editor). 'The prospectus of the *Guardian* was kept intentionally vague', argues Donald Read, 'so as to secure support from as wide a range of reformers as possible.'[30]

Indeed, far from promising to represent the interest of 'poorer communities', the prospectus makes it clear that the *Manchester Guardian* is aimed at 'the classes to whom . . . Advertisements are generally addressed.' Noting that no other Manchester newspaper was fully committed to represent the 'wealth and intelligence of this town', the prospectus promises to provide comprehensive information about commerce – and about the cotton trade above all:

> The commercial connexions and knowledge of the Conductors of the GUARDIAN will, they apprehend, give them the means of occasionally stating, with accuracy and effect, the condition of TRADE and its prospects, particularly as far as regards that most important branch of the Cotton Manufacture.[31]

It is an uncomfortable reality for the *Guardian* that the capital required for its start-up came largely from an industry whose own wealth was intimately bound up with the profits accrued from the slave trade,[32] and the prospectus clearly illustrates that the title was designed to be the house organ of cotton interests. That some of those involved in the paper's founding were active abolitionists does little to change the structural dependence of the title on a source of wealth that directly contradicts its own liberal values or, perhaps more accurately, that reflects the fundamentally compromised history of liberalism itself.

Far from praising the prospectus for its radicalism as Viner does, Archibald Prentice – Taylor's great friend at the time – later criticised its caution and suggested that, despite the wish of some of its backers for a more vigorous embrace of reform, it was felt that 'it was better not to make a broad declaration of political opinions which would give offence amongst the classes having advertisements to bestow.'[33] The prospectus was not a sign of radical intent but an expression of the commercial interests and moderate liberalism of its founders.

The political positioning of the *Manchester Guardian* was crucial. With its first appearance on 5 May 1821, it entered a crowded market with four Conservative-supporting titles on its right and two, the liberal *Manchester Gazette* and the radical *Manchester Observer*, pressing for reform. The great skill of Taylor was to set up the *Guardian* as a reliable source of parliamentary news, international reporting and liberal opinion that would appeal to a combination of its own natural constituency in the middle class, radical advocates of reform and more conservative readers concerned about the government's failure to deal adequately with demands for change. It was designed to be, above all, a bridge between moderate reformers and those to their right. Taylor wrote in the first edition of the paper that while the *Guardian* would make 'pointed animadversions on public questions', he hoped that 'even our political opponents shall admit the propriety of the spirit in which they are written, however fundamentally they may differ from their own principles and views.'[34] This approach paid off immediately with Taylor's fiancée Sophia Scott writing after the first edition had come out that the paper had been warmly received with 'encouragement from all parties', in spite of the serious political tensions in politics at the time.[35]

The fact is that while the *Manchester Guardian* was a passionate advocate of reform (albeit gradual), it was, according to Robert Poole, the biographer of the *Manchester Observer*, 'an opposition paper but never a radical one.' Taylor himself was 'an ally of the radical movement only in so far as he opposed its persecutors. He hoped and expected that radicalism would wither away in more benign political and economic conditions',[36] and he sought to position the *Guardian* as a title that would promote free trade and diminish the radical threat. The title sought to safeguard the interests of the Manchester business community, to seek the ear of the powerful and to promote its own reform agenda while distancing itself from the more insurrectionary voices that had dominated the previous decade. Taylor himself was an unreliable progressive voice: one moment attacking police spies and government corruption and then supporting Tory proposals soon after the paper's launch to restrict poor relief, perhaps reflecting his own Malthusian beliefs on population control.[37]

Indeed, one of the most immediate impacts of the *Guardian* was to squeeze the life out of the *Observer*, the top-selling title of the Manchester left and an organiser of the Peterloo protest. The *Observer* did not lack readers, but its support for the more militant wing of the reform movement together with its inability to attract advertising meant that it was both politically and financially vulnerable. The appearance of the *Guardian* only intensified the pressure on the *Observer*, making it harder to attract advertisers and presenting competition that, in the end, it was unable to withstand. The *Guardian*, argues Poole, 'helped to finish off the *Manchester Observer* as a local paper'[38] with the latter lasting less than a month following the first edition of Taylor's title. This was a foretaste of what was to happen to the Chartist press some 30 years later when, as James Curran has shown, a process of industrialisation, as opposed to any meaningful decline in popularity, led 'to a progressive transfer of ownership and control of the popular press to wealthy businesspeople, while dependence on advertising encouraged the absorption or elimination of the early radical press.'[39]

The *Guardian* enjoyed modest success to start with, but with a weakened *Gazette* (and a non-existent *Observer*) on the reform side, the title started to pick up circulation and advertisements – attracting an average of 100 ads per edition by 1825 – and Taylor was able to pay off his partners after only three years. Not only reformers but 'virtually the whole of the Manchester business community'[40] were avid readers. This success allowed him also to acquire in 1825 two Conservative Manchester papers, the *Manchester Mercury* and the *British Volunteer*, thus extending the impact of the *Guardian* amongst Tory readers. Poole argues that 'Taylor moved confidently among the Tory-dominated circles of the Chamber of Commerce and the Exchange and formed common political cause with the economic liberals among them', with Taylor even claiming credit for reforming the Manchester Tory party.[41]

This shift to the right had already infuriated some of the original backers of the *Guardian*, leading a deeply frustrated Prentice to conclude that the newspaper was, by 1823, the 'guardian of the commercial interests of the town and neighbourhood – a reputation much more valuable, in a pecuniary point of view, than the fame of being the advocate of popular rights.'[42] Rather than committing itself to pressing for working-class rights and universal suffrage, the *Guardian* adopted a relatively cautious and passive perspective in relation to radical demands for reform. Prentice describes this as a 'half-way' position: 'rather disposed to wait for the coming up of those who were in the rear [reform-minded Conservatives] than to march forward and to join those who were in advance.'[43] The bridge that Taylor was constructing through the pages of the *Manchester Guardian* was far more conducive to fostering relationships with moderate Tories than with working-class forces pushing to secure comprehensive social change.

THE *MANCHESTER GUARDIAN*: ON THE SIDE OF THE PEOPLE?

Taylor's *Guardian* was nevertheless a hugely significant addition to the Manchester publishing scene and was seen as innovative for its use of a regular leading article, its rigorous reporting of parliamentary debates, its hiring of the first dedicated reporter in Manchester, and its combination of news and opinion which Turner describes as a 'trend-setter in provincial journalism'.[44] Its journalism however, was hardly the incendiary advocate for reform that its later proponents would declare, nor was it firmly – as Katharine Viner argues in relation to its prospectus – 'on people's side'.[45]

The paper started brightly enough, with articles on policing, local corruption and some detailed reports of House of Commons debates on what it called the 'Outrage at Manchester' (it never referred to 'Peterloo' in these early days). Yet this was just as likely designed to attract readers from the rapidly declining *Observer* than it was a principled stand in support of working-class demands for electoral reform and, moreover, it was hardly that unusual given that most newspapers were extremely critical of the government's behaviour in relation to Peterloo.[46] Yet, even here, its political orientation was clear: the demand was not to stand down the yeomanry or to hold to account Hugh Hornby Birley, their commander at Peterloo (in whose circles Taylor was mixing in Manchester). 'We do not ask for vengeance, but enquiry' thundered an early editorial. 'It is due to the sufferings of the living; it is claimed by the memory of the slain; and, above all, it is demanded by the outraged and insulted majesty of the British Constitution.'[47] However justified and necessary it was, a public inquiry to restore the legitimacy of the rule of law was hardly in tune with more radical demands that had dominated the reform movement in the run-up to Peterloo.

Taylor had more opportunity to show off his reform credentials in relation to the biggest political issue of the time: the proposed repeal of the Combination Acts, legislation originally passed in 1799–1800 to restrict the collective organisation of working people into unions. The *Guardian* was firmly in support of repeal in 1823 but, once again, not because this might strengthen the bargaining rights of ordinary people, but because the Acts undermined free trade principles and actually risked *strengthening* working-class organisation. Republishing an article from the *Scotsman* that is 'exactly in accordance with our opinions', the paper argued that the laws 'instead of putting down combinations, have rendered them permanent and universal. They have given an illegal and dangerous character to what otherwise would have been legal and harmless.'[48] This was a view shared by many employers and MPs at the time: that repression had simply antagonised a nascent labour movement. It was a position much closer to Adam Smith than it was to Tom Paine.

The Acts were repealed in 1824 and led to a revival of working-class militancy for the first time in the *Guardian*'s lifetime. Far from celebrating repeal (indeed it failed even to report this), the newspaper – reflecting the business interests of its owner – railed against the excitement with which it was greeted by workers and complained instead of increased 'intimidation' and agitation. Indeed, the *Guardian* soon regretted this turn of events and worried that workers were getting above themselves and upsetting the natural order of things:

> Subordination will of necessity be observed by all those whose situation in life compels them to sell their labour, and because, in contests with their men, their masters, by their superior circumstances . . . are enabled to hold out longer than the former can possibly do.[49]

This position was greeted with outrage by a group of cotton spinners whose letter was published in the following week's edition. Referring to the 'better days of the *Guardian*', the letter asked: 'Is the press to be made the ready vehicle of abuse against the poor man, while the rich (for the self-same conduct) are not only screened and protected but absolutely eulogized?'[50] For perhaps the first time in its history, the paper's liberal credentials were publicly criticised for double standards that favoured the status quo.

In the end, the *Guardian* opposed the reintroduction of new Combination Laws the following year. However, the paper still condemned efforts by workers 'to obtain a mastery over their employers' as 'intrinsically and necessarily wrong' and reiterated its own support for an unfettered free market for labour, recognising the right for employers to 'purchase labour on the terms most favourable to themselves'.[51]

This was precisely the approach with which the *Guardian* approached the issue of slavery: that it is morally abhorrent but also that it undermines free trade principles. Despite (or perhaps because of) the *Guardian*'s connection to a cotton industry that had its roots in the slave trade, the newspaper confined most of its coverage of the issue in its first few years to parliamentary debates on abolition. In one of the few opinion pieces on the topic, the paper carries the thoughts of a 'most respectable and intelligent merchant' who identifies free trade, not organised resistance or solidarity, as the best way of defeating slavery. 'The unrestricted commerce of the world, and the competition of free labour . . . would gradually ameliorate the treatment of the slaves; and finally extinguish slavery itself,'[52] This chimes perfectly with an editorial by Taylor himself a few years later that condemns the 'harsh and brutalizing system of slavery' in the West Indies but warns the slave owners that they cannot keep expecting English people 'to be further taxed for the benefit of West Indian planters' if they [English consumers] do not also enjoy lower prices.'[53] Slavery poses, it seems, both a moral and a fiscal dilemma.

One further area in which one might have expected a significant amount of coverage from a newspaper wedded to free trade and enlightenment values was the government's restrictions on the freedom of the press and its 'taxes on knowledge'. This was a huge issue for the radical press facing a clampdown after Peterloo. 'The years 1819-21 brought 120 prosecutions for seditious and blasphemous libels, ending in numerous jailings,' argues Stanley Harrison. Although the radical press itself declined in this period, its supporters mounted 'one of the greatest counter-attacks in the whole press freedom story'[54] with the eventual release from jail, following blasphemy charges, of Richard Carlile, publisher of the *Republican* newspaper. This was a vivid and dramatic story of a brave tinplate worker, his family and his supporters, up against the might of the English state.

The *Guardian*, however, largely ignored Carlile and focused what little coverage of the topic there was on the short-sighted behaviour of his accusers and their counter-productive censorship: 'The public have, heretofore, felt little sympathy for Carlile, and no desire for his success.'[55] The paper argued against making him into a martyr and, when he was finally released in 1825, failed even to cover the story. The *Guardian* did occasionally report on trials of *Republican* sellers but spent more time discussing press freedom in relation to other countries – including India, Switzerland and France – than the UK, possibly because it felt less threatened in its own position as a reputable and well-resourced outlet. 'Free, spirited, and intelligent criticism on public events we unquestionably have' it declared[56] even while Carlile was languishing in jail and prosecuting societies were harassing radical bookshops. This might explain why, when it comes to the historic struggles for press freedom after 1821, the *Manchester Guardian* is virtually invisible in many key accounts.[57]

CONCLUSION

The two hundredth anniversary of the *Guardian* provides a real opportunity for its contemporary luminaries to celebrate the progressive values that marked its birth and that it claims to have nurtured ever since. Yet the story of its founding reveals a much more ambiguous commitment to democratic principles and radical reform. Far from challenging the legitimacy of the institutions that were responsible for the Peterloo massacre, Taylor attributed the violence to a few 'bad apples' and campaigned for a public inquiry that might embarrass the government but not directly challenge its authority. Instead of leading the campaign for universal suffrage and pressing for an extension of workers' rights, the *Guardian* infused the reform movement with a constitutionalist politics that diluted the more militant demands of a labour movement that, up until 1819, had provided the dominant voice for social change. In doing this, it expressed the dynamics of an emerging liberalism that involved 'a totalizing fusion of the political ideas of rule of law and civil liberties with the economic maxims of free trade and free markets.'[58]

Despite the many articles and timelines on the *Guardian*'s website in recent years that commemorate Peterloo and fetishize the role of John Edward Taylor, the title was not simply the brainwave of a single charismatic reformer but the product of a movement that required an institutional vehicle to disseminate its ideas. The *Guardian* provided middle-class reformers in Manchester with the opportunity to hegemonize the democratic movement after Peterloo and to 'consolidate their newly won influence'.[59] This echoes a more general shift in the balance of class forces and the overall consolidation of the power of the capitalist class after 1819 at the expense of the *ancien régime*. Peterloo, according to A.L. Morton, was a turning point that eventually generated limited reforms – those advocated by Taylor and his colleagues – whose eventual objective was 'the unobtrusive strengthening of the state apparatus'[60] and the replacement of working-class radicals with middle-class voices at the helm of the reform movement.

The *Manchester Guardian* exemplified this new political order. It railed against police spies and corrupt officials but it pursued reform on the basis that it would head off the most immediate threats posed by working-class militants; it supported the repeal of the Combination Acts not so much because they were an affront to the democratic right to organise but because they risked inflaming workers; it opposed slavery but assessed its brutal logic most often from a free trade perspective and failed to reflect critically on its own connections to the profits accrued from slave labour. The *Guardian* was, essentially, the voice of a 'modernising' wing of the Manchester business community that sought to establish dialogue with the powerful rather than to amplify the movements of the labouring poor. As David Knott notes in his account of the role of the press at the time: 'Pushing forward a radical agenda that threatened to shake the foundations of the political state was never part of the *Manchester Guardian*'s vision.'[61]

Above all, the *Manchester Guardian* served its purpose. It cohered business interests around a limited democratic agenda and articulated a 'respectable' voice advocating reform. In so doing, it provides us with a valuable example of the contradictions of liberalism as a set of values and structures that simultaneously express a desire for progressive change and that channel this appetite for change into actions that coincide with the interests of the status quo. According to E.P. Thompson, that there was not a revolution in England in 1831 was due, at least in part, to the 'deep constitutionalism of the liberal wing of radicalism.'[62] The *Manchester Guardian* played a not insignificant role in ensuring that this was the case at a critical time in English history. There are lessons here for the current day.

NOTES

1. Robert Poole, *Peterloo: The English Uprising* (Oxford: Oxford University Press, 2019), p. 2.

2. Katharine Viner, 'A Mission for Journalism in a time of Crisis', *Guardian*, 16 November 2017, www.theguardian.com/news/2017/nov/16/a-mission-for-journalism-in-a-time-of-crisis (accessed 8 May 2020).
3. Stephen Bates, 'The Bloody Clash that Changed Britain', *Guardian*, 4 January 2018, www.theguardian.com/news/2018/jan/04/peterloo-massacre-bloody-clash-that-changed-britain (accessed 2 July 2020).
4. Viner, 'A Mission for Journalism'.
5. A.L. Morton, *A People's History of England* (London: Lawrence & Wishart, 1989 [1938]), pp. 313–14.
6. Viner, 'A Mission for Journalism'.
7. John Saville, *The Consolidation of the Capitalist State: 1800–1850* (London: Pluto, 1994), p. 37.
8. E.P. Thompson, *The Making of the English Working Class* (New York: Vintage, 1966), p. 683.
9. Thompson, *Making*, p. 709.
10. David Knott, 'The Little Circle and Manchester Politics, 1812-46', unpublished PhD dissertation, University of Manchester, 2018, p. 121.
11. Knott, 'Little Circle', p. 72.
12. Alan Rusbridger, *Breaking News: The Remaking of Journalism and Why It Matters Now* (Edinburgh: Canongate, 2019), p. 18; Viner, 'A Mission for Journalism'.
13. David Ayerst, *Guardian: Biography of a Newspaper* (London: Collins, 1971), p. 15.
14. William Haslam Mills, *The Manchester Guardian* (London: Henry Holt, 1922), p. 31.
15. Ayerst, *Guardian*, p. 20.
16. Anonymous [A member of the Manchester Committee], *Notes and Observations* (London: Effingham Wilson, 1820), p. 171, pp. 166–7.
17. *Notes and Observations*, p. xiv.
18. *Notes and Observations*, pp. 175–6.
19. *Notes and Observations*, p. 194.
20. Donald Read, *Peterloo: The Massacre and its Background* (Manchester: Manchester University Press, 1958), chapter 10.
21. Morton, *People's History*, p. 315.
22. Morton, *People's History*, p. 314.
23. Thompson, *Making*, p. 711.
24. Viner, 'A Mission for Journalism'.
25. Sue Stennett, 'My Ancestor Founded the *Guardian*: Its Work Has Never Been so Vital', *Guardian*, 16 August 2019, www.theguardian.com/membership/2019/aug/16/peterloo-ancestor-john-edward-taylor-cp-scott-manchester-guardian (accessed 4 July 2020).
26. Michael Turner, 'The Making of a Middle-Class Liberalism in Manchester, c1815-32: A Study in Politics and the Press', unpublished PhD dissertation, University of Oxford, 1991, p. 79.
27. Turner, 'Making', p. 80.

28. Turner, 'Making', p. 80n.
29. Viner, 'A Mission for Journalism'.
30. Read, *Peterloo*, p. 172.
31. The *Guardian*, 'In the Wake of Peterloo: The Manchester Guardian Prospectus', 1821', 15 November 2017, www.theguardian.com/media/from-the-archive-blog/2017/nov/15/manchester-guardian-prospectus-1821 (accessed 4 July 2020).
32. According to Eric Williams: 'What the building of ships for the transport of slaves did for eighteenth century Liverpool, the manufacture of cotton goods for the purchase of slaves did for eighteenth century Manchester . . . It was this tremendous dependence on the triangular trade that made Manchester', *Capitalism and Slavery* (Chapel Hill: University of North Carolina Press, 1944), p. 68. Although the slave trade had been abolished in the UK in 1807, cotton produced by slaves was still essential to Manchester industry in the early nineteenth century.
33. Archibald Prentice, *Historical Sketches and Personal Recollections of Manchester* (London: Charles Gilpin, 1851), p. 204.
34. *Manchester Guardian*, 5 May 1821.
35. Quoted in Turner, 'Making', p. 83.
36. Robert Poole, 'The *Manchester Observer*: Biography of a Radical Paper', *Bulletin of the John Rylands Library*, 95:1 (2019), p. 98.
37. Poole, *Manchester Observer*, pp. 98–9. Prentice later criticised Taylor for 'regarding the multitude as intruders upon nature's feast, after the places at the table have been all taken, he can scarcely forgive the impertinence and seldom gives his warm sympathy to the intruders.' Prentice, *Historical Sketches*, p. 212.
38. Poole, *Manchester Observer*, p. 33.
39. James Curran in James Curran and Jean Seaton, *Power without Responsibility*, eighth edition (London: Routledge, 2018 [1981]), p. 41.
40. Ayerst, *Guardian*, p. 52.
41. Poole, *Manchester Observer*, p. 99.
42. Prentice, *Historical Sketches*, pp. 51–2.
43. Prentice, *Historical Sketches*, p. 245.
44. Turner, 'Making', p. 88.
45. Viner, 'A Mission for Journalism'.
46. See, for example, Hannah Barker, *Newspapers, Politics and English Society, 1695–1855* (London: Longman, 2000). Oddly enough, despite the emphasis placed by Alan Rusbridger and Katharine Viner on the significance of Peterloo for the *Guardian*, the paper failed to commemorate either the fifth, tenth or twenty-fifth anniversary of the massacre. The only mention of Peterloo fifty years later was a reader's letter saying how much more 'peaceful, happy, and gay' the country was today (17 August 1869). By its one hundredth anniversary, this had changed, and the *Guardian* provided a lengthy feature on 'The Meaning of Peterloo' which

talked about how it symbolised 'all the abuses and injustices that were associated with the ancient regime in England' (16 August 1919).

47. *Manchester Guardian*, 26 May 1821.
48. *Manchester Guardian*, 2 August 1823.
49. *Manchester Guardian*, 20 November 1824.
50. *Manchester Guardian*, 27 November 1824.
51. *Manchester Guardian*, 9 April 1825.
52. *Manchester Guardian*, 15 November 1823.
53. *Manchester Guardian*, 25 August 1827.
54. Stanley Harrison, *Poor Men's Guardians* (London: Lawrence & Wishart), 1974, p. 56.
55. *Manchester Guardian*, 5 January 1822.
56. *Manchester Guardian*, 7 September 1822.
57. There is not a single mention of the *Manchester Guardian* in William Wickwar's classic account of *The Struggle for the Freedom of the Press, 1819–1832* (London: George Allen & Unwin, 1928) although there are plenty of references to the more radical *Manchester Observer*. Similarly, the *Manchester Guardian* barely features in Curran's account of press freedom struggles in *Power without Responsibility* or in Harrison's *Poor Men's Guardians*.
58. Alexander Zevin, *Liberalism at Large: The World According to the Economist* (London: Verso, 2019), p. 11.
59. Read, *Peterloo*, p. 171.
60. Morton, *People's History*, p. 328.
61. Knott, 'Little Circle', p. 35.
62. Thompson, *Making*, p. 817.

2
The Political Economy of the *Guardian*

Aaron Ackerley

INTRODUCTION

'A newspaper', the *Guardian*'s most famous editor Charles Prestwich (C.P.) Scott intoned, 'has two sides to it. It has a business, like any other, and has to pay in the material sense in order to live'.[1] However, it was, he averred, also more than merely a business. It may be deemed 'an institution', a reflection of or influence on the whole community, or even, 'in its way, an instrument of government'. Writing in a special edition to mark the centenary of the paper's existence, the venerable editor was attempting to make sense of his own legacy, of the *Guardian*'s place within the media landscape and of the field of journalism more generally. Scott argued that a newspaper may 'educate, stimulate, assist, or it may do the opposite'. It had a 'moral as well as material existence, and its character and influence are in the main determined by the balance of the two forces'.

Scott was undoubtedly correct, and the interplay of editorial and business decision-making has been of central importance to all newspapers that have been run as commercial enterprises. The published output of a newspaper is what shapes its reputation. Yet the political economy of a title is just as important and covers a number of issues: its resources, including personnel, physical assets and property such as office buildings, printing presses and IT systems; its financial liabilities and endowments; its circulation; its sales and advertising revenue; and its ownership structure. Across the US press – at least among the most famous titles such as the *New York Times* and the *Washington Post* – the notion that the editorial and commercial worlds – referred to as 'church' and 'state' respectively – should be strictly separated long remained axiomatic, at least until recently, when a variety of factors such as the move to digital and plummeting print advertising revenues rocked the industry. This divide, however, has never been as clear-cut as such rhetoric implies, especially in relation to the history of the British press.

Depending upon the newspaper in question and the broader context it operated within at any particular moment, the balance of power between editorial and commercial concerns has varied. In some cases, one side was predominant. At elite Victorian newspapers – some of which survived to become the quality press of the twentieth century, such as the *Guardian* itself – the image presented to the public was usually of editorial taking precedence. Yet commercial imperatives always played an important role as well. At other types of newspapers, such as those that pioneered the 'New Journalism' that came out of the 1880s, the popular press that emerged at the end of the nineteenth century and the tabloids that are still with us today, commercial concerns were often at the forefront or were closely interwoven with the editorial direction of a newspaper. One can think of obvious examples such as Rupert Murdoch's *Sun*, but also the left-wing, partly TUC-owned *Daily Herald* of the 1930s. The latter underwent a radical overhaul to allow it to compete with popular commercial rivals such as the *Mail* and the *Express*, causing great consternation among those in the labour movement who wanted it to stick to its pedagogic mission and its championing of the Labour Party and the trade unions.

The paper known today as the *Guardian*, which for the first 138 years of its existence was called the *Manchester Guardian*, was for most of its life a relatively small circulation newspaper with a high-minded aspiration to educate its readership, improve public knowledge and promote a broadly liberal sensibility. Even as the paper transformed first into a truly national title and then into an international and vastly more expansive multimedia digital news company, these values have remained although they have evolved in response to broader social and cultural changes and financial pressures. When surveying the history of the *Guardian*, its political economy should be a central part of the story. Even when not directly influencing the editorial position of the paper, financial concerns always remained greatly important. Moreover, the status of the paper and its ability to wield influence have been defined not just by the power of the *Guardian*'s journalism and political commentary, but by factors such as the size and reach of its circulation, the geographical location of its office and its readership and the structure of the company.

The last of these issues has been of particular importance throughout the second half of the *Guardian*'s existence. Scott's centennial essay has become a widely cited text on journalistic ethics and practice, providing such memorable and influential dictums as 'Comment is free, but facts are sacred'. It has also served as a cornerstone for the direction of the Scott Trust, the unique ownership system that has maintained the *Guardian*'s independence since the mid-1930s. According to former *Guardian* editor Alastair Hetherington, '[t]he Scott Trust is worth attention both because it provides a greater guarantee of editorial freedom than any other and because it aims to maintain journalism with a high standard of accuracy and impartiality, as well as an open-minded approach.'[2] First formed in 1936 in the aftermath of C.P. Scott's death and that of the son who succeeded him as editor, Ted, the Scott Trust has controlled the *Guardian* and various other newspapers and assets ever since. The importance placed on the Trust by successive *Guardian* editors Hetherington, Peter Preston, Alan Rusbridger and Katharine Viner exemplifies how integral it has remained to the practical functioning and the self-image of the paper, and how it presents itself to the outside world.

This chapter will provide a brief historical account of the political economy of the *Guardian*, charting its financial status and commercial activities from its launch in 1821 to the current day. A recurring theme is the tension of a newspaper which has often aimed for high-minded journalistic, ethical and political ideals, whilst also attempting to maintain financial viability. Alongside an in-depth examination of the formation of the Scott Trust, the chapter mainly focuses on the period covering Alan Rusbridger's two decades as editor (1995–2015) and the ongoing tenure of his successor Katharine Viner (2015–present). This will help make sense of the current status of the *Guardian* and will provide useful context for the subsequent chapters in this volume. The financial health of the newspaper industry has ebbed and flowed over the centuries since a modern press arose and has had a significant impact on the orientation of the *Guardian* throughout its 200 years.

THE EARLY *MANCHESTER GUARDIAN*, 1821–1907

As discussed in the opening chapter, the *Manchester Guardian* was launched in 1821 in the wake of the Peterloo Massacre. John Edward Taylor had witnessed the violence enacted upon the peaceful protestors first-hand, and had written to *The Times* in London outlining what had happened. A prosperous cotton trader and supporter of moderate political reform, Taylor decided to launch a new weekly newspaper to provide a means of holding what he saw as an *ancien régime* to account, particularly in the Manchester and Lancashire region.[3] Taylor was a Nonconformist liberal – a worldview which was to remain important among those at the top of the *Guardian* until at least the mid-twentieth century – and was part of an influential group of elites who shared similar views who had begun meeting in Manchester in 1815, known as the 'Little Circle'. They had a common interest in the press as an instrument of democracy. Fellow member William Cowdroy Jnr was already the editor of the *Manchester Gazette* while Archibald Prentice served periods as editor of both the *Manchester Gazette* and the *Manchester Times*. Most of the Circle backed Taylor in his new venture, aside from Cowdroy who did not wish the *Gazette* to face competition for the same political demographic. Some space had been opened up, however, by the closure of the more radical Nonconformist *Manchester Observer* and in May 1821 the *Manchester Guardian* was launched as a four-page weekly newspaper.

Taylor remained owner and editor of the paper until shortly before his death in 1844, whereupon Jeremiah Garnett assumed the role of editor and – after a period of ownership by his brother-in-law Russell Scott – as laid out in John's will, ownership passed to John's son Edward – who also became editor in 1861.[4] Alongside Peter Allen, Edward Taylor also acquired the *Manchester Evening News* (*MEN*) soon after its launch in 1868, with the fates of the two papers remaining entwined for the next century and a half. The *MEN* moved into the *Guardian* offices at Cross Street in 1879. The first half century of the *Guardian* featured some financially precarious moments, such as in 1856 when newly purchased printing machinery proved to be inadequate for meeting the demands of the circulation, and emergency funds had to be canvassed by Taylor.[5] There were politically troublesome moments as well. The commercial interests of the paper – and of the capitalist class in the Manchester region more generally – centred on the cotton industry and played a role in shaping the *Guardian*'s stance on the American Civil War, where it offered support to the slave-owning South.[6]

Such a stance would have been unthinkable under the paper's most enduring editor, Charles Prestwich Scott, Russell Scott's son, who, at the request of his cousin and the then proprietor, also named John Edward Taylor, first joined the paper as London editor in 1871 and the following year became editor at the young age of 24. Even though Taylor could have, in theory, used his position to exert control, Scott was left free to do as he pleased. His strong personality and convictions were in stark contrast to Taylor's more reticent nature, and on the few occasions that the owner tried to influence Scott he was ignored, or the threat of resignation would be suggested until Taylor relented.[7]

Scott pushed the paper in a more radical direction even though some of its controversial positions led to financial challenges. For example, the *Guardian*'s opposition to the Boer War hit both advertising revenue and readership as the *Guardian* saw its circulation drop nearly one-seventh to 41,900 daily copies. However, many readers who disagreed with its position on the war nevertheless continued to buy it for its commercial news, and the losses were offset slightly by special newspaper trains set up to deliver to London and North Wales. Scott himself blamed the loss of 'casual sales' on the arrival of the *Daily Mail* into Manchester in 1900, due more to the latter's cheaper cost and sensationalist style than its pro-war stance. Even then, according to the *Guardian*'s managing editor, G.B. Dibblee, newsagents reported they sold more *Guardians* whenever delayed trains meant the *Mail* did not arrive on time.[8]

SCOTT FAMILY OWNERSHIP, 1907–36

The *Guardian* managed to ride out the hostility it had attracted for its opposition to the Boer War and the paper's steadfast ethical stance during the episode elevated its reputation among many liberals and radicals across Britain and beyond. Even so, while advertising revenue did steadily rise from the nadir of 1902, the drop in circulation continued, with 1907 seeing an average daily net sale 27 per cent lower than it had been in 1898.[9] Yet 1907 also saw C.P. Scott increase his dominance over the *Guardian*, when he became proprietor.[10] Taylor had died in 1905 and his will mandated that the trustees of his estate give Scott first refusal on the 'copyright' of the paper at a valuation of £10,000, and also recommended that they offer him the offices and printing works on reasonable terms. Yet the trustees were not obligated to sell to Scott due to the ambiguous wording of the document, likely the result of Taylor's anxieties about how Scott had been running the business. While he was happy with the title's editorial line, Taylor had recurrent concerns about the paper's commercial performance and the fact that Scott was often away from the office for extended periods, such as when attending Westminster as a Liberal MP until his retirement from parliament in 1906. After over a year and a half of legal wrangling, Scott ended up paying a much larger sum than he and his financial advisers assessed the assets to be worth: £80,000 for the copyright and £100,000 for the premises and plant. In total, Scott had to raise £240,000 to buy the paper, including paying off existing loans. His own fortune of £48,000 formed the whole of the ordinary shares of a new company, the Manchester Guardian Ltd., apart from the qualifying shares of the other members of the immediate family who served as directors. The remainder of the capital was raised in four per cent preference shares. The *MEN*, meanwhile, had passed down to the Allen family. Although the two papers remained housed in the same building, their connection was, temporarily, severed.

At the *Guardian*'s centenary dinner in 1921, Lord Robert Cecil described Scott's work as 'making righteousness readable'. John Scott, C.P.'s son and managing director of the paper, claimed at a staff celebration that his achievement was 'to make readable righteousness remunerative'.[11] Indeed, the *Guardian* emerged from the end of the First World War (a war about which the *Guardian* had argued against British involvement) in a strong financial position. Its circulation of nearly 70,000 by 1919 was higher than ever before – nearly double what it had been at the formation of the new company in 1907. Advertising revenue was healthy, and profits were rising. In response, the company capitalised £113,000 of its undistributed profits in March 1920, with the new ordinary shares allotted equally between Scott's two sons, Ted and John, and his son-in-law, C.E. Montague. At the age of 74, Scott decided to take none himself, aware of the creeping inevitability of death duties which could fatally wound the company.

The *Guardian*'s financial recovery was even more impressive given the emergence of a new competitor in its home region. In 1909, the *Daily News*, another liberal organ, began printing in Manchester, the second London paper to expand its operations in the north after the *Daily Mail*. The war had killed off the *Guardian*'s traditional quality rival in the Manchester and Lancashire area, the conservative *Manchester Courier*, which had printed its last issue in January 1916.[12] Even more importantly, the *Guardian* was formally reunited with the paper with which it cohabited in Cross Street. The *MEN* and the *Guardian* became stablemates in 1924 when the former was purchased by John Scott. C.P. Scott was delighted with the deal as it afforded the *Guardian* a financial safety net. Indeed, the *Guardian* was to rely on the more financially stable evening title in times of crisis throughout the remainder of the century.[13]

In a move that perhaps seems to better fit the reputation of the press barons than an icon of liberalism, Scott planned for a dynastic inheritance. His sons, Ted and John, were groomed for, and eventually assumed, the roles of, editor and manager. Though formally retiring in 1929 with Ted taking his place, Scott remained a regular fixture at Cross Street until his death in 1932. Ted was now fully in control but faced a daunting set of challenges. Britain had been suffering from economic difficulties and structural unemployment since the early 1920s, which was made worse by the Wall Street Crash of 1929 and the European financial crisis of 1931. This economic situation put great strain on the *Guardian*'s finances and its advertising revenue. Moreover, the economic and financial crises had contributed to political turmoil, with the formation of a National Government in Britain. Ted Scott believed that such a government undermined democracy and was increasingly drawn to more radical solutions for Britain's social and economic ills, finding sympathy with socialist ideas.

He staunchly opposed the National Government in the *Guardian*'s leader columns, even though he was aware this ran the risk of alienating some of the readership. This led Scott to question whether a change of cover price might be necessary, from twopenny down to a penny. With politics being in such an 'ugly shape', he believed the *Guardian* would 'be driven more and more to take an anti-property line. And that is fatal to a 2d. paper'.[14] Tragically, however, Ted Scott was to die in April 1932 while sailing on Lake Windermere with his eldest son,

Richard. Under his successor, William Percival Crozier, the *Guardian* moderated its political stance, and radical changes to the ownership structure of the paper were set in motion in the form of the Scott Trust.

THE SCOTT TRUST AND THE MOVE TO LONDON, 1933–93

The Scott Trust was created by Ted's brother John as a response to his death and the financial challenges this had caused for the *Guardian*. The Trust remained the holder of all ordinary shares and the trustees on the Scott Trust board drew no income or dividends from the company, apart from the three who drew salaries as employees of the company and one as a non-executive director. The Trust was to operate on a profit-seeking principle, but all profits were ploughed directly back into the company – and later its wider media group.[15] The original Trust deed required the Scott Trust board to continue the business on 'the same lines and in the same spirit as heretofore', but this left open lots of room for interpretation. In practice, the trustees appointed the editors and managing directors of the group's two principal newspapers, the *Manchester Guardian* and the *MEN*, the other group directors on both newspapers' boards and new members of the trust itself. The only instruction given to an editor upon their appointment was to 'carry on the paper in the same spirit as before', a tradition which persisted down the decades. Editorial policy continued to remain the preserve of the editor and was therefore rarely discussed by trustees, and usually only at the invitation of the editor.[16]

Although the overall structure and functioning of the Scott Trust remained stable until it was reformed as a limited company in 2008, the number of trustees and directors on its board and that of the *Manchester Guardian* and *MEN* gradually expanded over time. The *Guardian* was, for much of its history, centred on a number of interconnected families. It began with the Taylors, and expanded to include their relatives, the Scotts. The celebrated journalist C.E. Montague married C.P. Scott's daughter while deputy editor Allan Monkhouse was followed into the paper by his two sons Paddy and Allen. W.P. Crozier, a long-serving news editor and then editor of the paper, was joined by his daughter Mary who explained that she was 'born into it.'[17] Rather than this being solely due to nepotism, this family lineage occurred partly because those that stayed at the *Guardian* long-term felt the paper had an historic mission to promote and defend its own brand of liberalism, and most of the key figures during the late nineteenth and early twentieth centuries shared similar Nonconformist religious beliefs. This worldview was also shared among some of the *Guardian*'s readers around Manchester, and among liberals across the country who were its regular readers. For this reason, the *Guardian* attracted many journalists with values that matched the paper's own, a process which has in some respects persisted to the current day. It also historically led to continuity among those at the top of the paper. Even by the time Alan Rusbridger joined the paper in 1979, he remembers it as having had the feel of 'a family newspaper'.[18]

By 1981, when Hetherington wrote his account of his time at the paper, the boards had already expanded. Back when Hetherington was first appointed editor, former editor Alfred Powell Wadsworth and Laurence Scott, son of John, were members of both the Scott Trust and the Manchester Guardian and MEN Board, with Wadsworth chairing the Trust and Laurence the board. Alongside them, there were only four other trustees and four further directors. Hetherington describes Laurence as having never been a conventional proprietor or company chairman, 'rather the head of the family'. He added that from an editor's point of view, Laurence was 'a model manager with whom to work', who was 'shrewd on the business side and never interfered with editorial affairs'.[19] Richard Scott, son of Ted, became chairman of the Trust after Wadsworth's death. Richard was also serving as the paper's diplomatic correspondent in first Washington and then Paris, before finally retiring in 1974. Hetherington was therefore Richard's ultimate boss, but explained that 'the Trust's authority nevertheless stood above me'.[20] Laurence took the decision to appoint Hetherington as editor in 1956 as Wadsworth was seriously ill, though he did discuss the matter with the other trustees and directors. By 1975 there were ten trustees, which was the upper limit allowed by the Trust deed, and ten directors. Hetherington's successor, Peter Preston, was selected after a 'more systematic consultation', consisting of a joint committee drawn from the Trust and the board and an advisory group drawn from the editorial staff.

The centrality of the Scott family to the Scott Trust diminished as the decades passed, though the link has never been broken. However, its board, and that of the *Guardian* and MEN and its successors, remained filled with longstanding members of staff or others who had close associations with the *Guardian*. As we will see, the situation has changed somewhat in recent years as *Guardian* stalwarts have increasingly been joined by outsiders from the spheres of finance, business and technology. But for a long time, this lineage helped the *Guardian* maintain a sense of continuity and a consistency in its character and political sensibilities. Indeed, writing in the mid-1980s, Simon Jenkins, later to become editor of *The Times* and a longstanding columnist for the *Guardian* itself, stated that no other newspaper had gone to such lengths to ensure that its columns remained loyal to its journalistic tradition and the values of its early proprietors, with a corollary of this being that he doubted whether anyone with right-wing views would be appointed to the board of the Trust.[21]

Although the post-war period saw the age of the press barons come to an end and many newspapers were subsumed by multinational conglomerates, proprietorial control by no means disappeared within the British press.[22] Associated Newspapers, including the *Mail* titles, remained under the control of the Rothermeres, in the form of Esmond Harmsworth, who was admittedly far less editorially interventionist than his father. Among the quality titles, the *Telegraph* remained under the control of the Camrose and Burnham families until Conrad Black's takeover in 1986. *The Times* had an unusual system under the ownership of John Jacob Astor v and John Walter between 1922 and 1966, and under Roy Thomson between 1966 and 1976, with little proprietorial interference beyond the selection of editors and oversight of financial matters.[23] This changed drastically once the paper was acquired by Rupert Murdoch in 1981 as exemplified by his dismissal of the well-respected editor Harold Evans.

The rise of media conglomerates placed even more of an onus on commercial concerns which, while always a main concern of the press lords, had also been accompanied by their use of newspapers for propaganda purposes and to secure political leverage. As Hetherington explained, the *Guardian* editor's position was highly unusual, as there was – and remains – no proprietor above them, which allowed for much greater editorial freedom than was possible for most other editors. The financial support provided by the Scott Trust also offered at least some leeway for editors to pursue journalism on ethical rather than commercial grounds, though as Hetherington noted the editor still had to work 'in close conjunction with the management in commercial and financial matters, and must keep within his budget'.[24]

A mixture of financial and editorial imperatives lay behind the decision to transform the *Manchester Guardian* from a provincial newspaper (with an international reputation) to a truly national – that is to say, London-based – newspaper. The first step in this direction came when the paper dropped 'Manchester' from its name in 1959. As Carole O'Reilly has explored, the status of national newspaper was important for a variety of reasons.[25] The *Guardian*'s position outside of London was for a long time regarded by the newspaper itself, its journalists, and many of its readers as a virtue, though the paper also ranged far beyond Manchester in its coverage. Yet the fact that the *Manchester Guardian* was commonly labelled a provincial paper – including in prominent initiatives such as Political and Economic Planning's 1938 *Report on the British Press* and the 1947 *Royal Commission on the Press* – created economic and reputational problems. For example, the British newspaper industry was riven by a north–south divide even by the 1920s, with two separate bodies for newspaper owners that independently negotiated pay and conditions with the National Union of Journalists: the Newspaper Federation representing proprietors in the North and Midlands, and the Southern Federation the southern dailies. This was part of a wider pattern which dictated that newspapers based outside of London could not be classed as national regardless of the content of the paper itself.

By 1956, the *Manchester Guardian* was increasingly attracting new readers. Most lived in London and the South East, while sales in the North-West remained static. For example, in January 1956, 30,000 copies of the *Guardian* were being sold in London and the Home Counties, and this rose to 41,300 by July 1959.[26] Yet the paper was widely lampooned – notably by the satirical magazine *Private Eye*, the conservative magazine the *Spectator* and the comedy television programme *That Was the Week That Was* – because of its provincial status. This reputational harm and its influence over potential readers and advertisers heightened more important financial impacts. The *Guardian* was excluded from the Newspaper Proprietors' Association, which organised the national distribution of newspapers and conducted negotiations with trade unions.[27] But most harmful of all was the fact that the *Guardian* was unable to charge as much for advertising as the national, London-based titles. In particular, it did not attract as much of the prized display advertising as its quality rivals, which severely undermined the paper's financial security.[28] The decision to change the paper's title was taken by Hetherington and Laurence Scott to start to counteract these issues, but it was very unpopular with much of the readership, as letters received by the paper shows.[29] In 1960 the *Guardian* began to be printed in London for the first time, and four years later it relocated its main offices to Grays Inn Road in London, completing the shift. It was a complicated and contentious move, but it reshaped the *Guardian* as a national newspaper – with all of the extra status, influence and advertising revenue that this entailed.[30]

By the start of the 1980s, the *Guardian* was ninth in terms of circulation among national newspaper titles. As ever, it had been constantly on the brink of financial trouble, often being supported by the profits of the *MEN*. But gradually throughout the early 1980s its situation improved, due to Peter Preston's effort to modernise the paper and cut back where possible and, in conjunction with its business managers, his success in building up the paper's profitable classified advertising. The Scott Trust also began to invest in the *Auto Trader* classified advertising business from the early 1980s, which would eventually recoup sizeable financial rewards.[31] Moreover, the Scott Trust benefitted from a short-term cash injection in 1984, as did the rest of Fleet Street, when most national newspapers sold their holdings in the news agency Reuters. Previously a trust, it was floated on the market, and the *Guardian* received £26 million for its share.[32]

By the end of the decade, the *Guardian* had large, extremely profitable print sections from Monday to Wednesday carrying adverts for hundreds of jobs in media, education and public service.[33] This success came despite the launch of the *Independent* in 1986, a new quality title that tried to target a diverse range of political views across the political spectrum from the *Guardian* to *The Times*. Part of a raft of new print news ventures that were launched throughout the 1980s due to the introduction of new digital production techniques – such as Eddie Shah's *Today* – the *Independent* was the most successful and became an enduring rival for the *Guardian* in the quality newspaper market.

BUYING THE *OBSERVER*, THE MOVE TO DIGITAL AND A NEW MEMBERSHIP MODEL, 1993–2020

The competition from the *Independent* forced the hand of the Scott Trust. In 1993, what was now the Guardian Media Group was granted permission to launch a rival bid for the venerable Sunday newspaper the *Observer*, which had been placed onto the market after being beset by financial difficulties. Although the bid was successful, the *Observer* was to become a long-term drain on the Trust's finances. The intended strategy of merging it with the *Guardian* in a manner that would cut down on overheads was complex – both newspapers had their own proud histories, and the staff of the *Observer* continued to prize its distinct identity. This problem was compounded by an even greater challenge for Preston's successor in the form of transitioning online. The *Guardian*'s early digital efforts began under Preston with the Product Development Unit (PDU), later rebranded the New Media Lab. It was composed of people who Alan Rusbridger described as 'creatives', rather than journalists. After stints at the *Observer* and the short-lived *London Daily News*, Rusbridger had returned to the *Guardian* and launched the Saturday magazine and a daily tabloid features section, *G2*. Both were good sources of advertising revenue, and signalled the paper's future efforts to capitalise on such features and lifestyle content. Rusbridger was sent on a fact-finding mission to the US in the early 1990s to see what newspapers there were up to online. Rusbridger stressed to Preston in a note on his return that the internet was wild and chaotic, but that it offered a great opportunity for the *Guardian*.[34] The *Guardian*'s initial venture online appeared in 1995, one year after the *Daily Telegraph*, although this was still before other organisations such as the BBC which only launched a website in 1997. While early online *Guardian* efforts were often innovative, they were not yet a money-making proposition.[35]

As we have already discussed, the Scott Trust allows the editor great leeway to shape the *Guardian*, but its editors have always worked in the manner they feel befits the history and traditions of the paper. Rusbridger became editor in 1995 and later recalled:

> On most papers the proprietor or chief executive would find an editor, take him/her out to lunch and do the deal. On the *Guardian*

– at least according to a tradition dating back to the mid-1970s – the Scott Trust made the decision after balloting the staff, a process that involved manifestos, pub hustings and even (by some candidates) a little frowned-on campaigning.[36]

His mission statement when running was that he planned to boost investigative reporting and get serious about digital. His own view of the paper was – and is – that the *Guardian* takes editorial positions on an issue-by-issue basis, while sticking to a broadly liberal position overall. As part of this liberal ethos, the *Guardian*, Rusbridger believes, is duty bound to present a diverse range of opinions and beliefs, even political viewpoints which go against its own editorial line.

Looking back at the history of the paper, he notes that on some issues the *Guardian* has historically been quite radical (such as over the Boer War) while on others (such as its position on the US Civil War), the opposite was the case. In more recent times, it has advocated more radical policies on the environment without ever taking an anti-capitalist perspective. Under Rusbridger, its editorial position remained broadly in favour of a 'regulated, stakeholder-based capitalism' that mirrored the Scott Trust's own status as a profit-seeking company, but one with ethical imperatives. Indeed, Rusbridger described the Scott Trust as 'a very conservative institution', not in a political sense, but as regards how it operates and its need to keep the *Guardian* afloat.

Around 2007, Rusbridger and Liz Forgan, the chair of the Scott Trust Board, attempted to update the Trust's mission statement, while lawyer and fellow board member Anthony Salz codified it more explicitly in 2015.[37] The composition of the board members has changed compared to decades past. Although there is still a Scott family member present, the traditional family dynamic of the *Guardian* has largely disappeared. And while experienced *Guardian* journalists continue to feature on all of the companies' boards, often after stepping down from their previous journalistic positions, they have been joined by a host of figures from the worlds of finance, business and technology.[38] Rusbridger duly noted that there were recurrent tensions on the Guardian Board, Guardian Media Group Board and the Scott Trust between those who wanted to prioritise commercial and those who wanted to focus on editorial concerns.[39] Commercial pressures were certainly becoming ever more of an existential threat.

By the early 1990s, a big squeeze on newspapers began, that only accelerated over the following decades, as the new digital world supplanted the old order. Rupert Murdoch was using his deep pockets, having reaped success from the *Sun* and Sky Television, to undermine the competition. He started a price war, with the *Guardian* estimating that circulation of his own quality title *The Times* surged 80 per cent after he cut the cover price below what it cost to print and distribute. Murdoch could afford to bear the losses in the short-term, as long as it damaged competitors. The *Independent* seemingly fared worst, losing around £42 million a year (around £80 million when adjusted for inflation), while the *Telegraph* also lost £45 million in circulation revenues after cutting its own cover price to 18p. The *Guardian* stayed out of the price war, which in theory saved it around £27 million a year. It also shaved an inch and a half off the width of the newspaper, saving a further million a year in newsprint costs.

However, by this stage, the *Guardian*'s circulation had eroded by around 10,000 per day. Even more worryingly, the *Guardian* had an ageing readership – the average age being 43 – which preoccupied the paper's editorial and commercial staff 'rather a lot' as there was a large danger that the readership would become too old for the advertisements the paper carried.[40] The *Guardian* itself was profitable due to its advertising, although the £56 million a year generated through sales went directly to paying for the paper it was printed on and distribution. The newspaper division as a whole was losing nearly £21 million annually, mostly due to the fact that the *Observer* was eating up so much money. As Rusbridger later noted, despite its 'wonderful, romantic' history, the *Observer*'s commercial troubles consumed vast amounts of editorial, management and commercial time for the best part of the next decade.[41] Despite this, and cutbacks on news reporting seen across the media as advertising revenues dropped and journalists were increasingly laid off or forced to produce more content in less time – later described by the *Guardian*'s own Nick Davies as 'churnalism'[42] – the *Guardian*'s investment in reporting remained comparatively far more extensive than most of the UK press, and even led the way among the qualities. However, the proliferation of content on the *Guardian*'s website undoubtedly meant that quality levels varied more than had been the case in the print edition.

Rusbridger noted that the fact that the *Guardian* was owned by the Scott Trust meant that there was not the 'quarter-by-quarter financial reporting pressures that led so many newspapers to, almost literally, decimate their journalistic resources'.[43] Yet the *Guardian* was also not a charity. Rusbridger hoped that by producing impactful journalism, the paper's 'brand' would reap the benefits, potentially attracting more readers. To this end, slow, resource-intensive stories were pursued, resulting in some impressive results that brought the paper a lot of attention and acclaim, from its reporting on the WikiLeaks cables, to its breaking of the phone hacking scandal, to its publication of Edward Snowden's revelations on state surveillance. The money that could be channelled from other companies to subsidise the paper's journalism when necessary merely levelled the playing field with the 'billionaire press' as the wider media navigated the expensive shift to online. Even so, the sums available to the *Guardian* meant it would have been unable to survive disastrous investments such as Rupert Murdoch's acquisition of MySpace, and they were minute in comparison to the vast fortunes that were to be amassed by the new West Coast tech giants.[44] Although greatly reduced, the advertising revenue brought in by the print edition was still vital for the company.

With money needing to be found for the expansion of online operations, the print editions of the *Guardian* and *Observer* underwent a series of cost cutting changes. First, they moved to the slimmer, European-style Berliner format in 2005, a temporary solution which required new printers, while in 2017 both papers finally changed to tabloid size. By this time, the company's focus had long been firmly on the digital with both Rusbridger and the Scott Trust committed to a long-term survival strategy based on expanding the *Guardian*'s online presence to a large enough extent that digital advertising would make the business sustainable.

During the transition period, much like all other legacy media organisations, the Guardian Media Group's titles had been haemorrhaging money. To help secure the *Guardian*'s future, the Scott Trust Limited investment fund replaced the Scott Trust in 2008. There were also strategic considerations at play, as Rusbridger and others at the paper surmised that some of the company's other assets would no longer be as profitable, and hence as able to prop up the *Guardian* and *Observer*'s journalism, as they had in the past. To that end in February 2010, the Scott Trust sold its GMG Regional Media arm and its regional print titles to Trinity Mirror Group, who were expanding to become the dominant player in the ailing regional news sector. Alongside the sale of 31 other titles in the North West and the South of England, this severed the *Guardian*'s long connection with the *MEN*, which caused a lot of consternation among staff at the latter who felt that after helping to prop up the *Guardian* for so long, the *MEN* was being abandoned at a very precarious time.[45] Within a few years, another asset which had been a key factor in the continuation of the Scott Trust and the *Guardian* was offloaded, in the form of the GMG's 50.1 per cent stake in *Auto Trader*, which was sold to the venture capital firm Apax Partners for £619 million in March 2014.[46] As a result of these sales, the Scott Trust was left with a substantial investment of over £1 billion, though this was steadily eroded each year as the papers continued to run at a loss, particularly after the catastrophic crash in the digital advertising market in 2012.

Throughout this period, the *Guardian* had managed to expand its online reach in a very impressive fashion, with its nearly 39 million unique visitors in 2012 lagging only behind the *New York Times* and the *Mail Online*.[47] A major aspect of this rested on the deliberate decision to make use of the possibilities offered by being online to secure a more global audience and, in particular, a stake in the lucrative US market. While in part motivated by journalistic ideals of wanting to wield more influence and cover more important topics, there was an obvious commercial logic behind this effort. The *Guardian*'s UK demographic was not particularly affluent, especially in comparison with the other quality titles. This meant that it was unable to attract the extremely profitable advertisements targeted at high-income readers. The *Guardian*'s readership in the US, by contrast, lay in the higher income streams that would attract just this advertising.[48] The *Guardian*'s US office in New York was therefore greatly expanded in scope. The *Guardian* also launched an Australian operation, though via a more propitious path. A wealthy financial backer loaned the Scott Trust the required capital to help generate an alternative to the Murdoch-dominated media within the country, on the strict proviso that they would have no say over editorial matters.[49] This now gave the *Guardian* offices around the globe that enable truly 24-hour updates and the breaking of latest news for the website. The *Guardian*'s focus on online was reflected in its move from Farringdon Road to new offices at Kings Place, with a floorplan designed to allow the various departments of the organisation to work effectively together to produce content for the website.

Perhaps the most important recent development in the political economy of the *Guardian* concerns its shift to a membership model. It is startling that the *Guardian*'s online content continues to be free, in contrast to most of its direct competitors such as *The Times* and the *New York Times* which have implemented paywalls. Once again, this was a mixture of idealism and business strategy. Rusbridger and others at the paper such as Emily Bell were conscious of the fact that paywalls would deprive the less affluent of access to the best information, further entrenching inequality and undermining the public's ability to effectively engage in politics. But choosing not to implement a paywall also enabled the *Guardian* to amass a much larger volume of traffic to its website which, it was hoped, would eventually pay off in terms of advertising revenue. This strategy was not as successful as was originally hoped, so alternative ancillary means were turned to in the form of sponsorship deals, commercial partnerships and, most importantly, membership options.[50]

This was originally an idea floated by the US writer and commentator Clay Shirky at a Guardian Live event in March 2012.[51] First introduced under Rusbridger, the approach has been maintained under the current editor, Katharine Viner, as have the *Guardian*'s core values, still centred on C.P. Scott's famous essay written to mark the centenary of the newspaper in 1921.[52] Viner's own 'long read' on the 'mission for journalism' reasserted the paper's founding principles and once again placed the paper's history and the role of the Scott Trust front and centre.[53] In public messaging on the issue in the *Guardian* itself and through other platforms, Viner has continued to champion the paper's liberal character and its membership model – although the possibility that the latter could change in the future has been left open when the issued has been raised during interviews.[54] Various options have been offered for users to contribute to the *Guardian*, from yearly subscriptions to one off payments. Recently, some content has shifted to only being viewable by those with registered accounts on the website – though this is still free of charge. Regardless, in 2019 the Scott Trust was able to report a small operating profit for the first time in decades before the Covid-19 pandemic then hit leading to £25 million in projected losses and up to 180 job losses.[55] How the changes to the *Guardian* – driven by both idealism and commercial necessity, and often a hybrid of the two – will alter the company going forwards is unclear, but that it has already changed dramatically even when compared to only two decades ago is already evident.

CONCLUSION

This chapter has provided a brief overview of how the political economy of the *Guardian* has changed, from its launch in 1821 to the current day. The tension between the paper's ideals – which took an enduring form under the editorship of C.P. Scott – and the financial realities of remaining afloat have been a constant feature of that history. The rest of the story has been one of dramatic changes. From a weekly paper to a daily; from a family dynasty to control by the unique vehicle of the Scott Trust; from a provincial paper based in Manchester to a national one based in London; from a broadsheet to a Berliner to a tabloid; from a printed product to a vast multimedia website. Indeed, the *Guardian* can no longer really be called a newspaper. Though it still produces print editions six days a week and a print edition of the *Observer* on Sunday, the vast majority of its resources and its output are now online.

Yet even as traditional concerns such as printing and print distribution have receded in importance – though not yet disappeared – new logistical, financial and commercial imperatives have arisen and the conflict between securing the bottom line and championing liberal values remains as important as ever. The Scott Trust has divested most of its assets to feed into a new investment fund, while the character of the *Guardian* and its distinctive brand of journalism has already been changed by the move online, its vastly expanded readership and its efforts to reach audiences in Australia and especially the US. Whether the *Guardian* will manage to remain viable – at least in its current form – and whether the changes stemming from social media competition and a more unforgiving commercial environment fundamentally alter the essence of the *Guardian* remains to be seen.

NOTES

1. Originally published in 5 May 1921 edition of the *Manchester Guardian*. An online version is available at: Charles Prestwich Scott, 'CP Scott's Centenary Essay', *Guardian*, 23 October 2017, https://www.theguardian.com/sustainability/cp-scott-centenary-essay (last accessed 21 October 2020).
2. Alastair Hetherington, *News, Newspapers and Television* (London, Macmillan: 1985), p. 25.
3. Most of the wealth amassed by Taylor and his associates came from the cotton trade, and the *Guardian* has recently commissioned an academic research project to explore possible connections to the Atlantic slave trade. See Ben Quinn, 'Scott Trust commissions research into Guardian founder's possible links to slave trade', *Guardian*, 17 July 2020, https://www.theguardian.com/media/2020/jul/17/scott-trust-commissions-research-into-guardian-founders-possible-links-to-slave-trade (last accessed 25 October 2020).
4. A helpful outline of the Taylor–Scott family tree is available on the inside cover of David Ayerst, *Guardian: Biography of a Newspaper* (London: Collins, 1971).
5. Ayerst, *Guardian*, chapter 10.
6. Ayerst, *Guardian*, pp. 151–5.
7. Ayerst, *Guardian*, pp. 220–2, 244–54.
8. Mark Hampton, 'The Press, Patriotism, and Public Discussion: C.P. Scott, the *Manchester Guardian*, and the Boer War, 1899-1902', *Historical Journal*, 44:1 (2001), pp. 179, 195–6.
9. Ayerst, *Guardian*, p. 305.
10. Ayerst, *Guardian*, chapter 22.
11. Ayerst, *Guardian*, pp. 480–1.
12. Ayerst, *Guardian*, p. 481.
13. Chris Tryhorn, 'Manchester Evening News: Intertwined with the Guardian for 142 Years', *Guardian*, 9 February 2010, https://www.theguardian.com/media/2010/feb/09/manchester-evening-news-theguardian (last accessed 21 October 2020).
14. Stephen Koss, *The Rise and Fall of the Political Press in Britain: Vol. 2, The Twentieth Century* (London: Hamish Hamilton, 1984), p. 516.
15. Philip Schlesinger, *The Scott Trust* (Manchester: Guardian Media Group, 1994).
16. Hetherington, *News, Newspapers and Television*, pp. 25–6.
17. OHP/51 Mary Crozier, Guardian Oral History Project, Guardian News and Media Archive, London.
18. Alan Rusbridger, *Breaking News: The Remaking of Journalism and Why It Matters Now* (Edinburgh: Canongate Books, 2018), p. 21.
19. The only instance Hetherington mentions in regard to Laurence commenting on editorial conduct concerned the Lady Chatterley case

of 1961. Alastair Hetherington, *Guardian Years* (Manchester: Chatto and Windus, 1981), p. 37.

20. Hetherington, *Guardian Years*, p. 36.
21. Simon Jenkins, *The Market for Glory* (London: Faber and Faber, 1986), pp. 212–13.
22. Jeremy Tunstall and Michael Palmer, *Media Moguls* (London: Routledge, 1991).
23. Hetherington, *News, Newspapers and Television*, p. 26.
24. Hetherington, *Guardian Years*, p. 36.
25. Carole O'Reilly, '"The Magnetic Pull of the Metropolis": The *Manchester Guardian*, the Provincial Press and Ideas of the North', *Northern History*, 57:2 (2020), pp. 4–5 https://doi.org/10.1080/0078172X.2020.1800932 (last accessed 21 October 2020).
26. Geoffrey Taylor, *Changing Faces: A History of the Guardian* (London: Fourth Estate, 1993), p. 27.
27. O'Reilly, 'The Magnetic Pull of the Metropolis', p. 5.
28. Hetherington, *Guardian Years*, p. 145.
29. O'Reilly, 'The Magnetic Pull of the Metropolis'.
30. For details of the move, see Hetherington, *Guardian Years*, chapter 7.
31. Peter Preston, 'The Harder the Guardian Worked on Auto Trader, the Luckier It Got', *Guardian*, 26 January 2014, https://www.theguardian.com/media/2014/jan/26/guardian-auto-trader-harder-worked-luckier (last accessed 21 October 2010).
32. Rusbridger, *Breaking News*, pp. 394–5.
33. Rusbridger, *Breaking News*, p. 21.
34. Rusbridger, *Breaking News*, pp. 23, 26.
35. Scott Eldridge, 'Digital News, Digitized News: Exploring Online Newspapers, and Newspapers Online', in Martin Conboy and Adrian Bingham (eds), *The Edinburgh History of the British and Irish Press: 3: Competition and Disruption, 1900-2017* (Edinburgh: Edinburgh University Press, 2020), pp. 211–26.
36. Rusbridger, *Breaking News*, p. 32.
37. Interview with Alan Rusbridger, 18 August 2020.
38. See, for example, the current line ups of the Scott Trust board and the Guardian Media Group Board: 'The Scott Trust Board', *Guardian*, 11 June 2018, https://www.theguardian.com/the-scott-trust/2015/jul/26/the-scott-trust-board (last accessed 21 October 2020); 'GMG Board', *Guardian*, 1 February 2018, https://www.theguardian.com/gmg/2015/jul/23/gnm-board (last accessed 21 October 2020).
39. Interview with Alan Rusbridger, 18 August 2020.
40. Rusbridger, *Breaking News*, p. 32.
41. Rusbridger, *Breaking News*, pp. 32–3, 44.
42. Nick Davies, *Flat Earth News* (London: Chatto & Windus, 2008).
43. Rusbridger, *Breaking News*, p. xii.
44. Rusbridger, *Breaking News*, pp. xxii–iii.

45. Ian Herbert, 'End of the old guard: The sale of the Manchester Evening News', *Independent*, 22 February 2010, https://www.independent.co.uk/news/media/press/end-of-the-old-guard-the-sale-of-the-manchester-evening-news-1906267.html (last accessed 25 October 2020).
46. According to Rusbridger, the decision to sell *Auto Trader* came down to a simple calculation that eventually competitors – whether established rivals such as Murdoch or new online ventures – would eventually undermine its business model. Interview with Alan Rusbridger, 18 August 2020.
47. 'Most Read Online Newspapers in the World: *Mail Online*, *New York Times* and *The Guardian*', *Comscore*, 12 December 2012, https://www.comscore.com/Insights/Infographics/Most-Read-Online-Newspapers-in-the-World-Mail-Online-New-York-Times-and-The-Guardian (last accessed 23 October 2015).
48. In 2011, the average income of the *Guardian*'s US readership was estimated to be $81,000. In contrast, by 2016 the average income of British *Guardian* readers was only £24,000. Rusbridger, *Breaking News*, pp. 211, 241.
49. Rusbridger, *Breaking News*, pp. 337–8.
50. For a brief discussion of the *Guardian*'s use of donations from institutions and individuals such as Barclays Bank, the Joseph Rowntree Foundation, George Soros, the Bill and Melinda Gates Foundation and the Rockefeller Foundation, see Rusbridger, *Breaking News*, pp. 338–9.
51. Rusbridger, *Breaking News*, pp. 270–2.
52. C.P. Scott's centenary essay.
53. Katharine Viner, 'A Mission for Journalism in a Time of Crisis', *Guardian*, 26 November 2017, https://www.theguardian.com/news/2017/nov/16/a-mission-for-journalism-in-a-time-of-crisis (last accessed 21 October 2020).
54. 'The Media Show', *BBC Radio 4*, 6 December 2017, https://www.bbc.co.uk/programmes/b09gzjjd (last accessed 21 October 2020); Katharine Viner, 'Katharine Viner: "The Guardian's Read Funding Model is Working. It's Inspiring"', *Guardian*, 12 November 2018, https://www.theguardian.com/membership/2018/nov/12/katharine-viner-guardian-million-reader-funding (last accessed 21 October 2020); 'The Media Show', *BBC Radio 4*, 3 June 2020, https://www.bbc.co.uk/programmes/m000jmn8 (last accessed 21 October 2020).
55. Charlotte Tobitt, 'Guardian Groups Meets Target to Break Even At End of Three-Year Financial Turnaround Plan', *Press Gazette*, 1 May 2019, https://www.pressgazette.co.uk/guardian-group-meets-target-to-break-even-at-end-of-three-year-financial-turnaround-plan/ (last accessed 21 October 2020); Jim Waterson, 'Guardian announces plans to cut 180 jobs', *Guardian*, 15 July 2020, https://www.theguardian.com/media/2020/jul/15/guardian-announces-plans-to-cut-180-jobs (last accessed 25 October 2020).

3

Reflections from an Editor-at-large

Gary Younge

A BLACK JOURNALIST AT THE *GUARDIAN*

When I started at the *Guardian* on staff, there were only a handful of black journalists there. After about six months of shift work, I was offered a staff job on the Foreign Desk as the assistant foreign editor. Staff vacancies there are rare and coveted, so turnover is quite low. By that time I'd had some experience covering the South African elections in 1994 having been introduced to the *Guardian* initially through a bursary scheme aimed at racial minorities and those who are otherwise underrepresented in journalism and would benefit from assistance. Nobody had me down for that job, and when it was announced there were a few gasps in the office. It was a surprising choice in many ways but primarily because I was only twenty-five, which is quite young to be calling correspondents and saying 'How's that intro coming on?' So given my inexperience, it demanded a certain amount of humility. There were a handful of colleagues who resisted taking instruction from me and I had to work really hard to earn their respect.

Race was an important factor. Why wouldn't it be? There's a lot of racism in British society and it would be strange if the *Guardian* was immune. Generally speaking, it was very convivial: people were very pleasant and I was allowed to do quite a lot of stuff. But there was a moment where, in 1995, I edited a series on 'Black Britain', which didn't endear me to some of my other black colleagues who felt, not unreasonably, that they had been overlooked. The *Guardian* is actually quite a culturally conservative institution – people are there for a long time, and if someone comes in, then you're expected to wait your turn. But when I was doing that series, I had some conversations with white colleagues and was shocked by what they had to say about their black colleagues. Many assumed that they were all affirmative action hires and that none of them were any good, which was not true. They had effectively discounted them being there for any other reason than that they were black. I was actually shocked that they thought it and I was even more shocked that they said it to me.

There was a particular moment that crystallised some of these issues. It was just before the publication of the Macpherson report in 1999, the result of the inquiry into institutional racism following the murder of the black teenager Stephen Lawrence, by which time I'd been at the *Guardian* for a few years. An Asian colleague, Vivek Chaudhary, had been racially abused in the bar that was seen as the '*Guardian* pub'. If we won an award, our management would put a couple of grand behind the bar and everyone would head down the pub. The publican had spoken to a white friend of Vivek's about 'Pakis' moving in and Vivek had gone up and challenged him and the landlord had basically repeated it. Vivek saw in this all the things that the paper was writing about in terms of Macpherson: canteen culture, racist language and stereotyped assumptions.

Vivek raised this at a union meeting. I was travelling for work at the time but from all accounts, his contribution was met with a considerable amount of scepticism and a degree of vilification. He called for the chapel [the NUJ branch] to boycott the pub. The motion was passed but not without resistance and people saying, 'Well, how do we know that what you're saying is true? The publican has a disabled daughter and we're middle-class journalists so why are we beating up on him? We should set up a commission of inquiry to find whether this is true or not.' It felt as if Vivek, and not racism, was in the dock.

The motion was narrowly passed, but when I got back from my trip abroad, Seumas Milne turned to me and said: 'Look, we need you to intervene here.' I appreciated his intervention and was keen to show solidarity but initially bristled at the notion that I had to clear up a racist mess that I had nothing to do with. My initial response was: 'This isn't my responsibility. I'll boycott the pub, but why is it down to me?' But I did get involved and it was incredibly exhausting and distressing. We had this fight on our hands and it was very weird and ugly. Various colleagues would take me aside and talk in very opaque terms about their own views: 'I don't want to get into my private life, but you should know that I couldn't possibly be racist', and then it would turn out they had a black wife or they had black kids by someone who left them. It was as if it was my personal responsibility to fix this thing. And it was very rancorous, because lots of people were not observing the boycott.

Anyway, the black journalists ended up putting a note up on the wall – a letter to our colleagues within the building – saying that 'our understanding of the union is that you stand up for each other and it's disheartening to see people not showing solidarity. We just want you to know how really disappointed we are in you and we will not be going to that pub.' The idea was that if you want to go to a segregated pub, you go to a segregated pub, but we won't be there. This ended with the union officers opposing the boycott and a big union meeting, one of the biggest I'd ever been to, where the chapel voted to reaffirm its commitment to the boycott which led to the resignation of all the chapel's officers. I actually proposed the motion, which was seconded by Katharine Viner, that we reaffirm the boycott. Overall it was a particularly noxious episode.

Once I started in the newsroom after my stint on the Foreign Desk, I was advised (sometimes by the same people) either to write a particular story *because* it was about black people and I had special knowledge *or* to stop writing about black people because otherwise people would think that was all you could do. The latter suggestion, I think, often came from a genuinely supportive and even nurturing place. But it was wrong-headed all the same. 'You will become pigeon-holed' I was told – always in a passive voice, not realising that they were telling me not to write about something I knew a lot about, cared a lot about and could write well about.

This was a constant source of tension. The first column I ever wrote, which was about the Bosnian war, was returned to me with the question: 'Can you add an ethnic sensibility to this?' It was made clear by the then comment editor that my role was to write about 'black stuff'. So it was a struggle for a few years to make it clear that while I did want to write about race, I also wanted to write about other things.

Just because you're paranoid doesn't mean they're not out to get you. There really was the danger that someone would pigeonhole you, and it took a while to navigate the situation. Of course I always thought that race is important and interesting and I wanted to write about it: I wanted to write about the American Black Skiers Association going to a fascist part of Austria or about rap classes or whatever. But

I also wanted to write about Ireland and about strikes and about a range of things. So, there was always this assumption of a kind of expertise that was drawn through melanin, for which there was no office and no resources. It's not like it was established as a specialism, but nevertheless you were expected to produce endless copy about it when required and to keep it to yourself at other times. We never had a race correspondent as a specialist, which I lobbied for constantly, but there was always at least one black person in the office they would constantly go to for stories about race. They just never enjoyed the status or the salary of a specialist correspondent.

I do remember there was one article about a report that featured these spurious arguments about how black people have an Irish future, how Asian people have a Jewish future and stupid bullshit like that. I was asked 'maybe you know some people that we can interview.' And I remember thinking that I'm not actually paid to know black people or at least I shouldn't be. That happened a couple of times: 'we're doing a series on men of a certain age, but it turns out they're all white, so do you know any black ones we could interview?' That kind of thing.

In general, however, there wasn't an awful lot of casual racism at the *Guardian* that was aimed at me. But, there was one time when somebody used the phrase 'nigger in a woodpile' in our daily ten o'clock conference and nobody said anything. So I wrote to a senior member of staff pointing out that 'we write leaders saying that if somebody uses language like that they should be fired.' Now, I wasn't suggesting for a second that the person who said that should be fired, but they should be talked to. 'If it's only me who is offended, forget it. But if you were offended or thought, in retrospect, that it was offensive, then you should talk to him. It shouldn't come from me but from you.' I was quite explicit about it: this stops here if I'm the only person offended; otherwise, it has to come from their superior.

Two minutes later, I get a call from this person who made the comment. 'Oh, I'm such a cunt – I'm so sorry.' And it then became my issue and my problem because 'Gary has complained'. For me that was a completely reprehensible piece of management. So, while the *Guardian* is almost certainly more honest than most mainstream British newspapers, in terms of what is necessary, it's nowhere near honest enough.

The *Guardian* is an expression of a particular patrician form of British liberalism, and, as such, the racism one experienced there was mostly benign. It only occasionally came overtly to the surface when directly challenged or pointed out, regardless of how gently or strategically you did it. Those were the moments when you felt like a mask slipped and you were really being tolerated to a certain point. That didn't happen often, but then it didn't really have to. Whenever it did take place, it was both shocking and unsurprising.

I didn't know a black journalist there who didn't have to navigate tricky situations. But you also had to put it in context. Would you really be better off somewhere else that didn't even publicly aspire to equal opportunities and continually wrote reprehensible things about black people? You can resign from a job but you can't resign from racism. It's out there. As I've already said, the *Guardian* isn't immune. Where would you go? The *Telegraph* or *The Times*? The *Guardian* had its problems, but compared to what? Which other mainstream newspaper was going to publish work by black, left-wing writers? Ultimately, I had a successful career there for 27 or so years, so whatever problems I did experience there were navigable. But not everyone was so fortunate: some people found it really hard and at some moments it got quite unpleasant. On occasion it could be really draining.

Any criticism had to be coupled with a genuine desire to change the complexion of the paper. That was an aspiration that was embraced from the top, but was shaped, in no small part, by pressure from below. Joseph Harker was absolutely central to this work. Joseph thought that the Macpherson report provided an opportunity, a moment, at which to address underlying problems of racism. He convened the black journalists and secured a meeting with the editor Alan Rusbridger who was very receptive to the idea.

We talked about making sure that all posts should be advertised, because up to that point, an awful lot of recruitment was run in a very cliquey way – 'I met this guy' (and it was usually a guy), 'I was on this trip', or 'so and so is a good guy and gets a pint in'. These practices continue to mitigate against Black and Asian journalists, against women, particularly those with kids, or Muslims – there were all sorts of things that were very wrong. So it was important to establish some transparency in hiring practices and to look at what we were publishing and to ask ourselves why, if we're organising panels, there are no black people on them. So, some of it was about how there needed to be broader editorial responsibility and some of it was around newsroom culture. You could complain about the shortcomings of this approach and of particular meetings but at least they happened and they probably wouldn't have happened in most other newsrooms.

Katharine Viner built on that and, in terms of recruitment, ramped it up. Sure enough, as the years went on, the number of black journalists grew and became better organised. I found the younger generation more politically sophisticated, conscious and militant than my own which was great to see.

So, for the longest time, the discussion was mostly about hiring and then things like internships, where traditionally people would give their niece or their godchild or their friend's friend some type of work experience. The black journalists got a work experience scheme together that saw some quite impressive people like Reni Eddo-Lodge and Bim Adewunmi come through it and others who are doing very well. And then there was also the bursary scheme that I set up, which continues to be a conduit for a lot of talent including Randeep Ramesh, who is a chief leader writer, Tania Branigan, who is on the leader writing team, Charlie Brinkhurst-Cuff who is head of editorial at gal-dem and Hannah Azieb Pool, artistic director and CEO of the Bernie Grant Centre.

LIBERALISM AND THE RISE OF JEREMY CORBYN

There is something of the Kremlin in the *Guardian*: it's governed by a Trust which inherits a set of values, and its editors last for a very long time. So there is a certain tension between its conservatism and its liberalism, not least because there is a kind of glacial aspect to change there. Having said that, when pressed, it is able to move quickly and pre-emptively: just think about how quickly it moved to embrace the web compared to other titles. But generally, as the editor is called on to run the paper 'as heretofore', it's big on tradition and of course there is the weight of the Scott Trust's values and legacy that you are constantly applying at any moment. There is a sense of portentousness that I think the editors feel about certain decisions, for example that 'if we go tabloid, if we change to colour photography, if we add a supplement, what does that mean about our mission?' There is this weight about how to be liberal, and how to apply its core values to the present commercial and political moment.

So when it comes to orienting the paper in a certain direction, you're effectively trying to turn a tanker around. You are operating it with a cargo consisting of words, images and stories that reflect the values and precepts of *Guardian* or the Scott Trust and a staff roster that is less fluid than most because of a strong union and the relatively good benefits it offers. There is no travelling light from this history or reality. In contrast to the way in which Andrew Neil took over the *Sunday Times* and shifted it quite dramatically or when Piers Morgan became editor of the *Daily Mirror* and for a moment it turned to the left and carried front- page pieces by John Pilger – and then it didn't. There is none of that at the *Guardian*; you are moving with the full weight of the history even if the flipside of that is that you are not weighed down by purely commercial considerations.

To me, the *Guardian* is tied to a history of a kind of gentleman liberalism that is rooted in early nineteenth-century Northern England, and particularly to its cotton mill owners. So, first of all, you have to understand that it represents the liberal establishment, and is not particularly left-wing although, depending on the moment, it may end up in that position. If anything, actually, its centre of gravity always seemed to me to be to the left of the Labour Party leadership with a very broad range of political comment so that, in my time at least, it would cover that span from Paul Foot (or a version thereof) to someone like Simon Jenkins (and a version thereof). Tony Blair hated the *Guardian* and Alastair Campbell threatened to call a boycott of the paper. If you look at the leaders that were written during the Blair years, they are quite critical of New Labour. But at a time when Jeremy Corbyn and Boris Johnson were confronting each other, liberalism – relative to Corbynism – plays a scuppering role. It finds itself in the mainstream herd with the rest of the pack even if it is coming from a slightly different place.

However, the *Guardian* is perceived as a left-wing paper in relation to what else is on offer. People on the left, therefore, expect more from it – more from it than it has ever given and more than it probably would ever give. But because it's the one place where people on the left feel that they may see themselves or their worldview, then it disappoints more keenly precisely because they expect more from it.

While this tension has always been there, for most of the time that I worked at the paper it was never particularly acute. There would be moments when black people would be outraged about a particular leader or article. For example, there was a lot of friction with the Jewish community for a period over reporting from the Middle East. Support for the Liberal Democrats at the 2010 election drew quite a lot of flak. But for the most part, beyond a handful of activists who were convinced that the *Guardian* was not *a* problem but *the* problem, these credentials weren't seriously tested in my time there until Jeremy Corbyn was elected leader of the Labour Party.

My problem with most of the critiques as to how that played out is that they are too narrowly tailored. They scrutinise the *Guardian* as though it were an abstraction and fail to understand it within the fuller context of the British media and political culture as a whole or its historical role. That's not about letting anything or anybody off the hook but gaining a fuller understanding of what happened and why.

Corbyn's election presented a challenge to the entire media and political establishment. He became leader after 35 years of neoliberal political and economic hegemony, starting with Margaret Thatcher and then moving to Blairism and New Labour. That was the common sense that we had all lived with and that the people reporting on politics, including myself, had grown up with. Their sense of possibility was shaped by it; their contact books – soon to be made somewhat redundant by the emergence of Corbynism – were filled with people who, in one way or another, advocated for it. A set of received wisdoms prevailed about what is possible, about who voters are and what would happen. Most did not just believe this political project would fail; they 'knew' there was no possible way he could succeed.

This was illustrated quite clearly in 2017, when Labour defied expectations. Seven minutes before the polls closed, Piers Morgan tweeted his prediction: 'Conservatives to win by 90-100 seat majority'. Four minutes later, the *Sun*'s deputy political editor, Steve Hawkes, revealed the following: 'Rumour Tories could be looking at 400 seats'. Then comes the exit poll indicating that Labour's vote share had gone up, that they would win seats and that it would be a hung parliament. In pretty much every TV studio, the anchors turned to the people who said this could never happen to tell us what would happen next.

Meanwhile, employment in the media had followed the same oligarchic and elitist trends as the rest of the country. A 2019 report by the Sutton Trust and the Social Mobility Commission showed that while only 7 per cent of the country went to private school, 39 per cent of the elite did; while just 1 per cent went to Oxbridge, 24 per cent of the elite did.[1] The news media in general, and columnists in particular, came from more privileged backgrounds than the elite as a whole: columnists were more likely to have been to Oxbridge than Lords were! You wouldn't want to be too deterministic about that; some of Corbyn's inner circle fit that demographic too and many of his critics didn't. But you can see that in a moment of extreme and escalating inequality, that could be a problem when someone is elected who talks about redistributing wealth and power.

So secure was the consensus that he would lose, that the night before the by-election in Oldham West and Royton, the first edition of the *Daily Mirror* ran the headline: 'Dark Night of the Polls for Jeremy'. It suggested that Labour's lead could be slashed to 1,000. Labour not only won but increased its vote share by 7.3 per cent and came away with a majority of 10,722. The *Mirror* changed its headline for later editions to fit with reality but the claim was then that this was all because of a popular local candidate. So whatever happened, Corbyn couldn't be seen to win. It just wasn't possible. When the consensus is this strong, then nobody has to tell you what to write. The framing is clear.

So when Labour did better than expected in 2017, it was understood as a fluke and when it bombed in 2019, it was understood as inevitable. The chorus within the media and political class was 'I told you so', even though they had told us exactly the same thing two years earlier and had been completely wrong. After 2019, it's like they retreated to their ideological laagers feeling vindicated, with the four intervening years never having touched their sides.

Once again, you wouldn't want to be too deterministic about this. There were plenty of honest disagreements you could have with Corbyn's agenda, record and his capacity to lead a mainstream party. But our views don't emerge from a vacuum and the scarcity of voices and narratives that offered any kind of support, however critical, in no way matched the mood of the country. Even after the rout of 2019, around a third of the country voted Labour. Yet the proportion of columnists who backed Labour, however critically, didn't come anywhere close to that. Just to suggest that this was a necessary course correction in social democracy, replicated through much of Europe and the US and a response to the failure of the centre left to address the fallout of the financial crisis, as I did, left you isolated and marginalised.

I experienced this quite acutely: that it was reputationally damaging simply to *not* trash Corbyn – not to support Corbyn but just *not* to trash him. To take his leadership seriously was to risk not being taken seriously yourself. By doing so, you opened yourself to ridicule and you would be expected to then own his failures. I appeared on Radio 4's *Start the Week* in 2016 and Andrew Marr was like, 'Gary, you're a Corbynista, aren't you?' I wasn't even a member of the Labour Party and had reservations about the prospects for his leadership, which I raised in my work. But of course I did not say that if he wins, the world is going to fall apart. Instead, I argued that the Labour Party needed a course correction.

When I left the paper two months after the 2019 election, a colleague asked if I was leaving because of Labour's defeat, suggesting, I assume, embarrassment or perhaps petulance on my part. I thought this was really odd. First, my departure had been agreed a couple of months before the election had been called and announced six weeks before it took place. But secondly, nobody asked that of the columnists who had declared Corbyn's inevitable demise in 2017 or who had championed the Iraq War in 2003 and even insisted that there were weapons of mass destruction.

Finally, there is the ecology of the news business as a whole. The manner in which the news desks would take up the agenda of the *Today* programme and track the storylines of the TV news during the day was also important. Broadcast news would then pick up the headlines from the papers and it would all start again. It's a very fetid ecosystem and, given the right-wing bias of the mainstream press, the hostility was relentless. You would have to imagine stepping outside that completely and entertain a totally different kind of agenda in order to escape this insular logic.

The example that springs to mind is the video of Corbyn sitting down on the floor of a train because there were no seats. Sitting on the floor when all the seats are full isn't that rare. Anybody who has been on a train for any length of time knows what that is and yet I was staggered to see how credulous people were to think that somehow, Corbyn had made it up or that there were loads of seats and he was sitting on the floor for fun. Journalists interviewed all the people around him and they all said that there were no seats. But somehow Corbyn found himself in the dock and the issue was not the terrible state of our trains but whether he would choose to sit on the floor to make a point. I thought: 'Who do you believe? Richard Branson or all your own experience of travelling on trains?' It reminded me of the story of the dodgy lawyer in the film *Chicago*. A man is caught by his wife in bed with two other women and insists that he is, in fact, alone. 'Come on darling', he tells her. 'You gonna believe what you see or what I tell you?' The degree to which reality can be kind of warped and bent in the service of an idea – and to be in the middle of it as a journalist – was absolutely fascinating to me. There's a reason why they are called 'mainstream newspapers': they may swim in different parts of the river but ultimately they go with the flow.

As I've said, when it comes to the *Guardian*, that excuses nothing but it does, I think, explain a great deal. The issue I raised internally, repeatedly, was not that we should support Corbyn – newspapers should not act as adjuncts to political parties – but that we should be more curious about what he represented and why. It wasn't our job to predict the outcome but it was necessary to describe and interpret what we saw.

I recall in 2016 pointing out the extreme volatility of the moment to a colleague: 'If three years ago you could have called Brexit, Scotland's shift and Trump being the Republican nominee, then maybe you can say what comes next with Corbyn. But if you couldn't, then maybe there's a case for more humility.' He wasn't having it. In the run-up to the 2017 election, I wondered aloud what the large crowds flocking to meet Corbyn signified. 'I'm not saying they're going to vote or that they are representative', I said. 'I'm just wondering what they mean'. I was told that it meant nothing and that Michael Foot had drawn huge crowds in 1983 and look what happened to him.

Now the notion that Corbyn was a terrible thing for the Labour Party was a common stance in the paper but it was by no means either the prevailing or the dominant one. It was openly and frequently contested. There were lots of debates within the paper – the same kind of debates that were taking place within the Labour Party itself. A lot of people were sceptical but not cynical; doubtful but hopeful. And some of that came out in the coverage – not enough, but some. A range of studies have since shown that no news outlet, including the *Guardian*, reported on Corbyn fairly. They also show that the *Guardian* contained both more diverse opinions and more supportive opinions and coverage than virtually any other mainstream outlet.[2]

They don't deserve a medal for that. But it's simply not sustainable to claim that the coverage was universally bad; it wasn't. So, while I understood the disappointment from a huge section of the readership, and from within Labour, I found much of the vitriol and sanctimony that came with it disproportionate.

In the same way, people can be members of the Labour Party, a party that invaded Iraq and that did all of those terrible things, because they think that it also does good things. Some felt it provided a space where they could make a difference and offered the opportunity to persuade others and believed that it was better than the alternative. The *Guardian* is not that different. Ideologically, I never found it especially complicated to be there. As I pointed out earlier, the *Guardian* was not acting out of character historically. Its structural position was always much closer to the Parliamentary Labour Party (PLP) than to its grassroots.

So I think it's untenable to claim that the *Guardian* cost Labour the election. First, it assigns almost no agency to Labour itself, the mistakes it made, its internal rivalries that would have persisted had the *Guardian* existed or not, and secondly it takes no account of the precarity of the Corbyn project to start with. He did not expect to win when he stood in 2015 and the left did not have the capacity within the bureaucracy and the PLP to see it through.

Second, it assigns way too much power to a single news organisation and ignores the vast media network and accumulated biases in which it operates. But finally, while movements can be discredited in the media, movements themselves aren't built in the media. If your movement can be destroyed by the actions of a single news organisation, then it probably wasn't long for this world anyway. The *Guardian*'s shortcomings didn't help, for sure. How significant their coverage was is a worthwhile debate but I don't believe it was decisive.

INSIDE THE *GUARDIAN* NEWSROOM

Internally, the *Guardian* has long operated as a series of cantons. Things are a little more centralised under the current editor but different sections – features, the magazine, sport, news and so on – still retain a degree of autonomy. However, this was usually more of an administrative form of decentralisation. So, when Seumas Milne ran the comment pages or Victoria Brittain edited the *Third World Review* (see Chapter 4), you would see sections follow a certain kind of ideological dynamic.

What would come from the top, ideologically, would be a nod towards a certain trajectory. That could be a desire for light, lifestyle features, or fun – as opposed to heavy – issue-driven features; for more or less highbrow against lowbrow; more women, more from outside London – that kind of thing.

Occasionally, it would be directly political; more or fewer left voices, less from that particular freelancer, more about this issue. This bid for balance or recalibration was, of course, ideological. How could it not be? Sometimes it made sense to me. Sometimes it seemed to be guided by who had given a senior figure a hard time at a dinner party or on social media or elsewhere. But it never reached me as a writer. I was never told what to write, but section editors were often directed as to who could write what. I don't have a problem with that in principle. You can't run everything – that's what editors higher up the chain are for after all. The question is on what basis those decisions are being made, and who or what suffers as a result.

The balance of power inside the newsroom has definitely shifted in the last few years. If one thinks of Victoria Brittain, Seumas Milne, Richard Norton-Taylor and Duncan Campbell, there was a core of people on the left with some real influence. Now, I think there is still a sizeable left but it is probably weaker, younger and less experienced – much like the left elsewhere. I don't think that it's necessarily smaller, and they certainly contest for influence and continue to have some role in shaping content. But you also have to bear in mind that a significant core of the commentariat has remained exactly the same for two decades, including Jonathan Freedland, Polly Toynbee, George Monbiot and myself, notwithstanding a few breaks before I left.

The reference to Kremlinology I made earlier also relates to an opaque way in which things aren't said but kind of happen and then other things are said, but you're still not quite clear where they're said and what their consequences are. I remember having been there not very long and asking a question about what would happen to a *Guardian* person who was quoted in another publication trashing a different bit of the paper. 'Would they be fired?' I asked. 'Nobody gets fired here,' someone replied. 'You just find that they've fallen down a lift shaft and nobody knows where they are.' There is certainly an element of that as some people become non-people and others become mysteriously elevated. It has a good union; the employment for most is secure so there is relatively low staff turnover. That can lead to frustration and, in that sense, it's quite like the BBC.

Only very rarely did I experience any direct ideological pressure. For example, with one piece on Barack Obama close to the 2008 presidential election, I was strongly encouraged to be upbeat. There was a concern that I would be too negative because my view was that he was just ok. I had made the point in several columns that he wasn't a messiah and that, as a pretty mainstream Democrat, he hadn't promised any of the major reforms that his more enthusiastic supporters were always talking about. Nevertheless, I did see his election as a really big symbolic moment. I was asked, however, to focus on the latter and not the former: 'Could you sort of concentrate more on the symbolic stuff and a bit less on the substantial stuff because that's a downer?'

Once again, examples like that speak to a broader hegemonic process in which the dominant narrative – in this case a fairy-tale moment for western democracy – imposes itself on the actual narrative beforehand. That said, if that is the heaviest hand that you get in British journalism in 25 years, then I think you're probably quite lucky.

So I would argue that the *Guardian*'s relationship to Corbyn was in keeping with its historical role both as part of the liberal establishment and its contemporary role as a mainstream news outlet. While it has long provided a home for elements of the left, including myself, the *Guardian* was not, and never has been, a left-wing paper.

NOTES

1. Sutton Trust and Social Mobility Commission, *Elitist Britain 2019*, https://www.suttontrust.com/wp-content/uploads/2019/12/Elitist-Britain-2019.pdf (accessed 25 September 2020).
2. Media Reform Coalition, 'The Media's Attack on Corbyn: Research Shows a Barrage of Negative Coverage', 26 November 2015, https://www.mediareform.org.uk/press-ethics-and-regulation/the-medias-attack-on-corbyn-research-shows-barrage-of-negative-coverage (accessed 16 September 2020); Media@LSE, 'Journalistic Representations of Jeremy Corbyn in the British Press: From Watchdog to Attackdog', 1 July 2016, https://www.lse.ac.uk/media-and-communications/assets/documents/research/projects/corbyn/Cobyn-Report.pdf (accessed 16 September 2020).

4

Radical Moments at the *Guardian*

Victoria Brittain

There they were, one day after another, on the little sofa on the corner of the foreign news area on the first floor of the *Guardian*'s Farringdon Road office, in their West African robes, North African Islamic dress, Bangladeshi collarless tunic. These self-confident visionary leaders of movements across the world sought out the *Guardian* in the 1980s knowing they could tell their own stories in the paper's *Third World Review* (*TWR*), and believing the West would listen. The paper had a uniquely angled window on the world for the decade of *TWR*'s life.

Those three visitors to the small book-lined corner of the foreign department would belatedly become figures in the Western media a decade, or two, or three later, respectively, after *TWR* was no more. Ken Saro-Wiwa, the Nigerian writer and environmentalist who took on the power of Shell and the Nigerian military dictatorship for the destruction of the oil rich Ogoni Delta, was hanged in 1995 by the regime, causing worldwide outrage, which had his country barred from the Commonwealth. Rached Ghannouchi, the Tunisian intellectual Islamist leader, served two prison sentences, got a death sentence from the Tunisian dictator, Zine el-Abidine Ben Ali, and spent 22 years in exile before returning after Ben Ali's ousting at the start of the Arab Spring. Professor Muhammad Yunus, founder of the *Grameen* Bank, began micro loans to the poorest of the poor after the Bangladesh famine of 1974, transforming the rural economy and ultimately the discredited economic aid policies of the World Bank and Western donors. Yunus received the Nobel Peace Prize in 2006.

The three were already household names in the Global South, but only raised eyebrows, or indifference, in that busy *Guardian* newsroom of the 1980s, preoccupied with matters closer to home. It was a newsroom more comfortable when the Global South was presented to them in staff meetings with celebrities such as Bob Geldof on

Ethiopia's biblical famine, or Benazir Bhutto on the venal intricacies of Pakistan's political scene. No one ever commented to me on my guests, or what they wrote. The *Guardian* then was a series of fiefdoms vying for power and status, which flowed in mysterious ways from the editor's office. *TWR*, based in the Foreign department, subbed by the Features department staff on another floor, made up in Manchester, was too obscure inside the paper to attract any notice. Obscurity allowed us the gift of extraordinary independence. As then joint editor of *TWR*, I was new to the office, had been out of the UK for more than a decade and took the paper's mysteries for granted, absorbed in the world my visitors' words encapsulated for the paper.

The 1980s was a time of radical drama in the periphery, though mostly of minor interest in the West. Revolutions and liberation movements in small countries in Africa, Asia, the Middle East, the Caribbean and Central America had a hold on intellectual and political life across the Global South. Within international institutions such as United Nations bodies like the United Nations Children's Fund (UNICEF), the UN's Development Programme (UNDP) and the Economic Commission for Africa (ECA), the Commonwealth, the Non-Aligned Movement (NAM) and the Organisation of African Unity (OAU), a new narrative reflected these new currents, born of revolt against dictatorship, oppression and economic crisis. That narrative was barely reflected in Western media – the acronyms never made for an easy grasp – and stories of ideas of a pivotal moment did not lend themselves to regular news items.

Racism and xenophobia marked the decade's politics of Ronald Reagan and Margaret Thatcher, most notably in their support for South Africa's apartheid regime which was deepening repression of the majority at home and spreading death and havoc across Southern Africa with bombing raids and invasions. The Western side of the Cold War still played out in coups, assassinations and proxy wars across all the Southern continents. The unfinished business of decolonisation from Portugal and Spain was a running sore in East Timor then occupied by Indonesia, and Western Sahara, occupied by Morocco after General Franco's death in Spain. Military dictatorships supported by Washington gripped Latin America. And then there was the South's economic crisis. The *Guardian* reported many of these events on news and features pages better than many other papers, with several excellent staff and freelancers.

But in *TWR*, over an entire page once a week, people like my visitors writing from inside a special time of upheaval where they were participants, gave the *Guardian* a reputation as a radical voice. We published Wole Soyinka, Yoweri Museveni, Mahmood Mamdani and Ngũgĩ wa Thiong'o from Africa; Michael Manley and John La Rose from the Caribbean; Archbishop Paulo Evaristo Arns and Fidel Castro from Latin America; Yasser Arafat and Leila Sayigh from the Middle East; Eqbal Ahmed and Ahmed Rashid from Asia. In a diary column, I wrote short notices of new books, films, art exhibitions and meetings by the South in London. In response, a great tide of articles, cartoons, letters, books and photographs flowed in to *TWR* from all kinds of people living or working in the Global South. (When I left the paper some 15 years later, the then foreign editor, Ed Pilkington, read out with pleasure a rejection letter I had sent him in Nicaragua in 1986 regretting that *TWR* could not find space to publish his interesting article about refugees displaced by the US-backed Contra war against the Sandinista revolutionaries.)

Other visitors and writers were unknown – fleeing refugees, long term exiles, tortured former prisoners, communists, from South Africa, Brazil, Argentina, Chile, Iraq, Palestine, South Korea, India, Pakistan, Nigeria, Kenya, Turkey and many other places. They were poets, writers, journalists, academics, doctors, opposition politicians, guerrilla fighters. Many were shabby, angry and often desperate. One woman journalist from the Middle East came in with a story of death threats for what she had written about Iraq's oil industry, and a large suitcase. Then she asked if she could stay a night at my house. She stayed for more than a year.

AN EXPERIMENT

It was a senior Pakistani civil servant, journalist and poet, Altaf Gauhar, who, backed by a bank with Luxembourg and Abu Dhabi funds, in the late 1970s courted the *Guardian*'s editor, Peter Preston, into an experimental partnership producing articles about what they called the 'Third World'. It was Preston's deputy, managing editor Ian Wright, a former foreign editor and a former correspondent in

Vietnam, who took up the novel idea with enthusiasm. He backed the link with Gauhar and his media enterprises, *South* magazine and *Third World Media*. In 1978 Gauhar became joint editor with the late Michael Simmons, a gentle *Guardian* specialist in Eastern Europe, of the weekly page called *Third World Review*. Most of the copy came initially from Gauhar's influential network in the Global South and much of it was theoretical, around issues such as debt and agricultural reform and interviews conducted by Gauhar with presidents he knew personally, such as Julius Nyerere of Tanzania. Controversy soon lapped around the rapidly expanding Bank of Credit and Commerce International (which would later be closed down in a major international financial scandal). The relationship with Gauhar's media dwindled away and *TWR* was the *Guardian*'s alone.

TWR became my home in 1981 after seven years as a foreign correspondent, in Vietnam, Algeria and for five years in Kenya as the *Guardian*'s stringer for an East Africa in turmoil. To the west came the ousting of the Ugandan dictator Idi Amin by the army of neighbouring Tanzania to the south, followed by civil war and a succession of unstable military governments. To the north after the ousting of Ethiopia's Emperor Haile Selassie by young army officers who were self-declared Marxists, there was an ongoing war for independence by Eritrea, and another with Somalia which claimed a slice of the Ogaden Desert territory, and meanwhile swung from one Cold War patron, the Soviet Union to the other, the US. Neighbouring Sudan shouldered the greatest burden of war refugees in Africa, pouring over its borders from Uganda, Ethiopia and Eritrea, at the same time as the country lived through its own decades-old north–south civil war. Observing up close these exciting rapid-fire transformative events was a lesson for me in the shortcomings of most Western media coverage. We were all constrained by lack of local language skills, poor listening habits and the tendency to move in self-referential packs. We never knew enough.

NERUDA, THE GODFATHER OF *TWR*

Thirty years earlier, in November 1947, the Chilean poet and elected Communist Party Senator Pablo Neruda wrote an article in the Venezuelan newspaper, *El Nacional*. It led to his exile the following year and became my watchword for what *TWR* could be. 'The Crisis of Democracy in Chile is a Dramatic Warning for our Continent' was his title. Neruda opened with these words:

> I want to inform all my friends on our continent of the disastrous events which have taken place in Chile. I am aware that a large number of persons will be confused and surprised, since the North American news monopolies will no doubt (in this matter as in others) have produced the same result as everywhere else: to falsify truth and distort reality.[1]

Today the internet has totally altered people's ability to put their own reality out to the widest of worlds, but in the 1980s, as in Neruda's 1940s, gatekeepers held the keys to space in the powerful Western media, and events in the Global South were largely seen through Western eyes and written from that perspective, or else ignored.

Two small personal incidents soon emphasised for me the depth of distrust of Western media, including the *Guardian*, by significant people in the Global South and the unique position of *TWR*. During the Non-Aligned Movement summit in Delhi in 1983 I had an interview with the African National Congress Deputy President, Oliver Tambo. I was taken up to his very modest hotel room by Frene Ginwala, a South African lawyer who had organised safe houses and flights into exile for ANC leaders including Tambo after the 1960 State of Emergency in South Africa. In exile in London herself she was a discreet figure in ANC exile community communications – the source of my invitation to an interview, as she read *TWR*. A decade later Ginwala was elected Speaker of the National Assembly for the first 10 years of majority rule in South Africa. Tambo sat down on the bed and gestured to the two chairs for us and said kindly to me, 'don't worry my dear if they don't print what I say, they never do.' *TWR* did. The second was with another South African, the anti-apartheid activist, journalist and academic Ruth First, once detained for 117 days, and then living and teaching in Mozambique. Shortly before her assassination there by the apartheid regime in August 1982, I asked her during a visit to London if she would write an article for the *Guardian* about her academic work in Mozambique. She simply laughed and said, 'Why should I waste my time? The *Guardian* would never print what I would want to write.' Then she agreed that I could write what I had taken from our talk. It was published in *TWR*.

ECONOMIC IDEOLOGICAL WRESTLING

Gauhar and Wright had judged the moment of opportunity well for *TWR*. It was the perfect vehicle for new strands of international thinking, written from the perspective of the countries challenging Washington. A major ideological struggle was emerging between African leaders and intellectuals in the South, such as the Senegal-based Egyptian-French Marxist economist Samir Amin, and Western countries arrayed behind the World Bank over the way forward from the aftermath of the OPEC oil price surges of 1973–4 and 1979, and the mounting debt problems that had brought much of the Global South to its knees in the world recession.

Through the late 1970s radical demands for a New International Economic Order (NIEO) became part of every agenda of the Non-Aligned countries in UN and regional meetings. Its platform included regulation and control of multi-national companies by host countries; the right to nationalise them; a cartel of primary commodity producers similar to OPEC for the oil producing countries making prices stable; improved terms for the transfer of technology and other dreams of equity. NIEO was a threat to the established world order, which, in the usual way of the powerful, contested it by apparently not taking it seriously. In this context, the recession, induced by the policies of monetarism of Reagan and Thatcher, was a response to this threat – an effective way of controlling the high commodity prices and the power of both commodity producers and their own trade unions.

The former West German Chancellor, Willy Brandt, put a firecracker under general awareness of the looming economic and political crisis and its inevitable impact on the world, with the 1980 report of the prestigious North/South Commission. Its 18 members included Olof Palme the Swedish prime minister, Katharine Graham the president of the *Washington Post*, and Edward Heath the former UK prime minister from the North. The members from the South included Sir Shridath Ramphal, Secretary General of the Commonwealth, and intellectuals and ministers from Algeria, India, Tanzania, Malaysia and Indonesia – all prominent countries in a host of international institutions. These were mainly people who did not invite the term radical. However, their follow-up report *Common Crisis* in 1983[2] was a prophetic and radical call for emergency measures to halt 'international economic collapse and resulting anarchy'. It briefly got some respectful media stories, though no action.

Another landmark intervention into economic debate in 1980 – from the Economic Commission for Africa, headed by Nigeria's Professor Adebayo Adedeji – certainly did not get the media interest it deserved. The *Lagos Plan of Action*[3] was a radical blueprint for Africa to embrace self-reliance and put its weight behind the implementation of the NIEO to change the patterns of the world's economic relations. This challenge was effectively buried the following year with a World Bank report by American academic economist Elliot Berg – a diametrically opposed action plan for Africa's economic liberalisation. The *Berg Report*[4] had powerful outreach and was the blueprint for continuing the West's domination of Africa's economies (and most of the South) through the IMF and World Bank, mainly accepted without comment in the media.

Then, from the heart of the international establishment, in 1983 UNICEF published eye-opening research from work on the ground initially in 12 countries reporting the Impact of World Recession on Children. The following year UNICEF then reported on the devastating social and economic effects for children of the new orthodoxy of World Bank and IMF programmes imposed in return for loans, cutting or severely reducing spending on health, education, environmental programmes. The austerity mentality of Structural Adjustment Programmes (SAPs) meant rising poverty and inequality with worsening health, nutrition and education. Most importantly, SAPs robbed the countries concerned of their sovereignty. The power of these Western institutions and policies were a key trigger of the popular riots and challenges to various Western-allied regimes in the Global South which accepted SAPs and experienced the squeezing of the state and deepening poverty. The Western media rarely reported this huge story as the South saw it with such clarity as they lived it.

The impact of SAPs was nothing less than disastrous for most of sub-Saharan Africa and Latin America. The twenty-year rates of growth of per capita income, respectively 80 per cent and 36 per cent from 1960–80 declined to a miserable 9 per cent and *minus* 15 per cent from 1980–2000. Even austerity under the Tories never inflicted such pain at home.

The links between the West and the periphery were behind these World Bank/IMF policies, as Margaret Thatcher's Chancellor of the Exchequer once spelt out. As Nigel Lawson put it:

> The principal – though largely undeclared – objective of the Western World's debt strategy, ably coordinated by the IMF, was to buy time . . . Time was needed not only to enable the debtor countries to put sensible economic policies in place but also for the Western banks to rebuild their shattered balance sheets to the point where they could afford to write off their sovereign debts. For it was perfectly clear that the vast bulk of these debts would never come good – even though there was an understandable conspiracy of silence over admitting this unpalatable fact.[5]

A counter-narrative to the Western orthodoxy on the economic liberalisation agenda for Africa came consistently from UNICEF under James Grant, the director over this decade. Grant, a brilliant communicator, really got UNICEF taken seriously by leading the Child Survival and Development Revolution, which so expanded low-cost mass health actions like immunisation that child deaths were brought down by three million over the 1980s – in spite of SAPs. His team included well-known British academics such as Richard Jolly, who was Deputy Executive Director of UNICEF after years at the respected Institute for Development Studies, Frances Stewart from Oxford, and the distinguished Italian economist Giovanni Andrea Cornia. Here was the spine of intellectual resistance to the economic orthodoxies of the IMF and the World Bank that were ravaging Africa and Latin America. *Adjustment with a Human Face*, by these three authors, was published in two volumes in 1985 and 1987[6] and was the first widely popularised and respected critique of SAPs. UNICEF's research was an on-going critical resource reported in *TWR*.

Dissidents within the Bank and IMF and in senior UN positions were very ready to brief anonymously backing UNICEF's critiques, and international conferences and even visits to the ravaged South were organised for those who had the time to listen. *TWR* coverage of these intellectual battles was often written using political and academic luminaries of the Global South. Salim Ahmed Salim, in sequence Tanzania's foreign minister, defence minister and prime minister, then secretary general of the OAU, and Professor Adedeji with his degrees from Harvard and London were towering figures on a bankrupt continent, but too little regarded beyond it. Western leaders shunned public debate with them. In 1990 foreign secretary Douglas Hurd slipped away from a House of Commons conference with them before either spoke. And Adedeji was shunned the same year by the leaders of the World Bank and the IMF in a Washington conference where he said they were more powerful in Africa than the colonial powers had been.

THOSE COUPS

In the 1980s there was an avalanche of coups or coup attempts in 30 countries of the South – 18 of them in Africa. Sudan, Nigeria and Liberia had two each, Uganda three and Burkina Faso six. Most had their roots in popular dissent sparked by despair at deepening poverty as SAPs took hold, and rage at flagrant corruption among old elites supported by the West, or they were between competing military cliques.

Other coups were odder, as in the Seychelles in late 1981 when a group of 54 South Africans, led by the notorious mercenary, 'Mad' Mike Hoare, and including 27 members of the army arrived, apparently a rugby team on holiday. But as the last two men went through customs, an AK-47 was found under piles of toys said to be for distribution to local orphanages by the group which called itself part of a charity, Ye Ancient Order of Froth Blowers. In a six-hour gun battle at the airport the South Africans seized the control tower, talked down an Air India arriving flight, commandeered it and all except seven escaped back to South Africa in it. But it was not a joke, as some wrote. Tiny Seychelles was not just a tourist haven, but held a central position in the Indian Ocean, near the secretive strategic US military base on the island of Diego Garcia leased from Britain since 1966. Between 1968 and 1973, American officials and their British colleagues secretly removed the islanders, dumping them on Mauritius or the Seychelles without resources, and hiding their expulsion from Congress, Parliament, the UN and the media.

These events dramatized the destabilising reach of apartheid South Africa, and its allies in Washington and London. The previous Seychelles president, James Mancham, had had close ties with the apartheid regime, sold them landing rights, and was revealed by South African officials themselves as having been a useful source of information about what was discussed behind closed doors at OAU summits. The subsequent president, France-Albert René overthrew Mancham in a coup in 1977 while he was in London, and brought in socialist education and health programmes, and eco-tourism well before that was a popular concept. The then *Guardian* foreign editor, Campbell Page, accepted my brief telex request from Nairobi to go and report what I thought was important. This was the *laissez faire* of the *Guardian*, as assistant foreign editor John Gittings described things, at its best.

> I had for much of the time a great deal of freedom in reporting [for the *Guardian*] from China, and this was mainly positive but at times less so. When Ian Wright brought me in as a freelancer (I had been contributing to the *FT* after returning in 1969 from my two years with the *Far Eastern Economic Review*), China was a blank page on which I could write any words I liked. My five-parter in 1971, after my first visit to the mainland with the Society for Anglo-Chinese Understanding, went in without question. From 1976 to 1983 my fulltime job was teaching at the Polytechnic of Central London. If called in, I would hop on the Circle Line from Euston Square to Farringdon, usually around 4 or 5 p.m., quickly scan the wires and write whatever was required. I did that even for Mao's death.
>
> Once on the foreign desk as an assistant editor from 1983 to 1988, I would similarly quite often knock off stories in between or after my desk stint. However, I did have quite a few opportunities to travel to China and Hong Kong, and at that time I was free to write the way I wanted without being asked to catch up on stories from the wires or from our competitors. So for example I was able to write with some detachment, at times cynicism, eg about British pomposity in Hong Kong, rather than do it straight.
>
> There were downsides to the *Guardian*'s casual approach during this period and in one of them I was rescued by *Third World Review*. In 1985 I was sent to cover the 10th anniversary of the Vietnam reunification, and after the celebrations in HCM City stayed on for two weeks in Hanoi, covering a lot of interesting ground. But how the Vietnam revolution was now progressing was not of interest to the

Features department. I was only saved by *TWR*, which published two pieces – one on Vietnam's economic feature and an in-depth look at the country's medical capability. *TWR* also gave me the freedom to write on other subjects which probably would not have found a home elsewhere, including a fairly theoretical discussion on the transition to socialism and how views on it were changing in post-Mao China. Other subjects included consumerism in Beijing, and the shift from people's communes towards semi-private farming in rural areas. In 1984 we also produced under the *TWR* imprint a two-page supplement on the 35th anniversary of the People's Republic, with seven contributors including William Hinton (author of Fanshen),[7] and a foreword from the Chinese ambassador in London – how times have changed!

The build-up to Tiananmen from late 1986–87, when the reformist general secretary Hu Yaobang was sacked, was notable for increasingly vocal student and academic dissent, but although we did cover this it did not grab the paper's attention. I recall the foreign editor of the time telling me, I think in early 1989, that he couldn't understand what the students were going on about. This was a general attitude in the British media, and indeed government, towards the long development of radical thought and argument (which had started, unofficially, in the Cultural Revolution) among China's younger generation.

I went out to Beijing when Hu was removed; it was a critical turning-point, the start of the conservative backlash that would lead to Tiananmen Square (the democracy movement was sparked by his death). There was a lot to write, and I had good contact among dissenting intellectuals, but here again the *Guardian*'s relaxed approach had its downside. I was abruptly summoned back to London at a day's notice, because of a sudden gap on the foreign desk (which could have been filled in the office).

John Gittings was a China specialist writer and later a leader writer for the *Guardian*. This is taken from a memoir written for his family.

Two other tiny remote countries far from the Indian Ocean had coups and revolutions in the mid-1980s, which had loud echoes in *TWR* for their transformative ambitions. Maurice Bishop of Grenada in the Caribbean and Thomas Sankara of Burkina Faso in West Africa were surprise stars of the NAM summit in Delhi in 1983 with their identical energy of youth, and confidence in the ambitious transformation they would effect at home. Both believed in the possibility of change in the world economic and political order, the end of apartheid, rights and justice for Palestinians, the end of corruption among the elites of the South and ethical Southern leadership based on what they knew and respected in leaders like Fidel Castro in Cuba, Julius Nyerere in Tanzania and Lúcio Lara in Angola. Bishop and Sankara became instant soulmates when they met in Delhi, although they had no common language.

I spent many hours in the rural areas of both countries listening to earnest people full of hopes for transformed lives, in order to produce long accounts in *TWR*. In Grenada, a country of 91,000 people mired in deep poverty, Bishop introduced free public health, illiteracy dropped from 35 per cent to 5 per cent and unemployment went from 50 per cent to 14 per cent. Sankara changed the name of his country from the French colonial Upper Volta, to Burkina Faso, meaning 'the country of honourable men'. On my return from the trip when I had watched him make that announcement, along with compulsory group sport for all cabinet ministers, including women, and the replacement of the ministers' Mercedes cars with a Renault 5, I was surprised to see a notice on the *Guardian*'s foreign department board. The then chief sub had written: 'When you see Burkina Faso in Victoria Brittain's copy, please replace it with the country's proper name of Upper Volta.' Some people just did not want to know about these places. But the *TWR* postbag about them showed how far their reach really went with the readers.

Bishop and Sankara were assassinated, respectively in October 1983 (shortly after the Delhi meeting) and 1987, in violent coups led by their deputies. The Cuban military attaché who once said to me in Ouagadougou that 'this could all blow away with one puff, like a dandelion clock', was right. In both cases there were powerful foreign political interests ready to give that puff. These new leaders' ideas and policies were a threat to the *status quo* favoured by Western powers – the US in the first case and France in the second.

Ronald Reagan flew 6,000 US troops into Grenada on 25 October after Bishop's killing, using the fig leaf of a request from other Caribbean countries, and a threat to American students in medical school there. The US prime target was the Cuban workforce building a new international airport which was to give Grenada a much-needed real link to the outside world. It was too crude a demonstration of US military power in its own backyard by Reagan, and a helpful distraction from the deaths two days before of 241 US soldiers in a truck bombing of the Marines barracks in Beirut.

Twenty-five Cubans were killed, 59 wounded and 638 captured in the invasion of Grenada. In London Ken Gill, the only communist to become president of the Trade Union Congress, and head of the union which guaranteed the deposit on Wembley Stadium for Nelson Mandela's 70th birthday tribute, organised a memorial for the Cuban embassy. The grieving ambassador spoke, the ANC choir sang, and, as Ken and the Cubans knew I had been there with Bishop during his house arrest three days before he was killed, I was asked to read the list of the names of the dead Cuban workers. The Caribbean community in London packed the hall, stunned with grief at their hopes wiped out with Bishop. No one from the *Guardian* came.

Wole Soyinka said later in a speech printed in *TWR*:

> We know whose gun-ship helicopters, whose ubiquitous marines snuffed out the lamp of self-determination in Grenada, but what do we say of the consortium of black leaders who spread out the mat of invitation to Ronald Reagan? Who were these shameless so-called leaders who sent out the SOS which read: 'Recolonise us, *please*!'

Soyinka went on to open the fourth International Black Book Fair in London in 1985 urging people to celebrate Mandela. 'Let us at least be thankful and humbled by Nelson Mandela's giant fist thrust out beyond Robben Island to smash a loud resounding "No" in the teeth of apartheid.' He then linked Bishop to 'other heroes like Steve Biko, Walter Rodney and Malcolm X'.

By then, in the late 1980s, apartheid South Africa's regional destruction loomed as *the* dominating issue for the South in international summits of the UN, the OAU and the NAM. In 1986 the Commonwealth published *Mission to South Africa*,[8] detailed reporting of shocking realities by six elder statesmen and one distinguished woman, which was unanswerable. A UNICEF report estimated that in Angola and Mozambique a million people had been killed in South Africa's wars, 11 million were displaced and $60 billion of destruction caused. *TWR* carried articles and book reviews by South African lawyers, none more indelible than the testimonies of children arrested and tortured by the police, who in 1987 were brought to the Zimbabwean capital Harare by the ANC for a conference with Oliver Tambo and the rest of the ANC leadership in exile.[9] In fact secret negotiations were already starting among South Africans, while Mrs Thatcher was declaring at a Commonwealth conference that year that anyone who thought the ANC could ever be a government, was living in cloud cuckoo land. And one of my editors asked me, 'please, publish some right-wing views from Southern Africa'.

Victoria and *Third World Review* go together like debt relief and NGOs, liberation struggles and freedom fighters.

Heady days when the *Guardian* started to publish a page devoted to 'Voices from the South', Victoria and Michael Simmons – John Brown to her Queen – brought great gusts of vigorous argument and reportage that some of us subbing in Features had never heard of. Burkina Faso? Irian Jaya? Kampuchea? Where were they?

Production of the pages had a weird third-world belt-and-braces feel about them. These were the days of the dreaded Manchester parcel, when subbed copy, headlines and page schemes – all on paper – plus photographs and maps were entrusted to a courier who drove them up the motorway where he handed them over to the often-bemused subs in Dean Street.

God knows how they managed to hammer out sensible answers to the puzzle pages we sent them, chopping out what they hoped were the disposable bits so that yards of overmatter could fit the impossible spaces allocated and still make sense. Imagine the thrill when, two days later, page proofs arrived back by the same messenger, bringing yet another triumph for the weekly miracle.

Victoria began to disappear more frequently into these fascinating places we tramped over in the pages. Africa, naturally – Angola and Namibia, East Africa, Ethiopia, West Africa, the Middle East, the Indian subcontinent. She became the queen of ravaged hinterlands, flitting around the world – energetic, effervescent, enthusiastic, seemingly never thrown by lousy conditions, frustrating bureaucracy or terrible communications.

It all came to an end, in the great *Guardian* way of such things, Peter Preston decided *Third World Review* was a dated concept and had to go. Victoria fought hard but in vain.

Then, 1989, finis.

Doug Morrison was a senior sub-editor on the Features desk.

In 1989, as the *Guardian*'s Doug Morrison writes above, the then editor Peter Preston suddenly decided *TWR* was over. Did he really think it was 'dated' as Doug writes? The Global South was on fire on so many fronts and the only place that the experts were able to write about it in the Western press was *TWR*. On the cusp of Tiananmen Square, the release of Mandela, the first Gulf War, the *First Intifada* in Gaza and the West Bank, our readers would surely have wanted to hear those consistent 'Voices from the South' every Friday?

The truth was probably that Preston had had enough of the irritations *TWR* caused him. He was used to an early morning phone call from UK officials if the leader line was 'unhelpful' to the government, but he was interested in the paper's leaders, took part in leader conferences, sometimes wrote them himself and could respond to politely menacing hints. However, frequently on a Monday morning he would call me in to tell me that he had had complaints about the *TWR* Friday page, which he had probably not read carefully and was not really interested in. The Foreign Office, the World Bank, US embassy, South African embassy, Israeli embassy, officials and others he never mentioned to me, complained to him directly and repeatedly, demanded rights of reply, complained to journalists they knew on the paper and lobbied for the end of *TWR*. None of the paper's fiefdoms were interested to speak up for it.

TWR gave me a ringside seat in a unique decade of liberation movement and revolutionary struggles for economic and political transformation in some of the poorest places in the world. Thirty years ago, radical, clever people from the Global South gave *TWR* readers a coherent picture of realities in the periphery. It was unique; it is unforgettable.

* * *

Looking back now, it seems likely that *TWR* was dropped not just because the political frontline in the US, apartheid South Africa, Israel and the UK world of Margaret Thatcher attacked it constantly to the paper's editor. It was also because the consistent weekly reflection of the realities and analysis of the periphery, led by writing from that world and often critical of the emerging neoliberal global order, could not fit with the provincial middle England interests and views of the editor and most of the powerful fiefdoms inside the paper who depended on him. 'Dated' or 'boring' were the lazy, easy criticisms made by colleagues to dismiss *TWR*'s challenge to the dominant worldview, and the pages' almost equally important challenge to the notion that western journalists were the people to trust with agenda-setting.

Years later economic necessities involved in keeping papers afloat today means they are market-driven and would be likely to favour a *Style* section over the political flavour of *TWR*. Now *Guardian* readers do see a much greater diversity of writers and certainly many more women writers across the paper. But the internet and the huge commercial pressures it has brought to newspapers – combined with the post-Cold War US dominance of social, cultural, political and military spheres – has bled the paper's resources for foreign news beyond the US. Social media now brings, to those who want it, much great writing and news from the periphery. Bloggers, specialised online publications and cable channels, often with their own agendas, are all able to offer a considered analysis. This welcome proliferation of information is a real challenge for today's *Guardian*.

Newspaper reporters, caught in a 24-hour news circuit, under pressure from the great homogenising demands from editors reading on the internet what every other media outlet is carrying and required to do podcasts and video as well as writing, have lost the great gift of the *laissez faire* style *Guardian* of the 1980s: time. Before the days of instant communication, with all its miracles, working in or with the periphery as *TWR* did, meant hours, days, months or even years of direct communication and travel to build two-way trust: for *TWR* staff to understand the unknown stories people wanted to tell, and for those people to choose to tell them in the western press. *TWR* was a great experiment, initiated by Altaf Gauhar and Ian Wright and allowed by Peter Preston. While it lasted, *TWR*'s consistency gave, as Noam Chomsky once put it:

> a rare opportunity for Western readers to learn something about the lives, hopes and struggles of the great mass of suffering and oppressed people throughout the world, whose fate should be of no small concern to those who share in Western privilege and power.[10]

NOTES

1. Quoted in Victoria Brittain and Michael Simmons (eds), *The Guardian Third World Review: Voices from the South* (London: Hodder & Stoughton, 1987), p.x.
2. The Brandt Commission, *Common Crisis North-South: Cooperation for World Recovery* (Cambridge, MA: MIT Press, 1983).
3. Organization of African Unity, *Lagos Plan of Action for the Economic Development of Africa, 1980–2000*, 1980, www.web.archive.org/web/20070106003042/http://uneca.org/itca/ariportal/docs/lagos_plan.PDF (accessed 16 September 2020).
4. Elliot Berg, *Accelerated Development in Sub-Saharan Africa: An Agenda for Action* (Washington: World Bank, 1981).
5. Nigel Lawson, *Memoirs of a Tory Radical* (London: Bantam Press, 1992) p. 520.
6. Giovanni Cornia, Richard Jolly and Frances Stewart (eds) *Adjustment with a Human Face: Vol 1, Protecting the Vulnerable and Promoting Growth* (Oxford: Clarendon Press, 1987).
7. William H. Hinton, *Fanshen: A Documentary of Revolution in a Chinese Village* (New York: Monthly Review Press, 1966). It describes the land-reform campaign during the 1945 to 1948 civil war from inside the village where Hinton lived for months in 1948 and was described as perhaps the book that most changed American cold war perceptions of the Chinese Revolution.
8. Commonwealth Group, *Mission to South Africa: The Commonwealth Report* (London: Penguin, 1986).
9. Victoria Brittain and Abdul Minty (eds), *Children of Resistance, On Children, Repression and the Law in Apartheid South Africa – Statements from the Harare Conference* (Kliptown Books, 1988).
10. Communication from Noam Chomsky used in a farewell tribute *Guardian* page made for the author on leaving the paper.

5

The *Guardian* and the Israeli–Palestinian Conflict

Ghada Karmi

INTRODUCTION

It is well-known that the controversies arising from any attempt to report the Israeli–Palestinian conflict inflame passions such that journalists are forced to back one side or the other. Those who report on the conflict soon become aware that they have to pick their words with extra care in order not to provoke the ire of either side, but especially that of Israel and its supporters, who have the power to impede journalistic access to sensitive areas, and even end careers.

I recall a conversation with Martin Plaut, for many years the BBC's specialist on Africa, who had kept an interested eye on the BBC's reporting of the Middle East. He told me he would never accept a posting to Israel–Palestine because it would force him to withhold the truth about what Israel was doing to the Palestinians; and, in order not to offend, he would have to collude in what amounted to a lie.

These difficulties are not unique to the Israeli–Palestinian conflict. In any political situation where there is a need to disguise unpalatable facts because it would be damaging to have them come out, the side strong enough to suppress them will attempt to do so – with serious implications for those trying to uncover the truth. In the case of Israel–Palestine, there are added layers of complexity that have generated confusion about the true nature of the problem.

To begin with, the very term that conventionally describes what is happening between Israel and the Palestinians as a 'conflict' is misleading. It promotes the false concept of two, roughly equivalent, parties fighting it out. The reality, however, is of a Zionist colonising settler movement meeting resistance on the part of the native Palestinian population. A former senior leader writer at the *Guardian*, Frank Edmead, put it succinctly:

> At the receiving end Zionism looks like any colonial movement: settlers flowed in to acquire eventually much of the land and all the political power. Throughout most of the colonised world, including Algeria and other Arab lands, the indigenous people have checked or reversed that process.[1]

The Palestinians have not been able to do the same so far, not because they lacked the will, but because in Zionism, they faced a formidable challenge: a movement backed by the world's most powerful states, and a skilfully promoted narrative presenting the settlers as the authentic indigenous people from ancient times, and the Arab inhabitants of Palestine as late and illegitimate arrivals. Biblical justification through eliding the ancient Israelites with modern European Jewish communities so as to make them historically continuous, a preposterous and ahistorical claim, has, nevertheless, added credibility to this narrative for many people.

None of it, however, can alter the settler colonial nature of what befell Palestine from the time of the Balfour Declaration until today. There is no more 'conflict' here than there was between France and the Algerians, Belgium and the Congolese, or Britain and the nations it colonised. This misnomer in the case of Israel–Palestine obscures the reality and fosters the idea of equally valid claims to the land and its resources. Most importantly from the point of view of journalists reporting on the area, it sets the context in which events are interpreted and then understood by readers.

AN HISTORIC LACK OF CONTEXT

This obfuscation lies at the basis of the 'peace process' between Israel and the Palestinians since 1993. From the start this was predicated on the same myth of equivalence between the two sides and the need for 'compromise', as if such concepts could apply to a situation of colonisation, with the coloniser and the colonised natives pitted against each other. The same equivalence myth is at the basis of the 'two-state solution', whose very name suggests two nations with equally valid claims to the land trying to find a way to share it. This disguises the true situation of a settler movement that already holds 78 per cent of the natives' original land trying to acquire more of it by partitioning what remains with those natives.

One has only to imagine how different the recent history of Palestine–Israel would appear today had it been reported on this basis. And how much more sense one could make of events that seem otherwise incomprehensible or bewildering. The Palestinian Authority would then be described as an 'Israeli-controlled Palestinian administration', Hamas, as 'a Palestinian resistance organisation fighting against impossible odds', Gaza, as the 'Israeli-besieged Palestinian enclave', the West Bank as the 'colonised West Bank', and so on.

Adding to the confusion has been the lack of historical context usual in most news reporting. Thus, events seem to arise *de novo*, with no historical explanation. Writing in the 1930s, the *Daily Mail*'s Middle East correspondent, J.M.N. Jeffries, who noted the same phenomenon at the time, put it like this:

> Any first-class political question grows intricate if it is left without an effort to solve it for a number of years. It grows particularly intricate when one of the parties to the affair finds refuge in this passage of the years, taking advantage of all the secondary issues naturally or artificially produced during them to cloud the main issue that was clear at the beginning.[2]

In the more than 70 years of Israel's existence many layers have been added to the original story, making it almost impossible to distinguish cause from effect. In spite of much progress in enabling the Palestinian view to counterbalance this confusion, as we will see below, the Israeli narrative still sets the terms of thinking and interpretation of events in Israel–Palestine. That narrative has held sway since before the Israeli state was established, and indeed had to do so to promote Zionism to Western powers and their populations.

In fact, there is nothing complicated about what happened in Palestine after Britain took it over from Ottoman rule in 1917: a European settler movement, Zionism, aided, for its own imperial reasons, by Britain, the colonial ruler of Palestine at the time, was enabled by Britain to build itself up into a state-in-waiting, and develop a fighting force that expelled the majority of Palestine's native people in 1948. Thereupon, the settlers took their place and never allowed them back. That, in essence, is the basis of the Palestinian *Nakba*, and the origin of the Palestinian tragedy. Called the 'Palestine question' in Jeffries' day, it was later renamed, 'the Israeli–Palestinian conflict', a label that is with us to this day.

The events of 1948, an ignoble chapter among many in the history of Britain and that of the Zionist movement, were suppressed or covered up by the new state of Israel, and conveniently obscured by the Arab–Israeli War of 1967, which led to the extension of Israel's colonial project to the rest of Palestine. The post-1967 situation came to form the main subject of reporting on the Israeli–Palestinian conflict, as if there had been no problem between Israel or the Palestinians until then. The emphasis of news reporting on the 'occupation', the settlements, the status of Arab Jerusalem, and other consequences of the war was highly beneficial to Israel: it could now be called 'Israel proper', and therefore legitimate, inside the 1948 borders, and evade responsibility for the Palestinian refugees its establishment had created.

Yet, despite all these gains, Israel and its supporters continue to promote their own narrative of events, and, concomitantly to discredit anyone presenting an alternative that might implicate Israel. Israel's fear at the slightest provocation of what it calls 'delegitimization' seems exaggerated, but it is understandable, when one remembers how Israel was established: a state created on the back of expelling the native population, and supported by Western sympathy in the wake of the Holocaust that prematurely enabled its inclusion as a member state by the UN General Assembly in 1949. Since then, Israel has made strenuous efforts to hide this reality, projecting itself as a Western democracy, with a population of 'people like us', and an innocent target of mindless Palestinian 'terrorism'.

But denial of the truth makes it no less true. As Benny Morris, one of Israel's most prominent Zionist historians, puts it: 'This has to be clear: it is impossible to evade it. Without the uprooting of the Palestinians, a Jewish state would not have arisen here.'[3] Nevertheless, Israel has striven hard to hide evidence of these facts, insists on promoting the allegation that Palestinians fled of their own accord in 1948 for reasons unconnected with Israel, and has made its archives of that period inaccessible to researchers, with the aim of concealing the truth.[4]

Understanding the situation in Israel–Palestine in the context of settler colonialism and Western backing for the settler colony as part of larger geo-political considerations – as an ally during the Cold War, or in ensuring the supply of Arab oil to the West, for example – should form the basis of all journalistic reporting on the conflict. Such reporting would add a dose of honesty to the political discourse, clarify the real roles of the parties involved, and rid itself of the fear of offending that has crippled free speech on the origin of the conflict.

RESPONDING TO FLAK

Unfortunately, that has generally not happened, and the limitations on clear thinking and free expression have made covering what is conventionally known as 'the Israeli–Palestinian conflict' a uniquely daunting task. The *Guardian* and other news media, aiming to be impartial on the issue, have found it virtually impossible to avoid being accused of bias by one side or the other. James Rodgers, the BBC's foreign correspondent reporting on Gaza between 2002 and 2004, and the West Bank in subsequent postings, makes this point forcefully in his 2015 book, *Headlines from the Holy Land*: 'As almost anyone who has written or spoken in public about the conflict knows, to do so is to invite scorn, ridicule, abuse, or insult'.[5]

There is no doubt that it has been the common experience of press editors, TV stations, or any public outlet dealing with the conflict to find themselves on the receiving end of pressure and criticism. That pressure has tended to come overwhelmingly from the pro-Israel side. When researching this topic in relation to the BBC, Hilary Aked found what she called 'compelling' evidence of undue pressure on the organisation by pro-Israel groups, principally, the Britain-Israel Communication and Research Centre (BICOM) and BBC Watch, which monitors the BBC for anti-Israel bias. She describes one editor telling her that, following programmes or news reports that could possibly be construed as critical of Israel, '[w]e wait in fear for the phone call from the Israelis'.[6]

The *Guardian*'s experience, apart from the early days of the paper's pro-Zionist bias discussed later in this chapter, has been broadly in line with these assessments. A 2016 article by Chris Elliott, the *Guardian*'s readers' editor, noted that the Israeli–Palestinian conflict, while attracting one of the largest number of complaints of any one topic,[7] had both sides accusing it of bias. But the majority tended to come from the pro-Israel side, which also included the Israeli embassy. The embassy's complaint on that occasion was that, in reporting Palestinian attacks against Israeli targets, the *Guardian* often portrayed Palestinian perpetrators as victims. A *Guardian* headline like 'Three Palestinian teenagers shot dead on the West Bank', which implies they were victims, should have said that the youths had opened fire on Israeli soldiers first (and presumably provoked them into responding).

A more detailed editorial from 2006,[8] reviewing the *Guardian*'s record on reporting the Israel–Palestine conflict for that year, remarked it was the most controversial of editorial topics to cover. Every word that appeared was subjected to the closest scrutiny by both sides. While there was pro-Palestinian criticism, it was outweighed by 'orchestrated waves of complaints' from pro-Israel supporters. Campaigns of email bombardment have been a favourite tool of these pro-Israel groups. As the *Guardian*'s diplomatic editor, Ewan MacAskill, said of his experience:

> In January 2001, I wrote that the Israelis were behaving badly in the West Bank, and received 800 emails. Half of them were from the US, a quarter from Britain, and a quarter from Israel. A month or two later I wrote that it was not true that Israel had presented a generous offer at Taba, and I received hundreds of even worse emails.[9]

Even the *Guardian*'s usually pro-Israel commentator, Jonathan Freedland, was moved to say that '[a] lot of flak is coming my way, hundreds of emails, many of them pure hate mail.'[10]

While the paper had been an enthusiastic advocate of Zionism in its early years (of which more below), more recently some pro-Israeli voices have come to see it as too critical of Israel and part of a left-wing, liberal elite that agrees with the Palestinian narrative of the underdog with the implication that Israel is cast unfairly as the bully. For many supporters of Zionism, this anti-Israel posture is tantamount to antisemitism, of which the *Guardian* has often been accused.

To offset the accusations of anti-Israeli bias and antisemitism, the *Guardian* took the unusual step of commissioning an independent study of its coverage of Israel. A noted Israeli journalist, Daphna Baram, was entrusted with the task and the result, *Disenchantment: The Guardian and Israel,* was published in 2004.[11] Her study examined the *Guardian*'s archives for the period from the early-twentieth century up to 2002. She makes the point that no one at the *Guardian* attempted to interfere in her work, and she was given ready access to the paper's reporters and editors and its internal debates, which she describes as a 'courageous act'. The book is highly informative and well-documented, and I have made extensive use of her excellent research in this chapter.

In the end she arrived at several conclusions: that the conflict had consumed an inordinate amount of time and effort by the paper's staff to ensure a balance of views that would present it fairly; and, most importantly, she found no evidence of antisemitism or anti-Zionism. Attacks on the *Guardian* from the usual quarters did not abate, however, and the paper's editor at the time, Alan Rusbridger, was moved to point out with some exasperation that, given the *Guardian*'s unique self-criticism, which no other paper had ever displayed: 'The vitriolic nature and extent of the counter-response is unparalleled, utterly disproportionate, cynical and quite ugly.'[12]

Nevertheless, it didn't save the paper from being labelled antisemitic. Although such accusations were not new and were levelled at the paper whenever it published something critical of Israel, the process accelerated over time. Matters have deteriorated to the extent that, from the start of the twenty-first century, the *Guardian* has become the target of unrelenting attack for being allegedly anti-Israel and antisemitic. A 2014 *Times of Israel* blog described the paper as '[v]iciously and notoriously antisemitic'.[13] Apparently, the *Guardian*'s painstaking efforts at being impartial while still delivering high standard reporting of a complex and challenging conflict no longer counted for anything.

It is inevitable that a topic which excites such powerful reactions carries with it the threat of journalistic intimidation, and that in turn may lead to self-censorship, or avoidance of the subject altogether, with the result that such reporting becomes unbalanced or incomplete. Events during the editorship of Alastair Hetherington, the *Guardian*'s highly respected editor from 1956 to 1975, illustrate the point. It was mooted at the time that the paper came under economic pressure from parts of the Jewish community over its coverage of Israel.[14] Baram notes that Michael Adams and Harold Jackson, who both worked for the *Guardian* then, claimed to have seen a letter addressed to Hetherington from Lord Marks, a major Jewish businessman and founder of Marks and Spencer, threatening a boycott of the paper by Jewish-owned businesses. But the letter's existence could not be subsequently confirmed.[15]

Nothing makes supporters of Israel angrier than perceived critics of Israel who are themselves Jewish. The *Guardian*'s correspondent in Jerusalem between 2000 and 2002, Suzanne Goldenberg, is a case in point. During her time there, she reported on the 2002 Israeli invasion of the West Bank, which saw the Israeli Defence Force's (IDF) assault on the Palestinian refugee camp in Jenin. This seemed to have been a particularly brutal attack on what, in international law, is designated as a protected territory. The violence went on from 1 to 11 April, a ferocious attack on a camp long regarded by Israel as the source of Palestinian 'terrorists' and suicide bombers. The IDF released a formidable force of infantry, commandos, helicopters and armoured bulldozers on the camp. By the time they withdrew, they had left behind enormous devastation, with many dead and unburied corpses strewn in the narrow alleyways, thousands made homeless and some ten per cent of the camp destroyed by Israel's bulldozers. A dispute after the assault ended arose between the two sides over the numbers killed. The Palestinians called it a massacre of anything from 500 to several thousand people while Israel claimed that only 52 to 54 Palestinians and 23 Israeli soldiers had been killed.[16]

Goldenberg, covering the West Bank at the time, provided the *Guardian* with vivid on-site reports of the Jenin massacre, which left no doubt about the devastation and systematic abuse the IDF had inflicted, not just on the camp,[17] but along the whole length of the West Bank, especially the towns of Ramallah and Nablus, and villages around Jenin.[18] Three years later, when I worked in Ramallah, the destructive effects of Israel's West Bank invasion could still be seen in that town and in Nablus' historic old city. Goldenberg's reports were informative and impartial. She quoted her sources at all times and did not express her personal views.

It did not spare her a hate campaign by pro-Israel groups. Honest Reporting, a pro-Israel organisation established shortly after the start of the Second Intifada with the aim of scrutinising the media for anti-Israel bias, played a dominant part in the huge email barrage on Goldenberg. It was so overwhelming that it interfered with her ability to contact the *Guardian* during her assignment, and her email address had to be changed.[19] Another pro-Israel organisation, CAMERA, with aims similar to those of HonestReporting, wrote many years later of what it described as, Goldenberg's 'disgusting' role in 'disseminating the lies about the so-called "Jenin massacre"', and her 'despicable role in creating the Jenin massacre label', along with 'the entire stable of ant-Israeli *Guardian* journalists'.[20]

When she left Israel, HonestReporting went so far as to suggest that 'Goldenberg's incessant criticism of Israel's right to defend its citizens has undoubtedly emboldened Palestinian terrorists', a serious charge without foundation.[21] Yet the *Guardian* has made strenuous efforts to provide balance in its news reporting, (though not necessarily in its comment pages), and there is an active debate amongst its editors on the question of objectivity.[22] In a conflict as polarised as the Israeli–Palestinian one, this is a considerable challenge. Should all views be given equal weight and, on the American model, represent the claims of both sides equally and without judgement? The *Guardian*'s editors differed on this question, some believing that absolute objectivity is impossible, and others that it is better to judge views and events against a set of relevant and morally justifiable values. One Middle East editor put it like this,

> I think objectivity is not about being neutral and standing in the middle. It is a matter of looking objectively into the facts, approaching them with an open mind, and drawing conclusions, which should be fair.[23]

But for each side caught in the Israeli–Palestinian quagmire, 'objectivity' means that their view is the correct one and needs to be presented as such. To do otherwise is to be unfair, or worse, to be part of the other camp.

HIDDEN FROM VIEW: PALESTINIAN GRIEVANCES

Palestinians and their supporters have always felt unjustly treated by the Western media, their views not sufficiently aired or frequently misrepresented. Their criticisms of the *Guardian*, and other newspapers, all stem from this belief and their motivation in complaining of 'bias' is aimed at acquiring a platform for their side of the story, or at least getting a sympathetic hearing for it. They see the Zionist narrative as hogging the limelight, promoted with considerable funds and disseminated to reach all levels of western society. Indeed, while there is – justifiably – not a schoolchild in Europe who does not know about the Holocaust, few people are educated about the Palestinian *Nakba*, the catastrophic exodus of three-quarters of Palestine's native population as a result of Israel's establishment in 1948.

It is a longstanding Palestinian grievance that their case was always hidden or obscured from public view and they see the news media as complicit in this concealment. It is certainly true that the Palestinian case seemed to disappear after 1948, spoken of, if at all, as an issue of 'Arab refugees', whose origins few had any idea about. The *Manchester Guardian*, as the paper was known at the time, took the view that the refugees should be settled in Arab countries and not return to Israel. It was considered a predominantly humanitarian issue; and that more or less remained the situation until the founding of the Palestine Liberation Organisation (PLO) in 1964, and the start of Palestinian armed resistance to Israel after 1965.

At this time the Arab states, which had played host to the Palestinian refugees after 1948, brought up the need for their repatriation. Their request went unheeded, but it served to return the refugee issue to public attention. Soon after, the *Guardian*'s then editor, Alistair Hetherington, wrote a strikingly forthright article about these refugees, reversing the *Guardian*'s earlier position of settling them in Arab countries, and with a candour rarely repeated on this subject in the paper subsequently.

> 'Return' [for the Palestinian refugees] is no metaphor [unlike with the Jews]. Whatever caused them to leave in the first place ... the state of Israel was founded at their expense; if its population is to be enlarged, they have the first claim to be admitted ... it would be an acknowledgment by Israel of its responsibility for the existence of the refugees and its duty to right their wrongs. Since those responsibilities are absolute – not conditioned by any responsibilities that

> the Arab states may bear in addition – the offer would have to be unconditional too.[24]

These sentiments fell on deaf ears in Israel at the time, as they have done since. Its position has always been to reject all responsibility for the refugees' plight from the time of its establishment to the present day.

Back in the 1960s, no one outside the ranks of Middle East specialists knew much about the Palestinian issue in the UK. Growing up in England in that period, I remember that even the name, 'Palestine', slipped out of use. People thought I must have said 'Pakistan' when asking me where I came from. Throughout that time, it was virtually impossible for Palestinians to get a hearing in the media, and even when Palestine was featured in news reports or commentary, others spoke for the Palestinians, never they themselves.

J.M.N. Jeffries had noted the same phenomenon in his account of events in the 1930s referred to earlier in this chapter. Zionists in many walks of life and their British supporters, he says, have put over their case effectively in Britain.

> From voices which are familiar in their varying degrees and received in their varying degrees the public has heard over and over everything that is to be said for political Zionism ... From the Arabs the British public has heard little, despite all the endeavours the Arabs have made to present their cause ... [They] have never obtained in the newspapers and upon the platform one thousandth of the space or of the time which they needed to say all they had to say.[25]

In the wake of the 1967 Arab–Israeli War, the Palestine case was submerged by the triumphalism and adulation heaped on Israel. The *Guardian*'s coverage of Israel went along with the general mood, and it is doubtful that Alistair Hetherington would have made his earlier comments about the refugees after 1967. The *Guardian*'s editorial line started to veer towards sympathy for Israel's predicament with the newly conquered Palestinian territories. Hetherington thought they could be used as bargaining chips in peace negotiations, and understood Israel's need to annex some areas of occupied land. He exhorted Israel to make peace with the Arabs for its own sake.[26]

Yet this was also a time when the *Guardian* was publishing outspoken reports by its former staff correspondent, Michael Adams, from the newly occupied Palestinian territories. Adams, a supporter of the Palestine cause, did not hesitate to expose Israel's brutal treatment of the occupied people, the destruction of their villages, and the demolition of their homes. Although the paper published the articles, it eventually proved too much for the editor, and he never used Adams to report news from the region again.[27] Yet the Adams episode was the start of the *Guardian*'s willingness to cover Palestinian affairs, if only indirectly. It coincided with the appearance of the first Palestinian solidarity organisations in London: Free Palestine and, in 1972, the first Palestinian medical charity, Palestine Medical Aid, later to become Medical Aid for Palestinians (MAP), a successful charity that today operates in the West Bank, Gaza and the Lebanese refugee camps. In 1973 a small group of colleagues and I formed the first Palestinian lobbying organisation, Palestine Action, to publicise the Palestinian case. Despite its small size, it operated successfully until 1978.

In that period Hetherington became engaged with the idea of Israeli–Arab cooperation, which he thought, among other things, could be beneficial to the Palestinian refugees. He admired Israel's pioneering irrigation technology and steered the paper's line towards an alignment with the 'moderate' tendency in the Israeli Labour Party, the so-called 'doves' like Abba Eban, the then Israeli foreign minister, and Yigal Allon, Israel's sometime deputy prime minister. Hetherington had a romanticised view of these hard-nosed men who were in no sense moderate, but it fitted his increasing interest in promoting a peaceful outcome between the two sides as set out in UN Resolution 242.

The Palestinians at this time, no longer anonymous 'Arab refugees', thrust themselves into the limelight as a people engaged in a struggle for liberation. The PLO's guerrilla fighters captured the imagination of young people in many parts of the world, who flocked to join their ranks. The Palestinian leader, Yasser Arafat, became a world figure with his famous 'gun and olive branch' speech to the UN General Assembly in 1974. An Arab summit in Rabat in the same year recognised the PLO as the sole representative of the Palestinian people, and the first PLO representative, Said Hammami, was sent to London, to act as a quasi-Palestinian ambassador.

From then on, the *Guardian*'s attitude changed towards the Palestinian question, accepting the Rabat decision and exhorting Israel to start negotiations with the PLO to encourage the start of mutual understanding. To Hetherington's disappointment, many in the Jewish community saw this exhortation as hostile to Israel, and some thought it antisemitic.[28] In May 1976, the 'Palestine Report', an advertisement displaying various aspects of Palestinian culture in which Palestine Action was involved, appeared in the *Guardian*. It earned an approving editorial in the paper, signalling a change of direction in favour of the Palestinians who it thought should be regarded as a proper nation.[29] Peter Preston, who had succeeded Hetherington as editor, had no particular position on Zionism, but did not think Israel should receive special treatment. His views on Israel–Palestine were what was becoming the standard liberal position: Israel's right to exist within the 1948 territories, and the need to enter into negotiations with the PLO over the future of the West Bank and Gaza.

We activists turned to the *Guardian* as friendly to our position, with journalists like Martin Woollacottt and David Hirst writing for the paper, and tried to publish our articles in its pages. Although that did not happen for some years, when it did the paper published a good number of comment pieces by Palestinians and stood out in the British press as a home for the Palestinian point of view. Between 2002 and 2020, I and many friends were able to publish several articles in the paper. So far, at the time of writing in July 2020, two powerful comment pieces by Palestinians have appeared.[30]

The view we had of the *Guardian* corroborates the findings of Ruth Sanz Sabido, who carried out a study of coverage of the Israel–Palestinian conflict in the British press. Comparing the *Guardian*, *The Times*, the *Daily Mirror* and the *Sun*, she found that the *Guardian* had by far the largest coverage of the conflict since 1948.[31] On the occasion of Israel's seventieth anniversary, the paper mentioned the *Nakba* 45 times, compared with 6 mentions in *The Times* and four in the *Daily Mirror*. It also described the *Nakba* more often than the others as a violent event with deleterious long-term consequences for the Palestinians. The 2014 Israeli assault on Gaza was reported 17 times in the *Guardian*, twice in *The Times* and just once in the *Daily Mirror*.[32]

None of this is to suggest that the *Guardian* takes a partisan view on the side of the Palestinians. In a survey of how often the Palestinian voice was heard in the *Guardian*'s Comment is Free section, its print edition and *Observer* between October 2013 and November 2015, Ben White found that of the 138 op-eds on the Israeli–Palestinian conflict published in that period, 20 (15 per cent) were by Palestinians, as compared to 39 (28 per cent) by Israelis including state officials, and the rest by domestic and international journalists.[33] In 2016 White carried out a follow up survey for the year from December 2015 to November 2016, and found 20 comment pieces on the Israeli–Palestinian conflict, six by Palestinians, five by Israelis and another four by *Guardian* journalists, including the pro-Israel columnist Jonathan Freedland. None were from Palestinians in the Occupied Territories which would have been relevant to the topic.[34]

After our heyday of a decade ago, when it had been possible to obtain a *Guardian* platform for the Palestinian voice, it has become more difficult in recent years. On the centenary of the Balfour Declaration in 2017 I offered the editor of the *Guardian*'s 'The Long Read' a reflection on how the Declaration had affected my life as one of its Palestinian victims; he turned me down. I was disappointed that a topic so rarely presented from the Palestinian point of view should have been rejected. Instead, a reflection by a commentator on Balfour who was from neither side appeared in the same section. It has even seemed at times that either Israeli or Jewish critics of Israel, for example Oxford University's Israeli Emeritus Professor of International Relations, Avi Shlaim, who has written increasingly outspoken pieces against Israeli policy in the paper, have become more acceptable than Palestinian ones, perhaps because they might be less likely to provoke accusations of antisemitism against the paper.

There may be something in that, but it is more likely that the *Guardian* has still not shaken off its Zionist past and is still highly sensitive to Israeli flak. When the *Electronic Intifada*'s associate editor, and a seasoned European Union observer, David Cronin, tried to submit a piece to the *Guardian* in 2015 on how the Israel lobby operates in Brussels, he was told by the comment editor at the time, Matt Seaton, that the subject was 'too sensitive'. He then toned it down and resubmitted, but it was still rejected. In the same piece he had gone on to describe a conversation with a Hamas founding member, who wanted to learn how the Irish peace process worked, but this time Cronin was told by Brian Whitaker, the *Guardian*'s commissioning editor, that the paper had received too many submissions on Israel–Palestine, and he would be better off writing about the EU.[35]

THE *GUARDIAN*'S HISTORIC SUPPORT FOR ZIONISM

The *Guardian*'s Zionist legacy is longstanding. It dates from the paper's early days when it was the *Manchester Guardian*, and before political Zionism was established. Manchester was home to a large and prosperous Jewish community, on whose affairs the paper regularly reported. Even at that early time, three of its staff reporters were committed Zionists. But it was not until 1914 when the then editor C.P. Scott met with Zionism's most skilled advocate, Chaim Weizmann, that he fell under the spell of Zionism. From then on Scott became Weizmann's devoted sponsor and advocate, putting him in contact with leading political figures of the day and members of the cabinet who included the prime minister, David Lloyd George, and the foreign secretary, Arthur Balfour. Between 1915 and 1917, the paper published regular articles in support of Zionism.[36]

The next editor, W.P. Crozier, who had been a member of the paper's Zionist group during Scott's editorship, continued his predecessor's pro-Zionist tradition, only more fervently. As Baram puts it, he turned the *Guardian* into a tool of Zionist advocacy. The sufferings of Jews in Germany during the 1940s were covered extensively and sympathetically in the paper while, at the same time, its reporting on Palestine showed great sensitivity to every aspect of the needs of the growing Jewish settlement (*yishuv*) there.[37] Crozier's Zionist proclivities were greatly strengthened by his association with Lewis Namier, a professor of history at Manchester University and passionate Zionist, and their alliance came to influence the paper directly. Crozier saw himself and the paper as part of the Zionist effort, a partisan view never held so openly by any *Guardian* editor who succeeded him.

Over the subsequent decades, coverage of the Israel–Palestinian conflict evolved a more even-handed approach, as we saw above. It took account of Palestinian rights, which it saw as realistically fulfilled in the two-state solution. A *Guardian* editorial, written on the centenary of the Balfour Declaration which the *Manchester Guardian*'s editor had done so much to facilitate, took stock of the current situation. The Israel of 2017, with its right-wing government, illegal settlement building and military occupation of the Palestinian territories was not what the paper, in its enthusiasm for the Balfour Declaration, had envisaged a hundred years previously. While accepting that the Holocaust had made the creation of Israel 'morally justified', it also meant that an independent Palestinian state was equally justified:

> Balfour's original sin was to afford national rights to only one of the two peoples who claimed the land. This cannot be repeated. Palestinians need to be able to govern themselves in a state recognisable as such. The world's gaze will fall again on Israel and the condition of the Palestinians. To end a hundred years of conflict will need both sides to understand that neither can prevail through violence. Peace can be built only by equitably sharing the land they both crave.[38]

Aside from the reference to 'equitable sharing', which implies an equal division of the country between the two sides, something no two-state configuration has ever proposed, this editorial brings together all the strands of conventional liberal opinion on the conflict. It is a vision supported by 'moderates' on both sides, who earnestly want to see peace between Israelis and Palestinians. It includes liberal Zionists, and a majority of the well-meaning Western public, recognising on the one hand that Israel has a legitimate claim to a state of its own, even if the behaviour of its current right-wing government is objectionable, and on the other, acknowledging Palestinian suffering at the hands of Israel, to be remedied through the creation of a state of their own.

For a newspaper with this history of philo-Zionism and concern for Jewish sentiment, it has been galling for its staff to become the object of vilification by its pro-Israel critics, as outlined above. The main thrust of that hostility is focused on the question of Israel's legitimacy. In that sense, anything construed as a criticism of the Israeli state, its policies or people, raises fears of delegitimization of the whole Zionist project. Israeli hostility to the Boycott, Divestment and Sanctions (BDS) movement, a peaceful civil society initiative, is based on this fear.[39] Criticism of Israel's occupation of Palestinian land is rejected by Israel for the same reason.[40] This anxiety has now been taken to extremes: it covers any hint of anti-Israeli sentiment, extending to any support for the Palestinian side, the suppression of Palestinian history, and the plight of Palestinians under occupation, if it casts Israel or Zionism in a bad light.

To reinforce this defensive position, antisemitism has become a weapon in the hands of the Israeli state and its supporters. Any criticism of Israel can be designated antisemitic and so dismissed, a contention strengthened by the 2016 International Holocaust Remembrance Alliance (IHRA) definition of antisemitism that equates it with anti-Zionism. It is beyond the brief of this chapter to analyse the IHRA phenomenon, but since the adoption of its definition by the British and other European governments, negative comment on Israel – and by extension, anything supportive of the Palestinians – has been largely stifled.[41] For journalists writing in the *Guardian* (or any other mainstream newspaper), fear of accusations of antisemitism are a real concern, and it is easy to see how that can lead to dilution or suppression of inconvenient facts, and avoidance of the topic altogether.

It is worth noting that such anxieties are not new. Jeffries, reporting on Zionism in Palestine in the 1930s, felt he had to defend himself against possible accusations of antisemitism. In writing *Palestine: The Reality*, he predicted that '[i]t is quite possible I may be called an anti-Semite ... but I have never had any truck with anti-Semitism.'[42]

CONCLUSION

I have tried to show in the foregoing account that, apart from an early pro-Zionist phase, the *Guardian*'s coverage of the Israeli–Palestinian conflict has been the fairest and most balanced of all the mainstream British press. It has earnestly sought to represent the views and standpoints of both sides in spite of much provocation. But it has not strayed from its liberal position on the conflict which, however benignly formulated, amounts to affirming that Israel was a moral necessity and so had to be created in someone else's country, while the native inhabitants of that country must now be satisfied with a fifth of it; and those expelled by Israel in 1948 and their descendants can never return to Israel in case they threaten its 'ethnic makeup', and so must find their own solution.

In the end, this is an untenable position because it is unjust to the Palestinians and leaves the refugee issue, the heart of the problem, unsolved. As I have explained, it is a result of faulty thinking about the nature of the conflict which, if it were to be honestly reported as what it is – an old-style settler colonialist project, albeit with novel Biblical associations, that has robbed the indigenous population of its land, thrown them out, and intends to take the rest of it – would clear the fog of incomprehension about Israel–Palestine and pave the way to a lasting solution.

NOTES

1. Quoted in Daphne Baram, *Disenchantment: The Guardian and Israel* (London: Guardian Books, 2008), p. 105.
2. J.M.N Jeffries, *Palestine: The Reality* (London: Longman Green and Co, 1939), p. 5.
3. Ari Shavit, 'Survival of the Fittest', interview with Benny Morris, *Haaretz*, 7 January 2004, www.haaretz.com/1.5262454 (accessed 6 October 2020).
4. Hagar Shezaf, 'Burying the Nakba: How Israel Systematically Hides Evidence of 1948 Expulsion of Arabs', *Haaretz*, 5 July 2019, www.haaretz.com/israel-news/.premium.MAGAZINE-how-israel-systematically-hides-evidence-of-1948-expulsion-of-arabs-1.7435103 (accessed 6 October 2020).
5. James Rodgers, *Headlines from the Holy Land: Reporting the Israeli–Palestinian conflict* (London: Palgrave Macmillan, 2015), p. 2.
6. Hilary Aked, 'BBC bias? Reporting on Israel and the Palestinians', *openDemocracy*, 10 December 2012, www.opendemocracy.net/en/opendemocracyuk/bbc-bias-reporting-on-israel-and-palestinians/ (accessed 6 October 2020).
7. Chris Elliott, 'Accusations of Bias in Israel-Palestine Coverage', *Guardian*, 22 February 2016, www.theguardian.com/commentisfree/2016/feb/22/accusations-of-bias-in-coverage-of-the-israel-palestine-conflict (accessed 6 October 2020).
8. *Guardian* editorial, 'Fairness: Israel-Palestine', *Guardian*, 2006, www.theguardian.com/values/socialaudit/story/0,,1931205,00.html (accessed 6 October 2020).
9. Quoted in Baram, *Disenchantment*, p. 199.
10. Ibid.
11. Ibid.
12. Quoted in Baram, *Disenchantment*, p. 234.
13. Alan Simon, 'The Guardian. "Viciously and Notoriously anti-Semitic"', *Times of Israel blog*, 21 August 2014, blogs.timesofisrael.com/the-guardian-viciously-and-notoriously-anti-israel/ (accessed 6 October 2020).
14. Baram, *Disenchantment*, p. 116.
15. Ibid.

16. James Bennett, 'Death on the Campus: Jenin', *New York Times*, 2 August 2002, www.nytimes.com/2002/08/02/world/death-on-the-campus-jenin-un-report-rejects-claims-of-a-massacre-of-refugees.html (accessed 6 October 2020).
17. Suzanne Goldenberg, 'Toll of the Bloody Battle of Jenin', *Guardian*, 10 April 2002, www.theguardian.com/world/2002/apr/10/israel (accessed 6 October 2020).
18. Suzanne Goldenberg, 'Across West Bank Daily Tragedies Go Unseen', *Guardian*, 27 April 2002, www.theguardian.com/world/2002/apr/27/israel (accessed 6 October 2020).
19. Baram, *Disenchantment*, pp. 199–200.
20. CAMERA UK, 'Suzanne Goldenberg avoids mentioning her Jenin lies at the Guardian open weekend', 16 April 2012, www.camera-uk.org/2012/04/16/suzanne-goldenberg-avoids-mentioning-her-jenin-lies-at-the-guardian-open-weekend/ (accessed 6 October 2020).
21. Honest Reporting, 'The Guardian's Selective Memory', 15 August 2002.
22. Baram, *Disenchantment*, pp. 201–3.
23. Interview with Brian Whittaker, 2003; Baram, *Disenchantment*, p. 202.
24. Alistair Hetherington, 'Jordan Water and Arab Refugees', *Guardian*, 8 January 1964.
25. Jeffries, *Palestine: The Reality*, p. 5.
26. Baram, *Disenchantment*, p. 108.
27. Ibid., pp. 117–18.
28. Ibid., pp.136–7.
29. Quoted in ibid, p. 142.
30. Diana Butto, 'What We Palestinians Think Does Not Matter – All that Matters is Israel', *Guardian*, 2 February 2020; Ahmed Moor, 'Whether Israel Annexes the West Bank or Not, a Two-state Solution is No Longer Viable', *Guardian*, 20 July 2020, www.theguardian.com/commentisfree/2020/jul/20/israel-west-bank-two-state-solution-palestine (both accessed 6 October 2020).
31. Ruth Sanz Sabido, *The Israeli–Palestinian conflict in the British Press* (London: Palgrave Macmillan, 2019).
32. Ibid., p. 96.
33. Ben White, 'How the *Guardian* Continues to Exclude Palestinians from its Comment Pages', *Middle East Monitor*, 28 November 2016, www.middleeastmonitor.com/20161128-how-the-guardian-continues-to-exclude-palestinians-from-its-comment-pages/ (accessed 6 October 2020).
34. Ibid.
35. David Cronin, 'How the Guardian Told Me to Steer Clear of Palestine', *Electronic Intifada*, 11 March 2015, www.electronicintifada.net/blogs/david-cronin/how-guardian-told-me-steer-clear-palestine (accessed 6 October 2020).

36. Baram gives a detailed account of this crucial period in, *Disenchantment*, pp. 29–46.
37. Ibid, pp. 54–57.
38. *Guardian* editorial, 'The *Guardian* View on Israel and Palestine: Escape the Past', 1 November 2017, www.theguardian.com/commentisfree/2017/nov/01/the-guardian-view-on-israel-and-palestine-escape-the-past (accessed 6 October 2020).
39. Moshe Arens, 'The Real Goal of BDS: Deligitmising Israel', *Haaretz*, 9 February 2014, www.haaretz.com/opinion/.premium-delegitimizing-israel-1.5320415 (accessed 6 October 2020).
40. M.J. Rosenberg, 'Israel: Delegitimization is Just a Distraction', *Los Angeles Times*, 17 July 2011, www.latimes.com/opinion/la-xpm-2011-jul-17-la-oe-rosenberg-israel-20110717-story.html (accessed 6 October 2020).
41. Rebecca Ruth Gold, 'The IHRA Definition of Antisemitism: Defining Antisemitism by Erasing Palestinians', *Political Quarterly*, 28 July 2020, doi.org/10.1111/1467-923X.12883; Ash Sarkar, 'The IHRA Definition Is a Threat to Freedom of Expression', *Guardian*, 3 September 2018, www.theguardian.com/commentisfree/2018/sep/03/ihra-antisemitism-labour-palestine (accessed 6 October 2020).
42. Jeffries, *Palestine: The Reality*, p. 6.

6

The *Guardian* and Latin America: Pink Tides and Yellow Journalism

Alan MacLeod

Shocking pundits and bookmakers alike, Jeremy Corbyn was elected leader of the Labour Party in September 2015. Two years later, on a platform of what he called 'twenty-first century socialism', he led the party to one of its strongest electoral performances before losing a second general election two years later. The media had a great deal to do with his demise. Relentlessly attacking him for five years, the quiet, well-mannered vegetarian was transformed into a bloodthirsty terrorist, a national security threat, an antisemite, a communist spy and more. As discussed in chapter 11, the *Guardian* was far from blameless in this process.

To many in the UK, Corbyn and his ideas seemed like a bolt from the blue, a breath of fresh air and the beginning of something completely unique and novel. But, in reality, the same revolution had been brewing in Latin America for years; a progressive wave was washing over the region, as grassroots, left-of-centre people's movements were sweeping to power. This so-called 'Pink Tide' started in Venezuela with the election of Hugo Chávez, and soon spread throughout the continent. In 2002, Brazil elected long-time trade union leader, Lula da Silva. Soon after, new leftist movements were emerging and winning in Honduras, Uruguay, Paraguay and elsewhere. There was also the return of old faces from the political wilderness, like the Peronists in Argentina or the Sandinistas in Nicaragua. There were a few holdouts, like US-favourite Colombia, but, by 2011, the great majority of Latin Americans lived under avowedly left-wing governments. As the United States had its attention sed on the Middle East, its own backyard was in open revolt. Suddenly, the people of the region had elected bus drivers, peasant farmers and disabled shoe-shine boys to be their heads of state. It would be as if the former rail union leader Bob Crow had become prime minister of the United Kingdom.

Corbyn and his team knew all this, and had been watching closely and drawing inspiration. Corbyn, John McDonnell, Seumas Milne and Diane Abbott were frequent speakers at Latin America solidarity events, extolling the revolutionary changes being enacted. Indeed, the concept of 'twenty-first century socialism' was popularised by Chávez in 2005, and later used by new left-wing leaders like Lula, Bolivia's Evo Morales, Ecuador's Rafael Correa and Argentina's Néstor Kirchner, back when Corbyn was a mere blip on the national spectrum.

The results of twenty-first century socialism were truly extraordinary, exciting experts the world over. Poverty in Venezuela was halved under Chávez (1999–2013), with extreme poverty reducing by three-quarters.[1] The same can be said of Bolivia under Morales (2006–19).[2] Meanwhile, Lula's Bolsa Familia plan – cash transfers to the poorest citizens – pulled some 50 million people out of poverty.[3]

Far more important, however, was the political awakening and sense of inclusion fostered by the left's victories. People who had been oppressed for centuries found their voice, as a multiracial coalition of working-class people entered the political arena for the first time, with new programmes enabling to learn how to read, study at university and assert their democratic rights in the face of opposition from the oligarchical white elite that had dominated the region since the arrival of Christopher Columbus. 'For the first time in the region the leaders look like the people they govern', Cristina Fernández de Kirchner, president of Argentina between 2007 and 2015, told Oliver Stone, in his 2009 documentary, *South of the Border*, which explored the rise of the left.

While each government had its differences, they all saw themselves as part of a movement aimed at opposing neoliberalism and foreign interference in Latin America, realising that only through unity could true independence ever be achieved. Together, they started building institutions that would challenge the US and lay the groundwork for a modern, independent, progressive continent, and finally halt the bleeding from the open veins of Latin America.[4] They also rejected attempts to split them into 'good' and 'bad' lefts as Western governments and academics tried to do. Thus, Lula (a 'good' leftist) would openly campaign for a Chávez election win in Venezuela (the worst of the 'bad' left, in US eyes). 'Your victory will be our victory', he announced publicly in 2012, claiming Chávez had the full support of every leftist and every democrat in Latin America.[5]

However, the party was not to last, and the empire would strike back. In the wake of the 2008 financial crash and the 2011 Chinese slowdown (which hurt Latin America particularly badly), the right used the economic malaise to return to power. Sometimes this was done through electoral means, as in Argentina in 2015 and Uruguay in 2019. But in other countries, like Honduras in 2009 and Bolivia in 2019, far-right dictatorships came to power in US-backed coups (the Bolivian coup was spectacularly overturned the following year). And in Brazil, Lula's successor Dilma was impeached on highly dubious grounds in 2016. In the resulting election, Lula, the frontrunner by a wide margin, was jailed and barred from running, even from his cell, leaving the way clear for fascist president Jair Bolsonaro, who appointed Lula's judge as his Justice Minister. Lula himself blames the CIA and the US Department of Justice for masterminding events.

The United States has also conducted a campaign of economic war against those it has not been able to unseat, placing crippling sanctions on Cuba, Nicaragua and Venezuela, measures that have claimed the lives of over 100,000 in Venezuela alone, according to one American UN Special Rapporteur.[6] Venezuela, in particular, is in a terrible economic state. However, recent election victories in Argentina, Mexico and Bolivia show the left may be down but is not out in Latin America.

The emergence of a continent-wide progressive movement that not only championed but enacted many of the policies and values the *Guardian* claims it stands for, should have brought great interest and excitement at the outlet. For decades, the newspaper published important investigative journalism and covered Latin America well, with the likes of Richard Gott and Hugh O'Shaughnessy standing out. To this day, it still prints many important stories on the region, particularly in its comment pages. But far from embracing the 'Pink Tide', the *Guardian* has, for the most part, chosen to side with Western governments and reject it, often displaying a shocking lack of understanding of the continent. Indeed, the distortion with which it presents Latin America is so startling it often beggars belief, with regional specialists no longer able to rely on it for accurate information. As Professor Julia Buxton of Manchester University told me, many people simply 'don't see the *Guardian* as credible articulators of the reality of Latin America' anymore.

The newspaper's tone and outlook, often so conservative that it is indistinguishable from the *Daily Telegraph* in its reporting of the continent, has left a large opening for reader-supported alternative media like *Colombia Reports*, *Venezuelanalysis* or *Chile Today*. As Daniel Hunt of *Brasil Wire* told me, 'If the *Guardian* did its job properly, *Brasil Wire* would not have to exist.' Unfortunately, these outlets cannot possibly fill the gap of a major media organisation like the *Guardian*, meaning that the public has remained fundamentally misinformed about the region, as the following examples show.

VENEZUELA

Almost from the moment of his rise, the *Guardian* was hostile towards Hugo Chávez and the movement around him, showing little interest in his innovative social programmes that eradicated illiteracy, created a nationalised healthcare system from scratch, halved unemployment and greatly increased the country's Human Development Index (HDI) score.[7] Indeed, when he was briefly overthrown in a US-sponsored coup in 2002, the newspaper appeared to welcome it; its South America correspondent Alex Bellos misinforming readers that Chávez had actually 'resigned' after his snipers and supporters shot at peaceful demonstrators, killing 13 and firing on ambulances trying to aid the wounded.[8] All of this was untrue. It was actually oppositionists killing Chávez supporters, who Bellos told readers barely existed as a group inside Venezuela. Chávez 'antagonised almost every sector of society and failed to improve the lot of the poor', he wrote, just hours before a mass movement of over one million people spontaneously descended upon the presidential palace, demanding his return, a spectacular demonstration of people power that was caught on camera by an Irish documentary team, later becoming the movie *The Revolution will not be Televised*. Even 18 years later, the *Guardian* has neither apologised nor even corrected their mistakes. While the newspaper later published more accurate reporting on the coup from Duncan Campbell and Gary Younge, while the event was actually taking place, it effectively manufactured public consent for another US regime change operation in Latin America.[9]

In an era of neoliberal dominance and austerity politics, much of the Western left looked to Latin America, and Venezuela in particular, for inspiration. Professor Noam Chomsky, for instance, characterised the changes going on there as inspirational, even travelling to Venezuela in 2009 to embrace Chávez. 'I can see how a better world is being created and can speak to the person who has inspired it', he said in a speech in Caracas.[10] But instead of feeding that hunger, the *Guardian* began hiring journalists like Phil Gunson and Virginia López-Glass who are among the most committed and vocal opponents of the government. In 2005, it appointed its first Latin America editor for 20 years, Rory Carroll. This was an odd choice, not least because Carroll told journalist Pablo Navarrete that he knew nothing about the region and did not even speak Spanish.[11] Carroll spent much of his time in his penthouse in the exclusive Altamira district of Caracas, where he held parties for the Venezuelan elite and other wealthy, English-speaking expats. 'Imagine the contempt the *Guardian* (ostensibly a left-wing newspaper) must have for its readers to send such an underqualified person to report on the regional "Pink Tide" wave, that was at its height at that moment, and that had Venezuela at its epicentre', an incredulous Navarrete told me.

From Altamira, Carroll kept up a relentless flow of questionably sourced negative articles, so much so that activist organisations were formed in the United Kingdom to counter what they perceived as gross lies. Carroll was given the nicknames 'Rory Jackanory' and 'Carroll in Wonderland'.[12] The *Guardian*'s readers' editor came to his defence, arguing that the newspaper was not required to be neutral or balanced, with Carroll himself admitting that he was far from a 'champion of impartiality'.[13] Partiality and dishonesty, however, are two different things. In 2011, Carroll published an interview with Chomsky, headlined 'Noam Chomsky criticises old friend Hugo Chávez for "assault" on democracy', which began by claiming that 'Chomsky has accused the socialist leader of amassing too much power and of making an "assault" on Venezuela's democracy', framing the president as a power-hungry autocrat silencing dissent.[14] The story went viral and was picked up by other outlets, including the *New York Times*, keen to alert the world of the MIT professor's apparent change of heart towards Venezuela.

Yet Chomsky's supposed words were so unlike what he had said before that many readers were suspicious, contacting him for confirmation. An outraged Chomsky then complained vociferously about the article. 'Let's begin with the headline: complete deception. That continues throughout. You can tell by simply comparing the actual quotes with their comments. As I mentioned, and expected, the [New York] *Times* report of a similar interview is much more honest, again revealing the extreme dishonesty of the *Guardian*.'[15] Feeling the pressure, the *Guardian* took the unusual move of publishing the full transcript, but that made matters worse, showing conclusively the level of deceit necessary to frame his words as an all-out attack on Chávez. Chomsky now insists on the *Guardian* publishing a full transcript of any interview he does with them.

Chávez died in 2013, around the same time the Venezuelan economy began to falter. Breaking the tradition of not speaking ill of the dead, Carroll's obituary described him as a 'divisive leader' and a 'dictator who jailed opponents, sponsored terrorists and left his people hungry', providing no evidence for his claims.[16] The *Guardian*'s Gunson, meanwhile, said that he was seen 'as a hero by the poor and a socialist dictator by opponents' but made clear what the 'correct' opinion was:

> The debate continued as to whether Chavez could fairly be described as a dictator, but a democrat he most certainly was not. A hero to many, especially among the poor, for his populist social programmes, he assiduously fomented class hatred and used his control of the judiciary to persecute and jail his political opponents.[17]

Thus, even in his obituaries, Chávez was treated with scorn verging on hatred.

Compare that to US president George H.W. Bush, former head of the CIA and one of the masterminds of Operation Condor, the US-sponsored fascist takeover of Latin America, a plan whereby many of the region's governments were overthrown and replaced with genocidal dictatorships. Bush was also responsible for the Dirty Wars in Central America, partnering with figures like General Ríos Montt, since convicted of genocide and crimes against humanity. 'I'll never apologise for the United States of America. Ever! I don't care what the facts are', he was fond of saying.

The obituary of Bush in the *Guardian*'s sister paper, the *Observer*, mentions nothing of Latin America, instead glorifying him as an 'American patriot with a deep sense of duty'. He was, according to Simon Tisdall, 'quintessentially, a decent man', whose 'most admirable quality . . . [was] his deep sense of public duty and service'.[18]

Even when discussing recently deceased dictators like Saudi Arabia's King Abdullah, the *Guardian* found much to praise about him, describing him as a 'liberal' moderniser and, laughably, a counterweight to extremism. 'He was, in other words, not a bad man' and on the 'liberal' wing of the 'princely elite' concluded the paper's leader.[19] Chávez, on the other hand, was treated with a special venom even the world's worst human rights abusers were not subject to.

Since Chávez's death, the local opposition has led a near continual campaign of trying to overthrow his successor Nicolás Maduro. This has included demonstrations, direct legal and legislative challenges, and, most notably, sustained campaigns of violence, including attacking hospitals and maternity units, bombing kindergartens, destroying the Caracas metro, burning down free-to-attend public universities and even roasting Afro-Venezuelans alive in the street.[20] In short, their targets are any symbol of the collectivist social-democratic state the multiracial coalition of the left had been trying to build since 1998. The scale of the destruction was considerable; the government estimated that in 2014 alone, $15 billion worth of damage was done. For comparison, the 2020 Beirut explosion is thought to have cost Lebanon $5 billion.

Polls show that the opposition violence was deeply unpopular, with 11 per cent supporting and 86 per cent opposed to it.[21] Nevertheless, the *Guardian* has consistently backed the opposition's attempts to force Maduro out, misleadingly presenting the events as a people's movement enjoying support from the poor[22] and emphasising the supposedly peaceful nature of the opposition and the violence of the government. 'Venezuela's crackdown on anti-government street protests is a threat to democracy across Latin America', read one headline.[23] Thus, the *Guardian* wildly skewed events as a David vs. Goliath contest, where the opposition had 'only sticks and rocks',[24] while the government came equipped with 'army tank, helicopters and paratrooper regiments.'[25] Some of the only pushback to this dominant narrative came from the opinion pages, with associate editor Seumas

Milne flying out to Caracas himself, framing what he saw as a violent revolt of the elite.[26]

The government, knowing any serious response could be used to elicit an American military intervention, has been forced to allow the campaign to go largely unchecked, leading the opposition to grow bolder. In 2018, for example, one ex-military member of the opposition stole a helicopter, using it to bomb government buildings in downtown Caracas. Lopez-Glass described him as a 'patriot', also pushing a conspiracy theory that he might be a government plant, an idea that was immediately disproven as he led a public opposition demonstration the next week.[27]

One of the leaders of the campaign was opposition politician Juan Guaidó, who bizarrely declared himself president in 2019. Guaidó launched five coup attempts between January 2019 and May 2020, the last of which was in coordination with a contingent of American ex-Green Berets. A leaked contract between the two showed that he had promised to pay them a quarter-billion dollars for their services, and that the American mercenaries would then convert to his private death squad, destroying any resistance or protest to his rule. The contract makes clear that the group had the green light to kill essentially any Venezuelan they deemed to be hostile.[28]

The *Guardian*'s Latin America correspondent Tom Phillips consistently presented him as a charismatic, progressive, well liked social-democrat, surrounded by 'rapturous crowds'[29] and addressing 'packed auditoriums'[30] wherever he goes – the solution, in other words, to Venezuela's crisis. Phillips has even attempted to claim Guadó and Lula share the same politics, despite the fact that he has embraced far-right Brazilian president (and Lula's jailer) Jair Bolsonaro, something he claims he was 'amazed' by.[31] It is to Brazil we now turn.

BRAZIL

The 2016 impeachment of President Dilma Rousseff is now widely understood as having been a political power play by Brazil's oligarchy against the Workers' Party, with organised astroturfed protest movements attempting to give a veneer of legitimacy to the events. Dilma was impeached on the mundane charge of window dressing government accounts by moving money around to help facilitate social spending, an operation many previous administrations had done. Many of those impeaching her were facing far more serious corruption charges.

The judge who led the 'anti-corruption' crusade, Sérgio Moro, also presided over the trial of Lula in 2018. It is now known that Moro was secretly in constant contact with the prosecution, directing them on how to proceed with the sham trial. Moro barred the widely popular Lula, the runaway favourite for the 2018 presidential election, from running, even from his cell. Moro then took the job as Justice Minister in Bolsonaro's cabinet. Much of this was exposed by former *Guardian* employee turned strong critic[32] of the newspaper Glenn Greenwald.[33] Thus, the events of 2016 directly led to the rise of Bolsonaro and the return of fascism to Brazil.

At the time, however, the *Guardian* was relatively supportive of the right-wing putsch against the elected left-of-centre government. 'More than a million Brazilians protest against "horror" government', ran one headline, the article insisting that the crowd was a 'diverse' one, and that the extreme right was 'less in evidence' than in previous mobilisations. It also repeated one source who described the Workers' Party as a 'criminal organisation that is robbing state resources'.[34] The *Guardian* also presented the Movimento Brasil Livre, a right-wing libertarian group financed by the notorious American billionaires the Koch brothers, as a charismatic people's movement funding itself purely through T-shirt and sticker sales.[35] Why was the *Guardian* lionising groups that told them that Margaret Thatcher, Milton Friedman and Friedrich Hayek were their heroes, while they were attempting to overthrow a government that shared the same soft-left ideals the newspaper purportedly stands for at home?

In contrast, the many large counterdemonstrations against the attempt to force Dilma out were barely mentioned. As *Brasil Wire* wrote: 'Coverage of every Anti-Dilma protest contrasted with the *Guardian*'s rare mention of regular demonstrations and resistance against the coup.'[36] Thus, by ramping up any and all challenges to the government's legitimacy, and by giving the oxygen of publicity to all manner of right-wing groups, hiding their motives and sources of funding, the message conveyed was that the Workers' Party had to go and be replaced with a government more friendly to Western interests.

Indeed, if that was not clear enough, an editorial in the *Observer* spelled it out directly. 'Rousseff's duty is plain: if she cannot restore calm, she must call new elections – or step aside', it wrote, decrying the 'incompetence and illegality' of the Dilma regime.[37] That she had won re-election barely a year previously did not seem to matter. Instead, the *Guardian* presented conservative politician Michel Temer as 'the man who could fix Brazil', a figure in whom the 'country sees hope for salvation.'[38]

Once in power, Temer immediately conducted a privatisation firesale, along with a wholesale free market revolution, including decimating public spending, accelerating the destruction of the environment, raising the retirement age by 11 years, ending the eight-hour workday, relaxing anti-slavery laws and a myriad of other changes that attacked workers' rights. One 2017 poll found he had a three per cent approval rating.[39] While the *Guardian*'s editorial team quickly turned on Temer,[40] the outlet also published three letters from his ambassador to the UK, the message of each was that he was 'putting Brazil back on its feet'.[41] And with regards to the huge anti-Temer protests, it appeared uninterested, not publishing a single story on them.[42]

In 2018, ousted president Dilma Rousseff sat down with a number of *Guardian* staff in the UK, giving a two-hour interview where she warned of the dangers of a Bolsonaro presidency, and how Lula's imprisonment would assure his rise. Nobody, however, heard this warning, because the outlet did not publish anything from the exclusive interview, for reasons that are still unexplained.[43]

The phenomenon of *Guardian* foreign correspondents being ignorant of the country they are attempting to cover and largely interacting with only the elite, is not only limited to Venezuela. During the 2018 elections, which pitted Lula's last-minute replacement Fernando Haddad against Bolsonaro, Tom Phillips went on a tour of northeast Brazil and tweeted that he 'could not find a single Haddad voter' anywhere he went. Haddad won every northeastern state, and the region by a well over 2:1 ratio, on the back of an overwhelming working-class vote, begging the question of who Phillips was associating with. Imagine a foreign journalist travelling to Northern Ireland or Scotland during the 2016 EU referendum and not being able to find a single 'remain' voter. Phillips has since deleted the tweet.[44]

Consequently, while the *Guardian* now decries the Bolsonaro administration, accurately depicting it as a threat to its own citizens, public safety and a huge impediment to any meaningful action on climate change, it ignores its own role in smoothing his path to the presidency. Condemning the fallout from a right-wing coup that it broadly supported while it was going on is a relatively common occurrence in the newspaper, which did the same thing in Bolivia in 2019.

BOLIVIA

Polls showed that socialist incumbent Evo Morales was the front-runner in the October 2019 election by a clear ten points. As a result, the discussion inside Bolivia was not whether he would win, but if he would win by a wide enough margin (ten points) to avoid a runoff vote. Initial unofficial returns showed Morales ahead by 9.5 per cent, but when the country's far flung rural areas' totals came in, his overall victory rose to 10.5 per cent, enough to win outright in the first round. This should have surprised no one, as his strongest base has always been the rural poor (Morales himself was a coca farmer and peasant union organiser before entering electoral politics). The US-backed opposition and the Organization of American States, however, smelled a rat, claiming to find irregularities in the vote count, a claim that was almost immediately repudiated.[45]

Nevertheless, the Bolivian right quickly mobilised, conducting a campaign of intimidation aimed at the ruling Movement to Socialism (MAS) party, attacking and kidnapping elected officials. In the city of Vinto, for example, opposition groups kidnapped MAS mayor Patricia Arce, cutting her hair off, painting her body red and dragging her through the streets barefoot, all while abusing her on camera, forcing her to commit to leaving office. Morales' sister's house was also burned to the ground. Amid the violence, the *Guardian* excitedly reported that the country's notorious police had joined the 'mutiny' against the president, amid anger at his attempts to 'hang on to power after weeks of unrest over disputed election results',[46] thereby presenting the action as a legitimate uprising against a budding dictator. After the military appeared on television demanding Morales resign, or else they would take action, he fled to Mexico, stressing that he was choosing to leave in order to prevent a bloodbath against the left, something that had already started to take place.

The military picked Jeanine Áñez as his replacement, a little-known senator from a far-right party who gained four per cent of the vote. A strongly conservative Christian, Áñez had previously described Bolivia's indigenous majority as 'satanic', suggesting they should not be allowed to live in cities. Police and military units immediately ripped off and publicly burned their indigenous flag patches they had been made to wear under Morales, a symbolic gesture hinting of a return to a white supremacist state. Áñez immediately pre-exonerated the military and the police of all past and future crimes committed during the 're-establishment of order' – something roundly understood as a license to kill. They immediately used it, carrying out a number of massacres against Morales supporters, brutally suppressing public resistance against the coup.

While the *Guardian* did publish some opinion articles denouncing the coup,[47] the *Observer*'s editorial on the matter summed up their coverage. Blaming Morales solely for the violence and not mentioning any of the above details, it claimed that he was a 'victim of his own refusal to hand over power', and that it was his 'determination to grab a fourth consecutive term, and his alleged rigging of last month's elections for that purpose, which precipitated his downfall':

> To employ the past tense to describe Morales's presidency is to knowingly accept he is no longer Bolivia's leader. Yet this is a reality Morales himself is *unfortunately* refusing to acknowledge. After weeks of street protests, political defections, a police mutiny and a critical decision by the army to withdraw its support, Morales *voluntarily quit* last Sunday and fled into exile in Mexico (emphasis added).[48]

Assiduously avoiding using the word 'coup' to describe events, it chastised the 'authoritarian' Morales for describing it as such, and for calling the new administration a 'dictatorship', something that was, according to the paper's perspective, 'fanning violence between his supporters and security forces'. Indeed, the only time the editorial team used the word 'coup' was to warn that Morales must 'eschew any coup-making of his own'. Thus, it was not the semi-openly fascist[49] state shooting protesters that was the problem, but Morales drawing attention to it.

During the weeks of repression that followed, the *Guardian* displayed an unfortunate habit of describing the massacres merely as 'clashes'.[50] 'Bolivia Funeral Procession Turns Violent' ran one headline, reporting that 'marchers clashed with police'.[51] With such linguistic turns of phrase, the newspaper turned an armed police attack so brutal grieving pallbearers had to abandon the coffins in the street into a nebulous violent act with no clear perpetrator or victim. (The funeral, incidentally, was for victims of a previous police massacre.)

Nearly a month after the coup, the *Guardian*'s editorial board refused to use the word to describe the events, thereby tacitly endorsing them, advising the new government only to 'defend democracy' by 'living up' to its words, taking seriously the idea that the government wished to hold free and fair elections swiftly.[52] It also referred to Áñez's regime not as a dictatorship, but as an 'interim government' – exactly the phrase Áñez herself adopted to legitimise her rule.

Consequently, the *Guardian* worked to manufacture public consent for regime change in Bolivia by muddying the waters, presenting a classic Latin-American style military coup against one of the world's most progressive governments as a legitimate uprising against a budding dictator, at least until the dust cleared and the die was already cast.

COLOMBIA

One notable holdout from the progressive wave sweeping across Latin America is Colombia, where the US and UK-backed right-wing government maintained total control. This was down, in no small part, to the government's willingness to use extraordinary amounts of violence against its own population. Largely unknown outside the country, Colombia's civil war between the government and far-right paramilitary groups on one side, and leftist guerrillas on the other, has caused the current internal displacement of some 7.4 million people, according to the United Nations, and many more fleeing to neighbouring countries.[53] For reference, the conflict in Syria generated some 6.2 million internal displacements (and around 5.6 million more internationally).[54] The government and the death squads allied to it are thought to have been responsible for the large majority of the violence. Colombia is also far and away the most dangerous place to be an activist, according to Amnesty International, with more trade unionists killed inside the country than in all others combined.[55]

Throughout the twenty-first century, one man has dominated Colombian politics: Álvaro Uribe, president from 2002 to 2010 and a senator from 2014 to 2020. As president, Uribe worked closely with the Bush administration to carry out its 'Plan Colombia' drive, a radical militarisation of the drug war, which critics allege was actually a veiled attack on the rural population and the FARC guerrillas in service of huge Western agribusiness, mining and fossil fuel corporations, who wanted to clear the population off the land in order to exploit it.

Uribe oversaw a years-long policy of massacres, dubbed the 'false positives scandal', where government forces would kill anyone it wished, later claiming they were FARC guerrillas, allowing Uribe to impose his will nationwide and terrorise critics into silence. According to the *Guardian*, over 10,000 people were killed in this way during Uribe's eight year reign.[56] Despite the US working with him to eradicate cocaine production, internal American government documents name Uribe as an 'important Colombian narco-trafficker' himself, a high-ranking associate of the infamous Medellin Cartel and 'close personal friend' of the notorious drug kingpin Pablo Escobar (something which he has strenuously denied).[57] In August 2020, Uribe was arrested for allegedly trying to bribe a witness in a case against a paramilitary group.

The Labour government supported Uribe and Colombia, providing it with weaponry, over the strong protestations of the British trade union movement – the National Union of Journalists' general secretary writing that the government had Colombian blood on its hands, detailing Uribe's intimate connections with the right-wing death squads terrorising his fellow trade unionists.[58]

While the *Guardian* did report on the drugs and the violence in Colombia, it generally refrained from pointing the finger at the government. Indeed, throughout 2007, it worked closely with Uribe himself on a nine-part series singing the virtues of Colombia and its government (much of which it has now removed from its website). 'Welcome to the new Colombia', wrote Rory Carroll, noting that Uribe had 'ushered in a new era of peace and prosperity.'[59] Where once business executives fretted about being kidnapped, he wrote, now they worry only about 'having a hotel suite with Wi-Fi', writing approvingly that areas of Bogota are rapidly gentrifying and state-owned businesses are being privatised. 'We have no limitations on foreign investors', one executive told him. 'Here you don't have to talk about the possibility of investment; it's happening. You can observe how many foreign CEOs are based here.' The nation, Carroll claims, praises Uribe for his leadership and his 'security crackdown', casually noting near the end that threats against journalists have tripled and that millions of people have been forced out of their homes, but brushing it off as a mere footnote to conclude that Colombia is now a modern day 'El Dorado' that is 'glinting with promise'.

Another article extolled Colombia's decision to 'promote self-sufficiency' by expanding its coal and oil industries and 'actively wooing overseas investment', informing readers that the country has 'an extremely generous fiscal regime'.[60] Others promoted the nation's transport and communications sectors.[61] One, which detailed Colombia's privatisation drive and finance industry even included a quote from the now disgraced fraudster Allen Stanford: 'We know that Colombia has had difficulties in the past, but what many people don't know is that there are perhaps more investment opportunities here than in any other place of the world.' Stanford is currently serving a 110-year prison sentence in the USA for creating a giant Ponzi scheme. While Stanford's financial misdeeds might have finally caught up to him, there are no such penalties for journalistic malpractice.

To sum up, in article after article of relentlessly optimistic prose, the *Guardian* – an ostensibly left-wing newspaper – was glorifying a far-right president carrying out something close to genocide against his own people, mass privatisations, gentrification and the expansion of the fossil fuel industry. The series shared one central message: Uribe was to thank for this supposed Colombian miracle.

Whether the outlet was paid by the Colombian government for good coverage or not is unclear (the newspaper has not responded to enquiries). However, the praise of the government did not end there. The next year the newspaper's board released an editorial portraying him as a father-of-the-nation figure, a mix between Nelson Mandela and Winston Churchill, even using the word 'hero' to describe him.[62] It euphemistically noted that he had achieved peace and stability

through an 'aggressive military strategy, as controversial as it has been successful'. While the *Guardian* had condemned Morales for seeking an extra term in office, suggesting it was proof of a dictator in the making, it wistfully imagined a scenario where Uribe would 'use his recent triumphs to install himself in power semi-permanently.' 'His popularity means he would certainly win an election, and any referendum that might be held before it', the editorial noted, concluding that 'Mr. Uribe should think long and hard about what to do with his successes.'

In the end, Uribe chose not to run again, although in 2018, his handpicked protégé Iván Duque was elected president in a highly dubious election that saw an assassination attempt against Duque's leftist challenger Gustavo Petro, government-linked paramilitaries issuing death threats against anyone who dared vote for Petro, and more than 1,000 complaints of electoral fraud.[63] Mentioning none of this, the *Guardian* presented it as a fair democratic fight, even if it was more honest about Uribe's past by now.[64] In contrast, the Venezuelan election, occurring simultaneously, was presided over by over 150 international election observers, including foreign heads of state and current members of the British parliament, all of whom attested to the cleanliness of the process.[65] Despite this, the *Observer* editorial board dismissed the events as a 'sham poll', demanding, as they did with Dilma, that President Maduro 'must step aside' – presumably to let a leader more conducive to US and British interests to take charge like in Brazil.[66]

CONCLUSION

While the *Guardian* speaks the language of social justice and claims to espouse a left-of-centre political outlook nationally, when movements arise that push for a more equitable, progressive redistribution of resources, the outlet is sceptical, if not outright hostile. The lack of public knowledge about Latin America allowed for this campaign to work in a way that one against Corbyn could not, given its readership's first-hand experience. Ultimately, the *Guardian* has spent two decades demonising global south movements that put the lie to its progressive bona fides, while downplaying or even championing Washington-backed far-right regimes as champions of progress.

While the examples detailed might be particularly egregious or noteworthy, they are far from isolated cases, characterising the broad shape of the newspaper's coverage of Latin America. There is space for a more accurate view of the continent in the opinion pages, particularly in the 'Comment is Free section', allowing the publication to retain at least some credibility with those in the know. However, these articles rarely make it into the print edition.

Current editor-in-chief Katharine Viner describes the newspaper's mission as 'holding the powerful to account' and 'upholding liberal values'.[67] Yet when it comes to Latin America, it has attacked progressive movements attempting to further those values, while often failing to hold the region's right-wing rulers to the same standard. It has been necessary to do this, lest British readers are inspired, like Corbyn was, to try the same thing at home.

NOTES

1. 'Venezuela (Bolivarian Republic of): National Socio-Demographic Profile', *CEPAL*, http://interwp.cepal.org/cepalstat/Perfil_Nacional_Social.html?pais=VEN&idioma=english (accessed 9 August 2020).
2. Andrés Arauz, Mark Weisbrot, Andrew Bunker and Jake Johnston, 'Bolivia's Economic Transformation: Macroeconomic Policies, Institutional Changes,and Results', *Center for Economic Policy Research*, October 2019, www.cepr.net/images/stories/reports/bolivia-macro-2019-10.pdf (accessed 4 September 2020).
3. 'Lifting Families Out of Poverty in Brazil: Bolsa Familia Program', *World Bank*, 13 December 2005, www.documents.worldbank.org/en/publication/documents-reports/documentdetail/253131468237869685/lifting-families-out-of-poverty-in-brazil-bolsa-familia-program (accessed 5 September 2020).
4. Geraldine Lievesley and Steve Ludlum, *Reclaiming Latin America: Experiments in Radical Social Democracy* (London: Zed, 2009).
5. 'Lula a Chávez: tu victoria será nuestra victoria', *TeleSUR*, 6 July 2012, www.youtube.com/watch?v=GqBK49eWnkY (accessed 9 August 2020).
6. 'Former UN Rapporteur on Human Rights: US Sanctions Have Killed More than 100 Thousand Venezuelans', *Orinoco Tribune*, 2 March 2020, www.orinocotribune.com/former-un-rapporteur-on-human-rights-us-sanctions-have-killed-more-than-100-thousand-venezuelans/ (accessed 10 August 2020).
7. Alan MacLeod, *Bad News from Venezuela: Twenty Years of Fake News and Misreporting* (Abingdon: Routledge, 2018) pp. 43–7.

8. Alex Bellos, 'Ousted Chavez Detained by Army', *Guardian*, 13 April 2002, www.theguardian.com/world/2002/apr/13/venezuela.alexbellos (accessed 9 August 2020).
9. Alan MacLeod, 'Manufacturing Consent in Venezuela: Media Misreporting of a Country: 1998-2014', *Critical Sociology*, 2020, 46(2), pp. 273–90.
10. James Suggett, 'Noam Chomsky Meets with Chavez in Venezuela', *Venezuelanalysis*, 28 August 2009, www.venezuelanalysis.com/news/4748 (accessed 9 August 2020).
11. Pablo Navarrete, tweet, 25 January 2019, www.twitter.com/pablonav1/status/1088724996782993408 (accessed 14 September 2020).
12. Samuel Grove, 'Carroll in Wonderland: How the Guardian Misrepresents Venezuela', *Red Pepper*, 16 September 2008, www.redpepper.org.uk/carroll-in-wonderland-how-the/ (accessed 5 September 2020); Samuel Grove, 'Rory Rory Jackanory: The Guardian's Latest Chomsky Smear', *Venezuelanalysis*, 6 July 2011, www.venezuelanalysis.com/analysis/6331 (accessed 5 September 2020).
13. Siobhain Butterworth, 'Open Door', *Guardian*, 7 April 2008, www.theguardian.com/commentisfree/2008/apr/07/pressandpublishing (accessed 9 August, 2020).
14. Rory Carroll, 'Noam Chomsky Criticises Old Friend Hugo Chávez for "Assault" on Democracy', *Guardian*, 3 July 2011, www.theguardian.com/world/2011/jul/03/noam-chomsky-hugo-chavez-democracy?INTCMP=SRCH (accessed 9 August 2020).
15. Media Lens, '"Extreme Dishonesty" – The Guardian, Noam Chomsky and Venezuela', *Media Lens*, 6 July 2011, www.medialens.org/2011/extreme-dishonesty-the-guardian-noam-chomsky-and-venezuela/ (accessed 9 August 2020).
16. Rory Carroll, 'Hugo Chavez: Poor Boy from the Plains Who Became Leftwing Figurehead', *Guardian*, 5 March 2013, www.theguardian.com/world/2013/mar/05/hugo-chavez-poor-leftwing-figurehead (accessed 9 August 2020).
17. Phil Gunson, 'Hugo Chavez Obituary', *Guardian*, 5 March 2013, www.theguardian.com/world/2013/mar/05/hugo-chavez (accessed 9 August 2020).
18. Simon Tisdall, 'George HW Bush, an American Patriot with a Deep Sense of Duty', *Observer*, 1 December 2018, www.theguardian.com/us-news/2018/dec/01/george-hw-bush-american-patriot-deep-sense-duty (accessed 9 August 2020).
19. 'The Guardian View on Saudi Arabia after King Abdullah's Death', *Guardian*, 23 January 2015, www.theguardian.com/commentisfree/2015/jan/23/guardian-view-saudi-arabia-king-abdullah-death (accessed 9 August 2020).
20. MacLeod, *Bad News from Venezuela*, pp. 80–5.
21. MacLeod, *Bad News from Venezuela*, pp. 84–5.

22. Virginia Lopez and Jonathan Watts, 'Venezuela's Poor Join Protests as Turmoil Grips Chávez's Revolution', *Guardian*, 20 February 2014, www.theguardian.com/world/2014/feb/20/venezuelas-poor-protests-chavez-revolution (accessed 10 August 2020).
23. Dan Collyns, 'Venezuela Protest Crackdown Threatens Region's Democracy, Warns Vargas Llosa', *Guardian*, 10 April 2014, www.theguardian.com/world/2014/apr/10/venezuela-protest-crackdown-threatens-democracy-latin-america-mario-vargas-llosa (accessed 10 August 2020).
24. Virginia Lopez and Jonathan Watts, 'Venezuela's Poor Join Rising Tide of Protests', *Guardian*, 21 February 2014.
25. Jonathan Watts, 'Venezuelan Opposition Keader, Leopoldo López, Tells his Allies to Keep Fighting', *Guardian*, 21 February 2014, www.theguardian.com/world/2014/feb/21/leopoldo-lopez-venezuela-opposition-leader-popular (accessed 10 August 2020).
26. Seumas Milne, 'Venezuela Shows that Protest Can Be a Defence of Privilege', *Guardian*, 9 April 2014, www.theguardian.com/commentisfree/2014/apr/09/venezuela-protest-defence-privilege-maduro-elites (accessed 13 September 2020).
27. Virginia Lopez, 'Patriot, or Government Plant? Rumors Fly Over Venezuela Helicopter Attack', *Guardian*, 28 June 2017, www.theguardian.com/world/2017/jun/28/venezuela-helicopter-attack-oscar-perez-rumors (accessed 10 August 2020).
28. Alan Macleod, 'Guaidó's Mercenary Hit Contract on Venezuela's Maduro Mirrors Official US Bounty, Authorizes Death Squad Killings', *Grayzone*, 10 May 2020, www.thegrayzone.com/2020/05/10/guaido-mercenary-contract-venezuelas-maduro-us-bounty-death-squad/ (accessed 10 August 2020).
29. Tom Phillips, '"¡Sí se puede!" Shouts Rapturous Crowd at Juan Guaidó Rally', *Guardian*, 31 January 2019, www.theguardian.com/world/2019/jan/31/si-se-puede-shouts-rapturous-crowd-at-juan-guaido-rally (accessed 10 August 2020).
30. Tom Phillips, '"Our Only Enemy is Fear": Guaidó Calls on Venezuelans to Continue Protests', *Guardian*, 8 February 2019, www.theguardian.com/world/2019/feb/08/venezuela-juan-guaido-central-university-speech-maduro-protests (accessed 10 August 2020).
31. See www.twitter.com/tomphillipsin/status/1235205641284677632, www.twitter.com/tomphillipsin/status/1109695955722444480 (both accessed 10 August 2020).
32. Glenn Greenwald, 'Five Weeks After The Guardian's Viral Blockbuster Assange-Manafort Scoop, No Evidence Has Emerged – just stonewalling', *Intercept*, 2 January 2019, www.theintercept.com/2019/01/02/five-weeks-after-the-guardians-viral-blockbuster-assange manafort-scoop-no-evidence-has-emerged-just-stonewalling/ (accessed 2 September 2020).

33. Andrew Fishman, Rafael Moro Martins, Leandro Demori, Glenn Greenwald and Amanda Audi, 'Their Little Show', *Intercept*, 17 June 2019, www.theintercept.com/2019/06/17/brazil-sergio-moro-lula-operation-car-wash/ (accessed 9 August 2020).
34. Jonathan Watts, 'More than a Million Brazilians Protest Against "Horror" Government', *Guardian*, 14 March 2016, www.theguardian.com/world/2016/mar/13/brazil-anti-government-protests-dilma-rousseff-rio-de-janeiro (accessed 2 September 2020).
35. Bruce Douglas, 'Brazil Activists to Walk 600 miles for "Free Markets, Lower Taxes and Privatisation"', *Guardian*, 24 April 2015, www.theguardian.com/world/2015/apr/24/brazil-activists-march-free-markets-margaret-thatcher-rand-paul (accessed 2 September 2020).
36. 'The Strange Case of the Guardian and Brasil', *Brasil Wire*, 6 December 2018, www.brasilwire.com/the-strange-case-of-the-guardian-brasil/ (accessed 2 September 2020).
37. 'The Observer View on Brazil', *Observer*, 20 March 2016, www.theguardian.com/commentisfree/2016/mar/20/observer-view-on-brazil-olympic-games-corruption (accessed 2 September 2016).
38. Jonathan Watts, 'The Man Who Could Fix Brazil: Country Sees Hope for Salvation in Vice-president', *Guardian*, 3 April 2016, www.web.archive.org/web/20160403101327/www.theguardian.com/world/2016/apr/03/brazil-michel-temer-dilma-rousseff-impeachment (accessed 2 September 2020).
39. 'Approval Rating for Brazil's Temer Plummets: Poll', *Reuters*, 19 September 2017, www.reuters.com/article/us-brazil-politics-poll/approval-rating-for-brazils-temer-plummets-poll-idUSKCN1BU21S (accessed 2 September 2020).
40. 'The Guardian View on Brazilian Corruption: The Public Deserve a Voice', *Guardian*, 23 May 2017, www.theguardian.com/commentisfree/2017/may/23/the-guardian-view-on-brazilian-corruption-the-public-deserve-a-voice (accessed 3 September 2020).
41. Eduardo dos Santos, 'Michel Temer is a Legitimate President – and He's Putting Brazil Back on its Feet', *Guardian*, 3 September 2017, www.theguardian.com/world/2017/sep/03/michel-temer-is-a-legitimate-president-and-hes-putting-brazil-back-on-its-feet (accessed 4 September 2020).
42. '#15M: The Big Hush', *Brasil Wire*, 16 March 2017, www.brasilwire.com/15m-the-big-hush/ (accessed 1 September 2020).
43. 'The Strange Case of the Guardian and Brasil', *Brasil Wire*, 6 December 2018, www.brasilwire.com/the-strange-case-of-the-guardian-brasil/ (accessed 2 September 2020).
44. 'The Strange Case of the Guardian and Brasil'.
45. Guillaume Long, David Rosnick, Cavan Kharrazian and Kevin Cashman, 'What Happened in Bolivia's 2019 Vote Count?', *Center for Economic*

Policy Research, 8 November 2019, www.cepr.net/report/bolivia-elections-2019-11/ (accessed 2 September 2020).

46. Dan Collyns, 'Bolivian Police in La Paz Join "Mutiny" Against Evo Morales', *Guardian*, 9 November 2019, www.theguardian.com/world/2019/nov/09/bolivian-police-in-la-paz-join-mutiny-against-evo-morales (accessed 2 September 2020).
47. See, for example, Nick Estes, 'What the Coup Against Evo Morales Means to Indigenous People Like Me', *Guardian*, 14 November 2019, www.theguardian.com/commentisfree/2019/nov/14/what-the-coup-against-evo-morales-means-to-indigenous-people-like-me (accessed 2 September 2020).
48. *Observer* editorial, 'The Observer View on Evo Morales and Bolivia', 17 November 2019, www.theguardian.com/commentisfree/2019/nov/17/observer-view-on-evo-morales-and-bolivia (accessed 9 September 2020).
49. See Max Blumenthal and Ben Norton, 'Bolivia Coup led by Christian Fascist Paramilitary Leader and Millionaire – with Foreign Support', *Grayzone*, 11 November 2019, www.thegrayzone.com/2019/11/11/bolivia-coup-fascist-foreign-support-fernando-camacho/ (accessed 3 September 2020).
50. See 'Bolivia Protests: Five Killed in Rally Calling for Exiled Morales's Return', *Guardian*, 16 November 2019, www.theguardian.com/world/2019/nov/16/bolivia-protests-five-killed-in-rally-calling-for-exiled-moraless-return (accessed 2 September 2020).
51. Michael Williams, 'Bolivia Funeral Procession Turns Violent – In Pictures', *Guardian*, 22 November 2019, www.theguardian.com/artanddesign/gallery/2019/nov/22/bolivia-funeral-procession-turns-violent-in-pictures (accessed 2 September 2020).
52. 'The Guardian View on Bolivia: Respect the People', *Guardian*, 5 December 2019, www.theguardian.com/commentisfree/2019/dec/05/the-guardian-view-on-bolivia-respect-the-people (accessed 2 September 2020).
53. 'Forced Displacement Growing in Colombia Despite Peace Agreement', *UN Refugee Agency*, 10 March 2017, www.unhcr.org/uk/news/briefing/2017/3/58c26e114/forced-displacement-growing-colombia-despite-peace-agreement.html# (accessed 4 September 2020).
54. 'Syrian Refugee Children Stories: Life As a Refugee', *Save the Children*, www.savethechildren.org/us/what-we-do/emergency-response/refugee-children-crisis/refugee-stories (accessed 3 September, 2020).
55. 'Colombia: The Most Dangerous Place in the World to be a Trade Unionist', *Amnesty International*, 1 May 2003, www.amnesty.org.uk/press-releases/colombia-most-dangerous-place-world-be-trade-unionist (accessed 3 September 2020).
56. Joe Parkin Daniels, 'Colombian Army Killed Thousands More Civilians than Reported, Study Claims', *Guardian*, 8 May 2018, www.

theguardian.com/world/2018/may/08/colombia-false-positives-scandal-casualties-higher-thought-study (accessed 3 September 2020).

57. 'US Intelligence listed Colombian President Uribe Among "Important Narco-traffickers" in 1991', *National Security Archive*, 2 August 2004, www.nsarchive2.gwu.edu//NSAEBB/NSAEBB131/index.htm (accessed 2 September 2020).
58. Jeremy Dear, 'Blood on Britain's Hands', *Red Pepper*, 20 June 2008, www.redpepper.org.uk/Blood-on-Britain-s-hands/ (accessed 3 September 2020).
59. Rory Carroll, 'The Rebirth of a Nation', *Guardian*, 2007, www.theguardian.com/business/insidecolombia/story/0,,2095249,00.html (accessed 3 September 2020).
60. Fiona Walsh, 'Energy and Mining', *Guardian*, 6 June 2007, www.theguardian.com/business/2007/jun/06/fionawalsh (accessed 3 September 2020).
61. Fiona Walsh, 'Communications and Transport', *Guardian*, 5 June 2007, www.theguardian.com/business/2007/jun/06/fionawalsh (accessed 3 September 2020).
62. 'Out of the Jungle', *Guardian*, 4 July 2008, www.theguardian.com/commentisfree/2008/jul/04/colombia.drugstrade (accessed 3 September, 2020).
63. Alan MacLeod, 'Manufacturing Consent for the 2018 Elections in Venezuela and Colombia', *Media Theory*, 2:2 (2018), pp. 138–53: www.journalcontent.mediatheoryjournal.org/index.php/mt/article/view/65 (accessed 3 September 2020).
64. Joe Parkin Daniels, 'Colombia's Polarised Election Raises Fears for Fragile Peace', *Guardian*, 16 June 2018, www.theguardian.com/world/2018/jun/16/colombias-election-peace-ivan-duque-gustavo-petro (accessed 4 September 2020); Joe Parkin Daniels, 'Iván Duque Wins Election to Become Colombia's President', *Guardian*, 18 June 2018, www.theguardian.com/world/2018/jun/18/ivan-duque-wins-election-to-become-colombias-president (accessed 3 September 2020).
65. MacLeod, 'Manufacturing Consent for the 2018 Elections in Venezuela and Colombia'.
66. 'The Observer View on Venezuela's Need for Profound Change, Not a Sham Poll', *Observer*, 20 May 2018, www.theguardian.com/commentisfree/2018/may/20/observer-view-on-venezuela-critical-need-for-change-nicolas-maduro-hugo-chavez (accessed 3 September 2020).
67. Katharine Viner, 'A Mission for Journalism in a Time of Crisis', *Guardian*, 16 November 2017, www.theguardian.com/news/2017/nov/16/a-mission-for-journalism-in-a-time-of-crisis (accessed 4 September 2020).

7

The Origins of the *Guardian* Women's Page

Hannah Hamad

In a 1927 article for the (then) feminist political and literary UK magazine *Time and Tide*, in which she critiqued what she perceived to be the limitations of journalism for women at that time, US socialist feminist lawyer and journalist Crystal Eastman candidly opined that 'there is nothing more irritating to a feminist than the average "Woman's Page" of a newspaper, with its out-dated assumption that all women have a common trade interest in the household arts, and a common leisure interest in clothes and the doings of "high society".'[1] As this chapter demonstrates through its account of the early decades of the *Guardian* women's page, the co-existence of feminist commentary and debate with discourse on the domestic arts and advice on how best to adhere to the feminine norms of the day was arguably its defining characteristic. And the ideological tensions produced by this co-existence have coloured opinions on the raison d'être of newspaper women's pages ever since.

The *Guardian* was by no means the first UK newspaper to feature a women's page or section when it launched one in 1922. The *Illustrated London News*, for example, featured a regular column by Florence Fenwick Miller starting in 1886, which expanded into a full women's page in 1895.[2] In their account of women and journalism since the mid-nineteenth century, Deborah Chambers and others highlight both the potentialities and the pitfalls of the confinement of women's journalism to women's pages in the early decades of its presence in the profession, writing that 'women journalists were valued specifically as women, writing for women on topics concerning women's traditional role in the home'.[3] There was thus, they argue, a 'contrast between the fiction they wrote and the reality of their lives as paid employees in a male dominated profession'.[4] All the same it was the emergence and consolidation of women's pages that enabled the provision of 'a recognized space for discussing women's issues and granted a foothold for women in journalism'.[5] This was to become the case at the *Guardian* too, when the establishment of its own women's page made at least some space for women journalists (albeit within the bounds of what was possible in the context of an institution and a profession run and dominated by men) to set a women's agenda with the opportunity to take it beyond the concerns of domestic life and feminine beauty norms.

'MAINLY FOR WOMEN' – THE EARLY YEARS OF THE *GUARDIAN* WOMEN'S PAGE

The early decades of the *Guardian* women's page were dominated by the long editorships of the two women who pioneered the page during their respective tenures: Madeline Linford from 1922–39, and then Mary Stott from 1957–72.[6] The page originated in 1922 when Linford, the only woman then on the editorial staff of the *Manchester Guardian*, was asked by the paper's then editor C.P. Scott to institute and edit a 'women's feature'[7] which was to comprise three columns and would run daily.[8] That feature became 'Mainly for Women' and there followed a period of seventeen years during which Linford, undeterred by the low esteem in which her assignment was held by her male peers, carried out her task of producing a page (or more accurately, a portion of a page) that was intended to be 'readable, varied and always aimed at the intelligent woman',[9] and that was to be comprised of articles 'on subjects which are special to women'.[10] It is left to the *Guardian* reader to discover what kinds of subjects those might be. But setting the tone for an ideological double-bind that would go on to characterise newspaper women's pages for decades thereafter, Linford's tenure as women's editor gave rise both to landmark pieces of politically charged feminist journalism by established and emerging women writers on the one hand, and more advertiser friendly fare concerning domesticity, consumer affairs and feminine beauty norms on the other.

With respect to the former, feminist activist and writer Evelyn Sharp was an incumbent at the *Guardian* when she became the first regular columnist for Linford's new women's feature.[11] There she wrote alongside occasional columnists such as fashion writer Muriel Harris who in one article once noteworthily described make-up as 'the pastime of bores'[12] and Catherine Carswell whose importance as a feminist voice in early twentieth century women's writing was later recognised upon the re-publication of her 1920s novels *Open the Door!* and *The Camomile* by Virago in the 1980s.[13] Characterised by Mary Stott as a 'notable feminist, suffragist and commentator on the political aspect of women's life',[14] Evelyn Sharp was not only a feminist but also a pacifist, and she brought both commitments to her women's page writing. While in one column she would decry the cult of domesticity in what she called 'the fetish of spring-cleaning',[15] in another she would critique well-known anti-pacifism intimidation tactics as what she called the 'white feather complex'.[16] Over time though, Sharp became known for her expertise on children and childhood, eventually devoting a weekly column to this in Linford's women's page, in which she focused principally on issues concerning poverty among working class children in London.[17]

With respect to the latter, Winifred Holtby and Vera Brittain, both of whom of course went on to achieve major literary success, were emerging writers in the early years of Linford's women's feature. Both made early names for themselves writing feminist journalism for the *Guardian* women's page, which engaged with key debates about feminist concerns, albeit often adopting a highly classed mode of address in so doing that spoke rather specifically to educated women of some means and privilege. Indeed, as Mary Stott later wrote, from the vantage point of the post-second wave feminist 1980s: 'One outstanding difference between the *Manchester Guardian* women readers between the two World Wars and the *Guardian* readers of today is that in the 1920s and 1930s contributors discussed domesticity on the assumption that in homes like theirs there would be living-in domestic help.'[18] That being the case, the parallels between some of the feminist debates taking place in the earliest years of the *Guardian* women's page and some of those at the turn of the millennium start to become more explicable.

Holtby, for example, in attempting to intervene in debates about gender and the distinction between public and private spheres, wrote for the women's page in 1927 that 'women have been told they cannot both marry and have a home and have a career outside the home, that they cannot preserve both domestic and professional proficiency, that they cannot maintain a decorous and exquisite standard of taste in their own appearance and in their possessions, and at the same time perform useful service to the public.'[19] In lauding those few who demanded that 'we will have both', she in some ways anticipates the rallying cry of 'we can have it all' so familiar to later *Guardian* readers from feminist debates about the dilemmas of work/life balance in the women's page writings of millennial postfeminism under later editors like Libby Brooks, Kira Cochrane and others.[20] The following year, in 1928, Holtby also wrote convincingly on the vexed question of gendered personal pronouns, arguing for the adoption of pronouns 'without gender', thus again taking up and anticipating a long-running social and cultural debate about gender which continues today.[21]

Elsewhere across the lifespan of Linford's women's page though, readers were invited to consider all manner of what it offered up as quotidian domestic matters and consumer affairs. These might be the best means of achieving a 'brighter cabbage' in cooking with said vegetable;[22] the 'secure fixing of a broom handle' and the 'difficulty to the average housewife' that this has 'always presented';[23] or the problem of 'how to choose a teapot' given that 'few domestic articles in daily use sacrifice really worthy and solid qualities to appearance like the teapot.'[24] Unsurprisingly, feminine beauty norms of the day were also matters of interest to the readership, and thus 'a forecast of what women's issues were likely to come up in the next session of Parliament'[25] might sit alongside one of 1936's regularly running 'Beauty for the Busy Woman' series of articles, which advised (or body shamed) women on best practice in things like the 'use of cosmetics',[26] 'plucking',[27] 'slimming' and its 'treatments',[28] and how to deal with 'facial blemishes'.[29] All were usually accompanied by helpful illustrations that depicted the presumed average *Guardian* woman performing the self-surveilling labour of normative femininity.

In this way, and in line with feminist historian Angela John's characterisation of Linford's women's page as 'a mixture of continuity and change',[30] the disruptive anti-patriarchal potentialities of some of the more political writings on women's social issues, status and rights by writers like Sharp and Holtby were arguably offset by what sometimes comes across as the tacit acceptance of the *status quo* with respect to women's relationship to the domestic sphere and to normative femininity that characterised some of the other kinds of writing. All the same, the *Guardian* women's page under Madeline Linford's pioneering editorship, in John's words, 'became renowned, provoking debates about the necessity for a space dedicated to women.'[31]

Furthermore, and indicative of the political importance of such a space for women's journalism at this point in UK women's history, it is noteworthy that Linford's ultimate successor as editor of the women's page (although she was a very long time in coming due to the long hiatus between women's editors that accompanied the outbreak of the Second World War), attached such great significance to it. Writing long after her own retirement from the *Guardian*, Mary Stott proffered that 'a good case could be made for the claim that it was the *Manchester Guardian* Women's Page which, following quickly on *Time and Tide* (1920) and often quoting from it, kept feminism alive in the 1920s and 1930s, after the suffragettes had disbanded and the major battle for the vote had been won (1918),'[32] highlighting by way of illustration that 'the page carried regular reports on what measures of interest to women would be debated in Parliament, and on the women candidates who were standing for election.'[33]

Writing about it from a more personal perspective, Stott also attributed her own lifelong feminism to her youthful readership of Linford's women's page: 'I had been a devoted reader ever since I grew up; it had educated me as a feminist.'[34] It is unsurprising therefore that Stott was interested both in drawing parallels between her own period of editorship and Linford's, but also in identifying differences that mark their respective eras as distinct from one another. These differences Stott views (perhaps questionably) as 'social' rather than 'political',[35] thus arguably glossing over the extent to which the social and the political are mutually constitutive, and thus eliding important issues around race, class and sexuality. These were themes that became increasingly central to the feminist discourse that shaped the content of the page in her own period of editorship which spanned the 1960s and saw the rise to prominence on both the women's page and in society and culture at large of second wave feminism and the UK Women's Liberation Movement.

'WOMEN TALKING' – MARY STOTT, THE WOMEN'S PAGE AND SECOND WAVE FEMINISM

Mary Stott was hired to edit the women's page of the *Guardian* in 1957, at which time the paper was under the editorship of Alastair Hetherington.[36] She came into the role carrying thirty years' experience editing the women's pages of local and smaller publications like the *Leicester Mail* and the *Bolton Evening News*, and the women's publications of the Manchester-based *Co-Operative Press*.[37] And she continued the job of *Guardian* women's editor, all the while remaining prolific with her own writing both for the page and elsewhere, until her retirement from full-time editorial work in 1972.[38] Under Stott's editorship the focus of the *Guardian* women's page (including the focus of Stott's own writings) shifted over time, further and further towards increasingly politically charged engagement with women's issues, arguably well ahead of the mainstream rise to prominence of feminism and feminist discourse enabled by the subsequent emergence of the Women's Liberation Movement. In fact, writing in 1975 after Stott was awarded an OBE, but also in the year that was, in some respects, the high watermark for UK second wave feminism, fellow journalist Katharine Whitehorn neatly summarised a few of the ways in which the *Guardian* women's page under Mary Stott had, in her view, already been addressing many of the key concerns of second wave feminism in the years that preceded it, highlighting the impactful role played by the page on the emergence of some parts of the movement. As Whitehorn writes:

> Mary made her pages a forum for all the serious vital interests that women have. On it she fought all the battles for women's rights: to maintenance, to a place by their child's bed in hospital, to a decent return for their labour: hardly a pressure group in the fifties and sixties didn't get its impetus, or even its origin, on her pages.[39]

Born in Leicester in 1907, the roots of Mary Stott's feminism lay at once in the relatively moderate political environment of her upbringing (during her youth her parents were supporters of the Liberal Party),[40] the leftward political swing that accompanied her youthful encounters with the Independent Labour Party Guild of Youth,[41] and the heavy influence on her during her early life of the suffragettes. This manifested in her immense pride in having voted Labour in the 1929 general election as one of the generation of so-called 'flapper voters', which made her, in her own words, 'one of the first batch of women entitled to vote at twenty-one on the same terms as men.'[42] Stott's first foray into journalism came in 1925 through an uncle who worked as a journalist and chief sub-editor at local newspaper the *Leicester Mail*,[43] and who helped his niece to find a position there also.[44] Her entry into the profession was further enabled by her class background, growing up as she did in a four-storey family home in Leicester,[45] and educated as she was at Leicester's Wyggeston Grammar School for Girls.[46] This was also hugely compounded by the fact that Stott was a third generation journalist in her family and that both her father *and* her mother had been journalists.[47] She grew up, as she described it, with 'newsprint in the nostrils'.[48]

She began as a temporary copy holder, but soon thereafter, in 1926, aged just 19, Stott's employers appointed her to the role of women's editor.[49] She joined the *Co-Operative Press* in Manchester in 1931 with the remit to edit a section of the weekly periodical *The Co-Op News*. This section was largely concerned with reporting the activities of The Women's Co-Operative Guild, one of many women's organisations with which Stott maintained a lifelong affinity and affiliation.[50] From 1945 until 1950 she worked as a sub-editor (heretofore a job undertaken exclusively by men) on the *Manchester Evening News* before being dismissed in an explicit and unabashed act of gender discrimination. As Stott explained in an interview with BBC Radio 4 in 1994, she was sacked from her position in order to safeguard a masculine order of succession to the role of chief sub-editor, having been told outright by the editor that 'the successor has to be a man'.[51] There followed for Stott a seven-year long hiatus from journalism, spent in domesticity, and during which time she was principally occupied with motherhood and the raising of her daughter Catherine who was seven years old at the time that Stott lost her job on the *Manchester Evening News*.

Stott's return to journalism was specifically in order to work for the *Guardian*, which she recalled was 'the one paper I wanted to work for'.[52] Remembering this time in her life for the *Guardian* and *Observer* Oral History project, Stott explained something of the feminist nature of the approach that she took to her editorial role, asserting that 'I did want to campaign when there was something to campaign about and I wanted to use the women's page to do it.'[53] In 1962, Stott inaugurated 'Women Talking' which was a weekly opinion column that appeared on the women's page each Monday, very often authored by Stott herself.[54] It dealt with all manner of issues and debates of concern to women's lives, issues pertaining to women in both the public sphere and the domestic sphere, in various types of life situations across the class spectrum, and it addressed key concerns still relevant to feminist discourse and debate today, such as equal pay for equal work (or more specifically what we now refer to as the gender pay gap, wherein women still do not get equal pay for equal work), women's work/life balance, the politics of marriage and the politics of the body.

Stott's inaugural 'Women Talking' column offered up a defence of the continued necessity for women's pages in newspapers, focusing on the importance of covering issues that are of particular interest and importance to women,[55] albeit her page did this mostly from a heteronormative perspective that addressed women who were married and/or mothers. This was something that produced a degree of ambivalence about Stott and her feminism even amongst her fellow journalists, especially those attached to more radical publications such as feminist monthly magazine *Spare Rib*. Reviewing the first volume of Stott's autobiography for this publication in 1973, feminist writers Mandy Merck and Jane Caplan gave her due recognition for what they described as her 'instinctive' feminism, going on to describe her as 'a strong woman who created her own strength, a woman who really likes women in a generation of lots who don't, [and] a prime example of the sisterhood.'[56] But within the same review the authors are quick to turn their attention to what they highlight as Stott's omissions and shortcomings in her autobiographical musings on a number of topics of concern to second wave feminists, including things like marriage, motherhood, the nuclear family and feminist social reform. One of the reasons for their critique here seems to stem from the dissonance that they observed between Stott's apparent unwillingness or inability to acknowledge the intersections and overlap between issues of inequality that underpin feminist concerns, and those that underpin Marxist concerns (symptomatic of broader disagreements that were taking place at that time between socialist feminists and liberal feminists).

Specifically, Stott's championing of what she referred to as 'the joys of living in a . . . nuclear family' failed, in the evaluation of Merck and Caplan, to account for the gendered 'division of labour which makes it [such] an efficient server of capitalism.'[57]

Notwithstanding such critiques of the apparent narrowness of Stott's own feminism, the *Guardian* women's page in its final years under Stott's editorship in the early 1970s became an important site of consciousness raising for what was then unfolding in the UK to become the Women's Liberation Movement, and what the paper referred to as the 'new wave' of feminism. An important early publication on the women's page in this regard was Ruth Adam's 1970 article, 'The New Feminism',[58] which, in its impassioned description of the impact then being made in America by the National Organisation for Women, was one of the first sustained and serious takes on the new wave of women's liberation in the United States to be published in a UK newspaper.[59] During this period Jill Tweedie also emerged as one of the most important of the mainstream feminist commentators on the UK women's movement, principally through her contributions to the *Guardian* women's page in the last of the Stott years (but also beyond through the decade). Tweedie was prolific in her feminist writing from the embryonic stages of the movement. Some noteworthy examples from these early years include 'Feminists and the Right to Be Ugly', her impactful position piece responding to debates in the new feminist movement about the body politics of womanhood, and the political power of rejecting the trappings of normative femininity in one's personal appearance,[60] and 'The Words in Action', her *Guardian* write-up accompanying her participation in the first UK Women's Liberation march in London on 6 March 1971.[61]

THE WOMEN'S PAGE AFTER STOTT

Stott was succeeded as *Guardian* women's editor first by Linda Christmas from 1972–75 and Suzanne Lowry from 1975–78 who, between them, saw the *Guardian* through what was arguably the height of second wave feminism in the UK. They were followed by Liz Forgan who held the editorship of the women's page from 1978–81, at which point she left the newspaper to take up a commissioning editorship in television at the newly formed Channel 4. Forgan thus saw *Guardian* readers through a darker time for the women's liberation movement, as in some respects priorities shifted towards combating the real and ongoing social problem of men's violence against women. This took place in tandem with the high-profile case of the hunt for the serial murderer of women referred to colloquially in the news media and beyond as the 'Yorkshire Ripper'. Indicative of this was that in 1978 'freedom from intimidation by threat or use of violence' and 'an end to all laws, assumptions and institutions which perpetuate . . . male aggression towards women' was added to the list of demands made by the Women's National Coordinating Committee at the National Women's Liberation Conference that year.[62]

Forgan's four-year period as women's editor thus encompassed the most intense period at the intersection of the ongoing investigation into these serial murders of women, the larger and more generalised problem of male violence against women and this era of second wave feminism. One of the most noteworthy flashpoints in the way this manifested on the women's pages of the paper came with the December 1980 publication of Jean Stead's iconic 'Now is the Time to Stand up and Fight'.[63] This was a piece which she characterised at the time as 'a militant response to the menace of the Yorkshire Ripper',[64] whose crimes gave rise to a major cultural flashpoint around men's violence against women, which historically intersected with the Women's Liberation Movement and its campaigning. This, it turned out, was just days before the perpetrator of these crimes was finally apprehended, more than five years after the investigation began, and after the murder of thirteen women and the attempted murder of at least seven more. As Stead argued in the *Guardian* at the time: 'The search for the Ripper has become a focus for feminist thinking that will be far reaching.'[65] By the time Frances Cairncross took up the editorship of the women's page in 1981, Britain was two years into the first Thatcher government. The political tide had turned sharply, second wave feminism had peaked and the women's page, by now more than well established, and always socially relevant, was perhaps no longer the force for social change that it had arguably been in the most impactful years of first Linford's and then later Stott's editorship.

It is testament to the impact registered on women journalists of succeeding generations by the *Guardian* women's page in the Mary Stott years that Kira Cochrane, who edited the page herself from

2006–10, dedicated her 2012 book *Women of the Revolution: Forty Years of Feminism* to the memories of Mary Stott and Jill Tweedie,[66] elsewhere describing Stott as having 'revolutionised journalism' by 'widening all notions of what might be considered appropriate subjects for female writers'.[67] Despite the fact that likenesses of both Stott and Tweedie appear in Sally Raphael's 1994 painting 'Women's Page Contributors to the *Guardian*' displayed in the National Portrait Gallery, they are less well remembered today than they might be, considering their influence on women's journalism and their place in the history of the *Guardian*'s relationship to feminism and feminist discourse.

All the same, thinking about the place of the *Guardian* women's page in the context of the larger history of the twentieth century UK women's movements, it is worth remembering and emphasising that the contributions of this page to these movements over time were largely (though not exclusively) to particular strands of liberal feminism. This was a liberal feminism that envisioned a world in which it was possible for equality between men and women to be achieved in society through things like legal reform, political lobbying, issue-based campaigning and the belief that gendered inequalities could be eradicated if women were able to exist and move through the world on the same terms as men. The contents of the *Guardian* women's page over the years has done much to propound such beliefs. This has made it easier to continually renegotiate the page's relevance to the lives of its readers, as political tides turned in ensuing decades and feminist discourse began to give way to postfeminist discourse from the Thatcher years onwards. Even so, to *over* emphasise this would be to do a disservice both to those women writers who have used the page as a space to question some of the common sense assumptions made by liberal feminism about how to improve women's lives and to those more revolutionary voices that have continued to speak through its pages over the years, and who continue to do so today.

NOTES

1. Crystal Eastman, 'What Shall We Do with the 'Woman's Page'?' *Time and Tide*, 20 May 1927, p. 470.
2. Angela John, *Evelyn Sharp: Rebel Woman, 1869-1955* (Manchester: Manchester University Press, 2009), p. 144.

3. Deborah Chambers, Linda Steiner and Carole Fleming, *Women and Journalism* (London and New York: Routledge, 2006), p. 26.
4. Chambers et al, *Women and Journalism*, p. 26.
5. Chambers et al, *Women and Journalism*, p. 26.
6. The *Guardian* stopped running its women's page in 1939 upon the outbreak of war and as an upshot of the rationing of paper that accompanied it. See Margaret Holborn, 'Madeline Linford: A Pioneering Editor at the *Guardian*', *Guardian*, 8 January 2019, https://www.theguardian.com/gnmeducationcentre/2019/jan/08/madeline-linford-a-pioneering-editor-at-the-guardian (accessed 30 September 2020).
7. Mary Stott, 'Introduction', in Mary Stott (ed) *Women Talking: An Anthology from the Guardian Women's Page 1922–1935 1957–71* (London: Pandora Press, 1987), p. xvii.
8. Mary Stott, 'The Prime of Miss Madeline Linford', *Guardian*, 30 April 1971, p. 11.
9. David Ayerst, *Guardian: Biography of a Newspaper* (London: Harper Collins, 1971), p. 448; Stott, 'The Prime of Miss Madeline Linford', p. 11.
10. Stott, 'Introduction', p. xvii. See also Angela John, *Evelyn Sharp: Rebel Woman, 1869–1955* (Manchester: Manchester University Press, 2009), p. 144.
11. Angela John, *Evelyn Sharp: Rebel Woman, 1869–1955* (Manchester: Manchester University Press, 2009), p. 144.
12. Muriel Harris, 'On Make-Up', *Guardian*, 21 December 1922, p. 4.
13. Catherine Carswell, *Open the Door!* (London: Virago, 1986 [1920]); Catherine Carswell, *The camomile* (London: Virago, 1987 [1922]).
14. Mary Stott, 'Children's corner', in Mary Stott (ed), *Women Talking: An Anthology from the Guardian Women's Page*, 1922-35, 1957-71 (London: Pandora Press, 1987), p. 234.
15. Evelyn Sharp, 'The Rebel on the Hearth', *Guardian*, 27 February 1924, p. 4.
16. Evelyn Sharp, 'The White Feather Complex', in Mary Stott (ed), *Women Talking: An Anthology from The Guardian Women's Page, 1922–35, 1957–71* (London: Pandora Press, 1987), pp. 182-3.
17. The earliest women's page example of Evelyn Sharp's writing about children and childhood is 'Holiday Frocks for a Little Girl', *Guardian*, 14 June 1922, p. 4.
18. Mary Stott, 'Married to a House', in Mary Stott (ed), *Women Talking: An Anthology from the Guardian Women's Page, 1922–35, 1957–71* (London: Pandora Press, 1987), p. 49.
19. Winifred Holtby, 'Fashions and Feminism', *Guardian*, 9 March 1927, p. 8.
20. See for example, Sally Weale, 'The Right to Choose', *Guardian*, 2 December 2002, p. 64; and Viv Groskop, 'Having it All', *Guardian*, 3 March 2008, https://www.theguardian.com/lifeandstyle/2008/mar/03/women.fashion (accessed 30 September 2020).

21. Winifred Holtby, 'The Personal Pronoun', *Guardian*, 24 February 1928, p. 8.
22. 'Brighter Cabbage', *Guardian*, 18 June 1935, p. 8.
23. 'Fixing a Broomhead', *Guardian*, 15 September 1924, p. 4.
24. 'How to Choose a Teapot', *Guardian*, 5 September 1924, p. 6.
25. Stott, 'Introduction', p. xvii.
26. 'Beauty for the Busy Woman: The Use of Cosmetics', *Guardian*, 7 February 1936, p. 8.
27. 'Beauty for the Busy Woman: This Plucking Business', *Guardian*, 8 May 1936, p. 10.
28. 'Beauty for the Busy Woman: Slimming Treatments', *Guardian*, 3 April 1936, p. 8.
29. 'Beauty for the Busy Woman: Facial Blemishes', *Guardian*, 27 March 1936, p. 8.
30. John, *Evelyn Sharp*, p. 144.
31. John, *Evelyn Sharp*, pp. 159-78.
32. Mary Stott, 'Equal Citizens', in Mary Stott (ed), *Women Talking: An Anthology from the Guardian Women's Page, 1922-35, 1957-71.* (London: Pandora Press, 1987), p. 152.
33. Stott, 'Equal Citizens', p. 152.
34. Stott, 'Introduction', p. xvi.
35. Stott, 'Introduction', p. xvi.
36. 'The Papers of Charlotte Mary Stott', GB 106 7CMS, The Women's Library Archives, https://archiveshub.jisc.ac.uk/search/archives/1a0215b5-e8c6-3b93-a0ea-87cb1c6001e1 (accessed 30 September 2020).
37. Mary Stott, 'Introduction', p. xv.
38. Mary Stott, *Forgetting's No Excuse: The Autobiography of Mary Stott – Journalist, Campaigner and Feminist* (London: Virago/Quartet Books, 1975 [1973]), p. 48.
39. Katharine Whitehorn, 'Three Cheers for Mary', *The Observer*, 12 January 1975, p. 22.
40. Stott, *Forgetting's No Excuse*, p. 18.
41. Stott, *Forgetting's No Excuse*, p. 20.
42. Stott, *Forgetting's No Excuse*, p. 20. Indicative of this is that the cover art of the 1975 edition of her first autobiography *Forgetting's No Excuse* (originally published in 1973) depicted the book's title in the form of a cloth banner with the iconic purple, white and green colour scheme of the suffragettes. Stott, *Forgetting's No Excuse*, front matter.
43. Stott, *Forgetting's No Excuse*, 33.
44. 'The Papers of Charlotte Mary Stott', GB 106 7CMS, The Women's Library Archives, https://archiveshub.jisc.ac.uk/search/archives/1a0215b5-e8c6-3b93-a0ea-87cb1c6001e1 (accessed 3 October 2020); Oral history interview with Mary Stott (OHP/88, 26 July 2001), '*Guardian* and *Observer* Oral History Project', *Guardian* News & Media

Archive, https://www.theguardian.com/gnm-archive/oral-history-collection (accessed 3 October 2020).

45. Stott, *Forgetting's No Excuse*, p. 7.
46. Stott, *Forgetting's No Excuse*, p. 35.
47. Stott, *Forgetting's No Excuse*, p. 1.
48. Stott, *Forgetting's No Excuse*, p. 33.
49. 'The Papers of Charlotte Mary Stott', GB 106 7CMS, The Women's Library Archives, https://archiveshub.jisc.ac.uk/search/archives/1a0215b5-e8c6-3b93-a0ea-87cb1c6001e1 (accessed 3 October 2020).
50. 'The Papers of Charlotte Mary Stott', GB 106 7CMS, The Women's Library Archives, https://archiveshub.jisc.ac.uk/search/archives/1a0215b5-e8c6-3b93-a0ea-87cb1c6001e1 (accessed 3 October 2020). Stott's strong interest in the history of women's organisations can be seen in her 1978 book *Organisation Woman*, which relates the story of the formation, growth and significance of National Union of Townswomen's Guilds in the form of social history, arguing the case for a connection between the post-suffrage power of women to organise themselves via groups like these, and the growth of women's rights agendas that culminated in the women's liberation movement of the post-war decades. Mary Stott, *Organisation Woman: The Story of the Townswomen's Guild* (London: Heinemann, 1978).
51. Mary Stott interviewed by Sue Lawley, *Desert Island Discs*, BBC Radio 4, 25 September 1994, http://bufvc.ac.uk/tvandradio/trilt/index.php/prog/RT44EA32?bcast=120193129 (accessed 3 October 2020); see also 'The Papers of Charlotte Mary Stott', GB 106 7CMS, The Women's Library Archives, https://archiveshub.jisc.ac.uk/search/archives/1a0215b5-e8c6-3b93-a0ea-87cb1c6001e1 (accessed 3 October 2020).
52. Oral history interview with Mary Stott (OHP/88, 26 July 2001), 'Guardian and Observer Oral History Project', Guardian News & Media Archive, https://www.theguardian.com/gnm-archive/oral-history-collection (accessed 3 October 2020).
53. Oral history interview with Mary Stott (OHP/88, 26 July 2001), 'Guardian and Observer Oral History Project', Guardian News & Media Archive, https://www.theguardian.com/gnm-archive/oral-history-collection (accessed 3 October 2020).
54. Stott, *Forgetting's No Excuse*, p. 58.
55. Mary Stott, 'Women Talking', *Guardian*, 16 April 1962, p. 6.
56. Mandy Merck and Jane Caplan, 'Forgetting's No Excuse, Mary Stott,' *Spare Rib*, no. 13, July 1973, p. 42.
57. Merck and Caplan, 'Forgetting's No Excuse, Mary Stott,' p. 42.
58. Ruth Adam, 'The New Feminism', *Guardian*, 29 April 1970, p. 11.
59. Stott, 'Introduction,' p. 172, 175.
60. Jill Tweedie, 'Feminists and the Right to be Ugly', *Guardian*, 6 April 1970, p. 9.
61. Jill Tweedie, 'The Words in Action,' *Guardian*, 8 March 1971, p. 9.

62. Anna Coote and Beatrix Campbell, *Sweet Freedom: The Struggle for Women's Liberation* (London: Pan Books, 1982), p. 26.
63. Jean Stead, 'Now is the Time to Stand Up and Fight', *Guardian*, 3 December 1980, p. 10.
64. Stead, 'Now is the Time to Stand Up and Fight', p. 10.
65. Stead, 'Now is the Time to Stand Up and Fight', p. 10.
66. Kira Cochrane (ed), *Women of the Revolution: Forty Years of Feminism* (London: Guardian Books, 2012), front matter.
67. Eleanor Mills with Kira Cochrane, 'Mary Stott 1907-2002', in Eleanor Mills with Kira Cochrane (eds), *Cupcakes and Kalashnikovs: 100 Years of the Best Journalism by Women* (London: Constable & Robinson, 2005), p. 175.

8

Trans Exclusionary Radical Centrism: The *Guardian*, Neoliberal Feminism and the Corbyn Years

Mareile Pfannebecker and Jilly Boyce Kay

INTRODUCTION

A prominent strain of feminist commentary in the *Guardian* has played a curious role in the newspaper's political and cultural coverage since 2015. It combines the rejection of the rise of the left in the Labour Party under Jeremy Corbyn's leadership and, during the same period, the resistance against the emergent visibility and growing acceptance of transgender people in the British media landscape. In this chapter, we consider how a publication that is historically associated with social liberalism and progressive politics has, since the mid-2010s, increasingly given room to trans-exclusionary feminism, which positions women's rights at odds with trans rights, and insists on a feminism that operates along 'sex-based', biologically essentialist lines.

We make the case that the intensifying hostility to trans rights in the *Guardian* can be understood against the extraordinary political backdrop in which, under the leadership of Jeremy Corbyn from 2015 until 2019, the Labour Party departed from its commitment to neoliberal economics to propose a more radically left-wing politics. A feminism that prioritises 'sex-based' rights, and the protection of 'women's spaces' over all else came into alliance with a form of political centrism which dismissed the Corbyn project as a form of 'brocialism' that was intrinsically misogynist: together, they represent a centrist feminism reliant on an essentialist idea of womanhood. We argue that, in the pages of the *Guardian*, this centrist feminism is put to work to a specific political end: to allow liberal centrist commentary, at a time of political crisis, to claim the moral high ground via a quasi-left discourse, and so to disavow its complicity with the neoliberal status quo. With a view to understanding the particular, curious ways in which British centrism has sought to reassert feminism as a project of 'sex-based' rights, we contextualise the *Guardian*'s 'left feminism' in longer histories of its orientation to reformist rather than revolutionary politics. Ultimately, we argue that while transphobia occurs across the political spectrum, its particular crystallisation in mainstream feminist commentary in Britain points to a centrist radicalisation that uses escalating cultural proxy-battles to paper over the irreconcilable ideological and political ruptures that have challenged the centrist consensus since the economic and political upheavals of the 2008 financial crash, austerity, Brexit and the election of Trump in 2016.

THE *GUARDIAN*'S HISTORICAL RELATIONSHIP WITH FEMINISM

As other chapters in this volume attest, since its founding in 1821, the *Guardian*'s relationship to the left in Britain has been deeply ambivalent. On the one hand, it has been an important site for liberal-left politics that are otherwise broadly subordinated within the political ecology of British newspaper publishing, distorted significantly to the right as it is. On the other hand, it has functioned as 'capitalism's conscience'. At best, this indicates that it has been propelled more by the impulse to moderate the worst excesses of market-based liberal democracies than to radically supplant them with an alternative. At worst, this means that its apparent stance of admonition has actively diffused resistance and helped to affirm the status quo. The same can be said, we would suggest, for its relationship to feminism. Where British mainstream newspaper publishing has traditionally been overtly hostile to feminism, the *Guardian* has played an important and instrumental role in making visible and offering support for feminist activism. And yet this visibility and support does not function as an embrace of revolutionary feminist politics, nor to simply facilitate feminist 'progress'.

As Jane Chapman notes in her study of British newspaper coverage of the suffragette movement in the early twentieth century, while other publications, such as *The Times*, took a 'hard-line' position against women's suffrage, the *Guardian* was distinguished as 'the most energetic champion of feminism, democracy and left Liberalism' and yet the 'support' for women's suffrage was specifically aligned with constitutional reformism, and explicitly not with militancy.[1] Jilly Boyce Kay and Kaitlynn Mendes demonstrate that the *Guardian*, alongside other newspapers, now presents its unqualified and celebratory support for the suffragettes as part of the 'story' of British democracy. Yet at the time of their struggle in the early twentieth century, its reporting was frequently extremely hostile to militant suffragette tactics, which were abhorred as 'diseased' actions of protest, as opposed to the more sanctioned, gradualist reformism of the suffragists.[2] During the second wave period, as discussed by Hannah Hamad in her chapter in this volume, one of the best-known *Guardian* writers on women's issues was Jill Tweedie, who, when she presented a daytime women's television programme was billed as 'an exponent of women's lib (but not violently so)'.[3] This broad sketch points to the ways in which the *Guardian* has been instrumental both in the winning of legitimacy and respectability for feminism within mainstream political discourse and formal institutions, and in functioning to signify feminism as a non-revolutionary project.

The particular 'feminism' which has been historically mobilised and legitimised by the *Guardian*, then, has broadly been reformist and liberal. Other scholarship suggests that this liberal orientation has also worked to entrench white, middle-class, cis-gendered womanhood as the paradigmatic subject and agent of feminism. Terese Jonsson argues that the *Guardian* is characterised by a 'white feminism' which envisages itself as 'picking up the baton' from a specifically white feminist past, and which imagines feminism as a unified movement untainted by any of its own internal power struggles.[4] Particularly relevant for our analysis below is Jonsson's idea that this feminism sees itself and its subjects as 'innocent' which reifies a certain, bounded subjectivity of 'woman' as the feminist ideal and the basis of political mobilisation.[5]

TRANS IN THE *GUARDIAN* FROM THE MID-2010S TO THE PRESENT

In recent years, the *Guardian* has been a key part of the media terrain in which the 'debates' around transgender politics have played out. This is the case in quantitative terms – in the UK, it is second only to the *Mail Online* in terms of the number of news items it has published since 2014 with the terms 'trans', 'transgender' or 'transsexual'.[6] More importantly, however, alongside the *New Statesman*, it has been instrumental in defining the terms of mainstream feminist 'debate' around trans politics. This has occurred most markedly through its commentary pages and the online section previously known as 'Comment is Free', and now titled simply 'Opinion'.

Its commentaries claim to represent a range of different voices, and there is in fact no single, rigid position on trans issues – and indeed it is eminently possible to find trans-affirmative commentaries that complicate the picture we go on to sketch below. However, there are some clear, entrenched patterns of an increasing and hardening hostility to trans women in recent years, alongside the framing of feminism as a project defined by 'sex-based' rights, which explicitly names itself as 'left', and yet is largely divorced from materialist, redistributive politics.

The *Guardian*'s troubling history of pitting feminism against trans rights extends further back than the last decade; for example, the *Guardian* and *Observer* notably published some egregiously transphobic columns in the noughties, such as those by feminists Germaine Greer and Julie Bindel.[7] Indeed, the apparent dissonance between the newspaper's ostensibly socially progressive politics and its pattern of platforming trans-exclusionary voices played a key role in the political biographies of many trans writers at this time. Journalist and activist Paris Lees, for example, became politicised in part through reading a now-notorious 2009 *Guardian* article by Greer about trans women, which described them as 'people who think they are women, have women's names, and feminine clothes and lots of eyeshadow, [yet] who seem to us to be some kind of ghastly parody'.[8] Lees recalls thinking: 'hold on a minute, this is supposed to be a nice newspaper, they're supposed to be speaking up for people who are persecuted'.[9] Writer and journalist Juliet Jacques also noted how the *Guardian* in particular was 'setting the terms of the discussion' in the early twenty-first century, framing the defining characteristic of trans rights as its ostensible incompatibility with women's rights.[10]

In 2010, however, it seemed that perhaps the *Guardian* was open to expanding these narrow terms of 'debate'. At this time it began to publish 'A Transgender Journey', a blog series written by Jacques documenting her gender reassignment that ran until 2012.[11] Jacques has reflected on the more expansive affordances that the blog form allowed – for example, providing more room to develop complex narratives about trans identity than traditional newspaper publishing, with longer word counts and embedded hyperlinks – and on the sense of excitement and optimism that this entailed for the possibilities of trans politics. This blog series was able to enlarge the narrow terms of trans media visibility – which was, and still predominantly is, routinely reduced to questions of what constitutes a woman – and instead to speak to broader, structural issues of healthcare, employment, austerity and violence against trans people.[12] There were some other initiatives at around this time, which suggested that the *Guardian* was genuinely expanding possibilities for the public articulation of trans issues and the mainstreaming of trans-inclusionary feminism. In 2013, for example, it published a panel of four writers on the topic 'Why I'm trans . . . and a Feminist', including a contribution by Lees – who became a regular writer on trans issues.[13] Nevertheless, it is important to note that this inclusion and visibility of trans voices in no way represented an equalisation of status. Jacques notes that her blog was very 'low risk' for the *Guardian* – she was paid £90 per piece (Germaine Greer, on the other hand, was apparently paid £1000 for her columns).[14]

However, this period of (relative) openness to trans voices, and to expanding the terms of trans media visibility, was short-lived, both within the *Guardian* and the British centre-left media more broadly.[15] Since 2014, the centre-left British media, spearheaded by the *Guardian*, has increasingly narrowed the terms of debate around trans, again reducing the scope of trans issues to questions of what constitutes a woman, and who should be allowed access to 'women's spaces' – most notably, women's toilets and prisons. In many ways, we might say that British centrist feminism has been somewhat at odds with a trajectory of the broader turn to 'wokeness' and expanding repertoires of trans visibility in transatlantic media and popular culture. While in the US, the publication of an iconic *Time* magazine front cover in 2014 – depicting the US trans actress Laverne Cox with the headline 'The Transgender Tipping Point: America's Next Civil Rights Frontier' – seemed to signal a ruptural, positive change in the representation of trans people in mainstream media,[16] in the UK, at around about this time, when it came to trans rights, 'progressive' voices were taking another course.

A key moment came in 2017, when the then prime minister Theresa May announced a consultation on the Gender Recognition Act of 2004, with the intention to 'streamline' and 'demedicalise' the lengthy and invasive process of obtaining legal recognition for one's gender. In the context of alarmism about the implications of 'self-identification' that arose, the phenomenon of what came to be known as 'trans exclusionary radical feminism' (or 'TERF') emerged, a movement that involved the founding of multiple campaign organisations specifically to resist self-determination as well as social media interactions such as those on the Mumsnet 'Feminism' chat forum and Twitter.[17] While by no means homogeneous politically or ideologically, 'TERFs', or as they prefer to be called, 'gender critical feminists', are united in their rejection of various elements of trans women's right to live publicly as women and, in extreme cases, question their right to exist altogether.

In this context of an insurgent 'gender critical' feminism, an editorial published in October 2018, 'The *Guardian* view on the Gender Recognition Act: Where Rights Collide', was widely seen as marking an emboldened trans-hostile position.[18] This editorial ostensibly sought to present a 'balanced' view, considering both the need to challenge transphobia *and* misogyny. However, it was precisely the positioning of trans rights and women's rights as 'competing' that undergirded a notion of feminism as characterised by its commitment to 'sex-based' rights. It argued that:

> Gender identity does not cancel out sex. Women's oppression by men has a physical basis, and to deny the relevance of biology when considering sexual inequality is a mistake. [. . .] Women's concerns about sharing dormitories or changing rooms with 'male-bodied' people must be taken seriously.

The piece was met with despair by many trans people and their supporters. Significantly, *Guardian* journalists in the US published a vehement disavowal of the editorial's 'unsubstantiated', 'outdated' and 'offensive' arguments in response, which, they argued, 'promoted transphobic viewpoints, including some of the same assertions about gender that US politicians are citing in their push to eliminate trans rights'.[19]

These interventions by resistant *Guardian* staffers notwithstanding, the 2018 editorial marked a new phase in the publication's coverage of trans issues, in which the dominant theme was that the right to self-identification posed a threat to the safety and rights of cisgender women. A number of trans workers at the *Guardian* resigned at this time and, in early 2020, hundreds of staff and contractors from across the *Guardian* signed a letter to the editor Katharine Viner in protest at the newspaper's 'pattern of publishing transphobic content [which] has interfered with our work and cemented our reputation as a publication hostile to trans rights and trans employees'.[20] This leaked letter had itself been initiated in part as a response to an opinion piece written by regular columnist Suzanne Moore, in which she made sensationalist claims about women threatened by trans sexual predators and erroneous transitions:

> Male violence is an issue for women, which is why we want single-sex spaces. Vulnerable women in refuges and prisons must be allowed to live in safe environments – the common enemy here is the patriarchy, remember? How did we arrive at a situation where there are shocking and rising numbers of teenage girls presenting at specialist clinics with gender dysphoria, while some who have transitioned are now regretful and infertile?[21]

While the picture is complex, and there still are a number of writers at the *Guardian* who are supportive of trans rights, it is possible to trace a shift from a moment of cautious optimism and the tentative possibility of mainstreamed trans-inclusionary feminism in the early 2010s, to one where the *Guardian* became associated with trans-exclusionary feminism at the end of the decade, both in its workplace culture, and in its pattern of trans representation. Juliet Jacques notes that what were once 'below the line' attacks on trans identity, posted in the comments at the end of an article, are now 'above the line' in commissioned opinion pieces.[22] Prominent trans writers such as Jacques, Paris Lees and Shon Faye no longer write for the *Guardian*. Most recently, Jacques has written for the *Guardian* once more, but only to demand that 'liberals need to stand up for trans rights before it's too late'.[23]

ORIGINS OF BRITISH MEDIA 'TERF'ISM

There has been some speculation about the peculiar venom and media visibility of British 'TERF' ism in recent years. The origins of today's 'trans exclusionary radical feminism' on both sides of the Atlantic are generally traced to some factions of 1970s radical feminism in the US; revolutionary feminism in the late 1970s and 1980s, as one strand of the British Women's Liberation Movement, presents one plausible homegrown source. Given the general amnesia regarding most of the more radical ideas and demands of the woman's liberation movement, more explanation is required as to why, of all things, the relatively marginal hostility towards transgender people within some feminist circles in the 1970s and 1980s should find such resonance in the UK today. A cultural approach ventures that the middle- and upper-class white feminism that has been hegemonic in the UK in the aftermath of the women's liberation movement, and to which, as noted above, the *Guardian* has been a significant pillar, tends towards biological essentialism even in its moderate forms, and has thus quietly absorbed, or reproduced in parallel, what was once a radical fringe position. Additionally, Sophie Lewis has suggested that over the last three decades, middle-class white UK feminism has been less subject to the scrutiny that its US counterpart has experienced via feminists involved in protest movements (anti-globalization, anti-police brutality) during the same period.[24]

Yet, the extent to which the *Guardian* has offered a platform to anti-trans commentary in recent years may well be most convincingly explained by personal-institutional factors. As Juliet Jacques proposes, a group of editors and columnists who have been writing on feminist issues from a trans-exclusionary position since the idea arose in the 1970s, still wield significant influence now and encourage younger writers who agree with them.[25]

A further explanation points away from ideas per se and towards the techno-social functions of the internet. As Andrea Long Chu suggests in the American context, today's 'TERFs' are not the anachronistic revival of an outdated feminist past, but the purveyors of online confrontation that 'has as much to do with the ins and outs of social media ... as it does with any great ideological conflict'.[26] In the British case, as many commentators have stressed, the website Mumsnet has provided a platform for the fusion of parenting support with trans-exclusionary radicalisation.

Taking the above points together, a preliminary picture of UK 'TERFism' emerges where permutations of a trans-exclusionary stance cultivated as a quasi-political position in 1970s feminism have been quietly accommodated within the ossified structures of the liberal British culture and media landscape, and have since been amplified by the fusion with and parallel existence of online subcultures. This, then, would be a rough sketch of the cultural formation behind the backlash against emergent trans visibility and campaigning for trans rights. Yet, as we go on to argue, there is no understanding this peculiarly British media backlash and the *Guardian*'s role in it without also considering the extraordinary political backdrop.

CENTRIST FEMINISM AND THE CORBYN LEFT

It is at just this moment that members of the Labour Party shocked the liberal establishment by electing Jeremy Corbyn as leader by an overwhelming majority in September 2015. The *Guardian*'s position in Britain's right-wing dominated newspaper landscape, long-established as the 'left-liberal' alternative, was severely tested by this situation. Alex Nunns has documented how, in the run-up to the leadership election, as support for Corbyn grew among Labour members as well as the paper's wider readership, coverage failed to respond to this change of the centrist status quo. Beside a token smattering of commentary by supporters of Labour's left-turn, the paper was dominated by starkly hostile opinion pieces, negatively framed reports, negative and at times false headlines and critical editorials.[27] A report by *Media Lens* from 6 August 2015 points out that, 'in a spectacular instance of bias', the other three candidates in the leadership race only received very rare and mild criticism in the paper, where Corbyn was dismissed in a 'flood of disaster warnings'.[28] Even at the beginning of Corbyn's leadership, then, any conventional idea of the *Guardian* as the mainstream platform for the forging of pluralist left opinion crumbled to reveal a centrist institution desperately struggling, as Nunns puts it, to 'police the boundaries of a political field' in which a left-of-centre project was unequivocally 'out of bounds'.[29]

The failure of the paper's attempt to police the political imagination in 2015 set the scene for an anxious intensification of centrist feminism in its comment pages. From the start, there were negative reactions towards Corbyn from commentators at the *Guardian* couched in explicitly feminist terms. On the day of the election, Suzanne Moore, who often positions herself as a left feminist, complained about a 'new brocialism' that did not care enough about women's issues to elect a woman, that indeed Corbyn's election meant that 'men had won'.[30] Demands that a woman lead Labour for the first time had become more urgent again after Ed Miliband's defeat and during Harriet Harman's caretaker leadership, and some disappointment in this regard following Jeremy Corbyn's election over two women contenders, Yvette Cooper and Liz Kendall, was unsurprising. However, it quickly became apparent that negative feminist commentary about the new leader would outgrow initial complaints about his gender. Corbyn's initial shadow cabinet had more women than Harman's (52 per cent up from 47 per cent), meeting the cabinet gender parity promised in Corbyn's 'Working with Women' policy document which also pledged, amongst other things, to work towards universal free childcare and the end of Tory cuts to services for survivors of sexual and domestic violence.[31] Nonetheless, a consensus quickly took hold that Corbyn's leadership was a loss for women.

Corbyn's 'feminist manifesto' was barely mentioned in the paper when it was published: once in passing in a report with a headline that ridiculed Corbyn, and once in a report in the 'Life & Style' section.[32] Suzanne Moore's lament over the victory of 'middle-aged white guys' similarly did not comment on Corbyn's team's ambitious policies for women. Neither did Yvonne Roberts, who on the same day patiently explains to her readers that while some may claim that policies are what matter, it is women's numerical representation that makes the most difference, because 'gender, alongside race and class, shapes a different day-to-day experience that, consciously and unconsciously, is inextricably entwined in the politics a person espouses'. Would, she muses, a female version of the (Tory) chancellor have 'let the axe [of the cuts] fall hardest elsewhere', away from areas that hurt women most? Roberts concludes that 'nobody knows if a female-dominated cabinet would have opted for a very different agenda, but it's more than time we found out'.[33] As Helen Lewis had declared in a commentary a month earlier, feminist voters must be expected to put 'this aspect of their identity' over party loyalty when they go to the ballot box.[34]

Meanwhile Polly Toynbee worried about the loss of what she considered Harriet Harman's legacy of making Labour 'the choice for women', and tried to defend the interim leader's stance of abstaining on Tory welfare cuts, which included curbing child tax credit, a crucial source of income for many low-waged women, as prudent tactics.[35] Unsurprisingly, by October 2015, Gaby Hinsliff was able to write not only as if the new male leadership's political offer to women voters didn't matter, but as if it had never been made in the first place: 'Jeremy Corbyn just isn't that into us [female voters]'.[36] The direction of travel was clear: while explicitly feminist commentary at the *Guardian* insisted it cared about policies for women as well as their representation by female politicians, it was the latter that counted. Furthermore, there was an assumption that women, or at least feminist women, presented a unified constituency, to be adequately satisfied by a politics that has as its only feminist content the promise that women be represented by women.

Moore asserted this in blunt terms when the question of female leadership was raised once more in late 2019: 'This is not an argument about women being better, or even helping other women. It is an argument about basic representation.'[37] So, in the context of an editorial direction that was principally anti-Corbynist, centrist feminist commentary contributed by disqualifying the movement on the basis of the sex of its leader.

NEOLIBERAL CRISIS FEMINISM

The whole episode might be shelved as opportunistic, especially given that after Labour's general election defeat in 2019, there was no discernible outcry when the centrist candidate Keir Starmer was elected as party leader. The *Guardian*'s sister paper, the *Observer*, even ran an opinion piece before his election, putting him forward as the feminist choice.[38] That said, the position articulated by so many commentators is worth taking at face value for what it reveals about a mainstream feminism in crisis.

The feminism at stake fits a neoliberal mould even as it claims to occupy the space of the left; it is interested in substituting centrist female leaders for male ones into a political landscape that it would leave substantially unchanged. Here it is useful to recall Nancy Fraser's account of feminism as a movement that has lost its grounding in materialist politics, and which has become complicit with what she calls 'progressive neoliberalism'.[39] Looking back to the origins of the second wave, Fraser identifies two distinct dimensions of justice on which feminist struggle was based: 'redistribution' on the one hand, and 'recognition' on the other. For Fraser, any meaningful feminist struggle must continue to encompass both strands of justice – that is to say, fighting against the harms of material maldistribution as well as those of 'misrecognition' that arise from androcentric patterns of cultural value.

Since the 1970s, however, the 'recognition' strand has become dominant in a mainstream feminism that, stripped of its relationship to redistributive politics, has been compatible with the neoliberal economic order. Fraser suggests that the second wave's struggle against traditional authority has even unwittingly provided the 'feminist romance' that now invests flexible capitalism with 'a higher meaning and a moral point'. The result, Fraser argues, is that women are pacified in their daily struggles by their identification with a feminism which, following Luc Boltanski and Eve Chiapello, provides the true 'new spirit of capitalism'.[40]

Catherine Rottenberg points to the stunted political result of this in the rise of a 'neoliberal feminism' which on the one hand recognises (certain kinds of) gender inequality in the workplace and public life, and yet has no structural analysis, critique or solutions; individualised notions of 'leaning in' have displaced a feminist vocabulary and a politics of justice and liberation; accordingly, the 'neoliberal feminist subject is thus mobilized to convert continued gender inequality from a structural problem into an individual affair'.[41]

And yet, the manifestations of newly vigorous feminist protest movements around the world since 2008, culminating, for now, in #MeToo in 2017 and 2018, have shown that collective ideas of feminism are still attractive. However, in the case of #MeToo, in its dominant form, it appears that a simulation of collective organising, atomised on social media platforms, can take its place within a neoliberal culture that will accommodate the sort of activist pressure that does not threaten its economic structure in an ultimately failed promise of solidarity.[42] This involved the affirmation of individual suffering, in some cases, the punishment of some individuals, but either way, largely without the structural analysis and redistributive politics required to tackle sexual violence to which the most precarious and unprotected workers and non-workers are subject. Without addressing the complexities of #MeToo around the globe here, it is worth noting that this most recent flaring up of feminist protest culture under disorganised capitalism points to another, affective refiguration of its 'spirit'.[43] Where feminist identity politics affirms the experience of shared grievances without interest in structural change, it instead fosters what Wendy Brown memorably describes as 'class resentment without class consciousness or class analysis'.[44]

This simulation of the feeling of a political collective, characteristic, according to Jodi Dean, of 'communicative capitalism', is required to grasp the psychology of current liberal feminist journalism.[45] As evidenced above, it is heavily involved in the project of policing the boundaries of the neoliberal political normality identified by Nunns, but without wanting to identify with 'lean in' feminism's individualist ferocity at all. This makes sense as the contortions of a subjectivity that requires the 'feminist romance' of left political struggle identified by Fraser, and the affirmation of shared grievance identified by Brown, and is at the same time unwilling or unable to yield to the reality of political change. Indeed, where *Guardian* commentators have dismissed Corbynism, in the context of women's issues and beyond, they have generally done so from a position that claims mature left virtue in the form of the long-established Blairite line that left ideas must be smuggled past an inherently right-wing electorate piecemeal, and that a grown-up leftism thus never says what it wants out loud.

An only moderately novel twist to this narrative was to present Corbynism's explicit political programme for left politics as simultaneously an old man's obdurate 'purity' and childish, narcissistic 'virtue-signalling' in his millennial supporters. This position was prominently taken, for example, by the paper's executive opinion editor at the time, Jonathan Freedland, with reference to a piece by Helen Lewis published in the *New Statesman*.[46] True virtue, even true left politics, are accordingly found in centrist restraint: 'Free to Dream, I'd be Left of Jeremy Corbyn. But We can't Gamble the Future on Him', runs one headline to a Polly Toynbee commentary in August 2015.[47] By claiming the place of the left's rightful heirs, centrist commentators have been able to shrug off the duty to address the substance of any views to the left of their own.

Feminist commentary provided this virtuous and grown-up but left-at-heart Corbyn scepticism with an invaluable twist: that left projects in the hands of left men are rendered inherently worthless by their inevitable sexism. Established liberal feminist commentators thus refuse to engage with a left movement that is substantially supported by female voters, is organised by young women in crucial roles at grassroots level, and highlights women's issues as key political concerns. When, in the late 2010s, Julie Bindel declared in the pages of the *Guardian* that '[y]et again males on the left have let women down', the entire left was dismissed as a brocialist, male 'monoculture', and a leader with detailed political proposals to benefit women from all backgrounds scorned as fundamentally sexist.[48] One might even say that, by dismissing all left politics as male and sexist, such commentators installed a 'women's only space' in political discourse, not in order to raise 'women's issues', but in order to preserve the status quo and avoid political argument altogether.

Yet the political status quo after the crash of 2008 has been a precarious one, where mainstream feminism has struggled to present a plausible description of the lives the majority lead. As Susan Watkins has recently pointed out, advances in gender equality in work and education in countries around the world have come in lockstep with an unprecedented increase of socio-economic inequality overall, to such an extent that 'the mainstream-feminist model has been exhausted as a solution to median-income women's problems', even in its American heartlands.[49] A moment of crisis, however, is one when the affective rewards of an identity-based, essentialist feminism appear greatest, and it is this context, we suggest, that yields an explanation for the way anti-left and trans-exclusionary feminist journalism have coincided in the *Guardian* and elsewhere in the liberal media landscape.

Consider, in this light, Alice Echols' account of the emergence in the US of what she calls 'cultural feminism' in the mid 1970s as the dominant strain in the women's liberation movement. At the time a highly schismatic movement found solace in the cultural feminist's 'insistence upon women's essential sameness to each other and their fundamental difference from men' in the hope that 'even if women's political, economic, and social gains were reversed, women could build a culture, a space uncontaminated by patriarchy'.[50] Further, Echols details how cultural feminism, with its argument that 'one woman's power empowers all women', ended up converging with liberal feminism's long-established 'trickle-down' view of shared material gains, where one woman's business profits were viewed as a gain to all women, and even shared liberal feminism's aversion for confrontational, 'male', politics.[51]

Thus, essentialist feminism can work to paper over political and economic cracks with the understandably desirable idea of women's basic connectedness. However, this retreat into essentialism, as feminist critics within the movement already pointed out in 1970, only leads to a defeatist 'carving of an enclave in which we can bear the status quo more easily.'[52] An element of essentialist feminism at the *Guardian*, then, not only strengthened the hand of centrist critics of the Corbynist left in the second half of the 2010s. It also, we argue, spoke to a yearning for the romance of political struggle and the comforts of collective identification at a time of increasing political, socioeconomic and cultural uncertainty. This time round, neoliberal crisis feminism not only made the status quo more tolerable; it also actively propped it up.

CONCLUSION: TRANS EXCLUSIONARY CENTRIST FEMINISM

Trans-exclusionary commentary in the *Guardian* in the 2010s follows the same pattern. Here again we find a version of the self-affirming romance of feminism and the comforts of quasi-political collective identification in which feminism is construed primarily as the defence of women-only spaces against potential attacks. This became clearly apparent in controversy about the inclusion of trans women on women-only shortlists for positions in the Labour Party when a trans woman was elected as women's officer for her Labour constituency in Kent in February 2018.[53] Corbyn's unequivocal support for her inclusion was critiqued by trans-exclusionary voices, and confirmed a complaint already established in *Guardian* commentary that pointed to the 'regressive preoccupations' of men on the left's approach to feminism that it claimed privileged 'the rights of trans people and sex workers' over ordinary women's issues, once more ignoring Labour's substantial policy proposals on child care, social care and sexual violence amongst others.[54] Thus the figure of the male left sexist fuses with that of individual male perpetrators imagined to be invading women's spaces with violent intent – here represented by the implausible figure of the 'men's rights activist who might stand on a women-only shortlist to test the legalities'.[55]

The particularity of Britain's centrist, mainstream anti-trans discourse in the latter half of the 2010s, we argue, is the extent to which, alongside anti-left feminism, it provided a political simulation: the drama of moralist quasi-left struggle for a feminism that wants to assert its righteous injury with no discernible programme beyond policing the impossible ideal of a pure 'women's space' – even at the price of scapegoating a beleaguered minority. The current intensification of hatred directed against trans people in the media more generally, but especially on social media and in the broadsheets as inflected by social media, is beyond the scope of our chapter. There is, however, one more turn of the screw in the rhetorical logic of liberal anti-trans discourse that needs to be accounted for here.

Trans activism is frequently dismissed by some 'gender critical' feminists as a form of hyper-individualism that erodes the possibility of collective action through its focus on rights to personal identity and expression, against the rights of non-trans women who are seen to constitute a 'sex-class' with legitimate collective interests.[56] In this way, the right to gender self-identification is frequently framed as an effect of neoliberal ideology and an extreme manifestation of identity politics, while 'sex-based' feminism is framed as inherently characterised by its orientation to collective emancipation, sisterhood and solidarity.

While this position is rarely articulated directly in the *Guardian*, its pattern of framing trans issues as a matter of personal identity, individual choice and a question of the right to self-expression, nonetheless sets the discursive scene in which others, or the same writers on other platforms, can then make these claims.[57] As we noted earlier,

Juliet Jacques's *Guardian* blog in the early 2010s was significant not for contributing more 'positive' representations of trans people, but for articulating trans issues in more expansive political terms and linking them with broader questions of material and economic inequality. The *Guardian* has since played an insidious role in delimiting mainstream understandings of trans politics, and sometimes of explicitly equating 'sex class' feminism with the left, as the one force resisting neoliberalism in the guise of what Suzanne Moore terms American 'choice feminism'.[58] In this formulation, it is those 'leftwing feminists' who 'speak of our biology and our experience' that reject this 'feminism repackaged as capitalist attainment', leaving dubiously open the question of where trans people may fit into this picture.

If only cautiously, liberal trans-exclusionary feminism at the *Guardian* retraced the pattern already established when the agenda of the younger left was dismissed as narcissistic identity politics as we discussed above; an example that fuses the two was a rather detailed report in February 2020 on Tony Blair's view that too much 'trans rights identity politics', like that on the left of the party, was a youthful error detrimental to Labour's electability. The dismissal of 'identity politics' from the right and the centre is a familiar phenomenon; in the context of liberal trans-exclusionary feminism, it has the additional effect of endowing a rather simplistic sex-based centrist feminism with a touch of pseudo-left (sex) class consciousness.

As such, and as we have shown in this chapter, the *Guardian* has played a central role in the broader signification of trans politics as belonging to the sphere of recognition and identity, reducing it to questions of self-identification and the question of what constitutes a woman. At the same time, this trans-hostile feminism postures rhetorically as the 'real' left, and yet fails to engage with or support redistributive policies. Instead, this trans-exclusionary feminism has been put to ideological work in giving a 'progressive' feminist gloss to the *Guardian*'s broader anti-Corbynist, anti-left position. In keeping the focus of political energies trained on 'cultural' questions of gender identity at the same time as it cultivated hostility to a radical left alternative, it has played a key role in the shrinking of political imaginaries, in Nancy Fraser's terms, both of recognition and redistribution.

NOTES

1. Jane Chapman, *Gender, Citizenship and Newspapers: Historical and Transnational Perspectives* (Basingstoke and New York: Palgrave Macmillan, 2013), p. 148.
2. Jilly Boyce Kay and Kaitlynn Mendes, 'Gender, Media and Protest', *Media History*, 26:2 (2020), pp.137–52.
3. Jilly Boyce Kay, '"The *Sunday Times* among Them": *Good Afternoon!*, and the Gendering of Afternoon Television in the 1970s', *Critical Studies in Television*, 9:2, (2014), pp. 74–93.
4. Terese Jonsson, 'White Feminist Stories', *Feminist Media Studies* 14:6 (2014), pp. 1012–27.
5. Terese Jonsson, *Innocent Subjects: Feminism and Whiteness* (London: Pluto, 2020).
6. The *Mail Online* ran a total of 18,793 stories; the *Guardian*, 7,140. This information was gathered from the Nexis database, in a search for these terms in the time period 1 January 2014 to 31 August 2020.
7. Julie Bindel, 'Gender Benders, Beware', *Guardian*, 31 January 2004, https://www.theguardian.com/world/2004/jan/31/gender.weekend7 (accessed August 15, 2020).
8. Germaine Greer, 'Caster Semenya Row', *Guardian*, 20 August 2009, https://www.theguardian.com/sport/2009/aug/20/germaine-greer-caster-semenya (accessed 21 September 2020).
9. Hannah Ewens, 'Inside the Great British TERF war', *vice.com*, 16 June 2020, https://www.vice.com/en_uk/article/889qe5/trans-rights-uk-debate-terfs (accessed 21 September 2020).
10. Ibid.
11. Juliet Jacques, 'A Transgender Journey', *Guardian*, https://www.theguardian.com/lifeandstyle/series/transgender-journey (accessed 21 September 2020).
12. 'A Transgender Journey': Juliet Jacques & CN Lester in conversation. 24 June 2020, https://www.youtube.com/watch?v=v1yifIYGabI (accessed 21 September 2020).
13. Paris Lees, Jane Fae, CL Minou and Stuart Crawford, 'Why I'm Trans – and Feminist', *Guardian*, 18 January 2013, https://www.theguardian.com/commentisfree/2013/jan/18/trans-feminist-panel (accessed August 15, 2020).
14. Anthea Taylor, '"Steve is Twice the Aussie Icon You Will Ever Be": Germaine Greer, The Crocodile Hunter's Death, and Nationalistic Misogyny', *European Journal of Cultural Studies*, 22: 5–6 (2019), pp. 630–45.
15. For example, the *New Statesman* began to commission trans writers such as Jacques from 2012.

16. Notwithstanding all the limitations and problems of this visibility, as has been widely noted.
17. Ruth Pearce, Sonja Erikainen and Ben Vincent, 'TERF wars: An introduction', *The Sociological Review*, 68:4 (2020), pp. 677–98.
18. The *Guardian* view on the Gender Recognition Act: Where Rights Collide', 17 October 2018, https://www.theguardian.com/commentisfree/2018/oct/17/the-guardian-view-on-the-gender-recognition-act-where-rights-collide (accessed 15 August 2020).
19. Sam Levin, Mona Chalabi and Sabrina Siddiqui, 'Why We Take Issue with the *Guardian*'s Stance on Trans Rights in the UK', *Guardian*, 2 November 2018, https://www.theguardian.com/commentisfree/2018/nov/02/guardian-editorial-response-transgender-rights-uk (accessed 15 August 2020).
20. Patrick Strudwick, 'Hundreds of Staff at the *Guardian* Have Signed a Letter to the Editor Criticising its "Transphobic Content"', *Buzzfeed News*, 6 March 2020, https://www.buzzfeed.com/patrickstrudwick/guardian-staff-trans-rights-letter (accessed August 30, 2020).
21. Suzanne Moore, 'Women Must Have the Right To Organise: We Will Not Be Silenced', *Guardian*, 2 March 2020, https://www.theguardian.com/society/commentisfree/2020/mar/02/women-must-have-the-right-to-organise-we-will-not-be-silenced (accessed August 30, 2020).
22. 'A Transgender Journey': Juliet Jacques & CN Lester in conversation. 24 June 2020, https://www.youtube.com/watch?v=v1yifIYGabI (accessed 21 September 2020).
23. Juliet Jacques, 'Liberals Need to Stand Up for Trans Rights before it is too Late', *Guardian*, 24 September 2020, https://www.theguardian.com/commentisfree/2020/sep/24/liberals-stand-up-trans-rights-transgender (accessed 15 October 2020).
24. Sophie Lewis, 'How British Feminism became Anti-Trans', *New York Times*, 7 February 2019, https://www.nytimes.com/2019/02/07/opinion/terf-trans-women-britain.html (accessed 15 October 2020).
25. Juliet Jacques, 'Transphobia is Everywhere in Britain', *New York Times*, 9 March 2020, https://www.nytimes.com/2020/03/09/opinion/britain-transphobia-labour-party.html (accessed 15 October 2020).
26. Andrea Long Chu, 'On Liking Women', *n+1 magazine*, https://nplusonemag.com/issue-30/essays/on-liking-women/ (accessed 15 October 2020).
27. See Alex Nunns, *The Candidate* (New York and London: OR Books, 2018), pp. 182–3. Headlines included: 'Think before you vote for Jeremy Corbyn', 'Jeremy Corbyn caught looking gloomy on night bus', and 'Jeremy Corbyn suggests he would bring back Labour's nationalising clause IV' (in an article that negates just that claim in its first line).
28. The report identifies six instances of (mildly) negative comment on the other three candidates in total. MediaLens, 'Whitewash – the *Guardian*

Readers' Editor responds on Jeremy Corbyn' 6 August 2015, https://archive.is/Jxdwh (accessed 20 September 2020).

29. Nunns, *The Candidate*, p. 191.
30. Suzanne Moore, 'As Jeremy Corbyn Was Anointed Leader, Not One Female Voice Was Heard', *Guardian*, 15 September 2015, https://www.theguardian.com/politics/2015/sep/12/jeremy-corbyn-not-one-female-voice (accessed 15 October 2020).
31. These figures were noted in the paper's own data blog. George Arnett, 'Jeremy Corbyn's Shadow Cabinet – Older, More Rebellious and Less Male', *Guardian*, 14 September 2015, https://www.theguardian.com/news/datablog/2015/sep/14/jeremy-corbyn-labour-shadow-cabinet-statistical-breakdown (accessed 15 October 2020).
32. Nicholas Watt, 'Jeremy Corbyn Warns 'Naughty People' to Leave Labour Party Alone', *Guardian*, 28 July 2015, https://www.theguardian.com/politics/2015/jul/28/jeremy-corbyn-warns-naughty-people-to-leave-labour-party-alone; Olivia Marks, 'Do Mothers Need to Be in Bikinis to Push their Bugaboos?' *Guardian*, 3 August 2015, https://www.theguardian.com/lifeandstyle/womens-blog/2015/jul/31/the-bugaboo-bikini-ad-has-our-vision-of-motherhood-reached-peak-ridiculous?CMP=twt_gu (both accessed 15 October 2020).
33. Yvonne Roberts, 'Yet Again Men Hold Power: Why Can't Labour Change?', *Guardian*, 15 September 2015, https://www.theguardian.com/commentisfree/2015/sep/13/women-politics-power-labour-leadership-jeremy-corbyn (accessed 15 October 2020).
34. Helen Lewis, 'Labour Should Have Seen this Membership Debacle Coming', *Guardian*, 20 August 2015, https://www.theguardian.com/commentisfree/2015/aug/20/labour-membership-jeremy-corbyn-purge (accessed 15 October 2020).
35. Patrick Wintour, 'Anger after Harriet Harman Says Labour Will Not Vote Against Welfare Bill', *Guardian*, 12 July 2015, https://www.theguardian.com/politics/2015/jul/12/harman-labour-not-vote-against-welfare-bill-limit-child-tax-credits; Polly Toynbee, 'Those Who Flounce Out on Jeremy Corbyn Now Will Not Escape Blame When Labour Crashes', *Guardian*, 15 September 2015, https://www.theguardian.com/commentisfree/2015/sep/15/jeremy-corbyn-labour-mps; Polly Toynbee, 'Harriet Harman's Victory Was Putting Women's Lives at the Heart of Politics', *Guardian*, 17 September 2015, https://www.theguardian.com/commentisfree/2015/sep/17/harriet-harman-women-politics-legacy (all accessed 15 October 2020).
36. Gaby Hinsliff, 'The Women's Equality Party Has a Problem', *Guardian*, 22 October 2015, https://www.theguardian.com/commentisfree/2015/oct/22/womens-equality-party-problem-wep-ukip-eu-feminism (accessed 15 October 2020).
37. Suzanne Moore, 'Does Labour Really Want to Elect a Female Leader?', *Guardian*, 14 October 2019, https://www.theguardian.com/comment

isfree/2019/oct/14/labour-want-elect-female-leader-john-mcdonnell (accessed 15 October 2020).

38. Catherine Bennett, 'Why Should Keir Starmer Step Aside? His Rivals Have Few Feminist Credentials', *Guardian*, 26 January 2020, https://www.theguardian.com/commentisfree/2020/jan/26/why-should-keir-starmer-aside---his-rivals-have-few-feminist-credentials (accessed 15 October 2020).
39. Nancy Fraser, 'From Progressive Neoliberalism to Trump – and Beyond'. *American Affairs Journal*, I(4), Winter 2017, https://americanaffairsjournal.org/2017/11/progressive-neoliberalism-trump-beyond/ (accessed 15 October 2020).
40. Nancy Fraser, *Fortunes of Feminism: From State Managed Capitalism to Neoliberal Crisis* (London: Verso, 2013), pp. 298-99.
41. Catherine Rottenberg, *The Rise of Neoliberal Feminism* (Oxford: Oxford University Press, 2018).
42. See Mareile Pfannebecker and J. A. Smith, *Work Want Work* (London: Zed Books, 2020), pp. 80–81.
43. See Jilly Boyce Kay, *Gender, Media and Voice: Communicative Injustice and Public Speech* (Basingstoke: Palgrave Macmillan), chapters 2 and 3.
44. Wendy Brown, 'Wounded Attachments', *Political Theory* 21(3), 1993, p. 394.
45. Jodi Dean, *Democracy and Other Neoliberal Fantasies: Communicative Capitalism and Left Politics* (Durham: Duke University Press, 2009).
46. Jonathan Freedland, 'The Corbyn Tribe Cares About Identity, Not Power', *Guardian*, 24 July 2015, https://www.theguardian.com/commentisfree/2015/jul/24/corbyn-tribe-identity-politics-labour (accessed 15 October 2020).
47. Polly Toynbee, 'Free to Dream, I'd Be Left of Jeremy Corbyn', *Guardian*, 4 August 2015, https://www.theguardian.com/commentisfree/2015/aug/04/jeremy-corbyn-gamble-labour-future-yvette-cooper-best-chance (accessed 15 October 2020).
48. Julie Bindel, 'Jeremy Corbyn's Views on the Sex Trade Sum up the Male Left's Betrayal of Women', *Guardian*, 4 March 2016, https://www.theguardian.com/society/commentisfree/2016/mar/04/jeremy-corbyn-sex-trade-left-women-exploitation (accessed 15 October 2020). In the piece in question Bindel omits the fact that Corbyn's position was based on consultation with sex worker groups and the endeavour to lend a political platform to their petition.
49. Susan Watkins, 'Which Feminisms?' *NLR* 109, 2018, pp. 5–76.
50. Alice Echols, *Daring to Be Bad* (Minneapolis: University of Minnesota Press, 2019), pp. 244–5.
51. Ibid, pp. 278–79.
52. Quoted in Ibid, p. 244.
53. Rowena Mason, 'Labour to Clarify Policy Over Trans Women', *Guardian*, 1 February 2018, https://www.theguardian.com/politics/2018/feb/01/

labour-to-clarify-policy-over-trans-women-on-all-female-shortlists (accessed 15 Ooctober 2020).

54. Suzanne Moore, 'Men on the Left Are Sexist' *Guardian*, 14 August 2017, https://www.theguardian.com/commentisfree/2017/aug/14/men-on-left-sexist-labour-womens-rights (accessed 15 October 2020).
55. Mason, 'Labour to Clarify Policy Over Trans Women'.
56. Heather Brunskell-Evans, 'A Neoliberal Concept of Freedom Has Allowed Gender Identity Ideology to Take Hold', 2 December 2018, http://www.heather-brunskell-evans.co.uk/body-politics/a-neoliberal-concept-of-freedom-has-allowed-gender-identity-ideology-to-take-hold/ (accessed October 10, 2020).
57. It is important to note, for example, how Suzanne Moore writes articles for the *Spectator* which are often more openly trans-hostile than her regular *Guardian* column. For example, see 'How Progressive Misogyny Works', *Spectator*, 19 August 2020, https://www.spectator.co.uk/article/how-progressive-misogyny-works (accessed October 19, 2020).
58. Suzanne Moore, 'If we can't define what a woman is, how can we organise politically?', *Guardian*, 3 August 2020, https://www.theguardian.com/commentisfree/2020/aug/03/define-what-a-woman-is-organise-politically-suzanne-moore (accessed December 6, 2020).

9

The *Guardian* and Surveillance

Matt Kennard and Mark Curtis

INTRODUCTION

The *Guardian* has long been Britain's leading liberal newspaper. Through its embrace of the digital age, it has become a global brand, known for its independent and critical journalism. But its relative independence, evidenced particularly by its work on the early WikiLeaks revelations, increasingly made it a problem for the Anglo-American national security state.

This culminated in June 2013 when it began revealing secret US government documents leaked by National Security Agency (NSA) contractor Edward Snowden. The bombshell revelations continued for months and constituted the largest ever leak of classified material covering the NSA and its UK equivalent, the Government Communications Headquarters (GCHQ). They revealed programmes of mass surveillance operated by both agencies.[1]

According to the minutes of meetings of the Defence and Security Media Advisory (DSMA) Committee, the revelations caused alarm in the British security services and Ministry of Defence (MOD). 'This event was very concerning because at the outset the *Guardian* avoided engaging with the [Committee] before publishing the first tranche of information', the minutes of the 7 November 2013 meeting at the MOD note.[2]

The DSMA Committee, more commonly known as the D-Notice Committee, is run by the MOD – where it meets every six months. A small number of journalists are also invited to sit on the Committee. Its stated purpose is to 'prevent inadvertent public disclosure of information that would compromise UK military and intelligence operations.'[3] It can issue 'notices' to the media to encourage them not to publish certain information.

The Committee is chaired by the MOD's Director General of Security Policy, Dominic Wilson, who was previously Director of Security and Intelligence in the Cabinet Office.[4] Its Secretary is Brigadier Geoffrey Dodds OBE, who describes himself as an 'accomplished, senior ex-military commander with extensive experience of operational level leadership'.[5]

The D-Notice system describes itself as voluntary, placing no obligations on the media to comply with any 'notice' it issues.[6] This means that there should have been no need for the *Guardian* to have consulted the MOD before publishing the Snowden documents.

Yet Committee minutes note the Secretary saying that '[t]he *Guardian* was obliged to seek . . . advice under the terms of the DA Notice code.' It adds further that '[t]his failure to seek advice was a key source of concern and considerable efforts had been made to address it.'[7]

'CONSIDERABLE EFFORTS'

These 'considerable efforts' included a D-Notice sent out by the Committee on 7 June 2013 – the day after the *Guardian* published the first documents – to all major UK media editors, stating that they should refrain from publishing information that would 'jeopardise both national security and possibly UK personnel'. It was marked 'private and confidential: not for publication, broadcast or use on social media'.[8] Clearly the Committee did not want its issuing of the notice to be publicised, and it was nearly successful. Only the right-wing blog Guido Fawkes made it public.

At the time, according to the Committee minutes, the 'intelligence agencies in particular had continued to ask for more advisories [i.e., D-Notices] to be sent out'.[9] Such D-Notices were clearly seen by the intelligence services not so much as a tool to advise the media but rather a way to threaten it not to publish further Snowden revelations.

One night, amidst the first Snowden stories being published, the D-Notice Committee's then Secretary Air Vice-Marshal Andrew Vallance even personally called Alan Rusbridger, the editor of the *Guardian*. Vallance 'made clear his concern that the *Guardian* had failed to consult him in advance before telling the world', according to a *Guardian* journalist who interviewed Rusbridger.[10]

Later in the year, prime minister David Cameron again used the D-Notice system as a threat to the media. 'I don't want to have to use injunctions or D notices or the other tougher measures', he said in a statement to MPs. 'I think it's much better to appeal to newspapers' sense of social responsibility. But if they don't demonstrate some social responsibility it would be very difficult for government to stand back and not to act.'[11]

The threats worked. The *Press Gazette* reported at the time that 'The *FT* and *The Times* did not mention it [the initial Snowden revelations] . . . and the *Telegraph* published only a short [article]'. It continued by noting that only the *Independent* had 'followed up the substantive allegations' and that the BBC 'has also chosen to largely ignore the story.'[12]

The *Guardian*, however, remained uncowed. According to the Committee minutes, the fact the *Guardian* would not stop publishing 'undoubtedly raised questions in some minds about the System's future usefulness'.[13] If the D-Notice system could not prevent the *Guardian* publishing GCHQ's most sensitive secrets, what was it good for? It was time to rein the *Guardian* in and make sure this never happened again.

GCHQ AND LAPTOPS

The security services soon ratcheted up their 'considerable efforts' to deal with these exposures. On 20 July 2013, GCHQ officials entered the *Guardian*'s offices at King's Cross in London, six weeks after the first Snowden-related article had been published.[14] At the request of the government and security services, *Guardian* deputy editor Paul Johnson, along with two others, spent three hours destroying the laptops containing the Snowden documents.[15]

The *Guardian* staffers, according to one of the newspaper's reporters, brought 'angle-grinders, dremels – a drill with a revolving bit – and masks.' The reporter added that, '[t]he spy agency provided one piece of hi-tech equipment, a "degausser", which destroys magnetic fields, and erases data.'[16]

Johnson later claimed that the destruction of the computers was 'purely a symbolic act', adding that '[t]he government and GCHQ knew, because we had told them, that the material had been taken to the US to be shared with the *New York Times*. The reporting would go on. The episode hadn't changed anything.'[17] Yet the episode did change something. As the D-Notice Committee minutes for November 2013 outlined: 'Towards the end of July [as the computers were being destroyed] The *Guardian* had begun to seek and accept DA Notice advice not to publish certain highly sensitive details and since then the dialogue [with the Committee] had been reasonable and improving.'[18]

The British security services had carried out more than a 'symbolic act'. It was both a show of strength and a clear threat. The *Guardian* was then the only major newspaper that could be relied upon by whistle-blowers in the US and British security states to receive and cover their exposures, a situation which posed a challenge to security agencies.

The increasingly aggressive overtures made to the *Guardian* worked. The Committee chair noted that after GCHQ had overseen the 'symbolic' smashing up of the newspaper's laptops 'engagement ... with the *Guardian* had continued to strengthen.'[19] Moreover, he added that there were now 'regular dialogues between the Secretary and Deputy Secretaries and *Guardian* journalists'.[20] Rusbridger later testified to the Home Affairs Committee that Air Vice-Marshal Vallance of the D-Notice Committee and himself 'collaborated' in the aftermath of the Snowden affair and that Vallance had even 'been at The *Guardian* offices to talk to all our reporters'.[21]

But the most important part of this charm and threat offensive was getting the *Guardian* to agree to take a seat on the D-Notice Committee itself. The Committee minutes are explicit on this, noting that 'the process had culminated by [sic] the appointment of Paul Johnson (Deputy Editor Guardian News and Media) as a DPBAC [i.e. D-Notice Committee] member'.[22] At some point in 2013 or early 2014, Johnson – the same deputy editor who had smashed up his newspaper's computers under the watchful gaze of British intelligence agents – was approached to take up a seat on the Committee. Johnson attended his first meeting in May 2014 and was to remain on it until October 2018.[23] The *Guardian*'s deputy editor went directly from the corporation's basement with an angle-grinder to sitting on the D-Notice Committee alongside the security service officials who had tried to stop his paper publishing the Snowden material.

A NEW EDITOR

Guardian editor Alan Rusbridger withstood intense pressure not to publish some of Snowden's revelations, but agreed to Johnson taking a seat on the D-Notice Committee as a tactical sop to the security services. Throughout his tenure, the *Guardian* continued to publish some stories critical of the security services. But the situation changed in March 2015, when the *Guardian* appointed a new editor, Katharine Viner, who had less experience than Rusbridger of dealing with the security services.[24] Viner had started out at the fashion and entertainment magazine *Cosmopolitan* and had no history in national security reporting.[25] According to insiders, she showed far less leadership during the Snowden affair than Janine Gibson in the US (Gibson was another candidate to become Rusbridger's successor).[26]

Viner was then editor-in-chief of *Guardian Australia*, which was launched just two weeks before the first Snowden revelations were published. Australia and New Zealand comprise two-fifths of the so-called 'Five Eyes' surveillance alliance exposed by Snowden. This was an opportunity for the security services. It appears that their seduction began the following year.

In November 2016, the *Guardian* published an unprecedented 'exclusive' with Andrew Parker, the head of MI5, Britain's domestic security service.[27] The article noted that this was the 'first newspaper interview given by an incumbent MI5 chief in the service's 107-year history'. It was co-written by deputy editor, Paul Johnson, who had never written about the security services before and who was still sitting on the D-Notice Committee. This was not mentioned in the article.

The MI5 chief was given copious space to make claims about the national security threat posed by an 'increasingly aggressive' Russia. Johnson and his co-author noted that 'Parker said he was talking to the *Guardian* rather than any other newspaper despite the publication of the Snowden files'. Parker told the two reporters: 'We recognise that in a changing world we have to change too. We have a responsibility to talk about our work and explain it.'

Just four months after the MI5 interview, in March 2017, the *Guardian* published another unprecedented 'exclusive', this time with Alex Younger, the sitting chief of MI6, Britain's external intelligence agency.[28] This exclusive was awarded by the Secret Intelligence Service to the *Guardian*'s investigations editor, Nick Hopkins, who had been appointed 14 months previously. The interview was the first Younger had given to a national newspaper and was again softball. Titled 'MI6 returns to "tapping up" in effort to recruit black and Asian officers', it focused almost entirely on the intelligence service's stated desire to open itself up to recruitment from ethnic minority communities. 'Simply, we have to attract the best of modern Britain,' Younger told Hopkins. 'Every community from every part of Britain should feel they have what it takes, no matter what their background or status.'

Just two weeks before the interview with MI6's chief was published, the *Guardian* itself reported on the high court stating that it would 'hear an application for a judicial review of the Crown Prosecution Service's decision not to charge MI6's former counterterrorism director, Sir Mark Allen, over the abduction of Abdel Hakim Belhaj and his pregnant wife who were transferred to Libya in a joint CIA-MI6 operation in 2004.'[29] None of this featured in the *Guardian* article which did, however, cover discussions of whether the James Bond actor Daniel Craig would qualify for the intelligence service. 'He would not get into MI6,' Younger told Hopkins.

More recently, in August 2019, the *Guardian* was awarded yet another exclusive, this time with Metropolitan police assistant commissioner Neil Basu, Britain's most senior counter-terrorism officer.[30] This was Basu's 'first major interview since taking up his post' the previous year and resulted in a three-part series of articles, one of which was titled, 'Met police examine Vladimir Putin's role in Salisbury attack'.[31]

The security services were likely feeding the *Guardian* these 'exclusives' as part of the process of bringing it onside and neutralising the only independent newspaper with the resources to receive and cover a leak such as Snowden's. They were, we believe, acting to prevent any revelations of this kind happening again.

What, if any, private conversations have taken place between Viner and the security services during her tenure as editor are not publicly known. However in 2018, when Paul Johnson eventually left the D-Notice Committee, its chair, the MOD's Dominic Wilson, praised Johnson who, he said, 'had been instrumental in re-establishing links with the *Guardian*'.[32]

DECLINE IN CRITICAL REPORTING

Amidst these spoon-fed intelligence exclusives, Viner also oversaw the breakup of the *Guardian*'s celebrated investigative team, whose muck-racking journalists were told to apply to other jobs outside of investigations. One well-placed source told the *Press Gazette* at the time that journalists on the investigations team 'have not felt backed by senior editors over the last year', and that 'some also feel the company has become more risk averse in the same period'.[33]

In the period since Snowden, the *Guardian* has lost many of its top investigative reporters who had covered national security issues, notably Shiv Malik, Nick Davies, David Leigh, Richard Norton-Taylor, Ewen MacAskill and Ian Cobain. The few journalists who were replaced were succeeded by less experienced reporters with apparently less commitment to exposing the security state. The current defence and security editor, Dan Sabbagh, started at the *Guardian* as head of media and technology and has no history covering national security.[34] 'It seems they've got rid of everyone who seemed to cover the security services and military in an adversarial way,' one current *Guardian* journalist told us.

Indeed, during the last two years of Rusbridger's editorship, the *Guardian* published around 110 articles per year tagged as MI6 on its website. Since Viner took over, the average per year has halved, and is decreasing year by year. 'Effective scrutiny of the security and intelligence agencies – epitomised by the Snowden scoops but also many other stories – appears to have been abandoned', a former *Guardian* journalist told us. The reporter added that in recent years, it 'sometimes seems the *Guardian* is worried about upsetting the spooks.' A second former *Guardian* journalist added: 'the *Guardian* no longer seems to have such a challenging relationship with the intelligence services, and is perhaps seeking to mend fences since Snowden. This is concerning, because spooks are always manipulative and not always to be trusted.'

While some articles critical of the security services still appear in the paper, its 'scoops' have increasingly focused on issues more acceptable to them. In the years since the Snowden affair, the *Guardian* does not appear to have published any articles based on intelligence or security services sources that were not so to speak 'officially sanctioned'.

The *Guardian* has, by contrast, published a steady stream of exclusives on the major official enemy of the security services, Russia, exposing President Putin, his friends and the work of its intelligence services and military. In the Panama Papers leak in April 2016, which revealed how companies and individuals around the world were using an offshore law firm to avoid paying tax, the *Guardian*'s frontpage launch scoop was authored by Luke Harding, who has received many security service tips focused on the 'Russia Threat', and was titled, 'Revealed: the $2bn offshore trail that leads to Vladimir Putin'.[35]

Three sentences into the piece, however, Harding noted that 'the president's name does not appear in any of the records' although he insisted that 'the data reveals a pattern – his friends have earned millions from deals that seemingly could not have been secured without his patronage.' There was a much bigger story in the Panama Papers which the *Guardian* chose to downplay by leaving it to the following day. This concerned the father of the then prime minister, David Cameron, who 'ran an offshore fund that avoided ever having to pay tax in Britain by hiring a small army of Bahamas residents – including a part-time bishop – to sign its paperwork'.[36]

We understand there was some argument between journalists about not leading with the Cameron story as the launch splash. Putin's friends were eventually deemed more important than the prime minister of the country where the paper published.

GETTING JULIAN ASSANGE

The *Guardian* also appears to have been engaged in a campaign against the WikiLeaks publisher Julian Assange, who had been a collaborator during the early WikiLeaks revelations in 2010. One 2017 story came from investigative reporter Carole Cadwalladr, who writes for the *Guardian*'s sister paper, the *Observer*, and was titled, 'When Nigel Farage met Julian Assange'.[37] This concerned the visit of former UKIP leader, Nigel Farage, to the Ecuadorian embassy in March 2017, organised by the radio station, LBC, for whom Farage worked as a presenter.[38] Farage's producer at LBC accompanied Farage at the meeting, but this was not mentioned by Cadwalladr.

Rather, she posited that this meeting was 'potentially . . . a channel of communication' between WikiLeaks, Farage and Donald Trump, who were all said to be closely linked to Russia, adding that these actors were in a 'political alignment' and that 'WikiLeaks is, in many ways, the swirling vortex at the centre of everything'. Yet Cadwalladr's one official on-the-record source for this speculation was, according to her article, a 'highly placed contact with links to US intelligence', who told her that '[w]hen the heat is turned up and all electronic communication, you have to assume, is being intensely monitored, then those are the times when intelligence communication falls back on human couriers. Where you have individuals passing information in ways and places that cannot be monitored.' It was surely obvious that this was innuendo being fed to the *Observer* by an intelligence-linked individual to promote disinformation to undermine Assange.

In 2018, however, the *Guardian*'s attempted vilification of Assange was significantly escalated. A new string of articles began on 18 May 2018 with one alleging Assange's 'long standing relationship with RT', the Russian state broadcaster.[39] The series lasted for several months, consistently alleging with little or the most minimal circumstantial evidence that Assange had ties to Russia or the Kremlin. One story, co-authored again by Luke Harding, claimed that 'Russian diplomats held secret talks in London . . . with people close to Julian Assange to assess whether they could help him flee the UK, the *Guardian* has learned'.[40] The former Consul to the Ecuadorian embassy in London at this time, Fidel Narvaez, vigorously denies the existence of any such 'escape plot' involving Russia and was vindicated when the *Guardian* upheld his complaint against the newspaper for insinuating he coordinated such a plot.[41]

This apparent mini-campaign ran until November 2018, culminating in a front-page splash based on anonymous sources, claiming that Assange had three secret meetings at the Ecuadorian embassy with Trump's former campaign manager Paul Manafort.[42] This 'scoop' failed all tests of journalistic credibility since it would have been impossible for anyone to have entered the highly secured Ecuadorian embassy three times with no proof of their entry. WikiLeaks and others have strongly argued that the story was manufactured,[43] and it is telling that the *Guardian* has since failed to refer to it in its subsequent articles on the Assange case. The *Guardian*, however, has still not retracted or apologised for the story which remains on its website. The 'exclusive' appeared just two weeks after Paul Johnson had been congratulated for 're-establishing links' between the *Guardian* and the security services.

This string of *Guardian* articles, alongside the vilification and smear stories about Assange elsewhere in the British media, helped create the conditions for a deal between Ecuador, the UK and the US to expel Assange from the embassy in April 2019.[44] Assange, meanwhile, remains in Belmarsh maximum security prison where, at the time of writing, he faces extradition to the US, and life in prison there, under charges relating to the Espionage Act.

ACTING FOR THE ESTABLISHMENT

Another major focus of the *Guardian*'s energies under Viner's editorship has been to attack the leader of the Labour Party from 2015–19, Jeremy Corbyn. The context is that Corbyn appears to have recently been a target of the security services. In 2015, soon after he was elected Labour leader, the *Sunday Times* reported a serving general warning that 'there would be a direct challenge from the army and mass resignations if Corbyn became prime minister'.[45] The source told the newspaper: 'The Army just wouldn't stand for it. The general staff would not allow a prime minister to jeopardise the security of this country and I think people would use whatever means possible, fair or foul to prevent that.'

On 20 May 2017, a little over two weeks before the 2017 General Election, the *Daily Telegraph* was fed the story that 'MI5 opened a file on Jeremy Corbyn amid concerns over his links to the IRA'.[46] It formed part of a *Telegraph* investigation claiming to reveal 'Mr Corbyn's full links to the IRA', and was sourced to an individual 'close to' the MI5 investigation, who said 'a file had been opened on him by the early Nineties'. The Metropolitan Police Special Branch was also said to be monitoring Corbyn in the same period.

Then on the very eve of the General Election, the *Telegraph* gave space to an article from Sir Richard Dearlove, the former director of MI6, under a headline: 'Jeremy Corbyn is a danger to this nation. At MI6, which I once led, he wouldn't clear the security vetting'.[47] Further, in September 2018, two anonymous senior government sources told *The Times* that Corbyn had been 'summoned' for a "facts of life" talk on terror' by MI5 chief, Andrew Parker.[48]

Just two weeks after news of this private meeting was leaked by the government, the *Daily Mail* reported another leak, this time revealing that 'Jeremy Corbyn's most influential Commons adviser has been barred from entering Ukraine on the grounds that he is a national security threat because of his alleged links to Vladimir Putin's "global propaganda network"'.[49] The article concerned Andrew Murray, who had been working in Corbyn's office for a year but had still not received a security pass to enter parliament. The *Mail* reported, based on what it called 'a senior Parliamentary source', that Murray's application had encountered 'vetting problems'.

Murray later suggested that the security services had leaked the story to the *Mail*. 'Call me sceptical if you must, but I do not see journalistic enterprise behind the *Mail*'s sudden capacity to tease obscure information out of the [Ukrainian security service]', he wrote in the *New Statesman*.[50] He added that '[s]omeone else is doing the hard work – possibly someone being paid by the taxpayer. I doubt if their job description is preventing the election of a Corbyn government, but who knows?' Murray told us that he was approached by the *New Statesman* after the story about him being banned from the Ukraine was leaked. 'However,' he added, 'I wouldn't dream of suggesting anything like that to the *Guardian*, since I do not know any journalists still working there who I could trust.'

The *Guardian* itself ran a remarkable number of news and comment articles criticising Corbyn after he was elected in 2015 and the paper's clearly hostile stance has been widely noted.[51] Given its appeal to traditional Labour supporters, the paper has probably done more to undermine Corbyn than any other. In particular, its massive coverage of alleged widespread antisemitism in the Labour party has helped to disparage Corbyn more than other smears carried in the media.

The *Guardian* and the *Observer* have published hundreds of articles on 'Labour antisemitism' and, since the beginning of 2019, carried over 50 such articles with headlines clearly negative to Corbyn. Typical headlines have included 'The *Observer* view: Labour leadership is complicit in antisemitism', 'Jeremy Corbyn is either blind to antisemitism – or he just doesn't care', and 'Labour's antisemitism problem is institutional. It needs investigation'.

The *Guardian*'s coverage of antisemitism in Labour has been extensive (see Chapter 11), compared to the known extent of the problem in the party, and its focus on Corbyn personally suggests that the issue is being used politically. While antisemitism exists in the Labour Party, evidence suggests it is at relatively low levels. Since September 2015, when Corbyn became Labour leader, 0.06% of the Labour membership has been investigated for antisemitic comments or posts.[52] In 2016, an independent inquiry commissioned by Labour concluded that the party, 'is not overrun by antisemitism, Islamophobia or other forms of racism. Further, it is the party that initiated every single United Kingdom race equality law.'[53]

Analysis of two YouGov surveys, conducted in 2015 and 2017, showed that anti-Semitic views held by Labour voters declined substantially in the first two years of Corbyn's tenure, and that such views were significantly more common among Conservative voters.[54] Despite this, from January 2016 to September 2019, the *Guardian* published 1,225 stories mentioning Labour and antisemitism, an average of around one per day, according to a search on Factiva, the database of newspaper articles. In the same period, the *Guardian* published just 194 articles mentioning the Conservative Party's much more serious problem with Islamophobia. A YouGov poll in 2019, for example, found that nearly half of the Tory Party membership would prefer not to have a Muslim prime minister.[55]

At the same time, some stories which paint Corbyn's critics in a negative light have been suppressed by the *Guardian*. According to someone with knowledge of the matter, the *Guardian* declined to publish the results of a months-long critical investigation by one of its reporters into a prominent anti-Corbyn Labour MP, citing only vague legal issues. In July 2016, one of the authors emailed a *Guardian* editor asking if he could pitch an investigation about the first attempt by the right-wing of the Labour Party to remove Corbyn, informing the *Guardian* of very good inside sources on those behind the attempt and their real plans. The approach was rejected as being of no interest before a pitch was even sent.

A RELIABLE PUBLICATION?

On 20 May 2019, *The Times* reported on a Freedom of Information request made by the Rendition Project, a group of academic experts working on torture and rendition issues, which showed that the MOD had been 'developing a secret policy on torture that allows ministers to sign off intelligence-sharing that could lead to the abuse of detainees'.[56] This might traditionally have been a *Guardian* story, not something for the Rupert Murdoch-owned *Times*. According to one civil society source, however, many groups working in this field no longer trust the *Guardian*. A former *Guardian* journalist similarly told us that 'it is significant that exclusive stories recently about British collusion in torture and policy towards the interrogation of terror suspects and other detainees have been passed to other papers including *The Times* rather than the *Guardian*.'

The Times published its scoop under a strong headline, 'Torture: Britain breaks law in Ministry of Defence secret policy'. However, before the article was published, the MOD fed the *Guardian* the same documents that *The Times* were about to splash with, believing it could soften the impact of the revelations by telling its side of the story. The *Guardian* posted its own article just before *The Times*, with a headline that would have pleased the government: 'MoD says revised torture guidance does not lower standards'.[57] Its lead paragraph was a simple summary of the MOD's position: 'The Ministry of Defence has insisted that newly emerged departmental guidance on the sharing of intelligence derived from torture with allies, remains in line with practices agreed in the aftermath of a series of scandals following the wars in Afghanistan and Iraq.' Close inspection of the documents, however, showed this was clearly disinformation.

The *Guardian* had gone in six short years from being the natural outlet to place stories exposing wrongdoing by the security state to a platform trusted by the security state to amplify its information operations. A once relatively independent media platform had been largely neutralised by UK security services fearful of being exposed further. Which begs the question: where will the next Snowden go?

NOTES

1. 'Fighting Mass Surveillance in the Post-Snowden Era', Privacy International, 20 December 2018, www.privacyinternational.org/impact/fighting-mass-surveillance-post-snowden-era (accessed 26 September 2020).
2. The Defence Press and Broadcasting Advisory Committee, Minutes of a meeting held in the Ministry of Defence, 7 November 2013, www.dsma.

uk/dpbac-meeting-7-november-2013-minutes/ (accessed 26 September 2020).

3. 'How the system works', DSMA website, www.dsma.uk/how-the-system-works/ (accessed 26 September 2020).
4. www.gov.uk/government/people/dominic-wilson--2 (accessed 26 September 2020).
5. www.uk.linkedin.com/in/geoffrey-dodds-67883719 (accessed 26 September 2020).
6. 'How the system works', DSMA website.
7. DPBAC minutes, 7 November 2013.
8. 'D-Notice, June 7, 2013', Guido Fawkes blog, www.order-order.com/2013/06/08/d-notice-june-7-2013/ (accessed 26 September 2020).
9. DPBAC minutes, 7 November 2013.
10. Luke Harding, *The Snowden Files: The Inside Story of the World's Most Wanted Man* (London: Vintage 2014).
11. Nicholas Watt, 'David Cameron Makes Veiled Threat to media over NSA and GCHQ leaks', *Guardian*, 28 October 2013, www.theguardian.com/world/2013/oct/28/david-cameron-nsa-threat-newspapers-guardian-snowden (accessed 26 October 2020).
12. Dominic Ponsford, 'Guardian Spying Revelations Were in Breach of DA-Notice Guidance', *Press Gazette*, 19 June 2013, www.pressgazette.co.uk/guardian-spying-revelations-were-in-breach-of-da-notice-guidance/ (accessed 26 October 2020).
13. DPBAC minutes, 7 November 2013.
14. Julian Borger, 'NSA files: Why the Guardian in London Destroyed Hard Drives of Leaked Files', *Guardian*, 20 August 2013, www.theguardian.com/world/2013/aug/20/nsa-snowden-files-drives-destroyed-london (accessed 26 October 2020).
15. Luke Harding, 'Footage Released of Guardian Editors Destroying Snowden Hard Drives', *Guardian*, 31 January 2014, www.theguardian.com/uk-news/2014/jan/31/footage-released-guardian-editors-snowden-hard-drives-gchq (accessed 26 October 2020).
16. Ibid.
17. Paul Johnson, 'The Surreal Moment the Guardian Destroyed the Snowden Files', *Guardian*, 4 June 2018, www.theguardian.com/us-news/2018/jun/04/surreal-moment-guardian-destroyed-snowden-files (accessed 26 October 2020).
18. DPBAC minutes, 7 November 2013.
19. The Defence Press and Broadcasting Advisory Committee, Minutes of a meeting held in the Ministry of Defence, 8 May 2014, www.dsma.uk/dsma-committee-meeting-8-may-2014-minutes/ (accessed 26 October 2020).
20. Ibid.
21. House of Commons Home Affairs Committee, 'Counter-Terrorism', Seventeenth Report of Session 2013–14, p. 144.

22. DPBAC minutes, 8 May 2014.
23. Ibid and DPBAC minutes, 8 November 2018, www.dsma.uk/dsma-committee-meeting-8-november-2018-minutes/ (accessed 26 October 2020).
24. 'Guardian Appoints Katharine Viner as Editor-in-chief', *Guardian*, 20 March 2015, www.theguardian.com/media/2015/mar/20/guardian-appoints-katharine-viner-new-editor-in-chief (accessed 26 October 2020).
25. Ibid.
26. Jane Martinson, 'Janine Gibson Appointed Editor-in-chief of BuzzFeed UK', *Guardian*, 16 June 2015, www.theguardian.com/media/2015/jun/16/janine-gibson-appointed-editor-in-chief-buzzfeed-uk (accessed 26 October 2020).
27. Ewen MacAskill and Paul Johnson, 'MI5 Head: 'Increasingly Aggressive' Russia a Growing Threat to UK', *Guardian*,1 November 2016, www.theguardian.com/uk-news/2016/oct/31/andrew-parker-increasingly-aggressive-russia-a-growing-threat-to-uk-says-mi5-head (accessed 26 October 2020).
28. Nick Hopkins, 'MI6 Returns to "Tapping Up" in Effort to Recruit Black and Asian Officers', *Guardian*, 2 March 2017, www.tinyurl.com/y5jygzsh (accessed 26 October 2020).
29. Jamie Doward, 'MI6 Chief's Role in Abduction of Gaddafi foe Belhaj Set To Be Revealed', *Observer*, 19 February 2017, www.theguardian.com/world/2017/feb/19/mi6-mark-allen-review-role-gaddafi-libya-abdel-hakim-behaj (accessed 26 October 2020).
30. Vikram Dodd, 'Counter-terror Chief Says Policing Alone Cannot Beat Extremism', *Guardian*, 6 August 2019, www.theguardian.com/uk-news/2019/aug/06/counter-terrorism-chief-calls-for-greater-social-inclusion (accessed 26 October 2020).
31. Vikram Dodd, 'Met Police Examine Vladimir Putin's Role in Salisbury attack', *Guardian*, 7 August 2019, v (accessed 26 October 2020).
32. DPBAC minutes, 8 November 2018.
33. Dominic Ponsford, 'Guardian Set to Break up Six-Strong Team of Investigative Reporters as Journalists Told to Find Other Roles', *Press Gazette*, 19 May 2016, www.pressgazette.co.uk/guardian-set-to-break-up-six-strong-team-of-investigative-reporters-as-journalists-told-to-find-other-roles/2/ (accessed 26 October 2020).
34. 'Guardian Appoints Dan Sabbagh as National News Editor', *Guardian*, 18 January 2013, www.theguardian.com/media/2013/jan/18/guardian-appoints-dan-sabbagh-editor-national-news (accessed 26 October 2020).
35. Luke Harding, 'Revealed: The $2bn Offshore Trail that Leads to Vladimir Putin', *Guardian*, 3 April 2016, www.theguardian.com/news/2016/apr/03/panama-papers-money-hidden-offshore (accessed 26 October 2020).

36. Juliette Garside, 'Fund Run by David Cameron's Father Avoided Paying Tax in Britain', *Guardian*, 4 April 2016, www.theguardian.com/news/2016/apr/04/panama-papers-david-cameron-father-tax-bahamas (accessed 26 October 2020).
37. Carole Cadwalladr, 'When Nigel Farage Met Julian Assange', *Observer*, 23 April 2017, www.theguardian.com/politics/2017/apr/23/when-nigel-farage-met-julian-assange (accessed 26 October 2020).
38. 'Nigel Farage Tells The Truth About THAT Meeting With Julian Assange', *LBC*, 29 October 2017, www.lbc.co.uk/radio/presenters/nigel-farage/nigel-farage-tells-truth-about-meeting-assange/ (accessed 26 October 2020).
39. Stephanie Kirchgaessner, Dan Collyns and Luke Harding, 'Assange's Guest List: The RT Reporters, Hackers and Film-Makers Who Visited Embassy', *Guardian*, 18 May 2018, www.theguardian.com/world/2018/may/18/rt-journalists-visited-julian-assange-ecuador-embassy-london (accessed 26 October 2020).
40. Stephanie Kirchgaessner, Dan Collyns and Luke Harding, 'Revealed: The Secret Christmas Plan to Transfer Assange from the UK to Russia', *Guardian*, 21 September 2018, www.theguardian.com/world/2018/sep/21/julian-assange-russia-ecuador-embassy-london-secret-escape-plan (accessed 26 October 2020).
41. The *Guardian*, 'The Review Panel: Narvaez Decision', 20 December 2019, www.theguardian.com/info/2019/dec/20/the-review-panel-narvaez-decision (accessed 25 September 2020).
42. Luke Harding, and Dan Collyns, 'Manafort Held Secret Talks with Assange in Ecuadorian Embassy', *Guardian*, 27 November 2018, www.theguardian.com/us-news/2018/nov/27/manafort-held-secret-talks-with-assange-in-ecuadorian-embassy (accessed 26 October 2020).
43. Kristinn Hrafnsson, 'The Persecution of Julian Assange: Wikileaks Editor Says Media is Giving the U.S. Cover to Extradite Him', *Newsweek*, 7 December 2018, (accessed 26 October 2020).
44. www.twitter.com/senfeinstein/status/1072977963421978625?lang=en.
45. Tim Shipman, Sean Rayment, Richard Kerbaj and James Lyons, 'Corbyn Hit by Mutiny on Airstrikes', *Sunday Times*, 20 September 2015, www.thetimes.co.uk/article/corbyn-hit-by-mutiny-on-airstrikes-wgrvzpt3old (accessed 26 October 2020).
46. Claire Newell, Hayley Dixon, Luke Heighton and Harry Yorke, 'Exclusive: MI5 Opened File on Jeremy Corbyn Amid Concerns Over His IRA Links', *Daily Telegraph*, 19 May 2017, www.telegraph.co.uk/news/2017/05/19/exclusive-mi5-opened-file-jeremy-corbyn-amid-concerns-ira-links/ (accessed 26 October 2020).
47. Richard Dearlove, 'Jeremy Corbyn is a Danger to this Nation: At MI6, which I Once Ked, he Wouldn't Clear the Security Vetting', *Daily Telegraph*, 7 June 2017, www.telegraph.co.uk/news/2017/06/07/

jeremy-corbyn-danger-nation-mi6-led-wouldnt-clear-security-vetting/ (accessed 26 October 2020).

48. Tim Shipman and Richard Kerbaj, 'MI5 head Andrew Parker Summons Jeremy Corbyn for "Facts of Life" Talk on Terror', *Sunday Times*, 2 September 2018, www.thetimes.co.uk/article/mi5-head-andrew-parker-summons-jeremy-corbyn-for-facts-of-life-talk-on-terror-vwxncthlf (accessed 26 October 2020).
49. Glen Owen and Nick Craven, 'Corbyn's Ex-Communist Top Adviser is Banned from Entering the Ukraine for Three Years After Intelligence Officials Brand Him a National Security Risk "Over Links to Putin"', *Mail on Sunday*, 15 September 2018, (accessed 26 October 2020).
50. Andrew Murray, 'Is the "Deep State" Trying to Undermine Corbyn?', *New Statesman*, 19 September 2018, www.newstatesman.com/politics/uk/2018/09/deep-state-trying-undermine-corbyn (accessed 26 October 2020).
51. 'The Campaign to stop Corbyn – Smears, Racism and Censorship', *Media Lens*, 22 July 2019, www.medialens.org/2019/the-campaign-to-stop-corbyn-smears-racism-and-censorship/ (accessed 26 September 2020).
52. Rowena Mason, 'Three Labour Peers Quit Over Handling of Antisemitism Cases', *Guardian*, 9 July 2019, www.theguardian.com/politics/2019/jul/09/labour-peers-resign-over-handling-of-anti semitism-complaints-triesman-darzi-turnberg (accessed 26 October 2020).
53. The Shami Chakrabati Inquiry, 30 April 2016, www.labour.org.uk/wp-content/uploads/2017/10/Chakrabarti-Inquiry-Report-30June16.pdf (accessed 26 September 2020), p. 1.
54. Tom D. Rogers, 'YouGov Polls Show Anti-Semitism in Labour Has Actually Reduced Dramatically since Jeremy Corbyn Became Leader', *Evolve Politics*, 29 March 2018, www.evolvepolitics.com/yougov-polls-show-anti-semitism-in-labour-has-actually-reduced-dramatically-since-jeremy-corbyn-became-leader/ (accessed 26 September 2020).
55. Jessica Murray, 'Nearly Half of Tory Members Would Not Want Muslim PM – poll', *Guardian*, 24 June 2019, www.theguardian.com/politics/2019/jun/24/tory-members-would-not-want-muslim-prime-minister-islamophobia-survey (accessed 26 October 2020).
56. Lucy Fisher, 'Torture: Britain Breaks Law in Ministry of Defence Secret Policy', *The Times*, 20 May 2019, www.thetimes.co.uk/article/torture-britain-breaks-law-in-ministry-of-defence-secret-policy-2rl5dn2kd (accessed 26 October 2020).
57. Dan Sabbagh, 'MoD Says Revised Torture Guidance Does Not Lower Standards', *Guardian*, 20 May 2019, www.theguardian.com/law/2019/may/20/rewritten-mod-guidance-could-leave-door-open-for-torture (accessed 26 October 2020).

10

Corruption in the Fourth Estate: How the *Guardian* Exposed Phone Hacking and Reneged on Reform of Press Regulation

Natalie Fenton

INTRODUCTION

This chapter explores an important period in the *Guardian*'s history: the phone hacking scandal and the Leveson Inquiry into the culture, practices and ethics of the press. For four years (2009–13) the *Guardian* fought first to expose criminality and corruption in the press that had infected the police and the world of politics, and second to secure meaningful reform of press regulation. For this it received considerable praise. Then, without explanation, it dropped the issue, and when Parliament implemented the Leveson recommendations on the regulation of the press, it refused to participate. The effect of this was to make the newspaper complicit in the very cover-up it had set out to expose. This chapter reviews the events and examines a range of possible factors, including professional/industry dynamics, the state/security context and the commercial/business backdrop, that might explain why the *Guardian* changed its mind about such a crucial debate.

On 8 July 2009, the *Guardian* published an article by the freelance investigative journalist Nick Davies under the headline: 'Murdoch papers paid £1million to gag phone hacking victims'. The thrust of the story was that Rupert Murdoch's UK newspaper arm, News International (now News UK), had made secret payments to victims in an attempt to cover up the use of illegal voicemail interception by journalists at the *News of the World*, then Britain's biggest-selling paper.

As part of the cover-up, it was claimed, Murdoch executives had also misled the public, a parliamentary select committee and the press industry's own complaints body, the Press Complaints Commission. Grave as these allegations were for the company, they had wider implications. The Metropolitan Police had investigated hacking at the *News of the World* three years earlier and prosecuted only one journalist. On Davies's evidence it seemed that they had missed, or turned a blind eye to, much more extensive lawbreaking. Further, the deputy editor and then editor of the *News of the World* at the time the hacking occurred was Andy Coulson, who by 2009 had become director of communications for David Cameron, the leader of the opposition Conservative Party.

The allegations were at first fiercely denied on all sides, but the *Guardian* continued to report on the affair, revealing new evidence, and receiving important support from a *New York Times* investigation and the report of an inquiry by the House of Commons Culture, Media and Sport Select Committee.[1] News International's defences eventually crumbled, as did those of the Metropolitan Police and Coulson. The final breakthrough came in July 2011, when Davies revealed in the *Guardian* that *News of the World* journalists had illegally hacked the voicemail of murdered teenager Milly Dowler. This stirred a whirlwind of public fury. Within days, the *News of the World* had closed for good and a compromised David Cameron, by now prime minister in the coalition government, had ordered a public inquiry under a senior judge, Sir Brian Leveson.[2]

The *Guardian* played an important role in the inquiry, much of which was broadcast, and which commanded considerable public interest. The judge's principal mission was to make recommendations for reform of press regulation and the *Guardian* adopted a firm and clear stance on this. The Press Complaints Commission, having failed to detect phone hacking on its own account, had agreed to investigate once alerted by the *Guardian* report – only to surmise that there was nothing to find and it was the *Guardian*'s journalism that was at fault. The *Guardian* pointed to excessive industry influence over the PCC as the problem and insisted at the inquiry that any replacement body must be fully independent and have teeth:

> A new regulator clearly has to have teeth – the power to intervene and investigate meaningfully and to impose significant sanctions. I note that you [Lord Justice Leveson] have questioned the overly binary debate of statutory versus self regulation. We agree. If 'statutory regulation' implies some form of state control, or licensing of journalists, we would oppose it. The crucial issues, it seems to us, are funding and cost; the expertise/independence of those who run it and serve on it; and that it regulates the whole market – subject, of course, to the definitional difficulties of describing what the 'market' is, or will be. If statute can help make independent self-regulation work well, then we would welcome suggested use of statute to be scrutinised properly against concerns of press freedom.[3]

The inquiry report, published in November 2012, made detailed recommendations for regulatory reform, stressed the need for the system to be fully independent of both industry and government, and called for statutory underpinning of a reformed system.

Four months of political negotiations followed as the Conservatives, their governing partners the Liberal Democrats and the Labour opposition sought consensus on implementing the recommendations. During this period the *Guardian*'s role in events altered. Having been a leading player since Davies' first report in 2009, the paper now stepped back. By the time cross-party agreement had been reached in March 2013, and a Royal Charter on press self-regulation approved by all parties in Parliament, the newspaper had become a passive bystander on the issue. To the disappointment of politicians, campaigners, media academics, victims of press abuse and many of its own readers, it refused to engage with the new Leveson-compliant system. Later, when the press industry defiantly established its own (non-independent) self-regulator, similar to the discredited PCC, that did not meet Leveson standards, the *Guardian* also declined to join that organisation, the Independent Press Standards Organisation (IPSO).

To outward appearances, the paper had either changed its mind on the whole issue of independent regulatory reform – though no statement to that effect was ever made – or it had simply lost interest. And not only did the policy of the *Guardian* as an institution change, but its journalism also altered course. Its scrutiny of other papers' conduct and its criticism of their rhetoric all but ceased. No one knows what the result would have been if the *Guardian* had embraced regulation under the Royal Charter, but it is safe to say that the cause of reform and the drive for higher standards across UK journalism were significantly weakened by its refusal to do so.

The principal beneficiaries of that decision were the national newspapers whose power, and whose regulatory system, the *Guardian* had previously challenged. Meanwhile, IPSO, the PCC's replacement, is now the dominant regulator for the national press and continues along the lines of its predecessor in failing to protect members of the public whose rights continue to be traduced by bad journalism.[4] In this situation, it seems that the *Guardian* has abandoned its role as a champion of journalistic ethics, thus affording rival papers more licence to degrade the profession by fabrication, intrusion and collusion with politicians. It is no exaggeration to say that, by its retreat on these matters, the *Guardian* has made itself a silent accomplice in the very corruption it once seemed determined to root out. So, what lay behind this choice?

PROFESSIONAL/INDUSTRY DYNAMICS

The political journalist and broadcaster Peter Oborne has written that the British national press operates 'a system of *omertá* so strict that it would secure a nod of approbation from the heads of the big New York crime families.'[5] What this means, and few would seriously dispute it, is that newspapers steer well clear of investigating each other's conduct and indeed tend to avoid even reporting on each other's misfortunes. When this code was broken by Nick Davies and the editor who published his stories about hacking, Alan Rusbridger, they were not applauded by the industry, but shunned or, worse, denounced in leader columns. Even when the *Guardian* broke the story about the hacking of Milly Dowler's phone and it was the main story across broadcast news bulletins, several national papers chose to keep it off the front page. This was a sensational news story on their doorstep that was gripping and horrifying the public and it was clear that not only would most papers prefer it to go away, but that they deeply resented the *Guardian*'s initiative.

It would be easy to dismiss this as corporate rather than journalistic solidarity – the choice of executives and editors rallying around a peer organisation that was under attack. But little evidence has ever emerged that working journalists at other national newspapers – *The Times*, the *Daily Mail* and the *Daily Telegraph*, for example – took a different view from their bosses. Nothing suggests that there were any newsroom revolts, or even protests, over what amounted to a collective decision to isolate and shun the *Guardian*. If there is such a thing as journalistic solidarity across the national newspaper industry, it did not operate in favour of a paper that sought to expose wrongdoing and corruption in their midst – rather it upheld the *omertá*.[6]

And not only had the *Guardian* broken journalistic ranks, but this relatively small organisation had also taken on a global media giant in Rupert Murdoch's News Corp, a company of unbridled wealth and power known for its ruthlessness. As the Leveson Inquiry revealed, its tabloid journalists were well versed in dirty tricks, illegal activity and lies, and its broadsheets were not above playing a tough game. According to Nick Davies, John Witherow (then editor of the *Sunday Times*) had once responded to Alan Rusbridger about a story on his paper in the *Guardian*, 'I will always retaliate and I have many more readers than you do, so I can cause you much more pain.'[7] Rusbridger himself spoke about the 'fear, dominance and immunity . . . of this very big, very powerful company and the man who ran it'.[8] Those who crossed the company, the *Guardian* editor asserted, were likely to be put under surveillance themselves and ran the risk of seeing their private affairs laid bare to millions of people by papers whose legal departments would defend any action at any cost.

Further, by attacking and exposing the failures of the Press Complaints Commission, the *Guardian* was tearing off a veneer of accountability that had been carefully created, protected and polished by the big newspaper groups over a period of 20 years. Industry propaganda about the effectiveness and value of the PCC had been relentless, but the *Guardian*'s exposures gave new prominence to doubts and criticisms building over a long period. Rusbridger resigned from the Editor's Code of Practice Committee when the PCC declared that the problem of phone hacking had been limited to one rogue reporter, effectively rubbishing the *Guardian*'s investigation. When Nick Davies gave evidence to the Culture, Media and Sport Select Committee in 2009, he stated that the PCC had a 'real will to avoid uncovering the truth about phone hacking'.[9] In 2010, Rusbridger told the House of

Commons Select Committee: 'I believe in effective self-regulation, and I have made myself very unpopular within the industry because I think that sometimes the PCC has not been effective.'[10]

These were not passing emotions in the corporate national press. When editors and proprietors appeared before the Leveson Inquiry, many felt they had been humiliated and bullied and their resentment towards the *Guardian* can only have increased. As for working journalists, they never rallied to the cause of honest practice and ethical probity, either collectively or in any numbers as individuals. Nor did they show any interest in effective, independent regulation; instead, there was a surly sense of grievance, a feeling that all journalists were being condemned as criminals, and this too rebounded on the *Guardian*. Thus, by the time the Leveson Report was published in late 2012 the paper still faced the full wrath of the industry, and the desire to see it put in its place was as strong as ever. Rusbridger has written that not long after this – which was roughly the time when the *Guardian*'s change of heart first manifested itself – he met a senior executive from one of the big newspaper companies at the Savoy Hotel who explained to him that the industry would defy Leveson and Parliament and would set up a new regulator on its own terms. Rusbridger said he would think about it. The reply was: 'If you don't do what we want then I wouldn't want to be in your shoes.'[11]

STATE/SECURITY CONTEXT

Besides alienating the industry, the *Guardian*'s campaigning journalism, as we have seen, had implications both for the police and in the political world. The Metropolitan Police was gravely embarrassed. Its first response to Davies' 2009 story was to insist that hacking had been satisfactorily dealt with in 2006–7 and the matter was closed – a stance which, incidentally, perfectly suited the interests of the Murdoch company. It took more than a year, but eventually this defiance broke down, the case was reopened, and a series of high-level investigations were launched which would ultimately result in a string of convictions. The officer responsible for the initial denial, Assistant Commissioner John Yates, was obliged to resign. Meanwhile the public learned of an astonishing intimacy, at the very highest level, between the police and the Murdoch press. This prompted the resignation of the then

Commissioner, Sir Paul Stephenson. Either directly, through its own journalism, or indirectly, through the activities of the Leveson Inquiry it did so much to bring about, the *Guardian* had shaken the country's leading police force to its foundations.

In politics, Andy Coulson was initially the lightning rod in the storm. A senior figure in 10 Downing Street, he doggedly denied that he had ever been aware of the illegal hacking that had gone on under his nose when he was editing the *News of the World*, but the media wizard proved unable to shake off the doubts and in time he too had to resign. (He would later be convicted of conspiracy to hack phones.) Coulson's departure had the effect of moving politics in general, and some individual politicians, into the front line of suspicion. Questions were asked about David Cameron: how close was he to Rupert Murdoch and to the latter's CEO in Britain, Rebekah Brooks? What had he known about Coulson when he hired him, and why did he ignore warnings that the former editor was toxic? What were his relations with other press bosses and how much influence did he allow them? Many of the same questions were asked about previous prime ministers. Had any ministers – home secretaries for example – known about hacking? Could the failure of the police to properly investigate the *Guardian*'s allegations owe something to political influence? And how significant was it that a number of government ministers down the years had themselves been targets of hacking, including ministers with sensitive security responsibilities?

The PCC was also tangled up in politics, not least because virtually all of its chairs since its foundation in 1991 had been senior Conservative figures. The whole issue of regulatory reform raised profound concerns about the relationship between the press and the state. Rusbridger agonised over this in his second appearance in front of the Inquiry in January 2012, settling on the view that it was indeed possible to have press regulation set up by statute and still operate independently of government:

> There's a question about whether the regulator needs to be set up by statute or whether it could be something that recognises the powers of the regulator. I was trying to clear my own thinking on this and rang up the Irish ombudsman this morning because it looked to me as though the Irish Press Council had been set up by statute, and he

said, 'No, that's not quite right; it was set up in a piece of legislation in the Defamation Act that recognised the role of the regulator.' So that's one bit. The second bit is this mediation and adjudication role. As I understand the law, we should be talking about adjudication rather than arbitration, and there are parallels in law where it can be compulsory to submit yourself to adjudication before going to the courts . . . if you're saying that there would need to be a statute passed in order to give that force, I wouldn't be against the use of statute. If you made that it was written into law so that the powers this regulator had in order to be able to perform this adjudication function if the law needs to be changed by statute in order to do that, I would have thought that is something the industry ought to welcome, because it's going to help us out of this problem of libel. The third bit, which is the most wriggly and difficult bit, is how you deal with refuseniks and whether you need a statute in order to compel everybody in order to be able to then have the system that works for everybody, and I think that's the most difficult bit. In a way, it's connected with the first bit, i.e. do you set it up by statute or are you just recognising this organisation by [statute]?

[...] this debate about statute is a fairly central one. Again, I think most editors, most people in the industry [...], we all utterly reject anything that looks like state licensing and we reject anything that looks like politicians or the state having any kind of say in the content of newspapers. So I'm not surprised that [...] there's a kind of visceral rejection of it, but I think one of the things the Inquiry has done is to open this up as a more nuanced question than perhaps it would have seemed to us – I include myself in that – previously. In my previous answer about these different types of what we mean by 'statute', I hope I've shown that I have moved in my thinking and that there are significant challenges to all of us to think about that if we want to reap what could be the benefits of what I hope you'll propose as well as you know, I think what the blunt truth about our industry is that we've been under-regulated and over-legislated, and if we can get a better balance of better legislation and better regulation as a result of it, then that, to my mind, is a good thing.[12]

As Rusbridger noted, the rejection of the idea of the state having any kind of say in the content of newspapers was 'visceral' across the industry and the whole idea of government or parliamentary involvement with press regulation was widely viewed as taboo. There was much irony in this, considering for example the close relationship between newspaper figures and prime ministers and the role of politicians at the PCC, but there was no denying that, if change were to come, journalists, editors and proprietors would have to be persuaded that it would not usher in what they saw as unwarranted state influence. This would be the chosen battleground of the corporate newspapers.

When Sir Brian Leveson reported in November 2012, he emphasised that his recommendations were about enshrining press freedom and ensuring that any subsequent regulatory system was independent from government, albeit underpinned by statute. The scheme he proposed placed regulation at least two arms' length from government. A new public body would be created by statute, free-standing and independent of government influence, whose job would be to verify periodically whether press regulation – set up by the press itself – conformed to certain standards required to give the public protection from the effects of unethical journalism. No minister could meddle, nor could Parliament itself. Although Sir Brian declared categorically that '[t]his is not, and cannot reasonably or fairly be characterised as, statutory regulation of the press',[13] that is exactly how it was portrayed, at the fullest possible volume, by the mainstream press. Their strategy for defeating a measure that would have seen their journalism genuinely and meaningfully accountable before an independent body was to assert relentlessly, and in defiance of the facts, that this was, if not outright censorship, then a slippery slope leading inevitably to that fate. 'Freedom', indeed, became *the* narrative device to allow the industry to sidestep the problems thrown up by the hacking scandal, and freedom of the press meant *all* activities of the press.

It is important to note here that this rhetoric of freedom, while it may have tugged at the viscera of journalists, did not significantly alter the views of the majority of parliamentarians or the public. Although David Cameron's first response after the publication of the report was to say that he could not countenance legislation of the kind recommended, as it would be 'crossing the Rubicon', and although his party showed a persistent willingness to water down the reforms in ways desired by the newspaper chiefs, the parliamentary arithmetic was against Cameron. The Conservatives were constrained by the lack of a Commons majority while the Liberal Democrats and Labour strongly supported the Leveson scheme. The negotiations were long and tangled but after four months a unique cross-party agreement was reached on the terms of the Royal Charter. By this point, March 2013, the *Guardian* was at best lukewarm on the whole issue, and insofar as it articulated its reservations, these appeared increasingly influenced by the 'press freedom' arguments. The paper took special exception to the use of a Royal Charter, which had been chosen specifically to avoid legislation. This was, unarguably, an antique instrument, but no one has ever been able to make a substantive case that it was not up to the job required or that, in the context of the Leveson package of measures (which included some legislation), it was vulnerable to 'slippery-slope' abuse.

After Parliament approved the Royal Charter there came a hiatus. The corporate newspapers launched a long and doomed attempt to block it through the courts, and after that came to nothing, the cumbersome process began of establishing the new, independent recognition body, the Press Recognition Panel. The industry, meanwhile, was slowly shaping its successor body to the PCC. In this interval the *Guardian* remained uncommitted, but as it drifted something happened which may have influenced its thinking.

In June 2013 the *Guardian*, along with partner publications in other countries, began publishing the revelations of the National Security Agency (NSA) whistle-blower, Edward Snowden, about the scale of global surveillance. The British government and its security agencies, notably Government Communications Headquarters (GCHQ), were deeply implicated, and after a few weeks of dithering, David Cameron's government ordered the *Guardian* to hand over the files received from Snowden and to cease publishing their contents. The Snowden story had led to more than 100 interactions between the prime minister's office, the White House and US and UK intelligence agencies. The *Guardian* reported that the cabinet secretary, Jeremy Heywood, declared that '[a] lot of people in government think you should be closed down.'[14] The consequence was, in its way, sensational, as Rusbridger himself acknowledged:

> On Saturday 20 July three *Guardian* executives armed with angle grinders and drills took it in turns to dismember an array of circuit

> boards, drives and chips under the watchful instructions of the mysterious men from GCHQ.[15]

Just four months after the Royal Charter was approved by Parliament, therefore, the *Guardian* experienced unprecedented forms of state intervention and intimidation.

COMMERCIAL/BUSINESS FACTORS

At the time of the Leveson Inquiry, newspaper circulation and press advertising revenue had already been in steep decline for years, while increasingly desperate efforts to replace these revenue streams with online cash had not borne fruit. Every newspaper felt the pressure, and a good deal of evidence at the Inquiry was devoted to their financial woes. The *Guardian* was no exception. Indeed, as a small newspaper company without billionaire backing of the kind available to several of its rivals, it was especially vulnerable and felt keenly the accumulated power and dominance of the Murdoch empire (which at the time included over 40% of national newspapers in the UK).

In 2005 it had invested very heavily in a switch to a Berliner format, but while this brought short-term benefits, by 2011 those were wearing off. The paper was also establishing itself as a global online brand, and in this it had been more successful than any of its British rivals apart from the *Daily Mail*. Again, however, the expansion had been costly and was not matched by sufficient revenue increases. Although the paper's owners, the Scott Trust, still had at that time the buffer of its very valuable stake in *Auto Trader* magazine to help it fend off the worst, the *Guardian* itself was losing money and was unquestionably commercially vulnerable.

It was a business climate in which many editors and managers would consider ways of saving costs by cooperation with rivals, yet in 2009 the *Guardian* had all but declared war on the industry, and in particular on its richest and most powerful player, News International. As we have seen, those adversaries had more than once threatened the *Guardian* with ruin. Whether that was really in their power is doubtful, but it is certain that they were in a position to exclude the paper from any collective efforts they made to prop up income and slow the commercial decline. The evidence, however, suggests that this did not happen. Although the picture is far from clear, it seems likely that the *Guardian* group remained throughout the press regulation debates a part of the club of newspaper companies, the News Media Association (NMA), the body that ultimately controls IPSO. It is certainly a member at the time of writing in 2020. It has also been a member since 2012 of Newsworks, the collective 'news brand marketing' organisation which pools industry effort in the recruitment of advertisers. In 2017 it also joined the Murdoch and *Telegraph* papers in a joint online advertising sales club called The Ozone Project. And still more recently, in 2020, it participated, through the NMA, in a £35m government advertising and advertorial project designed to support mainstream newspapers during the Covid crisis – even though the scheme excluded from its beneficiaries even more vulnerable small independent publications.[16]

An indicator of the closeness that now exists between the *Guardian* and the organisations with which it was once in conflict, and of its possible commercial context, can be seen in the paper's response to the 'Leveson 2' debate and its role in the sequel. That the Leveson Inquiry would have a second phase had been foreseen from the outset: consideration of the criminal aspects of the scandal and their possible lessons had to be deferred in 2011 because prosecutions were pending, and the issues were *sub judice*. The power to decide when the time was right lay with the government and the Conservatives, in power in their own right from 2015, chose to delay. By 2018, however, a further delay was no longer practical and the government, responding to eager entreaties from the newspaper publishers, decided to ask Parliament simply to cancel Leveson part two. The affair was remarkable in many ways, but what concerns us here is the stance of the *Guardian*. Having exposed the criminality in the first place, the title might have been expected to press its investigation to the conclusion that was originally envisaged – in particular since no senior news executive, apart from Andy Coulson, had ever been prosecuted. It had emerged in the intervening years, moreover, that criminal conduct was rife in more newspapers than Nick Davies had initially reported, and although the role of senior figures had been explicitly admitted, again none had been prosecuted. Yet just as it abandoned the cause of regulatory reform, the *Guardian* also abandoned the pursuit of justice in the industry. Its explanation was revealing:

> Leveson 2 would ultimately end up like a driver learning to steer by looking in the rear-view mirror at the road behind rather than the one ahead. Newspapers today face an existential threat due to a combination of social, technical and economic factors. Their circulation has fallen by a third since the Leveson Inquiry. In the last decade hundreds of newspapers have closed. Digital disordering of news has sucked revenues out of print. While more people than ever have access to newspaper content, it is the platforms like Facebook that have hoovered up the profits. Tech giants stood by as the information economy became contaminated by fake news and malicious foreign actors.[17]

The cancellation of the second part of the inquiry was narrowly approved by Parliament after the government had offered what it presented as a more forward-looking alternative: a 'review' of the future of journalism. This would be chaired by Dame Frances Cairncross, with a *Guardian* executive, Matt Rogerson, on her panel of advisers alongside such mainstream industry figures such as the emeritus editor of the *Mail* papers, Peter Wright, and Ashley Highfield, former CEO of the regional newspaper group Johnston Press. Cairncross in due course produced a report whose principal recommendations were rejected by the government. It is not that cynical to suggest that the review's true purpose, at least in the eyes of the government, had already been served as soon as part two of the Leveson Inquiry was cancelled, and that the *Guardian* had been at best a dupe and at worst an accomplice.

CONCLUSION

The tenacity and courage shown by the *Guardian* in exposing the egregious behaviour of large sections of the national press and taking on the Murdoch empire was short-lived. Although it still remains outside IPSO, in all other respects the paper gradually retreated to its former relationship with the rest of the news industry. In other words, the whistle-blower in the national press packed away its whistle and conformed. This chapter has discussed some contextual factors that may help us to understand why this accommodation with press power happened.

The life of the whistle-blower is a lonely one, and as we have seen the *Guardian* experienced two or three years of animosity at corporate level from almost all its national rivals. Nor did working journalists rally to support a title that exposed large-scale criminality in their midst. Rather, it looks as though a journalistic cabal dedicated to washing other people's dirty linen in public did not like it when it happened to them. We have also seen how a rhetoric of press freedom, that at first the paper dismissed, later came to be adopted. The nuances of the debate throughout the Leveson Inquiry on the subject of the role of statute in press regulation were forgotten (or dropped), and within a couple of years a visceral opposition to any degree of state intervention became the *Guardian*'s official line – a position made easier by the Snowden affair. And then there are the unflinching demands of the market: the *Guardian* was a small, vulnerable player here and the financial threats of the twenty-first century were (and to some extent remain) existential. Getting back into bed with the big players was certainly the easy way to proceed and some may have seen it as the only one. But if the *Guardian* saved itself, it did so at the expense of other casualties.

At the time of writing the key question raised by Nick Davies's journalism in 2009 – who is running the country: the government or the press, and for whose benefit? – is more pressing than ever. At the same time the culture, practices and ethics of the national press remain unreformed with grave consequences for UK democracy. Newspapers break their own code every day with impunity, poisoning the flow of information to the public and, to borrow the words of the Leveson Report, wreaking havoc in the lives of innocent people.

NOTES

1. House of Commons, *Press standards, Privacy and Libel*, (Culture, Media and Sport: Second Report, 2010) http://www.publications.parliament.uk/pa/cm200910/cmselect/cmcumeds/362/36202.htm (accessed 15 September 2020).
2. See Binakuromo Ogbebor, *British Media Coverage of the Press Reform Debate* (London: Palgrave Macmillan, 2020) for a detailed account of the Leveson Inquiry and reporting of the press regulation debate.
3. Alan Rusbridger's statement to the Leveson Inquiry, *Guardian*, 16 November 2012, http://www.guardian.co.uk/media/2011/nov/16/

alan-rusbridger-statement-leveson-inquiry (accessed 15 September 2020).

4. Another press regulator IMPRESS was set up by a free speech campaigner Jonathan Heawood. IMPRESS is Leveson compliant and was recognised as an approved regulator on 25 October 2016. The Royal Charter system under which IMPRESS was endorsed didn't go as far as Rusbridger had said was acceptable in evidence to the Leveson Inquiry in terms of statutory recognition, statutory incentives and a differential cost regime. Yet the *Guardian* also refused to sign up to IMPRESS. Without a single national newspaper willing to support the new regulatory framework the system was essentially consigned to small independent media who understood the benefits and were not subject to pressure from powerful editors and owners of the national press (and had not engaged in phone hacking).
5. Peter Oborne, 'Does David Cameron Really Need This Tainted Man Beside Him?', *Guardian*, 4 April 2010, http://www.guardian.co.uk/commentisfree/2010/apr/04/david-cameron-andycoulson-election (accessed 15 September 2020).
6. Some former editors did occasionally break ranks to speak out against the practices exposed in the Leveson Inquiry and in support of the *Guardian* but as they had already largely left the profession, they had little to lose and the support of the general public to gain (e.g., former editor of *The Times* and *Sunday Times*, Sir Harry Evans; former editor of the *Independent*, Chris Blackhurst; former editor of the *Sun*, David Yelland; and former editor of the *Daily Mirror* Roy Greenslade). The occasional journalist was also brave enough to acknowledge what the *Guardian* had exposed but again these were usually those who operated as commentators or who had stepped out of the fray of mainstream national newspaper journalism. Most, however, sided with the Murdoch press: fearful of their future employment or aware that the dark arts of newspaper journalism may spread far and wide and that it wasn't wise to wash the industry's dirty linen in public.
7. Quoted in Nick Davies, *Hack Attack: How the Truth Caught up with Rupert Murdoch* (London: Chatto and Windus, 2014), p. 62.
8. Alan Rusbridger, 'Hacking Away at the Truth: Alan Rusbridger's Orwell Lecture', *Guardian*, 10 November, 2011, http://www.guardian.co.uk/media/2011/nov/10/phone-hacking-truth-alan-rusbridger-orwell (accessed 15 September 2020).
9. Nick Davies, *Uncorrected Transcript of Oral Evidence*, HC 275-vi, House of Commons, culture, media and sport committee, 21 April 2009, http://www.publications.parliament.uk/pa/cm200809/cmselect/cmcumeds/uc275-vi/uc27502.htm (accessed 15 September 2020).
10. House of Commons, *Press Standards*, Q1282).
11. Alan Rusbridger, *Breaking News: The Remaking of Journalism and Why it Matters Now* (Edinburgh: Canongate, 2018), p. 260).

12. Leveson Inquiry hearing, 17 January 2012, https://www.discoverleveson.com/hearing/2012-01-17/950/?bc=1 (accessed 15 September 2020).
13. Lord Justice Leveson, 'Closing Speech', 24 July 2012, https://www.discoverleveson.com/hearing/closingspeech/1118 (accessed 15 September 2020).
14. Luke Harding, 'Footage Released of Guardian Editors Destroying Snowden Hard Drives', 31 January 2014, https://www.theguardian.com/uk-news/2014/jan/31/footage-released-guardian-editors-snowden-hard-drives-gchq (accessed 15 September 2020).
15. Rusbridger, *Breaking News*, p. 315.
16. Brian Cathcart, 'Why is the *Guardian* Accepting a Dodgy Subsidy from This Dodgy Government?', *Bylinetimes*, 5 June 2020, https://bylinetimes.com/2020/06/05/why-is-the-guardian-accepting-a-dodgy-subsidy-from-this-dodgy-government/ (accessed 15 September 2020).
17. 'The *Guardian* View on Leveson Part Two: Look Ahead, Not Behind', *Guardian*, 1 March 2018, https://www.theguardian.com/commentisfree/2018/mar/01/the-guardian-view-on-leveson-part-two-look-ahead-not-behind (accessed 15 September 2020).

11
The *Guardian*, Corbynism and Antisemitism

Justin Schlosberg

INTRODUCTION

There is nothing especially new about the *Guardian*'s uncertain and somewhat fluctuating political consciousness, caught between being the token broadsheet of 'the left' as well as the vanguard of quintessentially liberal (centrist) values. Yet it was Jeremy Corbyn's leadership of the Labour Party from 2015 to 2020 which not only exposed and exacerbated this conflicting identity, but ultimately appeared to resolve it: the *Guardian* ended up editorially distancing itself from the left in a manner and to an extent that was without precedent.

This editorial (re)alignment was neither wholesale nor immediate. Indeed, the tone of the *Guardian*'s commentary on Corbyn's initial leadership candidacy in 2015 was remarkably different to how it evolved after he was elected.[1] It also carried both letters and occasional comment pieces in defence of Corbyn and, in keeping with tradition, endorsed Labour in both the 2017 and 2019 elections, offering qualified praise for the 'bold' pledges contained within the party's manifesto on each occasion.[2]

Yet, on the whole, comment pieces were aggressively hostile towards the Corbyn leadership; opinion editorials persistently critical; and the selection of issues and sources in news coverage overwhelmingly favoured the accounts and agendas of Corbyn's detractors. This editorial leaning was hardly out of step with the paper's entrenched and institutional culture of liberalism, or indeed a confluence of political economic pressures that, by 2015, were uniformly pushing in the direction of the political centre.

Of greater concern was a stream of flawed and inaccurate reporting on Corbyn, especially in the context of allegations of antisemitism.

Distortions and inaccuracies were systematic in nature and not easily explained as random, anomalous or an inevitable function of newsroom and news cycle pressures. At the same time, however, there exists no evidence of a conscious and concerted effort by the editorial team to delegitimise the Corbyn project, and the *Guardian*'s performance in this respect is too easily dismissed as just another front in the establishment war on the left. This chapter starts from the supposition that there were particular, and to some extent unique, drivers that oriented *Guardian* journalists towards certain sources and frames, and produced remarkable blind spots in relation to others. The Corbyn moment thus presents a challenge for scholars and activists alike to understand how and why alternative perspectives – and in some cases essential facts – were overlooked at a time of such acute political crisis and instability in Britain.

The chapter does not provide definitive answers to these questions, but rather attempts to sketch out some possibilities. It first examines the immediate historical context and the political economic backdrop to the *Guardian*'s journey back from market isolationism in the aftermath of the phone hacking scandal and Snowden revelations. Not unlike its dominant framing of the Corbyn movement, the *Guardian* itself was wrestling with the label of pariah newspaper throughout much of the five years preceding Corbyn's leadership.

This discussion is followed by a reflection on an in-depth case study of the *Guardian*'s coverage in relation to antisemitism in Corbyn's Labour. Based on data collected for a study on broadcasting and online news coverage over the summer of 2018,[3] the analysis documents straightforward examples of repeated inaccuracies and distortions in the *Guardian*'s online output. Both the particular context and language adopted in these examples suggests that journalistic failures were most likely the result of an instinctive deference to particular sources – especially within the Labour Party – combined with a tendency to view the Corbyn movement through the prism of populism.

BEYOND THE PALE

The *Guardian*'s coverage of Corbyn and Corbynism warrants special scrutiny because of the title's unique position as one of the most trusted and largest UK newspaper brands, as well as the sole traditional Labour-leaning broadsheet. This puts it on the front lines of consensus framing: the range and relative prominence of voices, perspectives and sources featured in the *Guardian* is likely to play a key role in shaping the contours and limits of 'acceptable' left-liberal discourse, and in drawing the definitional boundaries between the 'moderate' and the 'hard' in left of centre politics; and in distinguishing the mainstream from the extreme. This amounts to what scholars have traditionally termed definitional power or, perhaps more acutely, the power of legitimation.[4]

Of course, no newspaper operates in an editorial vacuum, and the *Guardian*'s news selection decisions are likely influenced by competitive as well as collective pressures. Ironically, the ascendance of Corbynism coincided with the end of a unique historical moment in which the *Guardian* itself had become well and truly ostracised from the mainstream press. Its rogue status was affirmed in 2013 when then editor-in-chief Alan Rusbridger was hauled before MPs and asked whether he loved his country. This occurred not long after the partner of one of his journalists was detained by the police under anti-terror legislation and, most extraordinary of all, security service personnel entered the *Guardian*'s office to oversee destruction of a hard drive containing source material.[5]

All this took place amidst the controversy and furore surrounding the paper's coverage of the national security files leaked by Edward Snowden. But the wider national press succeeded in pivoting the story towards one that centred on the *Guardian* itself, framing it as an irresponsible newspaper playing havoc with national security.[6] Even the *Independent* – a title hardly known for doing the state's bidding – published an extraordinary editorial lead condemning the *Guardian*'s decision to publish the leaks.[7]

The compliant reaction of the wider UK press to the Snowden revelations is very different to that of their counterparts in the US and, on one level, reflected little more than the peculiar ideological disposition of the British press.[8] But for Rusbridger, the chief cause had more to do with the *Guardian*'s lead role in exposing the phone hacking scandal at the former *News of the World* just two years earlier: 'They held the *Guardian* responsible for journalists being sent to prison and having their homes raided by police in the middle of the night.'[9]

Either way, the episode marked a period in which the *Guardian* found itself very much beyond the pale of mainstream news discourse. Crucially, however, the Snowden revelations precipitated a turning point at which the *Guardian* and the rest of Fleet Street closed ranks against further scrutiny and press reform. The first step was to join with the rest of Fleet Street in rejecting the system of 'recognised' self-regulation introduced by cross-party agreement, following the recommendations of the Leveson Inquiry in 2012. But perhaps the most crucial moment came in 2018, when the *Guardian* called for the government to scrap the planned second half of the Leveson Inquiry.[10] This stage of the inquiry was originally intended to get to the bottom of the very webs of institutional corruption which the paper had first uncovered. It marked an extraordinary concession to the rest of Fleet Street and the cementing of a transition that was already well underway by the time Corbyn became leader of the Labour Party in 2015.

THE POLITICAL ECONOMY OF ANTI-CORBYNISM

This about turn coincided with the peak of controversy surrounding Corbyn(ism). As Mike Wayne points out in Chapter 14, Corbyn was perceived by many of the *Guardian*'s chief commentators as a left-wing outlier whose disdain for Parliament (as well as the media) mirrored that of hard right figures such as Nigel Farage. From the outset of his leadership, the 'extreme' framing of Corbyn and Corbynism across the mainstream press was thus immediately resonant for an institution whose embedded liberal values were seemingly under assault from both sides of the political spectrum.

But there were pre-existing and wider political economic factors at play which pushed in the direction of both centrism and a closer alignment with the rest of the mainstream press. Under Rusbridger, the *Guardian* followed a strategic approach to the digital transition that avoided paywalls and sought to establish a leading presence online through a string of global news exclusives. Under his successor Katharine Viner, the focus has shifted towards capitalising on these gains through a membership model that has proved highly successful.[11]

Although this success was tempered by cuts announced in 2020,[12] declining revenues were not the result of members and subscribers rejecting the paper's coverage of Corbyn, as some critics assumed.

Indeed, revenue from both members and *ad hoc* donations increased substantially in the year to April 2020, as did its readership in general.[13] At first glance this seems at odds with the *Guardian*'s by now widely-recognised antipathy to the Corbyn project, not least given that its own consumer market research found that a majority of its readers backed Corbyn in the first leadership election.[14] But if we dig a little deeper it's easy to understand why the *Guardian*'s editorial stance towards Corbyn was not bad for business in the way that some had assumed. Crucially, a majority of those readers polled in 2015 who were aged 18–44 identified as either 'centre' or 'right of centre' in their political orientation, with the balance only slightly favouring 'left of centre' in older age groups.[15] If any consideration was indeed given to the title's core demographic in respect of its Corbyn coverage, this wouldn't have raised particular alarm bells.

Meanwhile, evolving market dynamics favoured a closer alliance with the mainstream press in lobbying for tougher regulation of tech monopolies. In 2011, Rupert Murdoch's attempts to broaden his grip on the UK news landscape was arguably the primary threat to the *Guardian*'s then fledgling business model.[16] His first bid to buy out Sky Plc coincided with the *Guardian*'s phone hacking exclusive, and the fallout from the latter eventually forced a withdrawal of the bid. But by 2015, there seems little doubt that the *Guardian*'s primary competitive threat stemmed not from Fleet Street but rather Silicon Valley.[17] The control over user attention, data and news consumption exercised by intermediaries like Google, Facebook and Apple was by far the biggest and shared obstacle to growth and sustainability for national newspapers, eclipsing even the BBC's dominance. Not surprisingly then, in the aftermath of the phone hacking scandal, the *Guardian* began to give increasing attention to stories critical of tech giants and social media over continuing scrutiny of its rivals in the mainstream press.

CLOSING RANKS WITH THE STATE

But it wasn't just the mainstream press that the *Guardian* had started to fall in line with under Viner's editorship. Following the aftermath of the Snowden revelations, the *Guardian*'s relationship with the security state began to look increasingly more cooperative than antagonistic.

Between 2016 and 2019 the paper was awarded three 'exclusives' with spy agency and counter-terror chiefs. These interview-based feature articles were largely devoid of the kind of interrogative scrutiny characteristic of the Rusbridger era.[18] This period also saw the departure of both of the *Guardian*'s most experienced defence and security journalists: Ewen MacAskill and Richard Norton-Taylor.

In 2019 three *Guardian*/*Observer* journalists were mentioned in documents leaked by the Integrity Initiative – a clandestine operation part-funded by the UK Foreign and Commonwealth Office which had been promoting anti-Corbyn narratives on social media.[19] One of the journalists – Carole Cadwalladr – spoke at an event co-hosted by the Integrity Initiative just three months prior to the leak, alongside the *Guardian*'s former special projects editor James Ball.[20] In the wake of the scandal, Cadwalladr tweeted a qualified criticism of the Integrity Initiative, whilst at the same time heaping scorn on the Labour front bench for its alleged 'silence' over allegations of Russian interference in British democracy.[21] But she did not initially declare her own participation in the Integrity Initiative event, nor directly answer the question of whether or not she knew of the organisation's existence prior to the leak.[22]

There is no evidence to suggest that Cadwalladr or any of the other journalists mentioned in the leaked documents were actively working with or for the Integrity Initiative, or had any knowledge about its wider activities, connections and funding. The concern, however, is that the journalists did not appear to raise or seriously engage with such fundamental questions even after the leak containing their names surfaced. In the context of the Corbyn leadership, this is particularly problematic because civil servants – especially from within the military and security apparatus – were instrumental in fermenting anti-Corbyn news stories. According to an investigation carried out by Declassified UK, an astonishing 34 major news stories attacking the Corbyn leadership between 2015 and 2019 were sourced directly from either active or retired civil servants.[23]

BLURRED LINES

The common thread of these stories was an association between Corbyn(ism) and extremism. Given the *Guardian*'s institutional and historical attachment to liberal values, combined with its own recent return to the mainstream fold, it is hardly surprising that its editors, journalists and columnists would, on the whole, instinctively apply the lens of extremism to the Corbyn project.

But there was a problem. Corbyn was elected leader on a policy platform that proved to be both unexpectedly popular amongst the general public and widely endorsed by experts. Pledges to comprehensively reverse austerity, resist war and tackle climate injustice chimed with the inclination of voters across a broad spectrum of the electorate, whilst Labour's economic plans attracted support from many of the world's leading economists.[24] Indeed, from a policy perspective, Corbyn was arguably more quintessentially 'moderate' than his political opponents within the Labour Party for whom, ironically, the term 'moderates' became established journalistic shorthand. On Brexit especially, Corbyn ended up adopting a centrist position between the relative extremes of the Conservatives' 'hard Brexiteers' and the Liberal Democrats' pledge to revoke Article 50.

Even the *Observer* was at pains to point out that Labour's 2019 election manifesto – widely derided as fanciful by the mainstream press – was hardly without precedent:

> The manifesto is not historically as startling as it will be caricatured as being. The Britain that Mr Corbyn and his supporters are imagining is a leftwing form of social democracy for which, with relatively few changes of policy, it might have stood at various times between 1945 and 1983.[25]

But the mainstream credentials of Corbyn's Labour were most dramatically exposed in the 2017 election, when the party won significant and wholly unexpected gains, with its share of the popular vote eclipsing that of even Tony Blair's last two election victories. What followed was a demonstrable upward shift in the intensity of mainstream media hostility. The period between July 2017 and December 2019 saw a spate of major news headlines doubling down on previous charges that Corbyn posed an immediate threat to national security. Of the 34 state-sourced articles identified by Declassified UK, 28 ran between the 2017 and 2019 elections compared to just six in the first two years of Corbyn's leadership. And according to a Loughborough University study, press hostility towards Labour during the 2019 election was more than double that of the 2017 election.[26]

EXTREMISM REDEFINED

The *Guardian* did not immediately buy in to this ramped up hostility and was among the first to comprehensively debunk claims that Corbyn was a former Soviet Union informant.[27] But it did devote substantial attention to the long-running controversy over antisemitism in Corbyn's Labour. This meta-story seemed to offer a more sustainable frame of extremism compared to that applied either to Corbyn's policies or alleged past associations with terrorists and enemy states. The ascendant narrative framed Labour under Corbyn's leadership as the political home of anti-Jewish racists and Corbyn himself as harbouring a dark and sinister hatred, or at least as being reluctant to tackle the problem for fear of alienating his political friends and allies. It was a framing that mapped squarely on to the logic of populism as defined by the political centre, which characterised 'illiberalism' – with all its underlying racist tendencies – as a phenomenon shared by political movements on the left as much as on the right.[28]

It is also important to note what was distinct about the antisemitism meta-story from what might be seen as wider efforts by the media to delegitimise the Corbyn left. First, unlike claims that Corbyn was a former Soviet spy, the antisemitism controversy was not entirely without substance. There were serious and unequivocal examples of antisemitic statements made by Labour members during the Corbyn leadership, however isolated and proportionately few in number (compared to the volume of complaints or the size of Labour's mass membership that swelled dramatically under Corbyn's leadership). There were also legitimate questions for journalists to ask of past statements by Corbyn himself which may have caused understandable offence.

And of course, it is perfectly understandable that professional journalists would be instinctively receptive to allegations that a major political party had become a vehicle for hatred against a minority community. When concerns were raised by prominent figures within the Jewish community and echoed by senior Labour MPs, it was both inevitable and entirely consistent with journalistic norms and ethics that the story would make headline news.

But we might equally expect professional journalists to be sensitive to the wider context of ideological hostility towards the Corbyn leadership and the obvious risks that such an issue could be exploited for political gain. Instead, claims by sources factionally and ideologically opposed to the Corbyn project were treated as gospel whilst alternative perspectives were marginalised or overlooked altogether. This pattern was most pronounced during the furore surrounding Labour's proposed adoption – or partial adoption – of the antisemitism definition promoted by the International Holocaust Remembrance Alliance (IHRA). It was an issue that saturated headlines during the summer of 2018 and marked the peak of coverage intensity over antisemitism that had built throughout the year.

Before elaborating on specific examples, it is important to situate and differentiate this particular story from much of the related coverage leading up to it. Prior to July 2018, most news stories about antisemitism in the Labour Party centred on controversial comments made by Corbyn or others in the party, often several years in the past. In conflict with professional journalistic norms, some of these stories were recycled over the course of Corbyn's leadership tenure. A Facebook comment that Corbyn made about a controversial mural in 2012 was first uncovered by the *Jewish Chronicle* in 2015[29] but only became a headline news story in April 2018. More remarkably, revelations about a Palestinian wreath-laying ceremony attended by Corbyn in 2014 became a story during the 2017 election campaign, only to resurface as a major headline in August 2018. At the time of writing, a Wikipedia page on the 'Corbyn wreath laying controversy' states that 'On 15 August 2018, a British political controversy was initiated when the *Daily Mail* claimed that, prior to becoming Labour Party Leader, Jeremy Corbyn had been present at a 2014 wreath-laying at a cemetery which contained the graves of many Palestinian activists'.[30] It makes no mention of coverage in the *Daily Mail* of the exact same story more than two years earlier.[31]

What this suggests is that, at least by the summer of 2018, the controversy surrounding antisemitism was starting to run out of fresh material. What's more, it was precisely at this point that the leadership had finally gained some degree of formal control over the party's bureaucracy, not least since Jennie Formby (a known Corbyn ally) was elected to the role of General Secretary in March 2018. Formby's tenure marked a dramatic increase in both the speed of investigations into antisemitism complaints, and the number of suspensions and expulsions imposed.[32]

REPORTING FAILURE

For a brief moment, it began to look as if the Labour Party was finally starting to get to grips with the problem as evidenced by Ivor Caplin, co-Chair of the Jewish Labour Movement in July 2018:

> There have been extensive discussions about how we deal with antisemitism and get it right and I am already starting to see the small steps that I wanted to see [...] I think we are starting to see the progress that I wanted to see.[33]

Caplin's comments were made two days before Labour announced proposals to adapt and incorporate the IHRA definition of antisemitism into its disciplinary code of conduct. This announcement appeared to both follow and invite further consultation with Jewish groups, as reported in the *Jewish Chronicle* immediately following Caplin's interview:

> The *JC* has seen a copy of the letter sent by Ms Formby on behalf of the Labour Party on Tuesday to the Board of Deputies, the Jewish Leadership Council and the Community Security Trust in which she confirmed the 'positive' nature of Monday's meeting and invited representatives of the three organisations to attend a 'feedback' meeting on July 17.[34]

The article was otherwise scathing in its report on claims that Caplin was 'played' by the Labour leadership. Yet even the *Sun* at this stage appeared to be corroborating the fact that the proposals were the product of positive discussion with the JLM:

> Figures from the Jewish Labour Movement (JLM) met with the party's general secretary Jennie Formby to discuss the new rules earlier this week, and Labour sources said they were 'positively received'.[35]

The Labour Party subsequently went on record to affirm that the proposals were made on the back of an 'open and inclusive' consultation in which 'a range of Jewish communal organisations, rabbis, academics, lawyers, trade unions, Palestinian groups, local Labour parties and members took part.'[36]

In spite of this, Labour's alleged *failure* to consult over the proposals became a key plank of the story as it quickly evolved. Writing in the *Guardian* on 27 July, columnist Jonathan Freedland asserted emphatically that the party 'drew up its code of conduct itself, without consulting the organized Jewish community at all'.[37] This was echoed a week later by Peter Mason, national secretary of the JLM, who told Sky News that

> Since the Labour Party adopted its own code of practice a month ago there have been no formal conversations with the Jewish community, there have been no invitations offered.[38]

So entrenched was this framing that BBC presenter Andrew Neil responded with apparent incredulity to a suggestion that the party had, in fact, consulted with Jewish groups at all:

> Andrew Neil: Who were these Jewish organisations? It wasn't the Board of Deputies was it?
>
> Peter Dowd MP: Yes they were.[39]

This portrayal of the Labour Party as a lone outlier, refusing to engage in consultation and rejecting consensus required an even more flagrant disregard of the facts in relation to the IHRA definition itself. In particular, it hinged on a framing of the definition as broadly consensual and widely adopted (at least to an extent beyond that which was initially proposed by the Labour Party). In fact, the definition had been mired in controversy ever since it was first developed by the European Monitoring Centre on Racism and Xenophobia (EUMC). The EUMC itself had cautioned that the 'working definition' has no legal weight and it was subsequently dropped by its successor body, the Fundamental Rights Agency. Its resurrection by the IHRA prompted concerns by leading experts including Professor David Feldman, Director of the Pears Institute for Antisemitism, who wrote in 2016 of 'a danger that the overall effect will place the onus on Israel's critics to demonstrate they are not antisemitic' and that the 'the greatest flaw of the IHRA definition is its failure to make any ethical and political connections between the struggle against antisemitism and other sorts of prejudice.'[40] Feldman raised particular concern about the illustrative examples, noting that even the House of Commons Home Affairs Select Committee had cautioned against adoption of the definition without qualification.

Virtually none of this essential context found its way into the *Guardian*'s online news reporting of the controversy. Instead, articles routinely characterised Labour's proposals as a 'failure' to adopt the definition in full (text emboldened by author):

> The rows over the summer about the party's handling of antisemitism complaints were sparked by a decision to implement a code of conduct that **failed** to adopt four of the 11 examples of antisemitism given by the IHRA.[41]

> Corbyn and the Labour party have been engulfed in controversy after **failing** to endorse the International Holocaust Remembrance Alliance's (IHRA) definition of antisemitism in its entirety.[42]

> The shift comes after weeks of discord between Labour's national executive committee (NEC) and the Jewish community after the party **failed** to adopt all 11 examples of antisemitism given by the IHRA, arguing that under one of them legitimate criticism of Israel could be deemed antisemitic.[43]

BEYOND CONSENT

The controversy also triggered a range of responses critical of the IHRA definition from Jewish groups, BAME groups, rabbis and QCs, which were all but ignored. For instance, no mention was made of a legal opinion by a leading human rights QC published at the height of the controversy, which slammed the definition as not fit for purpose.[44] In the same month, a joint statement by 84 migrant and minority communities warning of the definition's potential to 'silence public discussion' over Palestinian rights attracted no attention in the

Guardian's online coverage.[45] A similar joint statement on behalf of 36 Jewish groups from around the world received only a passing mention in the final sentence of an article with the headline 'Labour MP labels Corbyn an anti-Semite over party's refusal to drop code'.[46]

News reports and opinion pieces also contained repeated affirmations – by both sources and journalists – of the IHRA definition's broad take-up and acceptance both internationally and by public bodies and organisations within the UK. In fact, by the time the controversy had erupted in July 2018, none of the other major parties had adopted the definition, in spite of the Conservative prime minister's claims to the contrary.[47] As for local authorities, only around a third had adopted the definition more than two years after an explicit call by central government for them to do so. And internationally, the IHRA confirmed in a fact sheet published in 2018 that only eight countries in the world had formally adopted the definition – including only six of the 31 member countries of the IHRA.[48]

In other words, at most only a minority of UK public bodies, political parties and governments around the world had formally adopted the definition, which had attracted widespread criticism from a number of Jewish groups, other minority groups, academics and legal experts. Yet the coverage in the *Guardian*, as elsewhere, routinely characterised the definition as broadly consensual. This framing often involved wildly inaccurate statistical claims, such as when Nick Cohen asserted that the definition 'is accepted by thousands of public bodies'.[49]

Where numbers were not used, the language tended to emphasise the definition's wide acceptance and support, such as Jonathan Freedland's description of 'the near universally accepted' definition.[50] This was a sentiment echoed by Hannah Weisfeld and Alex Sobel two weeks later who described the definition as 'the closest thing that exists to a universally recognised definition.'[51]

By this point, such distortions were by no means limited to the opinion columns and comment sections. News reports began to adopt stock shorthand phrasing that subtly and repeatedly framed the definition as broadly consensual. The use of blanket qualifiers such as 'widely accepted in other countries'[52] echoed the assertions of prominently featured sources, such as a joint statement by the Board of Deputies of British Jews and the Jewish Leadership Council which referred to it simply as the 'universal definition'.[53]

It's important to note that the *Guardian* was by no means an outlier in this respect. In fact, the language it adopted closely mirrored that of other mainstream outlets including broadcasters. Sky News anchors and reporters, for instance, used a similar convention of referring to the definition as 'widely accepted' with little or no reference to the controversy and dissent it had courted:

> 'The widely accepted definition'[54]
>
> 'The widely accepted definition put forward by the IHRA'[55]
>
> 'The IHRA's widely accepted definition'[56]

BBC news presenters tended to be even more pronounced and explicit in framing the definition as universal:

> 'The definition accepted by more or less every country in the world'[57]
>
> 'It isn't just adopted by Jewish groups it's adopted by pretty much everybody'[58]
>
> 'why wouldn't you do what everyone else does, what's different about Labour?'[59]

But it is equally important to note that some outlets were relatively more balanced and nuanced in their coverage compared to the *Guardian*. The *Independent*, for instance, (second only to the *Guardian* in its volume of coverage on this issue) was notably more wide-ranging in its sourcing, and less prone to the kind of statistical inaccuracies that surfaced in the *Guardian*. Indeed, the *Guardian*'s online coverage included more unambiguous statistical errors than any other leading online news site.[60] This suggests that whilst the *Guardian*'s flaws were not quite exceptional across the mainstream media, they were equally not inevitable. It could – and should – have taken greater care in scrutinising contentious claims by its most vociferous sources, columnists and commentators.

HIERARCHY OF CREDIBILITY

Such flaws in the *Guardian*'s recent coverage have not been limited to its coverage of antisemitism in the Labour Party, or indeed the Corbyn leadership more widely. In 2018, the paper ran an exclusive headline claiming that a former campaign manager for Donald Trump held secret talks with Julian Assange whilst he was exiled within the Ecuadorian embassy in London.[61] The story has since been comprehensively debunked. According to former *Guardian* journalist Glenn Greenwald, its holes were visible even at the time of publication:

> [A]nalysts from across the political spectrum – including those quite hostile to Assange – expressed serious doubts about the article's sourcing, internal logic, self-evidently dubious assertions, and overall veracity, even as many media figures uncritically trumpeted it.[62]

But what was observed in the coverage of the IHRA controversy was a more subtle and systematic pattern of distorted coverage across a relatively wide sample, and attributable to a cross-section of the paper's journalists and columnists. This suggests the problem may have had something to do with an editorial groupthink and herd mentality that perceived and treated sources according to a hierarchy of credibility. In particular, the coverage was dominated by a combination of 'moderates' within the Labour Party and the leaders of mainstream Jewish organisations, especially the Board of Deputies of British Jews. The latter was frequently taken to represent the Jewish population as a whole, despite having no formal connection to either secular or strictly orthodox communities.[63] Yet as the self-proclaimed 'voice of the Jewish community', it is not hard to see why journalists instinctively would have viewed its charges against the Labour leadership as inherently credible and authoritative. At the same time, these charges were echoed and amplified by the centre-left majority of Labour MPs. They represented not only the Labour Party establishment but, perhaps more than any other mainstream political constituency, the ideology and values institutionally embedded in the *Guardian*.

What's more, much of this constituency had well-established and close relationships with journalists at the *Guardian*, going back to at least the early days of the Labour government under Tony Blair. At the heart of the spin culture associated with Blairism was a resigned belief that Labour could only win power through effective professional media management.[64] In contrast, Corbyn had spent his political life on the margins of the backbenches well beyond the Westminster media spotlight, and rejection of the Blairite model of communication was written into his political DNA.

Perhaps above all, Corbyn's political ascendance coincided with that of Donald Trump in the US and other hard right leaders from Modi in India to Bolsonaro in Brazil. Against this backdrop – and especially in the context of Brexit – it is easy to understand how Corbyn's Labour and those sources defending it came to be perceived by journalists as the left front of populism – tending towards the extreme and intrinsically less credible than their 'moderate' political counterparts.

Of course, none of this absolves professional journalists of their responsibility for recognising contentious claims, balancing sources and scrutinising even those considered intrinsically trustworthy. This is especially the case for a newspaper that trades on its reputation for news quality and as an antidote to the spread of fake news.

CONCLUSION

The IHRA controversy marked a profound turning point in the dominant media discourse surrounding antisemitism in the Labour Party and the Corbyn leadership more broadly. Up until July 2018, most of the headlines were based on discrete events and allegations of controversial statements predominantly in the past. Though these stories at times saturated the headlines, they did not attract the same degree of sustained attention as the IHRA controversy. The latter was also qualitatively distinct from previous coverage in that it was propelled by allegations labelling Corbyn definitively as a 'racist',[65] and the left of Labour as *institutionally* and *irrevocably* antisemitic.

The controversy eventually subsided after the party agreed to adopt the definition in full in September 2018. But it was quickly succeeded by another which similarly invoked the institutional character of antisemitism in Corbyn's Labour. Focused on the party's handling of antisemitism complaints, the dominant framing simultaneously targeted the leadership for not doing enough to address failures in the complaints process, *and* for undue interference in that process.[66] And like the IHRA controversy, it was a framing that required an extraordinary omission of countervailing evidence. This went beyond the demonstrable and radical improvements in complaints handling under Jennie Formby's tenure as General Secretary. Leaked emails that surfaced in May 2019 revealed persistent appeals by the leader's office to encourage swifter and more robust action by the complaints team prior to Formby taking over.[67] Such appeals were met with apparent obfuscation by former party staff whose factional opposition to the Corbyn leadership was laid bare in a report that was leaked in March 2020.[68]

That the *Guardian* failed to report at all on the leaked emails that surfaced in May 2019 was illustrative of a wider pattern of omission; one that was ultimately more problematic than the distortions and inaccuracies observed in the IHRA controversy. Ironically, in defence of its liberal values against the rise of populism, the *Guardian* appeared to disregard or undermine what has always been the very cornerstone of its liberalism: the sanctity of facts.

NOTES

1. Alex Nunns, 'How the Guardian Changed Tack on Corbyn, Despite its Readers', *Novara Media*, 8 January 2017, novaramedia.com/2017/01/08/how-the-guardian-changed-tack-on-corbyn-despite-its-readers/ (accessed 20 August 2020).
2. See editorial, 'The Guardian View on Labour's Manifesto: A Bold Step', *Guardian*, 11 May 2017, www.theguardian.com/commentisfree/2017/may/11/the-guardian-view-on-labours-manifesto-a-bold-step (accessed 20 August 2020); and 'The Guardian View on Labour's Manifesto: Bold Pledges for Anxious Times', *Guardian*, 21 November 2019, www.theguardian.com/commentisfree/2019/nov/21/the-guardian-view-on-the-labour-manifesto-bold-pledges-for-anxious-times (accessed 20 August 2020).
3. Justin Schlosberg and Laura Laker, *Labour, Antisemitism and the News: A Disinformation Paradigm*, Media Reform Coalition, 2018, www.mediareform.org.uk/wp-content/uploads/2018/09/Labour-antisemitism-and-the-news-FINAL-PROOFED.pdf (accessed 20 September 2020).
4. See, for instance, Philip Schlesinger, *Putting 'Reality' Together: BBC News* (London: Methuen, 1987); Gaye Tuchman, *Making News: A Study in the Construction of Reality* (New York: Free Press, 1978); Stuart Hall, 'The

Rediscovery of Ideology: Return of the Repressed in Media Studies'. In Michael Gurevitch, Tony Bennet, James Curran and James Woollacott (eds), *Culture, Society and the Media* (London: Methuen, 1982).

5. Glenn Greenwald, *No Place to Hide: Edward Snowden, the NSA, and the US Surveillance State* (New York: Metropolitan Books, 2014).
6. Julian Petley, 'The State Journalism Is In: Edward Snowden and the British Press', *Ethical Space*, 11:1/2, (2014).
7. Chris Blackhurst, 'Edward Snowden's Secrets May Be Dangerous: I Would Not Have Published them', *Independent*, 13 October 2013, www.independent.co.uk/voices/comment/edward-snowden-s-secrets-may-be-dangerous-i-would-not-have-published-them-8877404.html (accessed 20 August 2020).
8. Jens Branum and Jonathan Charteris-Black, 'The Edward Snowden affair: A Corpus Study of the British Press', *Discourse & Communication*, 9:2, (2015), pp. 199–220.
9. Interview with author, September 2014.
10. *Guardian* editorial, 'The Guardian View on Section 40: Muzzling Journalism', *Guardian*, www.theguardian.com/commentisfree/2017/jan/10/the-guardian-view-on-section-40-muzzling-journalism (accessed 20 August 2020).
11. Jim Waterson, 'Guardian Breaks Even Helped by Success of Supporter Strategy', *Guardian*, www.theguardian.com/media/2019/may/01/guardian-breaks-even-helped-by-success-of-supporter-strategy (accessed 20 August 2020).
12. Jim Waterson, 'Guardian Announces Plans to Cut 180 jobs', *Guardian,* 15 July 2020, www.theguardian.com/media/2020/jul/15/guardian-announces-plans-to-cut-180-jobs (accessed 20 August 2020).
13. Guardian Media Group Plc (2020). *Annual Report and Consolidated Financial Statements for the Year Ended 29 March 2020*, uploads.guim.co.uk/2020/07/15/1._GMG_Financial_Statements_2020_FINAL__pdf.pdf (accessed 20 August 2020).
14. Chris Elliott, 'Analysing the Balance of Our Jeremy Corbyn Coverage', *Guardian*, 3 August 2015, www.theguardian.com/commentisfree/2015/aug/03/analysing-the-balance-of-our-jeremy-corbyn-coverage (accessed 20 August 2020).
15. Ibid.
16. Binakuromo Ogbebor, *British Media Coverage of the Press Reform Debate: Journalists Reporting Journalism* (London: Palgrave, 2020).
17. Emily Bell, 'The Dependent Press: How Silicon Valley Threatens Independent Journalism'. In Martin Moore and Damian Tambini (eds), *Digital dominance: The power of Google, Amazon, Facebook, and Apple* (Oxford: Oxford University Press, 2018).
18. Matt Kennard and Mark Curtis, 'How the UK Security Services Neutralised The Country's Leading Liberal Newspaper', *Declassified UK*, 11 September 2019, www.dailymaverick.co.za/article/2019-09-11-how-

the-uk-security-services-neutralised-the-countrys-leading-liberal-newspaper/ (accessed 20 August 2020).

19. Paul McKeigue, David Miller, Jake Mason & Piers Robinson, 'Briefing Note on the Integrity Initiative', *Working Group on Syria Propaganda and Media*, 21, 2018, http://syriapropagandamedia.org/working-papers/briefing-note-on-the-integrity-initiative (accessed 20 August 2020).
20. Integrity Initiative, 'Tackling Tools of Malign Influence: Supporting 21st Century Journalism', *Frontline Club*, 1–2 November 2018, www.pdf-archive.com/2018/12/13/skillsharingdraft-nov12/skillsharingdraft-nov12.pdf (accessed 20 August 2020).
21. Carole Cadwalladr, tweet, 9 December 2018, twitter.com/carolecadwalla/status/1071825766797795330 (accessed 20 August 2020).
22. Piers Robinson, tweet, twitter.com/PiersRobinson1/status/107432695 5233820673 (accessed 20 August 2020).
23. Kennard and Curtis, 'How the UK Security Services…'.
24. Chris Giles, 'Economists and Academics Back Labour's Spending Plans', *Financial Times*, 26 November 2019, www.ft.com/content/d29b4cbe-0fa4-11ea-a225-db2f231cfeae (accessed 20 August 2020).
25. Editorial, 'The Observer View on the Labour Manifesto: A Bold Vision but is it Less than the Sum of its Parts?' *Observer*, 24 November 2019, www.theguardian.com/commentisfree/2019/nov/24/observer-view-on-the-labour-manifesto-a-bold-vision (accessed 20 August 2020).
26. David Deacon, Jackie Goode, David Smith, Dominic Wring, John Downey and Cristian Vaccari, *General Election 2019: Report 5*, Centre for Research in Communication and Culture, Loughborough University, www.lboro.ac.uk/news-events/general-election/report-5/ (accessed 20 August 2020).
27. Robert Tait, Luke Harding, Ewan MacAskill and Ben Quinn, 'No Evidence Corbyn Was a Communist Spy, Say Intelligence Experts', *Guardian*, 20 February 2018, www.theguardian.com/politics/2018/feb/20/no-evidence-corbyn-was-spy-for-czechoslovakia-say-intelligence-experts (accessed 20 August 2020).
28. See, for instance, Tom McTague, 'Boris Johnson Is Not Britain's Donald Trump: Jeremy Corbyn Is', *The Atlantic*, 14 November 2019, www.theatlantic.com/international/archive/2019/11/jeremy-corbyn-like-donald-trump-not-boris-johnson/601957/ (accessed 20 August 2020).
29. Marcus Dysch, 'Did Jeremy Corbyn Back Artist Whose Mural Was Condemned as Antisemitic?', *Jewish Chronicle*, 6 November 2015, www.thejc.com/news/uk/did-jeremy-corbyn-back-artist-whose-mural-was-condemned-as-antisemitic-1.62106 (accessed 20 August 2020).
30. Wikipedia, 'Corbyn Wreath-laying Controversy', en.wikipedia.org/wiki/Corbyn_wreath-laying_controversy#:~:text=On%2015%20August%20 2018%2C%20a,Atef%20Bseiso%2C%20both%20of%20whom (accessed 20 August 2020).

31. See, for instance, Kate Ferguson, 'Jeremy Corbyn Described Banned Terror Group Hamas As "Serious And Hardworking" and Calls For Trade Deal with Israel to be Suspended', *Daily Mail*, 29 May 2017, www.dailymail.co.uk/news/article-4551676/Jeremy-Corbyn-says-Hamas-hardworking.html (accessed 20 August 2020).
32. Peter Oborne, Justin Schlosberg and Richard Sanders, 'Were Labour's Antisemitism Failures Really Corbyn's Fault?', *Open Democracy*, 26 June 2020, www.opendemocracy.net/en/opendemocracyuk/were-labours-antisemitism-failures-really-corbyns-fault/ (accessed 20 August 2020).
33. LBC, *The Nick Ferrari Show*, 3 July 2018.
34. Lee Harpin, 'Jewish Labour Movement Chair Condemned Over Labour Antisemitism Meeting', *Jewish Chronicle*, 4 July 2018, www.thejc.com/jlm-chair-ivor-caplin-faces-criticism-over-labour-antisemitism-meeting-1.466577 (accessed 21 September 2020).
35. Natasha Clark, '"A Toothless Document": Jeremy Corbyn's New Antisemitism Rules Slammed as a "Racists' Charter" by Jewish Groups', *Sun*, 5 July 2018, www.thesun.co.uk/news/6701818/fury-as-it-emerges-labour-anti-semites-could-escape-punishment-if-they-tell-party-they-didnt-mean-to-be-offensive/ (accessed 20 August 2020).
36. Email response from Labour Party press office, 25 September 2018.
37. Jonathan Freedland, 'Yes, Jews Are Angry – because Labour Hasn't Listened or Shown any Empathy', *Guardian*, 27 July 2018, www.theguardian.com/commentisfree/2018/jul/27/jewish-anger-labour-listen-antisemitism-opinion (accessed 20 August 2020).
38. *Sunrise*, Sky News, 4 August 2018.
39. BBC Two, *Daily Politics*, 18 July 2018.
40. David Feldman, 'Will Britain's New Definition of Antisemitism Help Jewish People? I'm Sceptical', *Guardian*, 28 December 2016, www.theguardian.com/commentisfree/2016/dec/28/britain-definition-antisemitism-british-jews-jewish-people (accessed 20 August 2020).
41. Jessica Elgot, 'Antisemitism Row Risks Chances of Labour Government', *Guardian*, 1 September 2018, www.theguardian.com/politics/2018/sep/01/antisemitism-row-risks-chances-of-labour-government (accessed 20 August 2020).
42. Press Association, 'Antisemitism Row: Corbyn Has to Change, Says Gordon Brown', *Guardian*, 15 August 2018, www.theguardian.com/politics/2018/aug/15/antisemitism-row-corbyn-has-to-change-says-gordon-brown (accessed 20 August 2020).
43. Jessica Elgot and Heather Stewart, 'Labour Prepares the Ground for Compromise on Antisemitism Code', *Guardian*, 15 August 2018, www.theguardian.com/politics/2018/aug/15/labour-prepares-to-amend-antisemitism-code-ihra-israel (accessed 20 August 2020).
44. Anonymous, 'Government Definition of Antisemitism Not Fit, Says Geoffrey Robertson, QC', *The Times*, 31 August 2018, www.thetimes.

co.uk/article/government-definition-of-antisemitism-not-fit-says-geoffrey-robertson-qc-htx6trnmq (accessed 21 September 2020).

45. Peter Stubley, 'Antisemitism Definition at Heart of Labour Row "Will Silence Public Discussion", Say Minority Groups', *Independent*, 18 August 2018, www.independent.co.uk/news/uk/politics/labour-antisemitism-row-jeremy-corbyn-ihra-definition-bame-group-a8496906.html (accessed 20 August 2020).
46. Heather Stewart and Jessica Elgot, 'Labour MP Labels Corbyn an "Antisemite" Over Party's Refusal to Drop Code', *Guardian*, 17 July 2018, www.theguardian.com/politics/2018/jul/17/labour-agrees-to-fresh-antisemitism-consultation-after-stormy-debate (accessed 20 August 2020).
47. Georgina Lee, 'Conservative Party Rule Book Doesn't Mention Antisemitism', *Channel 4 News*, 20 July 2018, www.channel4.com/news/factcheck/factcheck-conservative-party-rulebook-doesnt-mention-antisemitism (accessed 20 August 2020).
48. The International Holocaust Remembrance Alliance, *Fact sheet: Working definition of anti-Semitism*, 16 March 2018, www.holocaustremembrance.com/sites/default/files/inline-files/Fcat%20Sheet%20Working%20Definition%20of%20Antisemitism_1.pdf (accessed 20 August 2020).
49. Nick Cohen, 'Why Has Labour Run the Risk of Alienating Progressive Jews?' *Guardian*, 7 July 2018, www.theguardian.com/commentisfree/2018/jul/07/labour-antisemitism-jeremy-corbyn (accessed 20 August 2020).
50. Freedland, 'Yes, Jews Are Angry'.
51. Hannah Weisfeld and Alex Sobel, 'Labour's Antisemitism Failure Means It Cannot be a Credible Critic of Israel', *Guardian*, 9 August 2018, www.theguardian.com/global/commentisfree/2018/aug/09/labour-antisemitism-credible-critic-israel (accessed 20 August 2020).
52. Toby Helm, 'Antisemitism: Corbyn and the Crisis that Won't Go Away', *Observer*, 5 August 2018, www.theguardian.com/politics/2018/aug/05/antisemitism-labour-jeremy-corbyn-crisis-wont-go-away (accessed 20 August 2020).
53. Jessica Elgot, 'Labour Jewish Affiliate in Row with Party over Antisemitism Code', *Guardian*, 11 July 2018, www.theguardian.com/world/2018/jul/11/labour-jewish-affiliate-in-row-with-party-over-anti-semitism-code (accessed 20 August 2020).
54. *Sunrise*, Sky News, 30 July 2018.
55. *Sunrise*, Sky News, 13 August 2018.
56. *Sunrise*, Sky News, 4 September 2018.
57. *Victoria Derbyshire*, BBC One, 4 September 2018.
58. *Daily Politics*, BBC One, 19 July 2018.
59. *Daily Politics*, BBC One, 18 July 2018.
60. Justin Schlosberg and Laura Laker, *Labour, Antisemitism and the News: A Disinformation Paradigm*, Media Reform Coalition, 2018, www.mediareform.org.uk/wp-content/uploads/2018/09/Labour-

antisemitism-and-the-news-FINAL-PROOFED.pdf (accessed 20 September 2020).

61. Luke Harding and Dan Collyns, 'Manafort Held Secret Talks with Assange in Ecuadorian Embassy, Sources Say', *Guardian*, 27 November 2018, www.theguardian.com/us-news/2018/nov/27/manafort-held-secret-talks-with-assange-in-ecuadorian-embassy (accessed 20 August 2020).
62. Green Greenwald, 'Five Weeks after the Guardian's Viral Blockbuster Assange-Manafort Scoop, no Evidence Has Emerged – Just Stonewalling', *Intercept*, 2 January 2019, theintercept.com/2019/01/02/five-weeks-after-the-guardians-viral-blockbuster-assangemanafort-scoop-no-evidence-has-emerged-just-stonewalling/ (accessed 20 August 2020).
63. Koser Saeed, 'Expose: Who are the Board of Deputies of British Jews?' *Spotlight*, 21 January 2020, spotlight-newspaper.co.uk/politics/01/21/expose-who-are-the-board-of-deputies-of-british-jews/ (accessed 20 August 2020).
64. Raymond Kuhn, 'The First Blair Government and Political Journalism'. In Raymond Kuhn and Eric Neveu (eds), *Political journalism: New challenges, new practices* (London: Routledge: 2002).
65. Margaret Hodge, 'I Was Right to Confront Jeremy Corbyn over Labour's Antisemitism', *Guardian*, 18 July 2018, www.theguardian.com/commentisfree/2018/jul/18/jeremy-corbyn-labour-antisemitism-margaret-hodge (accessed 20 August 2020).
66. Justin Schlosberg, 'BBC Panorama Investigation into Labour Antisemitism Omitted Key Evidence and Parts of Labour's Response', *Novara Media*, 22 July 2020, novaramedia.com/2020/07/22/bbc-panorama-investigation-into-labour-antisemitism-omitted-key-evidence-and-parts-of-labours-response/ (accessed 20 August 2020).
67. Alex Wickham, 'Leaked Emails Reveal Labour's Compliance Unit Took Months to Act Over its Most Serious Antisemitism Cases', *Buzzfeed*, 11 May 2019, www.buzzfeed.com/alexwickham/leaked-emails-reveal-labours-compliance-unit-took-months-to (accessed 20 August 2020).
68. Oborne, Schlosberg and Sanders, 'Were Labour's Antisemitism Failures Really Corbyn's Fault?'

12

Guardian Journalists and Twitter Circles

Tom Mills

This chapter examines the Twitter networks of 25 columnists writing for the *Guardian* and *Observer*. It analyses their tweets and retweets and the users they follow using data extracted from Twitter via its API in April 2020. Adopting the sorts of 'descriptive strategies' advocated by Mike Savage,[1] it uses a combination of social network analysis and correspondence analysis to analyse this data. First it examines the columnists' following of and interactions with each other. Then it turns to the Twitter accounts they most follow in aggregate, and then specifically the MPs they most follow. It then examines distinct following patterns among the columnists. It does this by first focusing on the different parties and party factions of MPs they tend to follow, and then by analysing only the Twitter users followed by five of the 25 columnists. The chapter concludes by reflecting on the findings in light of the debates around political balance, bias and sourcing at the *Guardian*, and its role as the dominant liberal-left media outlet in the UK.

COMMENT JOURNALISM, ONLINE PLATFORMS AND ELITE NETWORKS

Newspaper opinion journalism, a feature of the classic division between fact and opinion in the industry, includes newspaper editorials (anonymous articles setting out the editorial position of the paper on a given issue), commissioned opinion pieces written by outside experts or notable public figures, and regular opinion pieces by staff writers. While editorials have received some scholarly attention because of their usefulness as indicators of a newspaper's position on party politics and contentious policy issues,[2] there is relatively little research on either guest opinion writers or columnists, the latter of whom are the focus here. This is particularly the case in the UK where, like in the US, these journalists are significant as elite 'opinion formers'.

Alistair Duff's study, which involved in-depth interviews with ten leading British political columnists – among them the *Guardian*'s Polly Toynbee and then *Telegraph* columnist Boris Johnson – noted the 'slim knowledge base' at that time, and drew on a handful of sources to piece together the history of British newspaper columnists, notably Tunstall's research on the UK national press. It notes that columnists only became a significant feature of British journalism in the late 1960s, and that the rise of what has been termed the 'commentariat' accelerated as the commercialisation of the industry intensified in the neoliberal period.[3] From the late 1980s, there was a significant rise in the number of columnists employed in the UK national press, with an increase in lifestyle columnists in particular, but the number of political columnists also increasing.[4] By the 1990s, columnists had become, according to Duff, a 'British institution' while a decade later the *Guardian* columnist Martin Kettle would claim that the 120 political columnists who are read most intensively by 'politicians and the media village' represented the main opposition to the government.[5] While Kettle certainly exaggerates these columnists' antagonistic relationship with the government, Karin Wahl-Jorgensen in her study comparing Danish and British comment journalism, concurs that the commentariat should be considered a 'cohesive political force'.[6]

British columnists have comprised a mix of influential political commentators and celebrities and comedians producing lighter content. The former have usually been established reporters, often with some prior involvement in leader writing. These figures, who 'within the British journalistic profession . . . are undoubtedly an elite',[7] operate as part of what Wahl-Jorgensen describes as 'a top-down and professionalised vision of public debate'.[8] Aeron Davis, who has examined British networks of power, politics and publicity in detail, suggests that prestigious and well connected political columnists are especially influential in shaping how political elites understand and navigate political issues, conflicts and fault lines.[9] They can be seen as the most public facing members of a broader network of people and institutions that strongly shape elite political opinion and influence the broader contours of political common sense. Political scientist Peter Allen describes this 'relatively small group of "intensely involved" individuals who work in or around politics . . . [and] shape and drive dominant political discourse',[10] as 'perhaps wider in scope than the oft-referred to "political class", but more limited than "the elite" or "the establishment".'[11] Along with the commentariat, this group includes political reporters, pollsters, political consultants, think-tankers and prominent political scientists, as well as some current and former politicians who are well regarded in these networks.

The *Guardian* has a distinct role in this elite political micro-culture as the most prestigious national daily associated with the centre left in an industry that has long been highly skewed to the right. Its readership is largely middle class and university educated, but more significantly for our purposes the *Guardian* and *Observer* are both widely read by the liberal and centre-left political elite.[12] The *Mirror* has a wide readership, but little influence in elite circles, while the *Morning Star* has neither. The *Independent*, meanwhile, has been significantly diminished in recent years and has been more overtly centrist than the *Guardian*, usually supporting the Liberal Democrats. But though the *Guardian* is widely associated with the centre left, and has tended to be closely associated with the Labour Party, its core editorial politics have always been liberal rather than left-wing, and the paper has often had an antagonistic relationship with those situated to the left of its editorial and political centre of gravity – something that is even more true of its sister paper the *Observer*.

Both newspapers, as other chapters in this collection demonstrate, played an active role in the intra-left conflicts in the Labour Party under the leadership of Jeremy Corbyn. The *Guardian* initially lent its support to Yvette Cooper, the centrist candidate in the 2015 Labour leadership election, and its columnists were thereafter highly critical of the left-wing leadership. The antagonism from the comment pages in particular was noted by Corbyn himself, who in a *Vice* documentary aired in June 2016 is seen describing a column by the *Guardian*'s Jonathan Freedland as 'utterly disgusting subliminal nastiness', a remark that its target would later note 'was curiously out of character'. Freedland later recalls receiving a reassuring text message from a *Guardian* colleague after the documentary was aired that read 'Badge of honour!'[13] In the following years, the *Guardian* would come under fire from the left for its unfavourable treatment of Corbyn and his supporters, and its alignment with the then marginalised right of the Labour Party, even if a small number of its comment journalists were supportive of Corbyn, albeit neither strongly nor consistently.

In short, although the *Guardian* employs a number of left-wing columnists, and is often regarded as a left-wing newspaper, it is arguably very much part of the network of elite political opinion described, and critiqued, by Allen. Can this claim be substantiated empirically? Twitter provides an opportunity to evaluate networks of political communication and opinion formation in a way that was not previously possible. While data from the platform cannot provide a full picture, nor produce the sort of insights yielded by qualitative work, the widespread use of Twitter by those 'intensively involved' in formal politics, allows for a large scale and systematic analysis of communicative networks. Twitter is by far the most significant social media platform in UK journalism and is widely used for monitoring breaking news, gauging political opinion, identifying sources and promoting content.[14] Research suggests that journalists' Twitter networks correlate with their 'real world' professional interactions.[15]

Much early commentary and scholarship on journalism and social media assumed that platforms like Twitter would bring greater heterogeneity and openness to the industry. It focused for example on the use of user-generated content and the potential for greater dialogue and synthesis between journalists and their audiences. In this respect it failed to anticipate not only the acute, antagonistic modes of communication that would develop on social media, but also the inequalities of 'voice' that would emerge. Recent research has suggested that journalists continue to gravitate towards elites on Twitter and tend to interact mainly with other journalists.[16] Indeed, a recent review of research on journalism and social media suggests – somewhat ironically given the anxiety in the industry about online polarisation – that mainstream journalists may be more likely to operate in 'echo chambers' than the average citizen.[17]

Existing empirical work then seems to support the thesis that digital media reproduces existing power asymmetries, and suggests that network effects on platforms may even exacerbate the sort of elite-orientated reporting classically associated with journalist–sources relations.[18] This shouldn't be any surprise given the nature of

Twitter. The platform is a non-reciprocal network site on which users tend to follow those with more followers than them.[19] This means that it is characterised not only by a small number of highly active users, but also by highly skewed distributions of followers. For this reason, it has been suggested that Twitter 'better resembles a mixture of mass communication and face-to-face communication' than it does a horizontal social network.[20] Indeed, while much has been made of the egalitarian nature of social media compared to the closed and elite orientated world of traditional journalism, it is striking the extent to which broader prominence and status is associated with following and therefore reach.

METHODS, ANALYSIS AND DISCUSSION

The starting point for the present analysis was a list of *Guardian* and *Observer* columnists compiled from the *Guardian* website's contributor's index on 29 April 2020.[21] This yielded a total of 44 writers. So as to focus on the core columnists associated with the Guardian Media Group, only those listed writers who had (1) authored an article for the *Guardian* or *Observer* in the previous four months, and (2) whose author biography made some reference to a role at the *Guardian* or *Observer*, were included. This left 26 columnists, all but one of whom (Barbara Ellen) have Twitter accounts. The Microsoft Excel template NodeXL, which facilitates data extraction from Twitter via its API, was used to scrape data from these 25 accounts, including every Twitter account each of them follows. The timelines for each of the 25 columnists were also extracted (which is limited by Twitter to a user's last 3,200 tweets approximately). This scrape produced a dataset of 105,061 unique Twitter users followed by one or more of these 25 columnists, and a total of 62,567 tweets and retweets. The scope for substantive analysis of data at this scale obviously poses challenges, and a number of approaches have been taken that focus on a subset of these users or tweets. We begin with an analysis of the 25 columnists themselves and their relations with each other. Then we examine the 205 Twitter accounts they most follow, before looking specifically at which MPs they follow. Finally, we examine the Twitter users followed by only five of the 25 columnists to see what kinds of differences emerge between them.

Figure 12.1 is a visualisation of the follow connections between the 25 columnists. This is a fairly dense network. There are a total of 226 connections between the 25 users. If every columnist followed every other columnist in the network there would be 600. What network scientists call the 'graph density' of the network, therefore, is 0.377, which is to say that it is around 38% complete. At the core of the follow network is Jonathan Freedland, who is followed by 20 (80%) of his colleagues. The next most followed columnists are the *Observer*'s Nick Cohen and longstanding *Guardian* writer Polly Toynbee, who are both followed by 16 of their colleagues (64%). At the periphery, meanwhile, is author, think tanker and academic Timothy Garton Ash, as well as several of the more international *Guardian* columnists: Reza Aslan, Van Badham, Emma Brockes, Rebecca Carroll and Natalie Nougayrède.

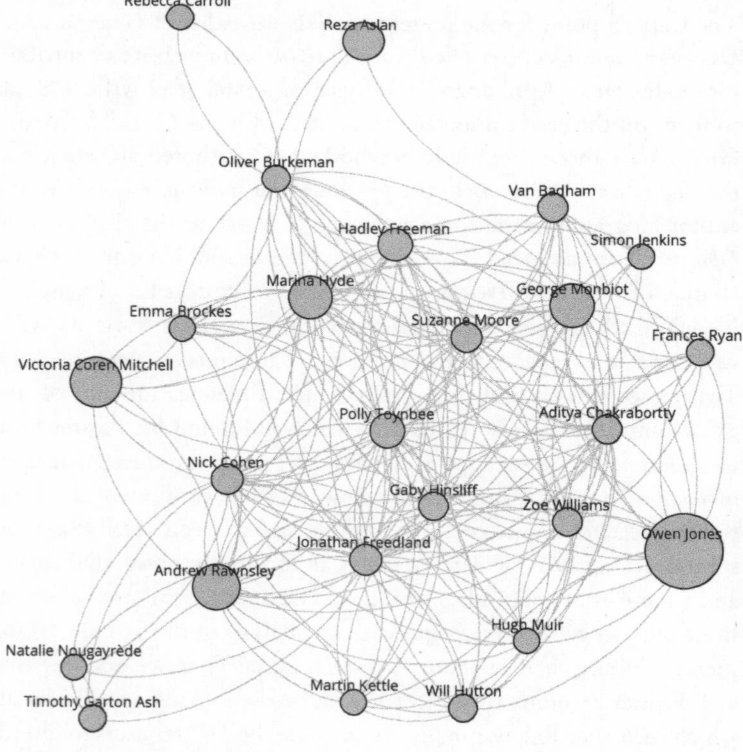

Figure 12.1 Directed Twitter follow network of 25 *Guardian* and *Observer* columnists. Nodes sized by number of Twitter followers.

There does not appear to be a very strong relationship between a journalists' centrality in this follow network and their overall following on Twitter. Owen Jones, Victoria Coren Mitchell and Andrew Rawnsley have the highest Twitter following among the 25 columnists, but are not particularly central in this network. This can be seen in Figure 12.1, in which nodes are sized according to their number of Twitter followers. Statistically, there is some relationship between the number of followers and the number of journalist followers, although the correlation is fairly weak (Spearman's rho: 0.487).

Since Figure 12.1 is a visualisation of a directed network, where users are positioned closer to nodes that follow them, even if they don't follow back, the visual structure can potentially be misleading. However, filtering for only reciprocated edges (meaning that only users who follow each other are connected) does relatively little to alter the overall network structure, as can be seen by comparing Figure 12.1 with Figure 12.2. In a reciprocated follow network, the American

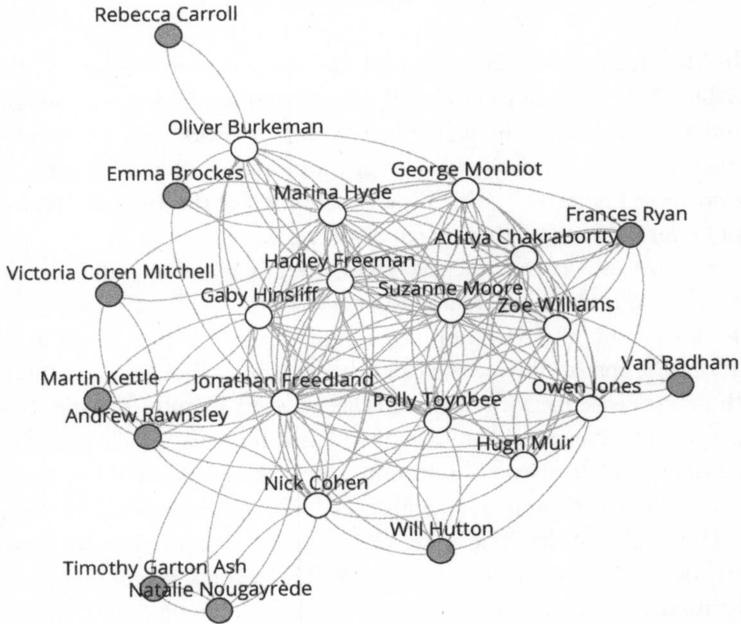

Figure 12.2 The giant component of the reciprocated follow network of 25 *Guardian* and *Observer* columnists. The core of the network is coloured white, and the more peripheral users grey.

religious studies scholar Reza Aslan and Simon Jenkins (who follows only six Twitter users) both drop out of the giant component (having no mutual connections to any other user). This reduces the network density to 0.336, meaning that a third of the 25 journalists are Twitter 'mutuals'.

In this network, Jonathan Freedland remains the most central user (with 13 mutual ties), though now jointly with Suzanne Moore. Next most connected are Gaby Hinsliff, Marina Hyde and Polly Toynbee, each of whom have 11, followed by Aditya Chakrabortty, Owen Jones and Zoe Williams, who have 10. All these more connected journalists are coloured white in Figure 12.2. These users are part of the maximally connected core of the network (in this case is a sub-network of 13 nodes connected to at least six other users). This makes the more peripheral columnists (coloured in dark grey) more readily identifiable.

CONVERSATIONAL CLUSTERING

In both these networks, while core and peripheral nodes are identifiable, there is not a particularly clear clustering of users – although those familiar with the columnists in this network may be able to interpret their proximity. A clearer clustering of the columnists is evident in Figure 12.3, which is a visualisation of the Twitter interactions between them, whether retweets, replies or mentions.

For this visualisation, the edges have been weighted according to the number of interactions, and clusters within the network – identified with a community detection algorithm[22] – are coloured black, dark grey, light grey and white. As can be seen, Emma Brockes and Oliver Burkeman together form one such cluster, as do Timothy Garton Ash and Natalie Nougayrède. Other than these couplets, which have the highest number of user interactions, the columnists form two large conversational clusters of roughly equal sizes. The larger of the two, colour coded white in Figure 12.3, contains the columnists most central in the mutual follow network. The second, colour coded in light grey, notably includes the more left-wing columnists. Also in this cluster is Polly Toynbee, likely because of her numerous interactions with Aditya Chakrabortty, and who is also notable for her frequent interactions with Will Hutton another member of this cluster who advocates a social democratic politics, but who has been highly critical of the Parliamentary left.

The clusters among our columnists that we start to see here more notably than in the follow networks (although Figure 12.3 has some clear similarities) are further explored in relation to their distinct following patterns below. Before that, though, we turn to analysing the Twitter accounts most followed by these columnists in aggregate.

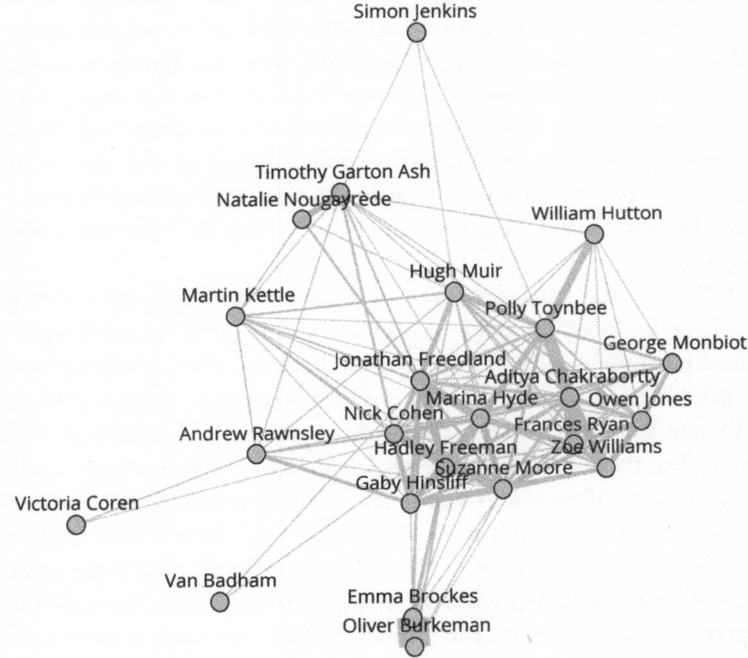

Figure 12.3 Conversational network of 25 *Guardian* and *Observer* columnists. Edges sized and shaped according to their intensity and nodes are coloured according to their cluster.

MOST FOLLOWED TWITTER USERS

In this section we focus on top 'followees': a total of 205 Twitter users followed by ten or more of the columnists (among them some of the columnists themselves). Before proceeding it is worth noting that these users make up only a fraction of the total accounts each individual columnist follows. As noted above, the 25 columnists together follow a total of 30,193 unique Twitter users. Eighty per cent of these are followed by only one of the 25. A total of 5,859 are followed by two or more, 2,833 by three or more, 1,672 by four or more, and so on until we reach the two users followed by 19 of our columnists: the current and former editors of the *Guardian* Katharine Viner and Alan Rusbridger respectively. It is important to note, therefore, that the journalists' networks may be more diverse than the following analysis implies, and also that the 205 most followed users are not necessarily the users at the core of each individual columnist's Twitter network. This is because a followee a columnist shares with nine or more other colleagues may not be widely followed by their other Twitter followees. In other words, the 205 accounts examined below are not necessarily those most prevalent on individual columnist's timelines, rather they are the users most followed by these *Guardian* and *Observer* columnists in aggregate.

The 205 top followees were categorised according to their current field and primary institutional affiliation. This is not always straightforward since in some cases individuals have recently moved from one organisation to another, or have changed occupation altogether. Gary Younge, for example, one of the contributors to this collection, who is among these 205 users, recently left the *Guardian* to take up a role as Professor of Sociology at Manchester University. In this case, his high following is plainly due to his former role. However, rather than assume whether a current or former field or organisation is the most significant, the coding has more straightforwardly been based on the person's primary activity and affiliation at the time of data extraction. This still relies on some subjective judgement since there are many different ways an occupational field can be categorised, aggregated and disaggregated, and it is not always clear which organisation should be considered most significant in cases where a person has more than one. One example is Andrew Neil, who is affiliated with *The Spectator* magazine, but who has the BBC as his primary institutional affiliation (his departure from the Corporation was announced later in 2020). In short, the coding is rather crude and has some limitations. In most cases, though, the categorisation is relatively clear cut, and the results are in any case reliable enough to provide a sense of the types of users most followed by the columnists in aggregate.

Table 12.1 displays the names, field and affiliation of the 18 most followed Twitter users. This already provides some revealing data. First, as already noted, the two most followed users are the *Guardian*'s two most recent editors. Moreover, the third most followed user is its former deputy editor Ian Katz, now director of programmes at Channel 4. Aside from these figures we see a mix of high profile journalists from the UK's most prestigious media organisations. Arguably Paul Waugh stands out here for his affiliation with HuffPost UK, although it is worth noting that he is also the presenter of the BBC's longest running political programme, Radio 4's *The Week in Westminster*, and is very much a political insider. The most followed political figures, with the exception of Conservative intellectual and Peer Daniel Finkelstein, are all from the right of the Labour Party.

Table 12.1 18 Twitter users most followed by 25 *Guardian* and *Observer* columnists.

User	*Field*	*Primary institutional affiliation*	*Following*
Kath Viner	Journalism	*Guardian*	19
Alan Rusbridger	Journalism	None	19
Ian Katz	Journalism	Channel 4	17
Amelia Gentleman	Journalism	*Guardian*	16
Daniel Finkelstein	Journalism	*The Times*	16
Janine Gibson	Journalism	*Financial Times*	16
David Lammy MP	Politics	Labour	16
Hugo Rifkind	Journalism	*The Times*	16
David Aaronovitch	Journalism	*The Times*	16
Paul Waugh	Journalism	HuffPost UK	16
Alastair Campbell	PR/Comms	Labour	16
Andrew Neil	Journalism	BBC	16
Robert Peston	Journalism	ITV	16
Rafael Behr	Journalism	*Guardian*	16
Tom Watson	Politics	Labour	16
Jon Snow	Journalism	Channel 4	16
Jess Phillips	Politics	Labour	16
Nick Cohen	Journalism	*Observer*	16

Table 12.1 gives some sense of the extent to which *Guardian* columnists follow their colleagues and peers, as well as revealing their

tendency to follow centrist politicians. In both cases this holds if we look at the top 205 accounts as a whole. Of these users, 27% are affiliated with the *Guardian* stable (n=55), while a total of 72% (those included) work in journalism. The number of users in each category is displayed in Table 12.2, along with the average number of followers in that category. Even these quite striking figures slightly underestimate the level of industry insularity, since a few users are former journalists who have moved into other fields (e.g. Gary Younge, Seumas Milne). Notably, the only businessperson to feature among these 205 users is Mumsnet founder Justine Roberts, who is the partner of the aforementioned Ian Katz.

Table 12.2 Professional field of 205 Twitter users most followed by 25 *Guardian* and *Observer* columnists.

Field	*n*	*Average followers*
Journalism	147	12
Politics	25	12
Academia	7	12
Literature/Publishing	6	11
PR/Communications	5	13
Comedy/Entertainment	5	11
Polling	3	11
NGO/Third sector	3	10
Law	2	10
Business	1	10
Sport	1	10

The insularity evident in Tables 1 and 2 is also illustrated by the data visualised in Figure 12.4, a TreeMap which shows the institutions with the highest aggregate following (that is the sum of the number of followers of every followee with that primary affiliation) among the top 205 accounts. Each of the institutions are sized according to that figure and coloured by their field (of which there are only two: journalism and politics in light grey and dark grey respectively).

While Figure 12.4 shows the focus of the columnists on the Labour Party. Further analysis shows that the specific orientation (also suggested by Table 12.1) is towards the right of that party, and towards centrists MPs more generally. Table 12.3 displays the MPs

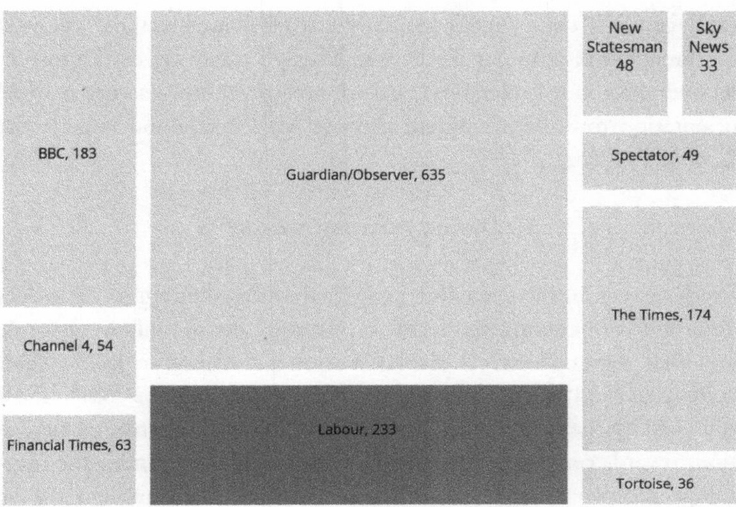

Figure 12.4 TreeMap displaying the aggregate following of the ten most prevalent organisations among the 205 Twitter accounts most followed by Guardian columnists.

Table 12.3 19 MPs from the 2017 and 2019 Parliaments most followed by 25 *Guardian* and *Observer* columnists

Name	*Party*	*Followers*
David Lammy	Labour	16
Jess Phillips	Labour	16
Tom Watson	Labour	16
Keir Starmer	Labour	15
Yvette Cooper	Labour	15
Stella Creasy	Labour	14
Caroline Lucas	Green	13
Chuka Umunna	Change UK	13
Ed Miliband	Labour	12
John McDonnell	Labour	12
Lisa Nandy	Labour	12
Liz Kendall	Labour	10
Luciana Berger	Change UK	10
Diane Abbott	Labour	9
Harriet Harman	Labour	9
Rachel Reeves	Labour	9
Stephen Kinnock	Labour	9
Wes Streeting	Labour	9
Rory Stewart	Conservative	9

(and former MPs) from the 2017 and 2019 Parliaments most followed by the columnists under discussion. Though members of the former left-wing Labour leadership team are present, there is a very marked orientation towards prominent centrist MPs inside and outside the Labour Party.

Distinct following patterns

We have seen in the preceding analysis that together our 25 *Guardian* and *Observer* columnists form a relatively dense online network, and that they collectively display a strong tendency to follow their colleagues and their industry peers. Looking at the MPs most followed by these journalists, meanwhile, shows their strong orientation towards centrist politicians. However, while examining the most followed accounts is very revealing of commonalities amongst the 25 columnists, what about potential differences that might be obscured in these data? The network analysis revealed not only more central and peripheral columnists, but also suggested there may be distinct clusters among them. To analyse whether these clusters might exhibit distinct following patterns and political orientation, we now examine first the groups of MPs each of our columnists most follow, and second the Twitter followees they share with just four of their colleagues (in other words the Twitter accounts followed by only five of our 25 columnists). In both cases correspondence analysis is used, a geometric data analysis technique that summarises and visually represents data from a contingency table.[23] Correspondence analysis is one of a family of multivariate statistical methods that also includes multiple correspondence analysis, a similar technique used for categorical data that was popularised by Pierre Bourdieu in his work on social capital and fields.[24] These approaches produce 'clouds' of points in a relational space that can then be qualitatively interpreted. In Bourdieusian analysis, multiple correspondence analysis is typically used to produce a representation of the space of a 'social field' in which individuals compete on the basis of different forms and amounts of 'capital'. More broadly though, these techniques are useful for social mapping since points can be interpreted in relation to other points based on their location. Significantly for our purposes, correspondence analysis also draws attention to differences, rather than commonalities, in the data.

We begin with the relationship between our columnists and the MPs (and former MPs) from the 2017 and 2019 Parliaments who they follow on Twitter. To do so, the Twitter handles of MPs were extracted from the columnists' followees using a 2019 and 2020 list of Twitter handles from the website, MPs on Twitter. The followed MPs were then aggregated to political parties and, in the case of Labour MPs, party factions. The Labour Party factions were identified using a document leaked to the press in 2016 that categorised the then Labour MPs in relation to their hostility to the party leadership. That document placed the MPs in five categories: core group, core group plus, neutral but not hostile, core group negative and hostile group. For clarity, these groups are renamed here: Labour Left core, Labour Left, Labour Neutral, Labour Right, Labour Right core.[25]

To conduct the correspondence analysis the starting point is a contingency table where the columnists (of which there are 21 since four follow no MPs in the data) are rows, the groups of MPs are columns, and each cell is the number of MPs that the given columnist follows in that party or party faction. Data in this table are the basis of a visualisation (Figure 12.5) that plots the columnists and the political groupings in a two dimensional space.

For those not familiar with correspondence analysis, a few basic principles will aid interpretation of this visualisation. First, it positions points close to other points with similar profiles. What this means is that columnists close to each other in Figure 12.5 tend to be following MPs in similar political parties and groupings, while political parties and groups that are close to each other conversely tend to have similar columnists as followers. Second, columnists and political groupings with less typical following profiles are located further from the origin (i.e. where both axes meet at 0 in Figure 12.5 – known as the barycentre in correspondence analysis terminology). This means that political groupings with a fairly even distribution of following among the columnists will tend to be closer to the centre, while those with a following concentrated among a smaller number of columnists (for example) will be positioned towards the edges of the visualisation. Third, points with negative associations will usually be positioned opposite sides of the origin. So in the case of Figure 12.5, columnists following the Labour Left are less likely to be following Change UK and *vice versa*. The final point worth noting is that in correspondence analysis the dimensions (i.e. the x and y axes) can be qualitatively interpreted. This is an important part of making sense of the 'social space' in which points are positioned.

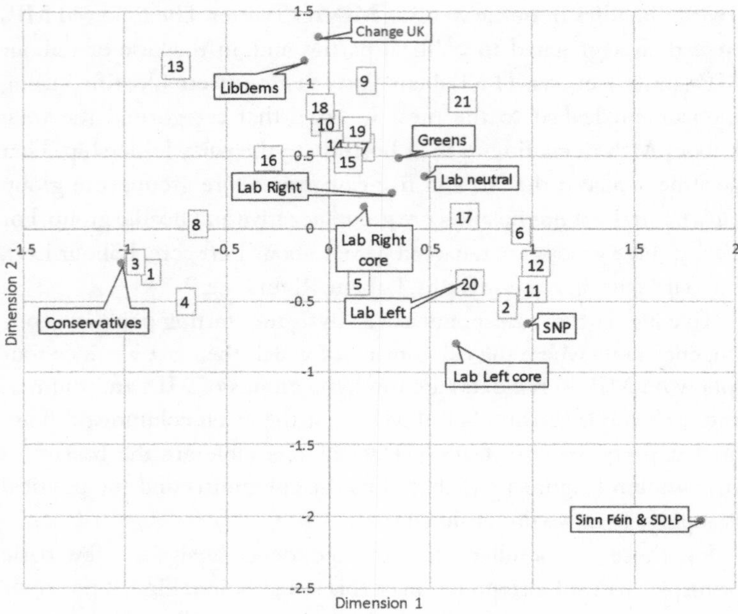

Figure 12.5 Cloud of *Guardian* and *Observer* columnists and political parties and factions. The columnists are numbered in order of their 'inertia', meaning those contributing more to the structure of the social spaces are numbered lower. 1. Gaby Hinsliff, 2. Owen Jones, 3. Marina Hyde, 4. George Monbiot, 5. Aditya Chakrabortty, 6. Van Badham, 7. Polly Toynbee, 8. Martin Kettle, 9. Nick Cohen, 10. Jonathan Freedland, 11. Frances Ryan, 12. Zoe Williams, 13. Timothy Garton Ash, 14. Hadley Freeman, 15. Andrew Rawnsley, 16. Hugh Muir, 17. Suzanne Moore, 18. William Hutton, 19. Victoria Coren, 20. Oliver Burkeman, 21. Emma Brockes.

In Figure 12.5, Dimension 1 is characterised most of all by the contrast between the Conservative Party at one pole, and on the other the Labour Left and to a lesser extent the national parties (hence why they are located on opposite ends of the y axis). Dimension 2, meanwhile, is characterised most by a contrast between those same left-wing factions and national parties at one pole, and the centrist political groupings on the other: Change UK and the Liberal Democrats. On the *Conservative v. left/national* axis (Dimension 1), the individuals with the largest contribution to the axis are former *Observer* political editor Gaby Hinsliff on the Tory side and Owen Jones on the left/national side. On the *centrist v. left/national* axis (Dimension 2) the individuals with the largest contribution are Owen Jones again on the left/national pole and Nick Cohen on the centrist side. Or to put it in simpler terms, according to this data, Gaby Hinsliff is (in relative terms) the most 'Tory' of the columnists, Nick Cohen is the most centrist and Owen Jones the most left-wing.

Turning to the specific positioning of the columnists in Figure 12.5, along with Gaby Hinsliff, Marina Hyde, Martin Kettle and George Monbiot all stand out for following Conservative MPs more than their colleagues (N.B. this doesn't mean they follow more Tory than Labour MPs, rather that they tend to follow more Tory MPs relative to their colleagues). So do Timothy Garton Ash and Hadley Freeman, though they are relatively closer to the centrist MPs than the former group of columnists. Most of the remaining columnists are positioned between the centrist parties and the Labour Right factions, towards the top right of the visualisation. Here we find the columnists who are the core of the *Guardian*'s editorial politics: Nick Cohen, Jonathan Freedland, Hadley Freeman, Andrew Rawnsley and Polly Toynbee, among others. In the bottom right quadrant, meanwhile, are those users who are more likely to follow the Labour Left or the nationalist parties compared to their colleagues. Here we find not just Owen Jones, but also Aditya Chakrabortty, Frances Ryan and Zoe Williams, among others. What this suggests is that while in aggregate the *Guardian* and *Observer* columnists have a strikingly insular and centrist orientation on Twitter, there are nevertheless some marked political differences between these columnists.

This is further illustrated by the final two visualisations, which are based on a correspondence analysis of our 25 columnists and the Twitter accounts followed by only five of them; an approach intended to uncover any general differences in following patterns beyond the field of formal party politics analysed in Figure 12.5. This analysis produced a cloud of 24 columnists and 327 followees. For ease of interpretation, given the high number of data points, the columnists and followees are displayed in two separate visualisations (Figures

12.6 and 12.7). Both, however, represent the same relational space and should be interpreted together. Figure 12.6 displays the 327 followees, which are distributed in a fairly even cloud across the four quadrants, although the bottom right section is slightly sparser and more dispersed (on account of the wider distribution of Natalie Nougayrède's shared followees – see Nougayrède's placement in Figure 12.7). Figure 12.7 shows the columnists, again positioned according to the similarity of their following profiles.

In a similar way to Figure 12.5, what we are analysing here is the extent to which columnists share followees with other columnists, and conversely the extent to which different followees share the same columnists. Recall that every followee in this analysis has five different columnists as followers. The number of these followees each columnist follows though will vary. Simon Jenkins does not follow any (which is not surprising given that he follows only six Twitter accounts), while at the other extreme it is possible, in theory, that a single columnist could follow all 327 of the followees (with their remaining four follows distributed among the other columnists). Additionally, it is also the case that the number of other columnists with whom a given columnist shares followees may vary considerably, even if the number of followees per columnist were constant. A columnist with four followees, for example, could potentially share them with a minimum of four and a maximum of 16 other columnists. One way of thinking about this is the followings being more distributed among the columnists, or clustered among particular sets of columnists, and this is what will determine the placement of both in the shared 'social space'. Our hypothetical columnist who follows all 327 followees, and shares a followee with every other columnist, would be located at the origin/barycentre. Those with more unusual follow patterns, meanwhile, like our hypothetical columnist who shares followees with only four others, would be further from the origin/barycentre. Columnists who share followees, meanwhile, will be positioned closer together.

To aid interpretation of this 'social space', a selection of followees have been labelled. Interpretation of the two dimensions of this analysis is less clear than in Figure 12.5, but taken together the followees appear to cluster into four distinct groups. In the top left of Figure 12.6 we find a concentration of left-wing organisations and commentators, while in the bottom left there is a notable concentration of more 'establishment' conservative and centrist figures. The top right quadrant, meanwhile, is less overtly political. It contains a number of celebrities, comedians, authors and other public figures. Finally, the bottom right quadrant is where the international – and particularly American – figures are concentrated. In broad terms then, we find users followed by the UK political commentariat mainly on the left side of the space, while on the right are accounts more followed by the *Guardian* and *Observer*'s lifestyle focused columnists and their international commentators.

Turning to the placement of particular columnists in the same space, there are some clear similarities, and noticeable differences if we compare Figure 12.7 with Figure 12.5. Again we see the *Guardian*'s

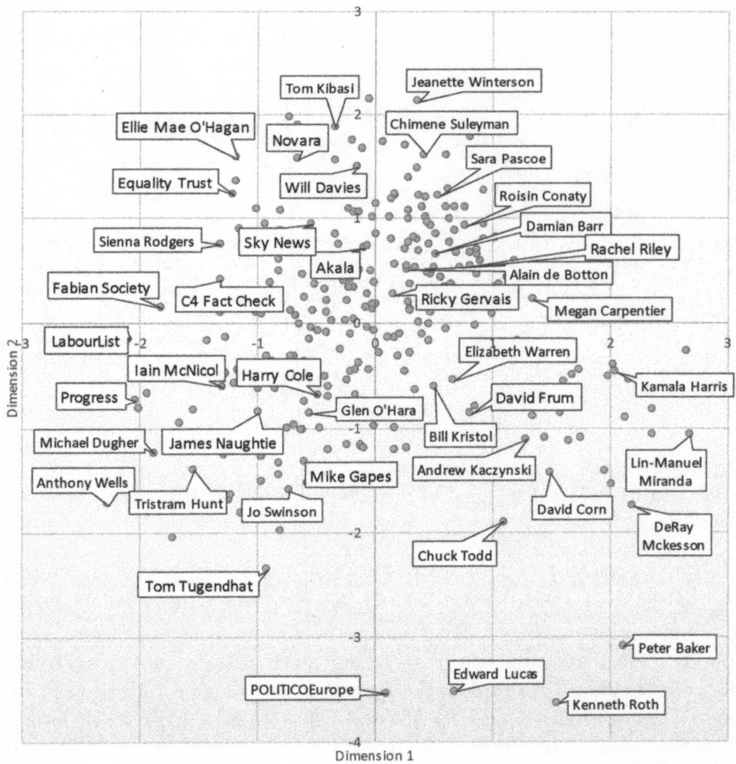

Figure 12.6 Cloud of 327 Twitter users followed by only five of the 25 Guardian and *Observer* columnists. A selection of users are labelled to aid interpretation.

left-wing columnists forming a cluster distinct from its core editorial figures, with Owen Jones, Frances Ryan and Zoe Williams again emerging as distinct left voices. This time, however, Will Hutton and George Monbiot, who were not found to be associated with the left in Parliament, are somewhat closer to the *Guardian*'s left columnists. Aditya Chakrabortty, meanwhile, appears to occupy something of a middle ground between the left and right factions, as does Hugh Muir, who likewise has a quite balanced following and who like Hutton was not at all associated with the Labour Left under Corbyn.

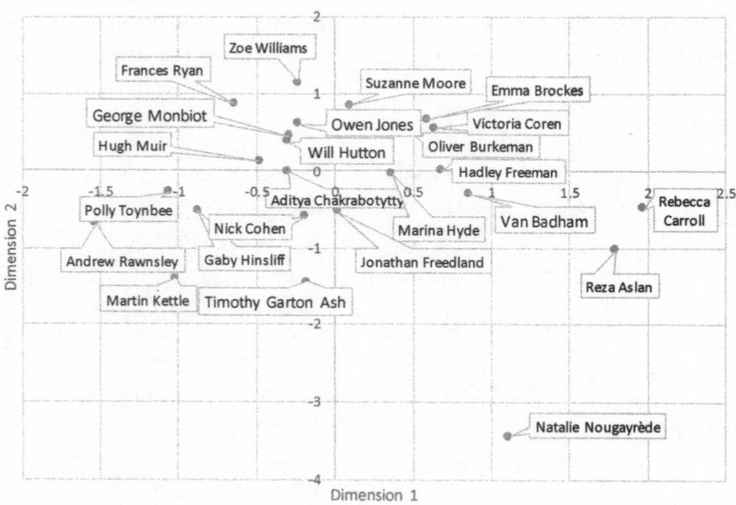

Figure 12.7 Cloud of *24 Guardian and Observer* columnists positioned according to their following of 327 Twitter users followed by four other columnists.

Notably contrasted with the left-wing *Guardian* columnists, meanwhile, are the more conservative and centrist writers in the bottom left quadrant, although in this analysis Hadley Freeman, Marina Hyde and to a lesser extent Jonathan Freedland, appear to have a more 'cultural' and international follow network, making them distinct from their more parochial colleagues in the bottom left quadrant. Finally, the less explicitly political columnists are located in the upper right quadrant, and the international commentators, who were fairly peripheral in the network analysis are mainly located in the bottom right quadrant.

CONCLUSION

Although this research has been somewhat exploratory, the results are very revealing about the nature of *Guardian* and *Observer* columnists' networks on Twitter, and arguably the broader political universe of which they are part. In line with the findings of recent work on journalists' Twitter networks, it reveals the columnists' aggregate following patterns to be highly insular. Judging by their most followed accounts, *Guardian* and *Observer* columnists have a very striking tendency to follow other journalists, and their colleagues in particular. Outside of journalism, meanwhile, politics is the field with the most aggregate attention, and here the particular focus is on the Labour Party most of all.

Further analysis, however, reveals that columnists' aggregate following is orientated most of all towards centrist politicians, and not only those in the Labour Party. In Table 12.2, we saw that Jess Phillips, a relatively inexperienced politician known best for her outspoken opposition to the Parliamentary left, had more followers amongst *Guardian* and *Observer* columnists than even the current Labour leader Sir Keir Starmer. A number of Labour MPs and former Labour MPs who are similarly most notable for their opposition to the former left-wing party leadership, meanwhile, are among the most followed politicians. Jeremy Corbyn himself was, at the time of data extraction, followed by only seven of the columnists – the same number as the prime minister Boris Johnson. Politicians with a higher aggregate following than both, who do not appear in Table 12.2, include the prime minister's brother Jo Johnson, the virulently anti-Corbyn Labour MP, Margaret Hodge, Change UK leading light Anna Soubry, the former Lib Dem leader Vince Cable, the Conservative rebels Jesse Norman and Nick Boles, and the Blairite Liam Byrne.

All this appears to substantiate claims from the left of a centrist bias in the editorial culture of the *Guardian* and *Observer*. The analysis, though, also reveals some notable differences among the columnists. A handful stand out for their closer association with the left, most consistently Owen Jones, Frances Ryan and Zoe Williams. The network analysis suggests that these columnists are hardly peripheral figures, but they do appear to be at odds with the core editorial culture at the *Guardian*. This itself is perhaps revealing. While the *Guardian* and *Observer* are often imagined to be the natural home of the left in the UK, even their most left-wing columnists have in recent years maintained a certain distance from, or at times have been notably at odds with, a political movement that enjoyed some considerable public support, yet found little or no support among the 'opinion formers' who hold sway in the world of formal politics.

NOTES

1. Mike Savage, 'Contemporary Sociology and the Challenge of Descriptive Assemblage', *European Journal of Social Theory*, 12:1, (2009), pp. 155–74; Mike Savage, 'What Makes For a Successful Sociology? A response to "Against a Descriptive Turn"', *British Journal of Sociology*, 71:1, (2020), pp. 19–27.
2. For example, Julie Firmstone, 'The Editorial Production Process and Editorial Values as Influences on the Opinions of the British Press Towards Europe', *Journalism Practice*, 2(2), 2008, pp. 212–29; Julie Firmstone, 'Editorial Journalism and Newspapers' Editorial Opinions', in *Oxford research encyclopedia of communication* (Oxford: Oxford University Press, 2019); Kimberly Meltzer, 'Newspaper editorial boards and the practice of endorsing candidates for political office in the United States', *Journalism*, 8(1), 2007, pp. 83–103; Aaron Reeves, Martin McKee and David Stuckler, '"It's the Sun Wot Won It": Evidence of media influence on Political Attitudes and Voting from a UK Quasi-natural Experiment', *Social Science Research*, 56, (2016), pp. 44–57, doi: 10.1016/j.ssresearch.2015.11.002.
3. Alistair Duff, 'Powers in The Land? British Political Columnists in the Information Era', *Journalism Practice*, 2:2, (2008), pp. 230–44; Jeremy Tunstall, *Newspaper Power: The New National Press in Britain* (Oxford: Clarendon Press, 1996).
4. Brian McNair, *Journalism and Democracy: An Evaluation of the Political Public Sphere* (London: Routledge, 2012), p. 68.
5. Martin Kettle, 'Don't Believe Everything You Read on the Comment Pages', *Guardian*, 17 December 2002, www.theguardian.com/politics/2002/dec/17/pressandpublishing.media (accessed 3 October 2020).
6. Karin Wahl Jorgensen, 'Playground of the Pundits or Voice of the People? Comparing British and Danish Opinion Pages', *Journalism Studies*, 5:1, (2004), p. 61.
7. McNair, *Journalism and Democracy*, p. 80.
8. Wahl-Jorgensen, 'Playground of the Pundits', p. 68.
9. Aeron Davis, *The Mediation of Power* (London: Routledge, 2007), pp. 106–8.

10. Peter Allen and David S. Moon, 'Predictions, Pollification, and Pol Profs: The "Corbyn Problem" Beyond Corbyn', *Political Quarterly*, 91:1 (2020), p. 80.
11. Peter Allen, 'Political Science, Punditry, and the Corbyn Problem', *British Politics*, 15:1 (2020), pp. 69–87.
12. Davis, *Mediation of Power*, p. 88.
13. Jonathan Freedland, 'What Did Jeremy Corbyn Mean When He Insulted Me?', thejc.com, 23 January 2020, www.thejc.com/comment/columnists/when-corbyn-insulted-me-what-did-he-mean-1.495769 (accessed 24 September 2020).
14. Marcel Broersma, Marcel and Todd Graham, 'Tipping the Balance Of Power: Social media and the Transformation of Political Journalism', pp. 89–103 in *The Routledge Companion to Social Media and Politics*, edited by A. Bruns, G. Enli, E. Skogerbo, A. O. Larsson and C. Christensen, (London: Routledge, 2015); Lasorsa, Dominic L., Seth C. Lewis and Avery E. Holton, 'Normalizing Twitter: Journalism Practice in an Emerging Communication Space', *Journalism Studies*, 13(1), 2015, pp. 19–36; Kristine Pole and Agnes Gulyas, *Global social journalism study* (Chicago: Cision, 2015), www.cision.com/us/resources/white-papers/2015-global-social-journalism-study/?clid=whitepaper-ty (accessed 5 October 2020).
15. Michiel Johnson, Steve Paulussen and Peter Van Aelst, 'Much Ado About Nothing? The Low Importance of Twitter as a Sourcing Tool for Economic Journalists', *Digital Journalism*, 6:7 (2018), pp. 869–88.
16. Kelly Fincham, 'Exploring Political Journalism Homophily on Twitter: A Comparative Analysis of US and UK Elections in 2016 and 2017', *Media and Communication*, 7:1 (2019), pp. 213–24; Folker Hanusch and Daniel Nölleke, 'Journalistic homophily on Social Media: Exploring Journalists' Interactions with Each Other on Twitter', *Digital Journalism*, 2018, pp. 1–23; Sophie Lecheler and Sanne Kruikemeier, 'Re-Evaluating Journalistic Routines in a Digital Age: A Review of Research on the Use of Online Sources', *New Media & Society*, 18:1 (2016), pp. 156–71; Logan Molyneux and Rachel R Mourão, 'Political journalists' Normalization of Twitter: Interaction and New Affordances', *Journalism Studies*, 20:2 (2019), pp. 248–66; Christian Nuernbergk, 'Political Journalists' Interaction Networks: The German Federal Press Conference on Twitter', *Journalism Practice*, 10(7), 2016, pp. 868–79; Nikki Usher and Yee Man Margaret Ng, 'Sharing Knowledge and "Microbubbles": Epistemic Communities and Insularity in US Political Journalism', *Social Media + Society*, 6:2 (2020).
17. Seth Lewis and Logan Molyneux, 'A Decade of Research on Social Media and Journalism: Assumptions, Blind Spots, and a Way Forward', *Media and Communication*, 6:4 (2018), pp. 11–23.
18. Richard Ericson, Richard Victor, Patricia M. Baranek and Janet B. L. Chan, *Negotiating Control: A Study of News Sources* (Toronto: University

of Toronto Press, 1989); Stuart Hall et al., *Policing the Crisis: Mugging, The State and Law and Order* (Basingstoke: Palgrave Macmillan, 2013); Edward Herman and Noam Chomsky, *Manufacturing Consent: The Political Economy of the Mass Media* (London: Bodley Head, 2008); Paul Manning, *News And News Sources: A Critical Introduction* (London: Sage, 2000).

19. Naghmeh Momeni and Michael Rabbat, 'Qualities and Inequalities in Online Social Networks Through the Lens of the Generalized Friendship Paradox', *PloS one*, 11:2, (2016), e0143633.
20. Marco Toledo Bastos, Rafael Luis Galdini Raimundo and Rodrigo Travitzki, 'Gatekeeping Twitter: Message diffusion in political hashtags', *Media, Culture & Society*, 35:2, (2013), pp. 260–70.
21. www.theguardian.com/index/contributors
22. Vincent Blondel, Jean-Loup Guillaume, Renaud Lambiotte and Etienne Lefebvre, 'Fast unfolding of communities in large networks', *Journal of Statistical Mechanics: Theory and Experiment*, 10, (2008): P10008.
23. Johs Hjellbrekke, *Multiple Correspondence Analysis for the Social Science*s (London: Routledge, 2018); Brigitte Le Roux and Henry Rouanet, *Geometric Data Analysis: From Correspondence Analysis To Structured Data* (Dordrecht: Springer Science & Business Media, 2004).
24. Pierre Bourdieu, *Homo Academicus* (Cambridge: Polity Press, 1988); Pierre Bourdieu, *The State Nobility: Elite Schools in the Field Of Power* (Stanford: Stanford University Press, 1998).
25. It should be noted that these party factions do not include a number of Labour MPs, and conversely a number of Labour MPs in the listed document are not in the dataset, since the document was drawn up in relations to the 2015 Parliament.

13
The *Guardian* and the Economy

Mike Berry

INTRODUCTION

This chapter uses the Great Financial Crisis (GFC) of 2007–8 as a case study to explore the contribution to public debate provided by the *Guardian*'s economic journalism. Its purpose is to map and unpack the range of arguments and debates within the *Guardian*'s coverage of the crisis and highlight what made it distinctive from reporting in other parts of the media.

I have chosen to focus on the GFC for three key reasons. First, the GFC represented a pivotal movement in British post-war economic history when the model of financialised capitalism pursued by Conservative and Labour governments since 1979 collapsed. If crises open up the intellectual and ideological space to think anew, what role did the *Guardian* play in highlighting alternative economic futures? Second, the GFC represented an interesting counterpoint to the previous crisis of British capitalism in the late 1970s. During that period the British press and broadcasting were a key site in an attempt to win elite and public consent for monetarism and supply side economics.[1] Newspapers such as *The Times* and *Telegraph* – and later the BBC – helped popularise the ideas of Fredrich Hayek and Milton Friedman, who argued that to control inflation and revitalise the economy it would be necessary to shrink the state and restrict the money supply. How then would the press and broadcasting respond to the implosion of the economic model they had done so much to popularise over decades? Third, the crisis has produced a series of major economic and political shocks which continue to reverberate more than a decade after the collapse of Lehman Brothers. These in large part are a consequence of the policy responses to the crisis – such as austerity and quantitative easing – which have sharply widened social inequalities and boosted contemporary political movements which espouse openly racist and/or anti-democratic attitudes.[2]

The chapter will begin by briefly tracing the background to the GFC, looking at the range of debate on why the financial system came close to systemic failure in 2008. It will then explore how the *Guardian* and other media outlets narrated the crisis and discussed whether the finance sector should be reformed. The chapter then moves on to discuss how the next stage of the GFC – the so called 'deficit crisis' – was reported. The chapter concludes by offering some brief comments on how the *Guardian* responded to the shift in debate on the economy created by the election of Jeremy Corbyn as Labour leader.

THE RISE AND FALL OF BRITISH FINANCE CAPITALISM

The near systemic collapse of the British banking system in 2008 had its roots in the deregulation and subsequent growth of the sector over the previous thirty years. After 1979, the Thatcher government enacted a series of reforms which supported the growth of finance.[3] These included the abolition of exchange controls and restrictions on consumer credit as well as the deregulation of the City through the 'Big Bang' reforms of October 1986. The decision by policy makers to prioritise the interests of the City had a profound effect on the structure of the British economy and patterns of regional development.[4] Inward capital flows increased markedly, pushing up sterling, damaging exports and widening the UK's trade deficit. As noted by Tony Dolphin, former senior economist at the Institute for Public Policy Research, the bias towards finance 'produced a casualness about the decline of manufacturing and the collapse of all competing sectors which is really quite jaw-dropping.'[5]

Such structural shifts accelerated in the 1990s with the rise of financial innovation – particularly securitisation[6] and derivative[7] trading. Between 1998 and 2009 the global value of over the counter derivatives (OTC) market – much of which went through the City of London – grew from $80,309 billion to $614,674 billion, equivalent to a rise from about 2.4 times to 10 times global GDP.[8] This growth in derivatives trading allowed banks to increase their balance sheet lending to households and businesses, and this extra credit – much of which fuelled the sharp rises in residential property values – came to underpin the growth in UK GDP, public spending and employment.[9] This temporarily obscured the weaknesses in other parts of the economy, especially the non-financial private sector and in particular manufacturing – which lost two million jobs between 1997 and 2010.[10] Replicating the Thatcher government, growth under New Labour became heavily reliant on consumer demand funded by housing equity release. Between 1997 and 2007 housing equity withdrawal was equal to 103.3 per cent of the growth in UK GDP, slightly less than the 104.2 per cent seen during Mrs. Thatcher's administration.[11] The debt fuelled growth after 1997 did however allow New Labour to undertake a major programme of public investment in areas such as health and education, which, as Engelen et al. note, functioned as an 'undisclosed regional policy' by boosting state and para-state employment in areas outside the South East where private sector job creation was 'weak or failing'.[12]

The consequence of this three-decade economic regime was to leave the British economy exceptionally vulnerable to a financial shock. The UK hosted the largest financial centre (as a proportion of GDP) of any major developed nation – one that was heavily leveraged and involved in risky business practices. Its manufacturing base had fallen as a proportion of GDP to nearly 40 per cent below the Eurozone average (10.1 per cent versus 16.1 per cent) and its productivity and research and development spending lagged behind key EU competitors such as France and Germany.[13] The UK was running a persistent current account deficit and suffered from extreme regional economic polarisation with much of the area outside London and the South East being heavily dependent on public spending. Just before the crisis, the IMF estimated that the UK housing market was overvalued by 20–30 per cent whilst household debt, which had become another of the economy's key motors of growth, was at record levels.[14]

If the previous thirty years had created a deeply unequal and precarious growth model for the UK, the proximate cause of its collapse was complex since different financial institutions had made different mistakes. Bradford and Bingley, for instance, expanded heavily in the risky buy-to-let and self-certification mortgage markets, so that when the markets turned in 2007 the bank found itself facing mounting losses. RBS, on the other hand, overpaid for the Dutch bank ABN AMRO which was later revealed to be full of toxic debt. However, as the 2009 House of Commons Treasury Committee report into the crisis concluded, underlying most of these failures were three common factors.[15] One was an increasing reliance on the wholesale money markets for funding. In their rush to expand, many UK banks had become increasingly dependent on borrowing from the money markets and when these seized up – due to concerns about the solvency of finance sector institutions – British banks were unable to roll over their liabilities. A second factor underlying the crisis was the increase in leverage amongst UK banks. In the decade leading up to the crash the banking sector saw a sharp increase in leverage ratios – assets in relation to equity – and this was the most important factor which distinguished those banks that failed from those that survived. The third factor underlying the crash was the failure of risk management in the face of increasing financial complexity. Key to this was a belief that securitisation – where banks increasingly packaged up their mortgages and sold them on to investors – had reduced systemic risk by distributing any potential losses widely amongst non-bank investors. However as noted by Adair Turner, the former chairman of the Financial Services Authority, when 'the music stopped . . . the vast majority of the losses . . . did not lie in the books of end investors intending to hold the assets to maturity, but on the books of highly leveraged banks and banklike institutions'.[16] It has also been argued that underlying these three immediate factors were a series of other issues that included failures by a range of actors such as regulators, credit ratings agencies and auditors. Others have argued that the crisis was the consequence of deeper structural factors such as the build-up of global trade and investment imbalances between China and America, the liberalisation of global capital flows or rising income inequality.[17]

THE *GUARDIAN* AND THE BANKING CRISIS

Unlike much of the press the *Guardian* entered the crisis unburdened by the ideological baggage of having supported the version of financialised capitalism which imploded so spectacularly in 2008. In fact, the paper's economics editor, Larry Elliott, had been one of the most consistent and prescient critics of New Labour's economic model.[18] When the financial crisis peaked in October 2008 the media primarily blamed the bankers.[19] Even newspapers traditionally supportive of the free market – such as the *Sun* – felt the occasional need to respond to public anger by featuring headlines such as:

> SCUMBAG MILLIONAIRES Shamed Banked Bosses 'Sorry' For Crisis (11 February 2009).

However in right of centre newspapers such as the *Sun* and *Telegraph*, almost an equal number of articles blamed the Labour government for its regulatory failures and claimed that the crisis was rooted in Labour 'over-spending'. Whilst very little blame was apportioned to Gordon Brown in Labour-supporting tabloids such as the *Mirror* and *Daily Record*, the *Guardian* was a regular critic. For example, in one comment piece, Elliott argued that the bank bailouts were only necessary 'because 11 years of grotesque government toadying to the City has left Britain in a parlous position and there was no alternative but to resort to concepts expunged from the New Labour lexicon'.[20]

What also distinguished the *Guardian* during this period was the depth of its analysis. For instance, unlike most newspapers, it highlighted the role played by credit ratings agencies, quantitative analysts and high frequency trading software. This depth was also visible in how it explained the mechanisms underlying the crisis. Whilst much of the press primarily explained the crisis in terms of individual moral failings – such as greed and risk taking – or the overextension of credit, the *Guardian* also focused on more technical aspects such as the role of derivatives, capital ratios and regulatory arbitrage in tax havens. The *Guardian* was also more willing than other newspapers to link the crisis to deeper structural issues. So the *Guardian* focused on arguments around global imbalances more than others newspapers and it was the only outlet to explain the crisis in terms of the build-up of inequality:

> It is the extremes of inequality in the west's most unequal countries that set off this nuclear explosion. Gargantuan bonuses in Wall Street and the City were earned from creating fairy money, imagined to be owned by people too poor to pay anything at all. If the poor had more money, it wouldn't have happened. If mega-bonuses had not inflated share prices and borrowing beyond reason, fantasy capitalism would have been avoided.[21]

Another distinctive aspect of *Guardian* coverage was its willingness to link the crisis to Britain's economic model – followed by consecutive Conservative and Labour governments since 1979 – where the interests of the City have been prioritised at the expense of other sectors of the economy. In this way it was the only part of the mainstream media which offered its readers the opportunity to understand how regional polarisation, public policy and Britain's oversized finance sector were linked:

> For the past 20 years, policy-makers in the UK have convinced themselves that the might of the City could compensate for the country's inability to make anything. The notion that the ever widening trade deficit was merely a temporary phase while Britain adjusted to a weightless, virtual, financially driven future has now been exposed for the grotesque fantasy it always was ... the bankruptcy of the City also represents the bankruptcy of New Labour economics ... Since 1997, ministers have convinced themselves that Britain had a comparative advantage in financial services and that therefore industrial policy should be based on giving the City what the City wants. The light-touch regulation of financial services was but one expression of the almost total obeisance to big capital.[22]

When it came to discussion of the bank bailouts, the *Guardian* mostly followed the perspective taken by broadcasting and all other newspapers: that essentially the bailouts and part-nationalisations were regrettable but that there was 'no alternative'. Whilst the *Guardian* didn't feature the strident New Right criticisms of public ownership that were common in other parts of the media, some of its columnists such as Michael White were fairly scathing of nationalisation as a policy:

> Labour leftwingers have understandably rejoiced at the sight of nationalisations, their long discredited recipe for anything that moved.[23]

On the whole, *Guardian* writers were suspicious of nationalisation as a panacea, although the newspaper did regularly feature arguments for more state influence over the part-nationalised banks. This suspicion of statist solutions to economic problems was, as we will see later, one of the key areas where *Guardian* writers diverged from Corbynite economic policy. Having said this, the *Guardian* was also the only part of broadcasting and the press where arguments for full temporary or permanent nationalisation of the banking system were even briefly entertained. John McDonnell put the case for full nationalisation in a letter (on 8 October 2008) and short comment piece the following day whilst the columnist Seumas Milne argued:

> Better surely to guarantee deposits and take over such banks once they've effectively failed, as in the case of Northern Rock and Bradford & Bingley, securely recapitalising them as fully publicly owned enterprises. They could then become the core of a newly accountable and publicly controlled banking sector able to channel investment where it's needed, rather than into reckless speculation in debt and housing bubbles.[24]

In terms of how to reform the sector, most of the press had little to say beyond restricting bonuses and vague calls for more regulation. The broadsheets – speaking to a more elite audience – did provide some analysis of some of the technical fixes designed to avoid a repeat of the crisis such as changes to capital adequacy ratios or regulating OFC derivative trades. But here again, *Guardian* coverage looked distinctive. For instance, it was the only part of the media to advocate for a 'Tobin tax' to reduce speculative activity and raise questions about whether the insiders managing the reform process would prioritise a return to 'business as usual' over systemic change.

> Brown himself can only regain lost trust if he realises quite what a monumental task that is, as well as for finance. That means far more than simply getting the City back on its feet, dusting down its worst excrescences and lopping off a few bank managers' heads (with their multimillion pensions intact). It will take more radical action and more resonant language. Alas, his committee of advisers consists of the City people who got us into this: the takers of the fattest pay, the sitters on each others' boards. Paul Myners, late of the *Guardian*, will be no radical steam cleaner as City minister, more of a feather duster. Brown needs a severe committee of those economists who

> were right when he was wrong – people to frighten the City, not to soothe its frightened feathers. Appoint the Richard Murphys, Will Huttons and Larry Elliotts not as City tsars but as City Savonarolas to flush out tax avoidance and evasion, to close down tax havens, to appoint honest nonexecutives to company boardrooms and institute a regime built on public trust.[25]

It was also the only mainstream news outlet to feature arguments that restricting bonuses was not sufficient and instead criminal sanctions should be brought in together with legally binding caps on lending:

> Bank executives responsible for reckless lending should be punished under criminal law and face fines, according to a politician who rescued Sweden's banking system from collapse in the 1990s. In an interview with the *Guardian*, Bo Lundgren, director general of Sweden's national debt office, the country's financial regulator, said US proposals to cap bankers' pay as part of the $700bn bail-out did not go far enough. He said laws should be introduced in the US and Europe making it a criminal offence for bankers to lend irresponsibly. He also proposed that banks should be made subject to legally-binding guidelines on lending.[26]

By the time the Government white paper on reforming the banking sector was published in July 2009, the non-broadsheet press had almost completely lost interest in the issue of banking reform. However, the *Guardian* reported extensively and critically on the white paper and took the opportunity to again step back and ask some hard questions about what role the financial system should play within the broader economy. For example, Will Hutton argued that the 'design of our financial system should be focused' on 'mobilising long-term equity and loan finance to build a balanced economy along with creating safe financial products for the saving and investing public'.[27] In another comment piece, Ken Livingstone went further and argued that the government should have introduced 'more radical measures' including 'nationalisation and direct control by government of the core of the banking sector' to direct investment to the 'cutting edge of the emerging new economy around the creative industries, the internet and environmental and the most technologically advanced manufacturing sectors'.[28] The former Labour MP Bryan Gould also offered a critical account of Conservative and New Labour approaches to the City and the impacts that these had on the rest of the economy:

> Macroeconomic policy was largely abandoned. Keynes was dismissed and forgotten. Interest rates were pressed into service to maintain the value of the currency and to underpin financial assets that might otherwise have been regarded as of dubious value. Little or no attention was paid to the competitiveness of the rest of the British economy, so that any thought of following an exchange rate policy that would stimulate exports, employment and investment simply never occurred to our policymakers; manufacturing in particular was allowed to continue its relentless decline. Most of our economic eggs were placed in the financial services basket and only City operators had access to the golden eggs among them. That is why the global crisis has hit the United Kingdom harder than anywhere else.[29]

If the banking crisis created the space for a reappraisal of the role of the finance sector in Britain's dysfunctional economic model, it wasn't an opportunity taken by most of the press and broadcasting. Instead the media largely functioned to channel the very real public anger than existed at the time into largely symbolic issues – like restricting former RBS chief executive Fred Goodwin's pension pot – whilst leaving the deep structural faults in the banking system, and Britain financialised economy, largely unexamined. The *Guardian*'s reporting was a clear outlier in this regard insofar as it was the only place where structural critiques and radical reforms were sometimes visible. Even here though, the lack of developed alternative models – reflecting the institutional weakness of left-wing economics – meant that although there was significant criticism of the current system, there wasn't much detail on what could replace it.

THE *GUARDIAN* AND THE DEFICIT DEBATE

The 2008 banking crisis precipitated a global recession and a worldwide surge in sovereign debt as governments attempted to maintain domestic demand and employment. In Britain, discussion over the banking crisis was quickly eclipsed by concerns about the public deficit which hit a peak of 9.9 per cent in 2009. The key drivers of the rise in the public deficit were the sharp contraction in tax revenues caused by the recession, and the fall in the housing market – which led to a sharp reduction in home equity release and other forms of consumer credit. Furthermore, the overhang of household debt accumulated in the previous decade and a half acted as a drag on economic activity which significantly prolonged the recession.[30]

Although Britain's deficit was high by international standards, its level of national debt was low, its reputation for debt management was outstanding and the maturity profile on its gilts was the longest in the world, making it well insulated from any market panic.[31] However, most of the media told a very different story. Almost all the media during the period produced alarmist and at times false accounts of Britain's public deficit. Right-wing papers, like the *Express* and the *Sun*, repeatedly claimed that the deficit had been created by Labour overspending – public debt had actually fallen as a proportion of GDP between 1997 and the GFC – rather than the recession:

> The extent of Gordon Brown's mishandling of the economy is now plain for all to see. He borrowed like a man possessed in the boom years when he should have been paying off debt.[32]

> Our plight is worse than most because we have spent and borrowed the money that might have helped us through [the recession]. Now Gordon insists the only way to avoid hellfire and damnation is to throw more taxpayers' cash on the flames.[33]

Furthermore, the media featured false accounts of the scale of Britain's debt and deficit. In 2009 the UK's debt burden stood at 63.3 per cent of GDP, lower than Italy's 116.6 per cent or Greece's 128.7 per cent, and was projected to remain below those countries in the foreseeable future.[34] But the *Mail*'s Peter Oborne claimed that:

> These latest official figures show that Britain's financial state is now far, far worse than countries such as Greece or Italy, which we have traditionally looked down upon and sneered at for their profligacy.

> Italy's indebtedness, though frightening, stands at little more than 100 per cent of GNP. Ours stands at twice that percentage and may well not be sustainable in the long term.[35]

The *Guardian* didn't reproduce such false narratives – or warn as many outlets did of national bankruptcy – but some of its writers did, along with the rest of the press and broadcasting, claim that the deficit represented a threat to economic stability through interest rate rises, potential gilt strikes and a run on the pound.

> The International Monetary Fund thinks the downturn will plunge the UK into the deepest deficit among the G20 countries next year, at 11% of gross domestic product . . . At this level, Britain's deficit starts to become unsustainable because financial markets would lose confidence and refuse to buy any more government debt except at very high rates of interest. This in turn would drive up the government's debt-service costs and add even more to the deficit. There could also be a further run on sterling if the country looks at risk of losing its AAA rating as a sovereign debtor.[36]

However, the *Guardian* was also the only major press outlet where readers could regularly see counter-arguments to the claims that the deficit represented a major economic crisis. When it came to what could be done about the deficit what was remarkable was the extraordinary degree of consensus across the whole press in favour of cuts to the state in order to 'balance the books'.[37] At right of centre titles, the key arguments from the 1970s – about the need to cut an unaffordable, bloated, unproductive public sector – were recycled but this time to defeat the danger represented by the deficit rather than inflation:

> We must freeze or even cut the cost of keeping six million state workers on the public payroll – or be abandoned by international creditors. There can be no sacred cows. The NHS budget has trebled in ten years. It must accept real cuts. So must every other Whitehall and town hall budget.[38]

Even the Labour-supporting *Mirror* accepted the unavoidability of cuts at some stage:

> We are heading for a new age of austerity. Whether Labour or the Tories win the next election, the country will be faced with making massive spending cuts. The reason is starkly simple. This year the Government will borrow £175billion – around £2868 for everyone in the UK.[39]

Its core argument – as a Labour supporting newspaper – was that only Labour could be trusted to carry out the inevitable cuts in a fair or 'compassionate' way that didn't damage vital public services. As one headline put it: 'THE REAL CHOICE: WHO DO YOU TRUST WITH A SCALPEL?'[40]

Guardian coverage was split, with many articles arguing in favour of deficit reduction via cuts to public spending. In one article Derek Brown argued that:

> Labour is portraying the Tories as the old enemy of the public sector but it too will have to slash spending if by some miracle it hangs onto power. [41]

However *Guardian* coverage also featured fewer pro-austerity arguments than in the other parts of the press or the BBC and also occasionally included alternatives. For example, the *Guardian* ran articles arguing that that a crackdown on tax evasion and avoidance could help close the deficit. An article penned by Larry Elliott, its economics editor, raised the issue of property taxes and noted the 'perverse' concentration on cuts when the deficit was caused by a 'collapse in tax revenues':

> It seems perverse that the current debate is all about which bits of spending should be cut rather than which taxes should be raised. There are plenty of ways to raise revenues. Darling could delay the introduction of the 50% tax rate but lower the threshold; he could prevent corporate tax avoidance by taxing companies on their turnover rather than their profits; he could deter speculative holdings of property through a land value tax.[42]

At times, it also featured Keynesian arguments, including an article from the Cambridge economist Ha Joon Chang, that the way to close the deficit was to boost economic growth:

> In the medium to long run, the most effective way to reduce the deficit is to revive growth, which will increase tax revenue and reduce welfare payments, rather than cutting welfare entitlements . . . In the British case, discussion of longer-term growth strategy has a particular urgency, as its engine of growth in the past few decades – the City – is going to slow down, with the forthcoming global tightening of financial regulation. Especially for the parts of the UK that have relied on government jobs funded by City taxes – Scotland, Wales, Northern Ireland and certain northern English regions – alternative sources of growth and jobs are even more urgently needed, as many of those jobs are going to disappear soon.[43]

So what explains the *Guardian*'s fractured response to the most politically important economic issue of the last decade? Interviews with *Guardian* journalists and editors revealed that two factors were paramount. First, there was a lack of easily sourced voices in the economics profession arguing against austerity. The economics correspondent Aditya Chakrabortty pointed out that even centre-left figures such as the Nobel prize winner Chris Pissarides were actually arguing that austerity was a 'good thing'.[44] This, Larry Elliott argued, reflected the weaknesses and unpreparedness of left economic thinking – in marked contrast to how the politicians and think tanks of the New Right were ready with a new economic programme as a response to Britain's economic problems in the 1970s. Second, Elliott argued that the schisms in the *Guardian*'s reporting reflected the divisions in the newsroom between reporters who were connected to opposing factions within the Labour Party at that time:

> It was happening inside the *Guardian* because there were two camps inside the government and it depends who your contacts were. So there was a big struggle going on between the Gordon Brown/Ed Balls faction and the Alistair Darling/Peter Mandelson faction. The Peter Mandelson and Alistair Darling faction thought that the budget deficit was the major problem and that Labour should go into the election with a clear commitment to bringing down the deficit . . .The Gordon Brown/Ed Balls camp said, one, economically this is not the right way to go forward and, two, politically it's a

very bad place for Labour to be in because we can't outbid the Tories in an austerity war if people want a Government who's going to be clamping down on public spending and capping the budget deficit . . . they'll choose the Tories. I was part of the Gordon Brown/Ed Balls camp but there were people on the *Guardian*, former Blairites or people who always hated Brown, of whom there were many on the *Guardian*, who were quite willing to take the Alistair Darling/ Peter Mandelson line. So that's why you got different views because Labour was at war with itself on this issue.[45]

Media coverage of the post-2008 public deficit was in many ways remarkable. Despite mainstream Keynesian macroeconomics advising against cuts to public spending – when the economy was struggling to recover from a recession and interest rates were close to zero – there was a strong consensus in favour of austerity across press and broadcasting. The *Guardian* did feature some dissenting voices who argued in favour of stimulus, such as a 'Green New Deal', or who suggested that taxation on the better off was a viable alternative to cuts to public spending. However, much of its coverage backed austerity. This in large part reflected the hardening of elite political consensus with Gordon Brown becoming increasingly isolated in arguing against austerity in the face of opposition from the press, broadcasting, the other political parties, his chancellor and much of his cabinet.[46]

POSTSCRIPT: THE *GUARDIAN* AND CORBYNITE ECONOMIC POLICY

In many respects it might be expected that the *Guardian* would have welcomed Labour's change in economic direction under the leadership of Jeremy Corbyn since many of the policies that his shadow chancellor John McDonnell was arguing for – such as the return of an interventionist state pursuing a targeted investment policy – had been long advocated by some of its key writers. Certainly, Corbynite economic policy was treated much more kindly by the *Guardian* than the party's positions on other issues including defence, foreign policy, Brexit and antisemitism.

Part of the reason for this is likely because it was much easier for *Guardian* writers to criticise these aspects of Labour policy. Labour's position on Brexit was contradictory, muddled and a direct affront to the pro-EU attitudes held by many of the paper's readers and leading columnists – its economics editor being a notable exception. Much of its foreign and defence policy was a hard sell to the public and a radical break from the traditional Labour Atlanticism which was still dominant within the PLP. The accusations that Labour had become tolerant of antisemitism or even institutionally antisemitic – however inaccurate or misleading – were easy to make bearing in mind the prevalence of the key institutional sources making such claims.[47] But to critique Labour's change of economic direction was harder. This was in part because many of the new policies were addressing glaring problems around inequality and precarity but also because Corbyn's opponents in the Labour Party had failed to outline any economic vision. This policy vacuum on the right of the PLP meant that the many New Labour aligned journalists at the *Guardian* were hamstrung by the inability to point to any kind of alternative.

The positive but cautious approach to Labour's change of economic direction could be seen in early editorials in the Corbyn era. For instance, the *Guardian* editorial on John McDonnell's speech at the 2015 Labour conference recognised that the shadow chancellor faced 'formidable obstacles', praised McDonnell as 'a cannier player than some had expected' and was generally optimistic about the new approach.

> Despite his protestations to 'be boring', Mr McDonnell is determined to break with orthodoxies that have reigned unchallenged for decades. He would ditch austerity in favour of allowing the government to invest and – he hopes – grow. He would do away with the presumption that business voices carry special authority, and instead approach them as vested interests. And he would rewrite a Bank of England mandate, set in the pre-crisis years when securing stable inflation was fondly imagined to be the only problem worth bothering with, to include growth, unemployment and wages . . .. Mr McDonnell's recruitment of progressive economists like Joseph Stiglitz and Thomas Piketty indicates an advance on the intellectual elegance point. His gamble is that the voters will take more kindly to his boldness than they did to Mr Miliband's barely audible murmur of dissent. Success is anything but assured. But with an impressive speech, Mr McDonnell has shown the world why Mr

Corbyn was so determined to have him, and earned a chance to give it a go.[48]

This is not to say that *Guardian* writers were uniformly enthusiastic about Labour's change in economic direction. A key critique made by columnists such as Martin Kettle, Suzanne Moore and John Harris was that Labour's economic policies were stuck in a rose-tinted 1970s time warp. All three were closely associated with *Marxism Today*'s 'New Times' thesis which had argued that, in the 1980s, the Labour Party had failed to adapt to a transformation in capitalism that had fractured social identities. Although heavily criticised at the time by many of the left for its embrace of market forces and consumerism – along with its rejection of class-based politics – it proved highly influential on a generation of New Labour policy makers.[49] For *Guardian* columnists associated with the New Times thesis, Corbyn represented an anachronistic throwback to the Labourism of the 1970s. 'Few politicians are less curious about the changes that have happened in Britain in his lifetime than Corbyn' argued Martin Kettle, while Suzanne Moore lamented that the Labour Party either looked 'back to the glory days of when we lost the miners' strike' or 'to that time Labour won elections. What it cannot do is offer an account of where we are now.'[50] According to John Harris:

> Labour is a 20th-century party adrift in a new reality. Its social foundations – the unions, heavy industry, the nonconformist church, a deference to the big state that has long evaporated – are either in deep retreat or have vanished completely. Its name embodies an attachment to the supposed glories of work that no longer chimes with insecure employment and insurgent automation. Its culture is still far too macho, and didactic; it has a lifelong aversion to analysis and ideas that has hobbled it throughout its existence, and now leaves it lacking any real sense of what is happening.[51]

Yet other *Guardian* writers recognised that this was a misleading picture which overlooked the ferment of new ideas that had been stimulated by the appointment of John McDonnell as shadow chancellor, including the party's consideration of a Universal Basic Income (UBI) and alternative models of ownership. Aditya

Chakrabortty, much of whose work concentrates on grassroots economics inspired in part by the Centre for Research on Socio-cultural Change (CRESC)'s ideas about the foundational economy,[52] recognised that Labour under Corbyn was generating new ideas on the economy:

> Behind the scenes, the party is doing much deeper thinking. I have seen an internal Labour report commissioned by McDonnell. It forms one part of what could be a far more radical programme after Thursday night. Some of the lines in it will give the *Daily Mail* stories for days – such as calling for an overhaul of the BBC Trust (which is 'dominated by appointees from the corporate and financial sectors') and hundreds of millions in public money to be spent on establishing workers co-ops. For the sympathetic reader, however, it contains some of the most imaginative thinking around economic democracy to come out of the party in decades (not saying much, sadly). In that, it sits alongside the speeches made by Corbyn's team last week about the need for 'industrial patriotism', and to give public backing to new sectors.[53]

Similar themes were explored in a 'Long Read' piece on the future of work authored by Andy Beckett which discussed Labour's interest in UBI and interviewed 'the new milieu of ambitious young activist intellectuals that has grown up around Corbyn's leadership'.[54] By the middle of 2019, even John Harris had begun to recognise that Labour and think tanks close to the leadership were producing significant new ideas:

> Even if it has yet to cohere into a convincing narrative, there is an abundance of good ideas in and around Labour and the left, from John McDonnell's plans to break up the Treasury and move a lot of its work to the north of England, through ideas about punishing companies that fail to pull their weight on climate change, and on to mounting a push to make co-operatives a central part of the economy . . . [Last week] I was in the basement of the HQ of the trade union Unite, speaking about a report jointly authored by the Runnymede Trust and the Corbyn-aligned think tank Class, about the modern working-class experience in London, and a set of policy

> proposals that ranged from a set of universal citizen entitlements to housing, transport and internet access, to the end of the sell-off of public land. Such organisations as the Institute for Public Policy Research and the New Economics Foundation are developing the central idea of the drastic redistribution of power into exciting, trailblazing work.[55]

Corbynite economics received a generally positive reception in *Guardian* editorials with leader writers seeing the commitment to state invention, redistribution, state investment and novel macroeconomic thinking as representing a welcome break from the New Labour era.

> Labour's economic policy has long displayed an understanding of the UK's structural problems, a point underlined last week by academics at the Policy Reform Group, whose recommendations largely mirror John McDonnell's blueprint of a national investment bank to raise infrastructure spending from 2% of GDP to the 3.5% norm for developed economies; to build more social housing; to reduce UK inequality to 1980 levels; and even to use 'helicopter money' – that is electronically created money – to boost demand. Labour aims to radically transform Britain; it is a change that is long overdue.[56]

CONCLUSION

This chapter set out to explore the *Guardian*'s economic journalism using the Great Financial Crisis – and to a lesser extent the rise of Corbynism – as case studies. Although there was clearly a diversity of opinion on economic policy amongst the paper's writers, some patterns could be observed. Prior to the 2008 crash, many writers – some of whom were closely aligned with New Labour – were either broadly supportive of, or at least acquiesced with, the core elements of the government's economic policy. The *Guardian*'s economics editor was a notable exception, and when the crisis hit Larry Elliott was one of the strongest voices criticising New Labour's economic model and arguing for a change of direction. Yet at this key moment, the *Guardian* was more equipped to critique rather than offer a developed alternative reflecting the fact that a) little new thinking had been done on the left on alternative economic policy, and b) most centre-left think tanks such as the IPPR and the Fabians had been supportive – or at least not critical – of New Labour policy.

The election of Jeremy Corbyn as Labour leader in 2015 radically shifted the public debate on economic policy. The *Guardian*'s response to this particular development was generally positive, with a few prominent exceptions. Certainly economic policy was one of the few areas where Corbyn's Labour didn't face a predominately hostile reception in the *Guardian*.[57] How durable the transformation in Labour's economic approach remains under the 'new management' of Keir Starmer is questionable. We will have to wait and see whether the *Guardian* remains broadly supportive of any Corbynite policies that endure or whether it shifts to the right as Starmer consolidates his grip on the party.

NOTES

1. D. W. Parsons, *The Power of the Financial Press* (Aldershot, Edward Elgar Publishing: 1989).
2. *Financial Times*, 'S&P: QE "Exacerbates" Inequality', *Financial Times*, 10 February 2016, https:// www.ft.com/content/b4e604c8-b61a-362e-b741-a78f7009a569 (accessed 30 September 2020); John Judis, *The Populist Explosion: How the Great Recession Transformed American and European Politics* (New York: Columbia Global Reports, 2016); Frances Ryan, 'Now It's official: The Less You have, the More Austerity Will Take From You', *Guardian*, 17 November 2017, https://www.theguardian.com/commentisfree/2017/nov/17/austerity-minorities-women-disabled (accessed 3 October 2020).
3. Aeron Davis and Catherine Walsh, 'The Role of the State in the Financialisation of the UK Economy', *Political Studies*, 64:3, (2016), pp. 666–82.
4. Will Hutton, *The State We're In: Why Britain is in Crisis and How to Overcome it* (London: Vintage, 1996); Davis and Walsh, 'The Role of the State'.
5. Cited in Heather Stewart and Simon Goodley, 'Big Bang's Shockwaves Left Us with Today's Big Bust', *Observer*, 9 October 2011, https:// www.theguardian.com/business/2011/oct/09/big-bang-1986-city-deregulation-boom-bust (accessed 4 October 2020).
6. Securitisation involves the process of taking assets (such as the revenue streams from loans, credit cards or mortgage payments), pooling them and then turning them into securities (or risk weighted tiers of securities) which can then be traded in secondary markets.

7. A derivative is a financial product whose value is based on the price of an underlying asset or group of assets. Common assets underlying derivatives include stocks, bonds, commodities, exchange rates and real estate.
8. Edward Engelen et al., *After the Great Complacence* (Oxford: Oxford University Press, 2011), p. 42.
9. Colin Crouch, 'Privatised Keynesianism: An Unacknowledged Policy Regime', *British Journal of Politics and International Relations*, 11 (2009), pp. 382–99.
10. Nicholas Comfort, *The Slow Death of British Industry: A 60-Year suicide*, 1952–2012 (London: Biteback Publishing, 2013).
11. Engelen et al, *After the Great Complacence*.
12. Ibid.
13. World Bank, *Manufacturing, Value Added (% of GDP)*, World Bank National Accounts Data, 2017, https://data.worldbank.org/indicator/NV.IND.MANF.ZS (accessed 30 September 2020).
14. International Monetary Fund, *World Economic Outlook (WEO) Financial Stress, Downturns, and Recoveries*, October 2008, http://www.imf.oFrg/external/pubs/ft/weo/2008/02/pdf/text.pdf (accessed 30 September 2020).
15. House of Commons Treasury Committee, *Banking Crisis: Dealing with the Failure of the UK Banks*, 21 April 2009, https://www.publications.parliament.uk/pa/cm200809/cmselect/cmtreasy/416/416.pdf (accessed 30 September 2020).
16. Cited in ibid, p. 33.
17. For example, Andrew Glyn, *Capitalism Unleashed* (Oxford: Oxford University Press, 2007); Lorenzo Smaghi, 'Has the Financial Sector Grown Too Big?' Speech at the Nomura Seminar, *The Paradigm Shift After the Financial Crisis*, Kyoto, 15 April 2020, https://www.ecb.europa.eu/press/key/date/2010/html/sp100415.en.html (accessed 30 September 2020); Graham Turner, *The Credit Crunch: Housing Bubbles, Globalisation and the Worldwide Economic Crisis* (London: Pluto Press, 2008).
18. Dan Atkinson and Larry Elliott, *Fantasy Island* (London: Constable: 2007); Dan Atkinson and Larry Elliott, *The Gods that Failed* (London: Nation Books, 2009); Larry Elliott, *The Age of Insecurity* (London: Verso, 1999).
19. Mike Berry, 'The "Today" Programme and the Banking Crisis', *Journalism*, 14:2 (2013), pp. 253–70; Mike Berry, 'The UK Press and the Deficit Debate', *Sociology*, 50:3, (2016), pp. 542–59; Mike Berry, 'No Alternative to Austerity: How BBC Broadcast News Reported the Deficit Debate', *Media, Culture and Society*, 38:6, (2016), pp. 844–63; Mike Berry, 'Austerity, Media and the UK Public' in Steve Schifferes, Sophie Knowles and Laura Basu (eds), *The Media and Austerity: Comparative Perspectives* (London: Routledge, 2018), pp. 43–62; Mike Berry, *The Media, the Public and the Great Financial Crisis* (London: Palgrave-Macmillan, 2019).

20. Larry Elliott, 'Now is the Witching Hour When We Find Out if We Are in for Systemic Meltdown', *Guardian*, 13 October 2008, https://www.theguardian.com/business/2008/oct/13/economics-economy (accessed 3 October 2020).
21. Polly Toynbee, 'In the Face Of Apocalypse, Heed Not Horsemen's Advice', *Guardian*, 7 October 2008, https://www.theguardian.com/commentisfree/2008/oct/07/brown.economic.policy (accessed 3 October 2020).
22. Larry Elliott, 'The Financial Crisis Has Exposed the Bankruptcy of New Labour Economics', *Guardian*, 8 October 2008, https://www.theguardian.com/business/blog/2008/oct/08/economics.creditcrunch (accessed 3 October 2020).
23. Michael White, 'Brown Wipes the Floor with David Cameron', *Guardian*, 8 October 2008, https://www.theguardian.com/politics/blog/2008/oct/08/pmqs (accessed 3 October 2020).
24. Seamus Milne, 'The Genie's Out: Now They've Shown What Can Be Done', *Guardian*, 9 October 2008, https://www.theguardian.com/commentisfree/2008/oct/09/banking.banks (accessed 3 October 2020).
25. Polly Toynbee, 'The Defibrillator Worked – Now for the Intensive Care', *Guardian*, 14 October 2009, https://www.theguardian.com/commentisfree/2008/oct/14/economy-creditcrunch1 (accessed 3 October 2020).
26. Tim Webb, 'Punish Reckless Lending, Says Regulator', *Guardian*, 7 October 2008, https://www.theguardian.com/world/2008/oct/07/sweden.banking.regulation (accessed 3 October 2020).
27. Will Hutton, 'O Lord Help Them Be Tough on the City – but not yet', *Guardian*, 8 July 2009 https://www.theguardian.com/commentisfree/2009/jul/08/alistair-darling-banking-reform-plans (accessed 3 October 2020).
28. Ken Livingstone, 'Facing Economic Facts', *Guardian*, 9 July 2009, https://www.theguardian.com/commentisfree/2009/jul/09/economic-crisis-state-intervention-banks (accessed 3 October 2020).
29. Bryan Gould, 'The Treasury's 23-year-old Mistake', *Guardian*, 9 July 2009, https://www.theguardian.com/commentisfree/2009/jul/09/financial-services-act-city (accessed 3 October 2020).
30. Ben Chu, 'Bank Blames High Household Debt for Depth of Britain's Recession', *Independent*, 16 September 2014, https://www.independent.co.uk/news/business/news/bank-blames-high-household-debt-depth-britain-s-recession-9734758.html; Fiscal Studies, *Revenues Including Forecasts*, 2012, http://www.ifs.org.uk/ff/revenues.xls (both accessed 30 September 2020).
31. Robert Neild, 'The National Debt in Perspective', *RES Newsletter*, 156, January 2012, https://www.res.org.uk/uploads/assets/uploaded/d3ae1512-fd3c-4eb6-9f5dc15be740bdae.pdf, pp. 20-22 (accessed 3 October 2020).

32. *Daily Express*, 'Each Day Brown Adds to Britain's Debt Nightmare', 22 July 2009, https://www.express.co.uk/comment/expresscomment/115603/Each-day-Brown-adds-to-Britain-s-debt-nightmare (accessed 3 October 2020).
33. The *Sun*, 12 January 2009.
34. Eurostat, *Government Debt as a Percentage of GDP*, 2014, https://tinyurl.com/yxa44avd (accessed 30 September 2020).
35. Peter Oborne, 'Borrowing to Save the Economy Is Like Trying to Sober up a Drunk by Giving Him Whisky', *Mail*, 20 February 2009, https://www.dailymail.co.uk/debate/article-1150764/PETER-OBORNE-Borrowing-save-economy-like-trying-sober-drunk-giving-large-whisky.html (accessed 3 October 2020).
36. Ashley Seager, 'Alistair Darling's Annual Deficit Forecast Likely to Be Spectacularly Shattered', *Guardian*, 26 March 2009, https://www.theguardian.com/politics/2009/mar/26/alistair-darling-budget-annual-deficit (accessed 3 October 2020).
37. See Mike Berry, *Media, the Public and the Great Financial Crisis*; *Steve* Schifferes and Sophie Knowles, 'The British Media and "the First Crisis of Globalization"', in Stefve Schifferes and Richard Roberts (eds), *The Media and Financial Crises: Comparative and Historical Perspectives* (London: Routledge, 2014), pp. 42–58.
38. The *Sun*, 6 July 2009.
39. Bob Roberts, 'Ten Ways for the Chancellor to Chop Billions and Get the UK Out of Recession', *Daily Mirror*, 3 July 2009, https://www.mirror.co.uk/news/uk-news/ten-ways-for-the-chancellor-to-chop-billions-790191 (accessed 3 October 2020).
40. Bob Roberts, 'Tory Spend Plan "Proof of Commitment to Slash Public Services"', *Daily Mirror*, 16 June 2009, https://www.mirror.co.uk/news/uk-news/tory-spend-plan-proof-of-commitment-790017 (accessed 3 October 2020).
41. Derek Brown, 'Week in Britain: I Can Cut Anything Deeper Than You', *Guardian*, 19 June 2009, p. 14.
42. Larry Elliott, 'Spending Cuts Are Not the Only Option: Taxes Can Be Raised too.' *Guardian*, 21 July 2009, https://www.theguardian.com/commentisfree/2009/jul/21/uk-debt-fiscal-cuts-tax (accessed 3 October 2020).
43. Ha-Joon Chang, 'Time to Broaden the Debate on Spending Cuts, *Guardian*, 19 October 2010, https://www.theguardian.com/commentisfree/2010/oct/19/spending-cuts-deficit-growth (accessed 3 October 2020).
44. Interview with the author, 8 December 2017.
45. Interview with the author, 8 February 2018.
46. Schifferes and Knowles, 'The British Media'.

47. Greg Philo et al, *Bad News for Labour: Antisemitism, the Party and Public Belief* (London: Pluto: 2019).
48. *Guardian*, 'Guardian View on Labour's Economic Policy: Careful Words, Bold Intent', *Guardian*, 29 September 2015, https://www.theguardian.com/commentisfree/2015/sep/28/the-guardian-view-on-labours-economic-policy-careful-words-bold-intent (accessed 3 October 2020).
49. John Saville, '*Marxism Today*: An Anatomy', *Socialist Register 1990* (London: Merlin Press, 1990), pp. 35–59; Ambavalaner Sivanandan, 'All that Melts into Air is Solid: The Hokum of *New Times*', *Race and Class*, 31(3), 1990, pp. 1–29.
50. Martin Kettle, 'It'll Take a General Election for Labour to Face up to its Crisis', *Guardian*, 22 September 2016, https://www.theguardian.com/commentisfree/2016/sep/22/general-election-labour-crisis-jeremy-corbyn; Suzanne Moore, 'Labour Needs to Address the Issues of the Present Before it Becomes the Retro Party', *Guardian*, 28 September 2016, https://www.theguardian.com/commentisfree/2016/sep/28/labour-needs-to-address-the-issues-of-the-present-before-it-becomes-the-retro-party (both accessed 3 October 2020).
51. John Harris, 'Whoever the Leader is, Labour May Never Recover from this Crisis', *Guardian*, 29 June 2016, https://www.theguardian.com/commentisfree/2016/jun/29/whoever-leader-is-labour-may-never-recover-crisis (accessed 3 October 2020).
52. Centre for Research on Socio-Economic Change, *Manifesto for the Foundational Economy*, CRESC Working Paper 131, 2013, https://hummedia.manchester.ac.uk/institutes/cresc/workingpapers/wp131.pdf (accessed 3 October 2020).
53. Aditya Chakrabortty, 'Britain's Economic Model Is Broken: This is Our First Post-Crash Election', *Guardian*, 6 June 2017, https://www.theguardian.com/commentisfree/2017/jun/06/britain-economic-model-broken-corbyn-may-understand-first-post-crash-election (accessed 3 October 2020).
54. Andy Beckett, 'Post-work: The Radical Idea of a World Without Jobs', *Guardian*, 19 January 2018, https://www.theguardian.com/news/2018/jan/19/post-work-the-radical-idea-of-a-world-without-jobs (accessed 3 October 2020).
55. John Harris, 'Labour Can Effect Positive Change, but not while its Internal Politics Are so Toxic', *Guardian*, 14 July 2019, https://www.theguardian.com/commentisfree/2019/jul/14/labour-positive-change-faction-fighting-antisemitism-brexit (accessed 3 October 2020).
56. *Guardian* editorial, 'The Guardian View on Labour's Radical Plans: Fix the Economy and Democracy', *Guardian*, 4 November 2019, https://www.theguardian.com/commentisfree/2019/nov/04/the-guardian-view-on-labours-radical-plans-fix-the-economy-and-democracy (accessed 3 October 2020).

57. Bart Cammaerts, Brooks DeCillia and Joao Carlos Magalhaes, 'Journalistic Transgressions in the Representation of Jeremy Corbyn: From Watchdog to Attackdog', *Journalism*, 21:2, (2017), pp. 191–208; Justin Schlosberg, *Should He Stay or Should He Go? Television and Online News Coverage of the Labour Party in Crisis*, Media Reform Coalition, 2016, https://www.mediareform.org.uk/wp-content/uploads/2016/07/Corbynresearch.pdf (accessed 30 September 2020).

14
The *Guardian* and Brexit

Mike Wayne

BREXIT AS CONJUNCTURE

'Brexit' is both the term coined for the result of the 2016 Referendum on the UK's future relationship with the EU (Brexit as 'event') and the subsequent chaotic and polarised path cut by successive political leaderships of the dominant parties (Brexit as process). Brexit is also a tailor-made example of what Antonio Gramsci described as a 'conjuncture'. Much more than an elastically defined temporal moment, a conjuncture is, as Stuart Hall noted, a 'condensation of contradictions', a zone of convergence where long germinating problems intensify, the established settlements crack apart and new possibilities (both good and bad) emerge.[1] The conjuncture indicates 'spatial relations and entangled temporalities'[2] writes John Clarke, and that is certainly true of the UK's long history vis-à-vis the European continent. For Gramsci it is the moment when 'incurable structural contradictions' that are 'organic' or essential to a mode of production (such as capitalism) and that stretch across a long history, reach 'maturity'. Then 'the political forces which are struggling to conserve and defend the existing structure . . . [make] every effort to cure them, within certain limits, and to overcome them.'[3] However, Brexit is about far more than simply the UK's relationship with the EU.

In a crisis, at the political level, social classes become 'detached from their traditional parties'[4] because the relationship between represented and representatives is breaking down. Brexit saw former Conservative and Labour Party voters moving over to the challenger party for conservatism, the United Kingdom Independence Party (UKIP) in the years leading up to 2016 and in the years afterwards as well. The Conservative Party then won 52 of the 54 seats in the 'Brexit' general election of 2019 in long-held Labour Party seats in areas that had voted heavily to leave the EU in 2016. To rescue itself, the Conservative Party has undergone 'UKIPisation' under the leadership of Boris Johnson. In doing so, it has produced a significant rupture with the majority opinion of the British capitalist class, a rather small part of the electorate that nevertheless constitutes a significant power bloc. As Will Hutton, writing in the *Guardian*'s sister paper, the *Observer*, noted: 'The CBI may represent British-based and British owned capitalism, but it is judged no longer significant enough for the Tories to heed. Our capitalism has fractured.'[5] Gramsci argued that some national newspapers (he specifically cites *The Times* in England and *Corriere della Sera* in Italy) can have important leadership functions for political parties, functioning as an alternative 'intellectual High Command'.[6] We shall see that the *Guardian* had a crucial leadership function for the faction of the Parliamentary Labour Party implacably opposed to Jeremy Corbyn and intent on mobilising Brexit as a wedge issue. The *Guardian* helped win credibility back for Corbyn's 'centrist' opponents amongst Labour party members and voters who read the paper and who continue to trust it as a 'progressive' outlet.

For liberalism, the transformation of conservatism has been a horror show that has seen a long-term partner in the management of British capitalism tear up a decades-old policy consensus on Britain's future as a (sometimes fractious) partner in the European project. That project began in the 1950s as an economic nexus of trading arrangements (very acceptable to mainstream conservatism) but became increasingly a broader political and cultural project of unification (increasingly problematic for conservatism). Temporalities became 'entangled' indeed. At the same time as dealing with this new conservatism's attempt to re-vivify Thatcherism's combination of nationalism with a globally facing capitalist economy orientated towards America and the world outside Europe, liberalism was faced with the ascendancy of Jeremy Corbyn to the leadership of the Labour Party in 2015. For liberalism, Corbyn represented a left-wing mirror image of the 'populist' right represented by UKIP, its leader Nigel Farage and increasingly the UKIP wing *within* the Conservative Party (culminating in Boris Johnson's leadership). While fighting this neo-conservatism's anti-EU critique, liberalism's strategic leadership groups in the political and media class simultaneously worked furiously to defeat Corbyn's leadership of the Labour Party. They operated on a number of different fronts, but Brexit was undoubtedly the most significant and harmful to the Corbyn leadership. Labour's defeat in the general election of 2019 has for the time being removed the possibility of a left-wing challenge to the dominant political cultures of conservatism and liberalism. Despite the fact that this challenge offered little more than a social-democratic route out of the crisis, even this very modest re-direction of the policy agenda was unpalatable for the collective intellectual mood of liberalism.

What we may call 'nationalistic' neoliberalism and 'progressive' or liberal neoliberalism are the latest mutations respectively of the older philosophies of conservatism and liberalism. They are joined by their shared commitment to capitalism and belief in the inviolability of market forces which, as 'laws of nature', are best left alone to work their magic, with states relegated to providing the legal framework for the market. This is the basis of their alliance. Gramsci calls this joint leadership the formation of a 'historical bloc'; that is the forging of precisely this *intra-ruling class* alliance that can then project its interests as the universal interests, 'the motor force of a universal expansion, of a development of all the "national" energies', drawing the 'subaltern' classes into its programmes and initiatives and persuading the subaltern classes to leave the running of things to them, 'the leaders', as much as possible.[7]

A spectrum of force and the winning of consent by leadership and ideological means facilitates the durability of the settlement within and between classes. Some prospect of meagre economic concessions from the dominant to the subaltern groups is also crucial to seal the compact. Where leadership by consent is in the ascendancy, Gramsci calls this 'hegemony' – i.e. moral and political leadership is preferred and efficacious. Conservatism and liberalism compete for leadership of capitalism, offering some distinctive touches to the tiller of state activity within the overall capitalist settlement. But when moral and political leadership weakens due to those incurable structural contradictions, and when the prospects of even meagre economic prospects for the subaltern groups declines (as it did after the 2007–8 worldwide crash), intra-ruling class unities may start to fray.

Yet an economic crisis does not in itself explain why the historic settlements between conservatism and liberalism have failed *in the way that they have*. We have to look in more detail at their respective political cultures and, crucially, their *differential* relations to the contradictions of capitalism. One major fault-line where this has occurred runs through the tension between capitalism's national and international activities. At the national level, conservatism dominated the state, both its repressive institutions (law and order) and its ideological institutions (the spectacle of reactionary romanticism embodied in the military, monarchy, the 'Mother of parliaments', etc).[8] It was conservatism that provided the rich imagery of 'the nation' as a point of identification in the context of a mode of production whose expansionary dynamic *cannot* be contained within the nation-state. Liberalism has always played second fiddle to that at the national level, yet it has an important political role in helping to calibrate the force/consent spectrum and communicating to conservatism when it might be a good moment to make tactical reforms to safeguard long term shared strategic objectives. As Thomas Macaulay warned in 1831 on the eve of the Great Reform Bill, 'Reform that you may preserve.'[9]

Capitalism has, however, always been international, although the extent of that has waxed and waned according to historical circumstances. It has taken two distinct forms at an international level just as it has at a national level: a force model, through colonialism and imperialism (something that conservatism is most comfortable with but which liberalism has also intermittently supported and sometimes critiqued), and a *consent* model, through international governance and supranational institutions (something which liberalism is most comfortable with but which conservatism has intermittently supported and sometimes critiqued). The historical circumstances of the last forty years have been to extend and deepen liberalism's preferred model of hegemonic internationalism using the more subtle compulsions of economic power to discipline populations to accept the 'rationality' of market forces. The result of liberal internationalism has been that democratic leverage by national publics over their respective state representatives has weakened as those representatives have willingly been drawn into ever more global networks, relationships, forces, obligations, trade deals and institutions that have insulated them from whatever forms of democratic pressure bourgeois democracy has hitherto allowed at the national level.[10] But ideologically it has been much easier to present these trends as forms of 'progress' (especially, it seems, to the middle class) than the (military) force model.

The EU is of course the key example that concerns us here. It is a trend that has led to a bitter disagreement between significant wings of conservatism and liberalism in the UK. The disagreement centres on different strategies for containing and channelling rising popular discontent, especially since the 2007–8 global crash, ensuing austerity, weak to zero economic recovery and the drying up of those meagre economic concessions. Two different contrasting options have emerged: should globalisation be accelerated (liberalism's answer to the crisis) and national sovereignty and identities 'pooled'? Or should globalisation be partially decelerated, with some reassertion of national 'controls' (on immigration, rather than capital flows) and identities? Notice that each of these options play to the respective strengths of liberalism and conservatism respectively.

This disagreement – wherein tactical differences have now become strategic – has rent the historic bloc that has governed the UK since the rise of Thatcherism in the 1980s. But the bloc does not disintegrate. Gramsci identifies the importance of civil society institutions within capitalism that function as relatively independent networks of support and as a source of 'molecular' initiatives, a 'line of defence'[11] that can strive and strain to repair hegemony (moral and political leadership). The *Guardian*, as a leading organ of 'progressive' neoliberalism, has played a key role in this 'game of thrones'. To understand how the *Guardian* participated in this effort, we must now explore the reach of liberalism into the Labour Party membership even after they had, apparently, moved decisively to the left.

BREXIT: CORBYN'S ACHILLES HEEL

The vertical split between the two wings of the historic bloc was beginning to open up the prospects of a horizontal split between the hegemonic clusters (conservatism and liberal neoliberalism) and various subaltern social strata. A key moment was the Scottish Referendum of 2014, which came relatively close to breaking up the British state as the subaltern Scots rebelled against decades of rule from the neoliberal centre (Westminster). A second moment was Corbyn's election as leader of the Labour Party in 2015, when the subaltern membership was able to choose the leader for the first time on a 'one member one vote' basis. Their choice, against a range of uninspiring continuity candidates, was a break from the neoliberal 'capitalist realist' politics cemented in place by former leader Tony Blair which still dominated the Parliamentary Labour Party.[12] *Three* days after Corbyn won the leadership vote, leading *Guardian* columnist Rafael Behr wrote an article describing Corbynism as 'a kind of Faragism of the left', as not competent in professional politics and as representing a 'contempt for Parliament'. The result was 'bad for all moderate politicians' we were told. Many of the readers' comments below the line were critical of Behr. The emerging gap between the *Guardian*'s editorial line and sections of its readership reflected the one that had opened up between the PLP and the party membership. But there was one point of attack that Behr made which received less attention below the line and that was his argument about Corbyn's 'obvious dislike for a European project he sees as the conduit for corporate interests and pro-austerity economics'.[13]

In fact, it was on precisely the question of the EU that liberal neoliberalism would manage to reconnect with the membership inside the Labour Party, Labour supporters and the readership of the *Guardian* (as we will see there is considerable overlap between these three constituencies). The gulf that was opened up between the moral and political leadership of liberal neoliberalism and the Labour Party membership and it would appear, some of the *Guardian*'s readership, was re-sealed on the terrain of the EU. Conversely, the connection between Corbyn and his support base (in the membership, amongst Labour Party supporters and the paper's readership) was eroded by an extensive, long-term and co-ordinated campaign to push Corbyn towards the EU while constantly criticising him for his lacklustre and tardy support for the EU.

It was Gramsci who understood the role of intellectuals in shaping arguments, giving strategic direction and channelling the passions that affect political outcomes. The leadership organs of intellectuals are 'permanent persuaders',[14] key institutions in shaping the meanings, values and interpretations of the political and cultural scene. Behr's article crystallised very early on some of the main lines of attack on Corbyn that would, in time, get more and more traction in political discourse: Corbyn as outside the traditions of Parliamentary democracy; Corbyn's lack of leadership skills; Corbyn's supposedly inflexible self-righteous moral rectitude (a subtle recoding of the more positive framing of Corbyn as someone having integrity); and above all, Corbyn unwilling or unable to stop our catastrophic break with the EU.

Yet the *Guardian*'s leadership role and efficaciousness in driving a wedge between Corbyn and his support base, could only come to fruition if there was some basis already there to do so, some already existing sentiments which could give liberal neoliberalism a way back in, some purchase to exercise once more the moral-political leadership over the support base which had been threatened by the election of Corbyn. And it was indeed soft left positive sentiments towards the EU within the Labour Party membership that provided precisely that possibility. These sentiments were in time orchestrated into political passions that subtly re-ordered the priorities of many Labour members away from the politics of wealth redistribution and towards an identification with the EU. As we have seen, *Guardian* columnist Rafael Behr argued that Corbynism was the mirror image of Faragist/UKIP nationalism. But actually, in some ways, the Remain cause was the mirror image of culturally driven investments in national distinctiveness and assertiveness. Like nationalist Leavers, EU Remainers were powerfully motivated by cultural drivers (such as the 'progressive' values of the EU, often conflated with Europe itself) and less interested in the EU's neoliberal base.

Initially though, Corbyn's opponents tried to overthrow him through a 'vote of no confidence' by the Parliamentary Labour Party in 2016, immediately after the Leave campaign won the EU referendum. In the *Guardian*, Polly Toynbee described Corbyn's performance in the referendum as 'dismally inadequate, lifeless and spineless, displaying an inability to lead anyone anywhere.'[15] Never mind that the 35 per cent of Labour voters who joined the 61 per cent of Conservative voters in the Leave camp, had been built up decisively in the years of the Conservative-Lib Dem austerity government between 2010–15. Never mind that 32 per cent of Liberal Democrat voters also voted Leave![16] The Liberal Democrat leadership escaped all blame for the referendum outcome. When the 'no confidence' vote failed (given that it had no constitutional validity), Corbyn's opponents triggered a new leadership contest which Corbyn won comfortably against Owen Smith in September 2016.

Labour went into the 2017 general election explicitly accepting the referendum result and promising to negotiate a deal that retained the benefits of the Single Market and Custom Union. It would have been more honest (but perhaps poor negotiating tactics) to have later crafted a position acknowledging that such a deal would be difficult, but that short-to-medium term economic disadvantages fell well short of liberalism's catastrophism. However, with the Remain campaign demoralised and adrift at that point, Labour was able to focus on the real cause for inequality in the UK: the neoliberal policy agenda pursued by successive national governments. The unexpected early general election called by Theresa May also meant that the media had only had two years to build up its attacks on Corbyn, and many of them, especially the right-wing sourced complaints, had proved relatively ineffective. This is not to say that the *Guardian* had not been productively busy with an extensive two-year anti-Corbyn campaign.[17] Despite this, the Labour Party made a net gain of 30 seats and the Conservatives had a net loss of 13 seats, wiping out the small majority Theresa May had inherited from David Cameron's 2015 general election victory. While this unexpectedly strong showing boosted Corbyn's credentials for a brief period, it also, in one of those dialectical reversals at which the cunning of history so excels, laid the basis for Corbyn's defeat. With the Conservatives no longer retaining their Parliamentary majority, the Remain campaign was re-energised. Now it was once more feasible to think of frustrating and blocking the 2016 EU referendum result and having a new vote.

The identification with the EU amongst the Labour Party membership, despite twice having voted for a break with neoliberalism by supporting Corbyn's leadership, allowed liberal neoliberalism to win back its leadership position amongst the membership. The 2017 party conference season saw the launch of the Labour *Campaign for a Single Market* backed by right-wing openly anti-Corbyn MPs such as Chris Leslie, Chuka Umunna and Stella Creasy and pulling in wider support from less hostile MPs such as David Lammy. By the 2018 Labour Party conference, Labour's leadership was flooded with 150 motions on Brexit, 84 of which specifically called for a people's vote. These motions drew inspiration from a plethora of organisations such as Another Europe is Possible, Love Socialism, Hate Brexit, Labour for a Socialist Europe and Open Labour.

On the eve of the September 2018 conference, a YouGov poll found high levels of support for a second Brexit vote amongst trade union members. GMB members supported a second vote by 56 per cent, Unite members by 59 per cent and Unison members by 66 per cent. These levels of support indicate the political hegemony of liberalism within the trade union wing of the labour movement. YouGov also found that a whopping 86 per cent of Labour members wanted a second referendum, whilst only 8 per cent were opposed to a 'people's vote'.[18] This higher majority for a second referendum from the Labour Party membership is likely explained by the fact that Labour Party membership was, by this stage, skewed towards the middle class and skilled workers, with 77 per cent of the membership falling into the ABC1 categories of social class identification according to one study.[19] This push for a second referendum in turn fed into a deepening class-culture fissure between the membership and important segments of Labour's electoral popular base in northern smaller towns. By the time of the 2019 general election, Labour officially backed a second referendum on a deal. To repeat: Labour went on to lose 52 long-held Labour Party seats in heavily Leave voting areas.

The results of two years of pressure from the Labour membership and critique from Corbyn's opponents was the following:

1. The liberal neoliberals within the Parliamentary Labour Party and beyond, in civic organs such as the *Guardian*, won back their moral and political leadership over the membership.
2. Their pressure and critique made it impossible for Corbyn to strike a compromise deal with Theresa May's government (or assorted plans by groups of cross-party backbenchers) that might have neutralised the issue of Brexit for the time being at least and cleared the way for a UK election on domestic policy issues.
3. Corbyn's continual changes made him look weak and vacillating and failed in any case to win him a moment's respite from those who were opposed to his leadership in the first place.

Instead of treating the EU question as, for the time being, a second order issue and a tactical issue to be neutralised prior to winning government power, overturning the 2016 EU result became the strategic goal of both the neoliberals and the Labour Party membership.[20] This robbed

Corbyn of the shield that had hitherto protected him from a sea of enemies.

THE READERSHIP OF THE *GUARDIAN*

In this context, the *Guardian* could merge its hostility to Corbyn with its enthusiasm for the EU and gradually bring wider layers of people onto this terrain. It could do so because its readership overlaps significantly with electoral support for the Labour Party. According to a YouGov survey, 73 per cent of *Guardian* readers voted for Labour in the 2017 election, 12 per cent for the Lib Dems and 8 per cent for the Tories.[21] It is therefore a reasonable assumption that a significant chunk of the Labour Party's membership also reads the *Guardian*. The social class of the Labour Party membership maps nicely onto the *Guardian*'s readership, where 85 per cent of the readers of the *Guardian* and *Observer* papers are ABC1s.[22] According to the *Guardian*'s own survey of its readership, presented for advertisers, 60 per cent of its readership self-identify as 'progressives' which, we are told, means that they are 'forward-looking individuals who are curious about the world and embrace change and technology'.[23] These are the 'progressive' middle classes for whom the EU question and the referendum was much more than a tricky tactical question that could not really be posed before Labour actually got into power and were on the other side of the negotiating table. It was instead an existential question that touched on their very identity as progressives, differentiating themselves from regressive nationalism by investing in multilateral co-operation (albeit without any democratic accountability), international exchange and cosmopolitanism. Indeed, for the 'progressive' middle class, the Brussels bureaucracy, as overlords of a particular governance model of international capitalism, seemed to be reason incarnate.

RHETORICAL TROPES: SUNDERING CORBYN FROM HIS BASE

Contexts mapped, it is time to drill down into the discursive strategies of the *Guardian*. I analysed a sample of *Guardian* opinion pieces between July 2017 and November 2019, just before the general election of that year. I chose opinion pieces because it is the title's explicit purpose to articulate opinions, to make arguments, to interpret events, to criticise and to be permanent persuaders. Using the newspaper archive *Nexis* I filtered for pieces that had 'Corbyn' in the headline (I also dipped into the *Guardian*'s Sunday sister paper, the *Observer*). I went through one month at a time, scanning the news reportage items that were also coming up along with the opinion pieces to provide context. I noted that between June 2017 and February 2018, the reportage was fairly mixed in terms of positive and critical articles about Corbyn. There were quite a few *mea culpas* by various writers, such as Owen Jones, who had lost faith in Corbyn before the 2017 election, Zoe Williams and even to a lesser degree Rafael Behr. Here there was some measure of contestation internal to the *Guardian*. But the tone of the coverage became more uniformly hostile from March 2018 onwards, the month that the accusations of antisemitism in the Labour Party began in earnest. From March 2018 the *Guardian* mounted a disciplined, indeed relentless, anti-Corbyn campaign. I chose 29 articles, one for each month between the two general elections, by 21 writers, that included *Guardian* staff writers and guest opinion pieces. In the space available, I want to explore three key themes of the campaign, which as we have seen, Rafael Behr, in a hostility foretold, already anticipated three days after Corbyn's election to the leadership of the party.

1. Brexit as Existential Crisis

For the leadership within the intellectual cadres of liberal neoliberalism, a change in the UK's relationship with the EU was unthinkable. No doubt the intellectual leaders really felt and meant this, but it did also have a more instrumental and grubby political advantage which was to press down hard on a faultline in the electoral bloc that made up Corbyn's popular support. Looking at the young people chanting Corbyn's name at the Glastonbury music festival two weeks after the June 2017 election, liberalism's older leaders spotted the potential for the EU to become a wedge issue. And they had young representatives who they could recruit to their cause. Michael Chessum, a Labour and Momentum activist and national organiser for Another Europe is Possible, warned in the *Guardian* that: 'Labour cannot expect to demoralise its activist base by choosing to implement a policy they regard as a fundamental affront to their values, and then just talk about school funding instead.'[24] Clearly EU 'values' were more important than the values underpinning the need for a redistribution of wealth.

The economic and normative importance of the EU for middle class young people was highlighted by Femi Oluwole, co-founder of the pro-EU, Our Future, Our Choice! In his *Guardian* opinion piece, Oluwole argued that leaving the EU:

> will make us much poorer, cut us off from our closest friends and leave us unable to address problems that require international cooperation to solve – such as climate change and rampant inequality. It will deny us opportunities and deprive us of the right to live, work, and love anywhere in Europe. It will rob us of the internationally engaged Britain we know we want.[25]

Many of these assertions reveal a complacent investment in a status quo that is already producing inequality and lack of action on climate change. Some are bizarre (cut off from friends?) while others assume that there is only one form of leaving the EU. This was a key feature of the Remain position in fact, returning to the binary of the EU Referendum rather than a post-Referendum world of compromise between a split country. This meant, as columnist Steve Richards put it as early as August 2017, that 'there will be only two options for Labour to contemplate over the next 12 months: the government's version of Brexit or no Brexit.'[26]

Given that for liberal neoliberalism, the only good Brexit was a no-Brexit, Labour's position was assailed continuously as a muddle, confused, deceitful or precisely what I have suggested it should have been: 'too tactical' as a *Guardian* editorial put it. 'Corbyn combines deference to the referendum outcome with reluctance to sound too enthusiastic about Brexit. It is not an easy balance. The longer this goes on, the likelier it gets that frustration and disillusionment build on both sides.'[27] It was the task of liberalism's intellectual leaders to ferment precisely that outcome in order to weaken Corbyn. One of the very few articles I found in the *Guardian* that was critical of the EU came from Holly Rigby, a teacher and Labour Party member. She articulated the left-wing critique of the EU ('neoliberal free trade for the rich and punishing austerity for the poor') rarely to be found in the pages of the *Guardian* and gently lampooned the class interests tacitly expressed in the defence of the EU ('Aperol spritz, discounted Zara coats and Erasmus study programmes').[28] Rigby noted that: 'Asking Labour to campaign for remain in a second referendum in leave-voting, post-industrial cities such as Stoke would make Corbyn part of the same political elite they feel have betrayed them.' Of course, this was what liberalism's champions were pushing Labour and Corbyn towards. We can note that in the 2016 Referendum, Stoke on Trent North voted 72.12 per cent Leave. In the 2019 general election, Stoke on Trent North, long held by Labour went Conservative with a 7 per cent swing against Ruth Smeeth. Stoke on Trent Central, which likewise heavily voted for Leave in 2016, went from Labour to Conservative with a 5.6 per cent swing.

2. Corbyn the Incompetent

So certain were the cheerleaders of Remain that it was obvious that Labour should swing behind a second vote and campaign for staying in the EU, that many commentators concluded that the only possible reason Corbyn did not do so was either that he was an incompetent leader or that he secretly wanted Brexit (or both). For Simon Jenkins, Corbyn was a man with a 'meagre reserve of parliamentary talent.'[29] His reluctance to be dragged along in the slipstream of the Remain campaign was interpreted as indecisiveness. He was not a leader because he had spent thirty years on the back benches.[30] He was passive, an absence where agency should be: 'Brexit politics has happened around him, not with or through him.'[31] The *Guardian* even gave credence to leaks by the civil service to the right wing press that called into question Corbyn's physical or mental fitness for office.[32] Against this, there was a minority stream of articles suggesting that Corbyn was on an evolving journey in relation to the EU. 'Where has Corbyn been?' wrote Polly Toynbee. 'On a journey, say those close by. A lifetime of instinctive "capitalist club" Euroscepticism has been shed.'[33] But this theme petered out in impatience as the anticipated buckling in front of the liberal juggernaut failed to happen with sufficient speed and enthusiasm.[34] Corbyn the incompetent was very much the dominant message. Another sub-theme of this category was the idea that Corbynism could exist without Corbyn, as if the problem were *really* a leadership skills deficit and not a policy agenda problem. There is such a thing as liberal 'dog whistle' politics just as much as there is the right-wing coded racism of conservatism. The liberal version as applied to Corbyn, launched relentless *ad hominem* attacks on Corbyn's professionalism, intellect and leadership capacity that grew to intensely vitriolic passion in the *Guardian*'s readership base. LindaD66 for example opined below the line: 'Corbyn is without any doubt one of the stupidest MPs we have'.[35] Such personal attacks bracketed off the political problems of trying to hold together the increasingly fragile electoral coalition that made up Labour's vote.

Of course, this is not to say that Corbyn was flawless. He made mistakes and he had his personal weaknesses no doubt. There is, however, often enough very little correlation between the personal qualities of political leaders and the outcomes of elections. The election of Donald Trump in the US and Boris Johnson are examples of that. Corbyn's *political* weakness was a reflection of the contradictions of the situation. The personal attacks disguised liberalism's agenda and no doubt also provided psychological absolution for all those who should have known better after the outcome of the 2019 election result. In the end it was, apparently, all the fault of a weak leader, not a 'stupid' fetishization of the EU.

3. An Illegitimate Left

Corbyn was assailed by liberalism as a representative of an illegitimate left well outside the traditions of parliamentary democracy, even though Corbyn had spent most of his professional life as a constituency MP. There was an extraordinary recycling of Cold War themes in this discourse. The theme was spotted and critiqued by the *Guardian*'s economic editor Larry Elliott, a lone voice of EU scepticism on the paper. '[B]randing Corbyn a 1970s Marxist throwback or banging on about his support for Venezuela is not going to cut it.'[36] At that point, this discursive framing of Corbyn probably did have waning efficacy. Liberalism's guns were depleted of ammunition in the months immediately after the 2017 general election. But as Corbyn's position weakened, so his opponents returned again and again to this theme. For Martin Kettle, Labour has been 'radically transformed into a party in the leader's own far-left image' which if it had been true, would have solved many of Corbyn's problems.[37] For Rafael Behr, there was a symmetry between the political forces apparently tugging at the seam of sensible centrist politics. Both right and left were turning political parties into 'intolerant sects'.[38] When some of Corbyn's senior staff tried to oust Tom Watson from the post of deputy leader, having undermined the leadership since his 2015 election alongside Corbyn, Andrew Rawnsley in the *Observer* juggled images of 'Stalin's henchmen' and the 'Soviet dictator' with Mafiosi gangsterism ('capos' 'drive-by shooting', etc).[39] For Will Hutton, Labour's 'leadership is too indiscriminately critical of all business and wedded to the socialist transformation of capitalism. Not even the Chinese and Cuban Communist parties believe that.'[40] Of course the 2017 and 2019 Labour Party manifestoes fell a long way short of the socialist transformation of capitalism, along the Chinese, Cuban or any other model for that matter. The idea that Corbyn represents an illegitimate political tradition (one with its roots outside British constitutionalism) was connected to other sub-themes. One, alluded to by Hutton, was the idea that Corbyn represented a return to outdated, 1970s politics that were no longer applicable. Another was that an intrinsic left-wing authoritarianism was evident in the so-called idolatry of Corbyn by his supporters and their inability to accept fair criticism from the impartial media (or Labour's MPs) who were after all only doing their job. Liberalism framed these responses as 'blasphemies against the supreme leader'[41] by 'Corbynite zealots'.[42] The left was apparently as fanatical as religious fundamentalism, a position that, in the circumstances, somewhat over-egged liberalism's claims to be a defender of autonomous critical reason. This theme of political illegitimacy also allowed liberalism to participate subtly in the right-wing smears that Corbyn was a terrorist sympathiser,[43] indicating once again liberalism's own role within a historic bloc with a long history of colonial violence and deadly policy blunders. Corbyn himself has been on the right side of that history.

CONCLUSION

In the two or more years before the 2019 general election, the *Guardian* acted as if there was a choice between Corbyn's Labour Party, the Tories and some imagined alternative. There was not, at least at that stage. But in its discrediting of the Corbyn project, the practical grounds for the imagined alternative were being laid, namely the return to the policy agenda of liberal neoliberalism. Out of power at the top of the Labour

Party, liberal neoliberalism remained very much in power in the PLP and wider civil society. Gradually it reasserted its leadership credentials, its moral-political will over the membership and the relatively small readership of the *Guardian*. As part of a nexus of power, the *Guardian* helped to isolate Corbyn, demolish his personal legitimacy, separate him from his base, shift him towards a second referendum, amplify the voices of MPs defining Labour as a 'remain' party and fracture a chunk of Labour's electoral coalition along class lines. If we keep our nose only to the Brexit grindstone, we fail to see the bigger picture: this was hegemony in action.

NOTES

1. Stuart Hall, *The Hard Road to Renewal: Thatcherism and the Crisis of the Left* (London: Verso, 1988), p.130.
2. John Clarke, 'A Sense of Loss? Unsettled Attachments in the Current Conjuncture', *New Formations*, issue 96–97, 2019, p. 132.
3. Antonio Gramsci, *Selections from the Prison Notebooks*, (eds) Quintin Hoare and Geoffrey Nowell-Smith (London: Lawrence and Wishart, 2003), p. 178.
4. Gramsci, *Prison Notebooks*, p. 210.
5. Will Hutton, 'How Could it Be that the Tories Have Turned Their Back on the Best of British industry?', *Observer*, 17 November 2019.
6. Gramsci, *Prison Notebooks*, pp. 148–9.
7. Gramsci, *Prison Notebooks*, pp.181–2.
8. See Mike Wayne, *England's Discontents, Political Cultures and National Identities* (London: Pluto Press, 2018) for a more extensive discussion of the hegemony of conservatism and liberalism in the UK.
9. Thomas Macaulay, 'Speech in the House of Commons', *The Liberal Tradition: From Fox to Keynes*, (eds) Alan Bullock and Maurice Shock (Oxford: Clarendon Press, 1956), p. 32.
10. See Belén Balanyá et al, *Europe Inc: Regional & Global Restructuring and the Rise of Corporate Power* (London: Pluto Press, 2000).
11. Gramsci, *Prison Notebooks*, p. 235.
12. 'Capitalist Realism' is the term associated with Mark Fisher and refers to the idea that realistic politics today must accept that neoliberal capitalism is the only game in town.
13. Rafael Behr, 'This Faragism of the Left Will Leave Behind a Loathing of all Politics', *Guardian*, 15 September 2015, www.theguardian.com/commentisfree/2015/sep/15/faragism-left-protest-britain-eu-jeremy-corbyn (accessed 26 October 2020).
14. Gramsci, *Prison Notebooks*, p. 10.

15. Polly Toynbee, 'Dismal, Lifeless, Spineless – Jeremy Corbyn let us Down Again' *Guardian*, 25 June 2016, www.theguardian.com/commentisfree/2016/jun/25/jeremy-corbyn-referedum-campaign (accessed 26 October 2020).
16. Peter Moore, 'How Britain Voted at the EU referendum', YouGov, 27 June 2016, www.yougov.co.uk/topics/politics/articles-reports/2016/06/27/how-britain-voted (accessed 15 June 2020).
17. 47 anti-Corbyn headlines from the *Guardian* between July 2015 and May 2017 have been collated by some enterprising soul at www.theguardian.fivefilters.org/ (accessed 15 June 2020).
18. Jim Packard, 'Poll Shows 86% of Labour Members Want a New Brexit vote', *Financial Times*, 22 September 2018, www.ft.com/content/dc56ee36-bea4-11e8-95b1-d36dfef1b89a (accessed 26 October 2020).
19. Tim Bale, 'Inside Labour's Massive Membership Base', *Labour List*, 6 October 2017, www.labourlist.org/2017/10/tim-bale-inside-laboursmassive-membership-base/ (accessed 15 June 2020).
20. Conversely, left-wing proponents of Leave around, for example, The Full Brexit website, also made the tactical mistake of prioritising Brexit above the election of a Corbyn government. Their enthusiasm for Brexit assumed that the Leave vote was an indication of class consciousness on the part of the working class. It was much more heterogeneous than liberalism (for whom Leave is a racist bloc) was willing to admit. But certainly the conservative right had succeeded in articulating the question of sovereignty to immigration in the minds of many Leave voters, something The Full Brexit website and *The Morning Star* underplayed in their enthusiasm for following through on the Referendum result.
21. Freddy Mayhew, 'How Daily Newspaper Readers Voted by Title in the 2017 General Election', *Press Gazette*, 14 June 2017, www.pressgazette.co.uk/how-daily-newspaper-readers-voted-by-title-in-the-2017-general-election/ (accessed 15 June 2020).
22. The *Guardian* and *Observer* reader profile 2012 can be accessed at www.image.guardian.co.uk/sys-files/Guardian/documents/2012/08/22/Printreaderprofile.pdf (accessed 15 June 2020).
23. The *Guardian* and *Observer* reader profile, https://image.guardian.co.uk/sys-files/Guardian/documents/2012/08/22/Printreaderprofile.pdf (accessed 6 December 2020).
24. Michael Chessum, 'If Corbyn Helps the Tories Deliver Brexit, it Will Be a Disaster for Labour', *Guardian*, 9 April 2019, www.theguardian.com/commentisfree/2019/apr/09/corbyn-tories-brexit-labour-voters (accessed 26 October 2020).
25. Femi Oluwole, 'Dear Jeremy Corbyn…' *Guardian*, 5 February 2018, www.theguardian.com/commentisfree/2018/feb/05/jeremy-corbyn-young-people-brexit-radical-change (accessed 26 October 2020).

26. Steve Richards, 'Now Jeremy Corbyn Must Say No to Brexit', *Guardian*, 21 August 2017, www.theguardian.com/commentisfree/2017/aug/21/jeremy-corbyn-say-no-to-brexit (accessed 26 October 2020).
27. *Guardian* editorial, 'The Guardian View on Labour and Brexit: Too timid, too Tactical', 8 June 2018, www.theguardian.com/commentisfree/2018/jun/08/the-guardian-view-on-labour-and-brexit-too-timid-too-tactical (accessed 26 October 2020).
28. Holly Rigby, 'For People Suffering Under Austerity, Corbyn is the Answer, Not the EU', *Guardian*, 22 November 2018, www.theguardian.com/commentisfree/2018/nov/22/austerity-corbyn-eu-brexit-peoples-vote (accessed 26 October 2020).
29. Simon Jenkins, 'Corbyn's man of the future act is hooked on dogmas of the past', *Guardian*, 28 September 2017, www.theguardian.com/commentisfree/2017/sep/28/jeremy-corbyn-dogmas-past-labour (accessed 26 October 2020).
30. Helen Lewis, 'If Corbyn is Not to Appear a Passenger in His Own Party, He Must Learn to Lead', *Guardian*, 1 April 2018, www.theguardian.com/commentisfree/2018/apr/01/if-corbyn-is-not-to-appear-a-passenger-he-must-learn-to-lead (accessed 26 October 2020).
31. Martin Kettle, 'If Corbyn Gets His Hands Dirty He Can Avert a Hard Brexit', *Guardian*, 30 January 2019, www.theguardian.com/commentisfree/2019/jan/30/corbyn-avert-hard-brexit-tory-may-deal-labour (accessed 26 October 2020).
32. Gaby Hinsliff, 'Civil Servants Should Discuss Corbyn – as Long as it's Behind Closed Doors', *Guardian*, 2 July 2019, www.theguardian.com/commentisfree/2019/jul/02/civil-servants-discuss-corbyn-journalists-labour (accessed 26 October 2020).
33. Polly Toynbee, 'Corbyn Has Seen the Light on Brexit', *Guardian*, 23 November 2017, www.theguardian.com/commentisfree/2017/nov/23/jeremy-corbyn-brexit-tories-labour-eu (accessed 26 October 2020).
34. Paul Mason, 'Corbyn Has Taken a Brave Step: Now He Must Rule Out any "Labour Brexit"', *Guardian*, 15 August 2019, www.theguardian.com/commentisfree/2019/aug/15/jeremy-corbyn-labour-brexit-second-referendum?CMP=fb_cif (accessed 26 October 2020). For Mason, Corbyn's 'journey' was to head back to the backbenches and let someone else take over. Mason, an independent journalist and a former excited Corbyn supporter, swam, like others in the 'left/liberal' media commentariat, with the tide of power.
35. Comment in response to Polly Toynbee, 'This Government Really is Stupid. Labour Must Get Smart on Brexit', *Guardian*, 20 December 2018, www.theguardian.com/commentisfree/2018/dec/20/government-stupid-labour-brexit-referendum-jeremy-corbyn (accessed 26 October 2020).
36. Larry Elliott, 'Labour Has a Once-in-Generation Opportunity', *Guardian*, 5 October 2017, www.theguardian.com/commentisfree/2017/

oct/05/labour-opportunities-tories-radical-change-corbyn-marxist-throwback (accessed 26 October 2020).

37. Martin Kettle, 'Could Corbyn Solve Brexit and Save Britain?', *Guardian*, 27 September 2018, www.theguardian.com/commentisfree/2018/sep/27/jeremy-corbyn-solve-brexit-labour (accessed 26 October 2020).
38. Rafael Behr, 'Deal or No Deal, both Labour and the Tories Will Split Over Brexit', *Guardian*, 12 February 2019, www.theguardian.com/commentisfree/2019/feb/12/deal-no-deal-labour-tories-brexit-may-corbyn (accessed 26 October 2020).
39. Andrew Rawnsley, 'The Failed Watson Plot Exposes What Really Scares Corbyn and his Coterie', *Guardian*, 22 September 2019, www.theguardian.com/commentisfree/2019/sep/22/failed-watson-plot-exposes-what-really-scares-corbyn-and-his-coterie (accessed 26 October 2020).
40. Will Hutton, 'How Could it Be that the Tories Have Turned their Back on the Best of British Industry?', *Observer*, 17 November 2019, www.theguardian.com/commentisfree/2019/nov/17/how-could-it-be-that-the-tories-have-turned-their-back-on-the-best-of-british-industry (accessed 26 October 2020).
41. Behr, 'Deal or No Deal'.
42. Rawnsley, 'The Failed Watson Plot'.
43. Marina Hyde, 'Come on, Jeremy Corbyn, Give us the Full Jack Nicholson', *Guardian*, 17 August 2018, www.theguardian.com/commentisfree/2018/aug/17/jeremy-corbyn-jack-nicholson-a-few-good-men (accessed 26 October 2020).

15

'I'm not "racist" but': Liberalism, Populism and Euphemisation in the *Guardian*

Katy Brown, Aurelien Mondon and Aaron Winter

With the resurgence of Black Lives Matter (BLM) protests, and their spread to the United Kingdom in Spring 2020, the *Guardian* adopted a mostly unambiguous approach to the movement, offering broad support, whether in its editorial, news or opinion pieces. This was even the case when the statue of slave trader Edward Colston was toppled in Bristol, with an editorial stating that it was 'a long time in going'.[1] This not only departed from many instances of mainstream coverage and reactions, which were more cautious and warned against illegal acts for example, but also from the approach the *Guardian* itself had taken in the past when discussing racism and the resurgence of the far right in particular.

Discussions of racism, in the *Guardian* and mainstream media more broadly, are usually couched in post-racial terms, whereby racism is constructed as an extreme, and the racist as the other, the anomaly, the residue of a bygone era. Such politics are limited in time, place and ideology to precise occurrences, whether they be terrorist attacks or racist expressions of a biological nature mimicking Nazism and fascism. As such, the term is mostly used to describe what we have called elsewhere, occurrences of 'illiberal racism' or what Alana Lentin calls 'frozen racism'.[2] This, we argue, takes us away from more liberal articulations of racism, which are not only more common, but also core to many of our institutions and systemic oppression and rarely addressed in the mainstream media, at least until the BLM protests and wider public outcry.[3]

Normally, liberal articulations take the form of cultural racism (or what others have called 'new racism'), which is not based on the explicit superiority of one race over another, but instead on the essentialisation and incompatibility of cultures.[4] Liberal articulations of racism are positioned in opposition to illiberal ones: if we oppose illiberal racism, we cannot be racist ourselves. This form of self-justification is used extensively in liberal societies, and even by those on the far right, to excuse their own liberal approach to racism. We see this logic replicated widely in mainstream circles, and in the media in particular. The effect of this is that it diverts attention from, conceals and even enables systemic racism by pointing the finger at extreme occurrences, as well as legitimising far right attempts to become more acceptable and mainstream.

In this chapter, we argue that liberal articulations of racism are not only core to the process of mainstreaming far-right politics, but that these tropes have become intricately linked to the production of news and the shaping of public discourse, including on the left. We contend that the limitation of racism to its extreme and illiberal forms has led to an obfuscation and deflection of its mainstream presence and systemic operation within our societies, and the impact this has on those at the sharp end. Contributing significantly to this process is the euphemisation of racism through its labelling as 'populism' and, crucially, what is termed the populist 'hype', something we turn our attention to first.[5] We then move on to explore the way in which the *Guardian* navigates the tensions between liberal and illiberal articulations of racism in its coverage and the effects and impact this can have on its readership, particularly in terms of euphemisation and amplification. Finally, we explore the issues of platforming, false equivalence and free speech, actively stoked by the far right and bought into by the *Guardian*, often providing coverage of the far right either on its own terms or in a positive light.

While this chapter is interested in broader trends regarding the *Guardian*'s uneven coverage of racism, it builds on our research on the *Guardian*'s series on 'The New Populism'.[6] The corpus,[7] coupled with Brown's methodological approach combining Discourse Theory, Critical Discourse Studies and Corpus Linguistics, allows us to explore the way in which such news coverage feeds into and sustains these harmful logics.[8] While examples are sourced from a range of articles, Simon Hattenstone's piece entitled, '"We're reactivating the people's army": Inside the battle for a hard Brexit' forms one of the core articles from which we draw, owing to its relevance to many features discussed here and those relating to populism in particular.[9]

POPULISM AND THE POPULIST HYPE

The use of 'populism' to describe a range of phenomena has proliferated vastly over recent years, and we now see the term applied extensively in political commentary, public discourse and academic analysis. In November 2018, as part of 'The New Populism' series, the *Guardian* even asked, 'Why is populism suddenly all the rage?'. In the piece, they noted that '[i]n 1998, about 300 *Guardian* articles mentioned populism. In 2016, 2,000 did', and asked 'What happened?'[10] Despite their differences, the dominant definitions of populism, which identify it as a thin ideology or a discourse,[11] both acknowledge that it is only part of the bigger political, ideological and discursive picture. However, such tempering of its significance through situating it within this wider frame is becoming increasingly rare, leading to what has been termed 'populist hype'.[12] The concept underscores the dangers of the uncritical diffusion of 'populism', particularly as a term to describe reactionary right-wing parties and movements. Indeed, a skewing of the meaning of populism, an exaggeration of its significance and the apocalyptic way it is posed as a threat to democracy feed into the notion that right-wing populism is 'itself a disease rather than [...] a mere symptom',[13] with serious implications for the level of self-reflection on the current state of liberal democracy. Therefore, the overuse and misapplication of the term, and consequent skewing of its meaning, has serious implications in both exaggerating and downplaying certain aspects of politics, and has been particularly rife in media coverage.

Indeed, it is often the case that the 'populist' (far) right is discussed as if it has risen and exists in a vacuum, as if its success can only be attributed to its own political nous or the demands of the electorate *qua* 'the people' *qua* the (white) working-class. Interestingly, its defeat is often celebrated on the other hand as a victory for democracy, for all that's good in liberalism, for us *qua* 'the good people' *qua* the liberal *Guardian* readers. This of course ignores the most basic concepts within social sciences and media studies such as power structures and relations, and in particular the ability for some to set the agenda.[14] This is especially the case when it comes to matters of national importance, or more precisely, those where an individual, no matter their expertise in a particular field, is required to think beyond their immediate practical knowledge and thus rely on mediated sources of information. Based on this research, what we argue here is that without the space and coverage provided by mainstream elites (media, politicians and academics), it is highly unlikely that the far right could have found itself in such a strong contending position. This is also why we turn our attention here to the *Guardian*, a centre/centre-left newspaper, rather than to the right-wing tabloid press or even Murdoch-owned broadsheets. While the latter are often seen as the mouthpiece of reaction, we argue that mainstreaming trends can be best observed in what would traditionally be thought of as opposed to such politics: if your adversaries are abiding by your rules, then you must be winning the culture wars.

To analyse the corpus, we draw on the early warnings of Annie Collovald,[15] whose prescient work was anchored in a particular context where Jean-Marie Le Pen of the far-right Front National (FN) had reached the second round of the French presidential elections in 2002. In particular, Collovald critiqued the increasing predominance of 'populism' as a descriptor for the party:

> As well as offering a new way of classifying the FN, which is much fuzzier and much less stigmatising than the previous labels of fascism and extreme right that it replaces, the term [populism] legitimises extremely harmful notions that it is 'the people' [*groupes populaires*] who support this party.[16]

Here, Collovald identifies two key problems with the use of 'populism' in this context, relating to the euphemisation of the party and the legitimisation of its position as representing the will of the people. With fewer negative connotations than other descriptors and the blame placed on 'the people', she argued, our focus is deflected away from the party itself, its ideology and the system/environment that allowed it to garner some success. Although centred around a specific event, we see these trends replay frequently in various contexts, including in the *Guardian*.

As highlighted, one of the main problems with populist hype is the way in which 'populism' or 'populist' has come to replace, or euphemise, more accurate terminology and qualifications, and particularly those associated with racism. In our corpus, we see significant reluctance from the *Guardian* to call phenomena racist, frequently employing perspectivisation strategies of distancing. Indeed, in 523 instances of racis*,[17] 235 (45 per cent) references were either quoted or formed part of reported speech. Of the remaining examples, 157 were within opinion pieces or letters, leaving only 131 (25 per cent) to occur in regular articles. This practice of distancing is also evidenced for instance in Hattenstone's description of Orbán: 'Farage tweeted his support for Orbán, who has been accused of Islamophobia and antisemitism'.[18] Despite his clear record of both, the article avoids directly stating it, instead choosing to sit on the fence through the language of accusation.

Clearly racist phenomena, as defined per academic standards, are often defined 'populist', and the ambiguity associated with the term induces further euphemising effects. Although 'The New Populism' series attempts to address the issue of definitions, particularly in Peter C. Baker's intervention which problematises the overuse of populism,[19] we see that this is often lost in the content of many articles. Again, Hattenstone's piece provides an illustrative example through positive framing and actor-led definitions. Indeed, of Farage the journalist asks, 'Is he Britain's greatest populist politician?', using positive predication which encourages similar sentiment to be expressed in the response from the participant. Equally, he states, 'I ask Peter Bone what populism means to him. "Doesn't populist mean what most people want?" he says', thereby inviting involved actors to define the term for themselves, inevitably manipulating its meaning towards positive connotations and directly reinforcing the Brexit Party's claim to represent 'the people's army'.[20]

As evidenced in the above examples, by referring to such phenomena as 'populist', a simplistic narrative is constructed which places the demands of the electorate as the driving force. Within the corpus, we see these tropes of illiberalism limited to the working class played out time and time again. It is presented as an undeniable truth, despite much evidence to counter this narrative.[21] For instance, in a *Guardian* comment piece, the former prime minister and leader of the Labour

Party, Gordon Brown claims that '[t]he basic building blocks should be self-evident: radical measures to end the economic insecurity that is the breeding ground for populism; no truck with divisive nationalisms or with intolerance and racism from whatever quarter it comes.'[22] Here, we see this simplistic topos played out as common sense, deflecting attention from the normalisation of these discourses by figures such as Brown himself, for instance in his far-right inspired slogan, 'British jobs for British workers', used during his leadership. In placing illiberalism and racism almost exclusively among the working class, the message is that it is 'theirs' not 'ours', creating dangerous false distinctions: if it was not for the working class, we would not have racism and could achieve enjoyment of our liberal democracy – something which of course, borrowing from psychoanalytic theory, is simply unachievable. It is to this distancing that we now turn.

I'M NOT ILLIBERAL BUT... LIBERAL VS. ILLIBERAL RACISM

In the previous section, we noted that the way in which the *Guardian* referred to racism and racist ideas, euphemistically or overtly, was usually through distancing, whether it was in a quotation or attributed to an individual, such as Nigel Farage. While this raises the issue of platforming, which is examined in the next section, it also ensures that the racism that is articulated and amplified is anathema to the paper's liberal identity and discourse. This can take the form of the illiberal masses ('the people', often the white working class 'left behind') or far right 'populists'. It depends on the distinction between illiberal and liberal articulations of racisms, and more precisely, the ways in which liberals deny their racism by displacing it onto more overt and unacceptable illiberal forms.

Illiberal racism is what is commonly defined as 'real' racism in hegemonic discourse. It is represented by traditional or historical forms of racism, such as slavery, segregation, Nazism and race science, which have been defeated and rejected by the post-war and post-civil rights liberal order. When it does appear in our contemporary context, it is usually represented by the extreme right as a remnant of this old order: extreme, unacceptable and often individualised, as is the case for example after white supremacist attacks. In the corpus, we see the use of 'racist' as a descriptor (free from quotation or reported speech) often in limited contexts epitomising illiberalism, such as South African apartheid, Nazism, blackface, Jobbik's discourse in Hungary, Trump's racist comments towards four congresswomen, racist chants in football stadiums, etc. These are generally condemned unequivocally, but there are some exceptions. When historical icons and institutions are accused of illiberal racism, they are often excused as 'of their time'. This allows for the affirmation of the unacceptability of their racism today, and division between the bad past and progressive present, but paradoxically does not require their rejection.

This has been most obvious in the case of Winston Churchill. In February 2019, *Guardian* columnist Simon Jenkins not only defended Churchill (and Gladstone), but, using a current reactionary talking point, criticised identity politics and anti-racists who rejected his legacy:

> The current cult of identity politics is to rifle through the past careers of great men and women, not to ascertain accuracy but to sort them into friends or foes. Churchill has been accused of racism. He undoubtedly expressed racist views but they were uttered in very different times, in which such ideas were deemed acceptable by many.[23]

Here, mitigation strategies are used consistently to diminish Churchill's racism, attempting to depict him as a mere reflection of society at the time and to discredit those challenging his legacy as lacking commitment to accuracy in pursuit of a Manichean agenda. Central to the piece is the idea of balance and rationality in the approach to history, which Emmy Eklundh identifies as an exclusionary logic: 'rationality is used as a proxy to devalue or exclude certain groups from the political sphere, and [. . .] when we are discussing emotions, we are simply using a euphemism for describing groups who are not deemed worthy of inclusion.'[24] Eklundh highlights the development of rationality as a mode of exclusion within democratic theory, so we can see how core features of liberalism are used here to defend illiberalism. Another mitigation strategy frequently used in defences of Churchill, is his role in defeating the Nazis,[25] the symbol of illiberal racism, and ushering in the post-war liberal order against which it and liberal racism are defined.

This brings us to liberal racism, which includes those articulations of colour-blind, post-racial racism that distinguish themselves and deny being racist in contrast to 'illiberal' forms of racism. Liberal racism does not see itself or liberalism as being racist, instead evoking illiberal racism to justify its self-appointed non-racist position. In fact, it treats liberalism as the antidote or bulwark against racism. Yet, at the same time, it weaponizes liberalism and liberal tropes, such as freedom of speech, women's rights and LGBTQ+ rights, against racialised groups, something most notable in the case of Muslims.[26] In doing so, it not only denies the racism often core to liberal practice, but justifies the lack of action on structural inequalities and the continuity of less overt forms of systemic and coded racism. In fact, it often uses the threat of the far right to push 'moderate' politicians and policies. This includes structurally racist ones about Islam and immigration because such illiberal actors are seen as far worse.

For example, on 22 November 2018 the *Guardian* published an interview with Hillary Clinton asserting that 'Europe must curb immigration to stop rightwing populists'.[27] Not only did the paper give a platform for this particular analysis legitimising xenophobia, but this was the eye-catching headline in an already reactionary and racist political landscape. A day later, the *Guardian* published another article in which Clinton 'criticised the US media over its coverage of Donald Trump, calling on the press to "get smarter" about holding to account a president who is a master of diversion and distraction'.[28] The irony that anti-immigrant politics, and the illiberal threat of the far right, were the diversion and distraction that were bought into and legitimised was lost. A few days later, on 26 November, left-wing columnist Paul Mason argued that 'Liberals must learn the politics of emotion to beat rightwing populists', and that '[a]ttachment to place and identity can be part of a radical democratic project that speaks to people's hearts'[29] – an implicit acknowledgement, of the need to engage with (rather than agitate against) the racial, national and even nativist politics the right have weaponised.

Critically, liberal platforming and the push for moderate versions of far-right ideas, even if only to fend off a challenge, play a role in legitimising and mainstreaming such ideas. It became even more explicit when, in a September 2019 article, the former US Ambassador to the UN, Samantha Power, was interviewed and blamed the same refugees targeted by the far right and racists, for the illiberal backlash against themselves: 'The exodus of refugees has destabilised the region and Europe, prompting a racist backlash exploited by populist politicians'.[30] The topos of backlash here places refugees as the instigators and politicians (also note the use of 'populist' here) as only responding to the reaction prompted, thereby completely obscuring the power dynamics at play.

With such arguments, the lines between illiberal and liberal articulations of racism become blurry and difficult to maintain. Despite this, the *Guardian* and other mainstream media partake in openly reinforcing these distinctions, which in turn legitimise the positions of those who attempt to straddle the mainstream-extreme divide. For instance, in December 2018, as Nigel Farage gained more mainstream legitimacy and the more illiberal far/extreme right exerted greater influence in UKIP, *Guardian* columnist Martin Kettle urged readers to: '[l]ook at the lurch to the racist right within Ukip, which has driven even Nigel Farage to resign from it'.[31] With this argument and the hyperbole of 'lurch' to intensify the distinction, Kettle effectively affirmed Farage's own strategy to define himself as the more liberal, acceptable alternative to the old, illiberal far/extreme right, which he outlined in a 2016 interview:

> I destroyed the British National Party – we had a far-right party in this country who genuinely were anti-Jew, anti-Black, all of those things, and I came along, and said to their voters, if you're holding your nose and voting for this party as a protest, don't. Come and vote for me – I'm not against anybody, I just want us to start putting British people first, and I, almost single-handedly, destroyed the far right in British politics.[32]

We see this argument replicated in Hattenstone's piece, with an embedded video entitled, 'How Ukip normalised far-right politics', which effectively distances Farage and the party from the label of far right and suggests that it is only since his resignation that UKIP have shifted to this position. In the video, as an image of Farage in front of the 'Breaking Point' poster appears, the narrator states: 'Yes, they had some off-piste moments, but their actual policies were mainly about low taxes and bashing Brussels.'[33] The casual dismissal of this racist poster as an 'off-piste moment' serves to minimise its importance, play down the power of discourse as opposed to 'actual policies' and deny the centrality of racism within the party long before Farage stepped down.

It may seem to be a paradox or contradiction that liberals would platform and amplify the ideas of those they denounce and displace racism onto, but it is this very process that is necessary for liberalism, centrism and liberal racism to function and flourish. We can see how the two work together through the alignment of liberals, the establishment and far right around defending statues of slave traders and racists during the BLM protests in the summer of 2020.

'ACTIVISM': LIBERAL PLATFORMING, FALSE EQUIVALENCE AND FREE SPEECH ON THE FAR RIGHT

As already noted, the *Guardian* has repeatedly given voice to racist and far-right figures and ideas in interviews and articles. This platforming and the resulting amplification do not only fulfil the function of deflecting from liberal racism, but also allow the paper to represent its journalism as adhering to liberal principles of objectivity, balance and free speech. This is based on the belief that it needs to represent the democratic 'will of the people' and promote a diversity of ideas – something that is skewed by populist hype and its exaggeration of the prevalence of far-right support amongst 'the people'. That is not to say that the *Guardian* does not take a negative position on matters of racism and the far right. However, when it does, its commitment to liberalism seems to matter more and requires platforming 'bad' ideas, even if this leads to their legitimisation in order to affirm liberal virtues and deflect from their sins.

This has been particularly striking in the context of Brexit and a reactionary culture war, which includes attacks on the media and demands for 'free speech', and has targeted the *Guardian* for representing the 'woke' left *and* liberal metropolitan Remainer elite. This is something that the newspaper often tries to reject and overcome through a variety of methods such as self-defence, self-parody and self-flagellation. Prior to Brexit, perhaps reading the signs, the *Guardian* published the quiz: 'Are you part of the dreaded metropolitan elite?'[34] In 2019, post-Brexit, it published a piece headlined: 'The left-behind v the metropolitan elite? That's a lazy, harmful cliché'.[35] Between these two events, some *Guardian* writers have also tried to address this, as we have discussed in the previous two sections, through perpetuating 'populist hype' and reaching out to the 'white working class' as they have constructed it. In one example, the paper published an op-ed by pro-Brexit *Spiked!* associate Joanna Williams which argued: 'Liberal elite, it's time to strike a deal with the working class'.[36] They have also reported on and engaged with far-right ideas and figures, often using euphemisms and more neutral language, that they may assume, in their elitist minds, are representative of the white working class.

One of the ways that the *Guardian* addresses such criticism is through the representation and platforming of racist and reactionary ideas and figures in what they may see as objective, neutral and balanced ways in line with their liberal centrism and journalistic identity. This can be done through euphemisms, and the use of less stigmatising language such as 'populist' (as highlighted earlier) and 'activist' to describe racists and the far right. The *Guardian*'s coverage of the German state election in Thuringia, where the far-right AfD finished second, provides a clear example of this process.[37] Populist hype can already be witnessed in the headline – 'Far-right AfD surges to second place in German state election' – and body of the article, which focuses far more on the AfD than it does on the actual winner, Die Linke, its radical left opponent. Despite the fact that the leader of the Thuringian section of the AfD, Björn Höcke, is well known to be on the more extreme right of the party, the opening line states that '[a]nti-immigrant populists beat Angela Merkel's Christian Democrats (CDU) to second place'. In September 2019, Höcke threatened a ZDF journalist who compared his quotes to those of Adolf Hitler with 'massive consequences', something the *Guardian* itself reported on.[38] The court in Thuringia eventually threw out the case, ruling that Höcke 'could legally be termed a "fascist", saying that such a designation "rests on verifiable fact"'.[39] Despite the evidence, the *Guardian* steered clear of such language which not only euphemised Höcke's politics but demonstrated a lack of solidarity with their German colleagues.

In October 2018, the *Guardian* published Arwa Mahdawi's criticism of the *Sunday Times*' use of the term 'Hipster Fascists' to describe Generation Identity.[40] However, there are many examples of similar approaches within the corpus; for instance, we see headlines such as 'Meet Thierry Baudet, the suave new face of Dutch rightwing populism',[41] descriptions like that of Brexit Party chairman Richard Tice 'with his Dr Kildare good looks'[42] and no fewer than four articles on Steve Bannon on the second day of 'the New Populism' series portraying him as a key shaper of European politics despite much evidence of his failure to do so.[43] Beyond humanising these figures, such generous descriptions and coverage feed into the legitimisation of their ideas.

We see this particularly in the way in which English Defence League founder 'Tommy Robinson' (Stephen Yaxley-Lennon) is framed. Concordance analysis revealed that 'activist' was among the top two collocates (second to 'right') of 'Tommy Robinson' within the corpus, signifying a dominant mode of reference with euphemising effects. This is also evident in Hattenstone's piece where Robinson is referred to as a 'far-right activist'.[44] Furthermore, in an article in which he is described as an 'anti-Islam campaigner', the reporters state that Robinson 'frequently complains of being smeared as a racist, insisting he does not care about skin colour and that his objection is to Islamist political ideology rather than people'. The article then attempts to challenge this by listing some of the illiberal racist things Robinson has been recorded as saying, such as: 'Somalis are backward barbarians', British Muslims are 'enemy combatants who want to kill you, maim you and destroy you', and refugees are 'raping their way through the country'.[45] Not only does the *Guardian*'s euphemisation and sanitisation of language help serve this self-image, but its revelations about racism and corruption reinforce Robinson's claims about persecution. This is best illustrated by the piece 'Tommy Robinson: from local loud mouth to international far-right poster boy',[46] in which he is promoted as the latter, an 'international brand' and 'global cause celebre' throughout the article.

The coverage of Tommy Robinson, and in particular his 'activism', introduces a further key element of the *Guardian*'s engagement with the 'other side', through the construction of false equivalences, as if 'two sides' must always be voiced in a polarised social and political landscape. The two sides may be Brexiteer and Remainer, right and left, or racist and anti-racist. In the context of the latter, Tommy Robinson is merely another activist in a democratic battle over ideas and beliefs (Islam) as opposed to targeting racialised people (Muslims). This distinction feeds off both defences of Islamophobia and an ideologically loaded free speech debate which has been weaponised by reactionaries as a way of getting platforms and airing their ideas in the mainstream.[47]

We believe that this has been one of the most significant methods through which the far right has been legitimised and mainstreamed by liberals, libertarians and conservatives such as *Spiked!* and *Quillette*. In this discourse, the inclusion in debate of racists and the far right represents the true 'diversity of ideas'. For concerned liberals, airing these views is seen as both necessary for a truly free society and the most effective way to defeat them through exposure to the 'marketplace of ideas', as if speech and power was equally distributed and as if the far right comes to such debates with an open mind. For the far right and racists, who normally hate 'diversity' and whose aims are a direct threat to diverse communities, this is a blessing as it allows them to attack and shame opponents on the left for being illiberal and fascistic for their refusal to engage in debates about whether the humanity of some should be up for discussion. This reversal of 'illiberal' and 'liberal' corresponds directly to the construction of reverse racism, when white people are claimed as victims because of an alleged anti-racist hegemonic power structure, where anti-racists and anti-fascists are the real racists and fascists. In this free speech narrative, dominant ideas are claimed to be from the 'woke' left and thus reactionaries must fight bravely for the representation of their ideas. Robinson's representation of himself as an activist and censored victim trying to expose Islam's 'bad ideas' fits within this narrative and is dangerously echoed and thus legitimised by the *Guardian*.

A similar trend is at play with the way in which both Brexit and Trump have been commonly represented as a white working class revolt as opposed to a white, elite-driven consolidation of conservative power. It is a mistake for the *Guardian* to buy into these narratives and to attempt either to achieve balance between, for example, Brexit and its opponents or to overcompensate for a liberal reputation in a manner which ultimately benefits the status quo. One example of this is the paper's response to a letter condemning 'cancel culture' in *Harper's* magazine in August 2020.[48] Instead of merely reporting on or challenging the letter's argument that free speech is under threat, particularly one signed by major authors on a prestigious platform, it presented 'both sides' of the debate in the piece: 'Is free speech under threat from "cancel culture"? Four writers respond' that featured short articles by Nesrine Malik, Jonathan Freedland, Zoe Williams and Samuel Moyn.[49] While Malik expressed clearly why the letter was a mistake, the *Guardian*'s decision to adopt that language and to pursue a pseudo-debate in a media landscape already saturated by the reactionary view only served to legitimise a false equivalence that not only served the right's attack on anti-racism and trans rights, but was now being aired on yet another high-profile platform.

CONCLUSION

In a media landscape tilting ever increasingly in favour of reactionary forces and interests, it should be of great concern for democracy to see one of the major mainstream centre-left newspapers react so naively and irresponsibly to the culture wars waged by the right. This is not to say of course that there does not remain some solid quality journalism in the *Guardian*, as demonstrated by its investigative reporting in particular and some of its opinion pieces from important, anti-racist contributors such as Nesrine Malik, Gary Younge, Afua Hirsch, Angela Saini and Priyamvada Gopal.

However, in a context where the balance of 'good' and 'bad' opinions has become an apparent norm, the lack of a clear stand on issues such as racism and immigration risks creating some dangerous false equivalences and feeds into the mainstreaming of far-right ideas. As the reactionary hold on the political system tightens and much-needed media reform aimed at providing real democratic dissemination of information appears increasingly unlikely, news outlets like the *Guardian* have a crucial role to play. This rests on a choice between the kind of democracy it wishes to support: a reactionary democracy, where racist, sexist, transphobic and classist voices are afforded the same space as their opponents or a democracy that does not tolerate that the humanity of some can be debated or treated as a matter of discussion.

NOTES

1. *The Guardian* (2020) 'The Guardian View on Colston's Statue: A Long Time in Going', *The Guardian*, 8 June. https://www.theguardian.com/

commentisfree/2020/jun/08/the-guardian-view-on-colstons-statue-a-long-time-in-going (accessed 29 September 2020).

2. Aurelien Mondon and Aaron Winter, *Reactionary Democracy: How Racism and the Populist Far Right Became Mainstream* (London: Verso, 2020); Alana Lentin, *Why Race Still Matters* (Cambridge: Polity, 2020).
3. It is still unclear whether the latest shock to white supremacy will last or whether the hope generated by widespread protests and replicated in countless statements by organisations, both public and private, acknowledging their role in upholding racist hierarchies, will be swallowed up by the news cycle as a new crisis could quickly take our attention away from longer term issues.
4. See amongst others Eduardo Bonilla-Silva, *Racism Without Racists: Color-blind Racism and the Persistence of Racial Inequality in the United States* (New York: Rowman and Littlefield, 2006).
5. Jason Glynos and Aurelien Mondon, 'The political logic of populist hype: The case of right-wing populism's 'meteoric rise' and its relation to the status quo'. In Paolo Cossarini and Fernando Vallespín (eds) *Populism and Passions: Democratic Legitimacy after Austerity* (Abingdon: Routledge, 2019).
6. Katy Brown and Aurelien Mondon, 'Populism, the media and the mainstreaming of the far right: The Guardian's coverage of populism as a case study', *Politics*, online first, 2020.
7. This is composed of any article containing populis* in the year following the start of 'The New Populism' series (20 November 2018-19), in total 1548 articles.
8. Katy Brown, 'When Eurosceptics Become Europhiles: Far-right Opposition to Turkish Involvement in the European Union', *Identities*, 27:6 (2019), pp. 633–54.
9. Simon Hattenstone, '"We're Reactivating the People's Army": Inside the Battle for a Hard Brexit', *Guardian*, 12 January, 2019, https://www.theguardian.com/world/2019/jan/12/were-reactivating-the-peoples-army-inside-the-battle-for-a-hard-brexit (accessed 29 September 2020).
10. Matthijs Rooduijn, 'Why is Populism Suddenly All the rage?', *Guardian*, 20 November, 2018, https://www.theguardian.com/world/political-science/2018/nov/20/why-is-populism-suddenly-so-sexy-the-reasons-are-many (Accessed 25 September 2020).
11. See amongst others: Cass Mudde, *Populist Radical Right Parties in Europe* (Cambridge: Cambridge University Press, 2007); Ernesto Laclau, *On Populist Reason* (London: Verso, 2005).
12. Glynos and Mondon, 'The Political Logic of Populist Hype'.
13. Ibid., p. 84.
14. Maxwell McCombs, *Setting the Agenda: Mass Media and Public Opinion* (London: Wiley, 2014).
15. Annie Collovald, *Le populisme du FN: un dangereux contresens* (Bellecombe-en-Bauges: Ed. du Croquant, 2004).

16. Ibid p. 10.
17. This excludes organisation names, book names and instances with the prefix 'anti-'.
18. Hattenstone, '"We're Reactivating the People's Army"'.
19. Peter C. Baker, '"We the People": The Battle to Define Populism', *Guardian*, 10 January, 2019. https://www.theguardian.com/news/2019/jan/10/we-the-people-the-battle-to-define-populism (accessed 29 September 2020).
20. Hattenstone, '"We're Reactivating the People's Army"'.
21. Gurminder Bhambra, 'Brexit, Trump, and "Methodological Whiteness": On the Misrecognition of Race and Class', *British Journal of Sociology*, 68(S1), (2017), pp. 214–32; Danny Dorling, 'Brexit: The Decision of a Divided Country'. *BMJ*, 354: i3697, 2016; Aurelien Mondon and Aaron Winter, 'Whiteness, Populism and the Racialisation of the Working Class in the United Kingdom and the United States', *Identities*, 26:5 (2018), pp. 510–28.
22. Gordon Brown, 'We Are Becoming a United Kingdom in Name Only: Politicians Must Heal the divide', *Guardian*, 18 November 2019, https://www.theguardian.com/commentisfree/2019/nov/18/gordon-brown-united-kingdom-nationalists-election (accessed 25 September 2020).
23. Simon Jenkins, 'The Churchill Row is Part of the Glib Approach to History that Gave Us Brexit', *Guardian*, 14 February 2019, https://www.theguardian.com/commentisfree/2019/feb/14/winston-churchill-history-brexit-john-mcdonnell (accessed 29 September 2020.
24. Emmy Eklundh, 'Excluding Emotions: The Performative Function of populism', *Partecipazione e Conflitto*, 13:1 (2020), p. 115.
25. Aurelien Mondon and Aaron Winter, 'Auschwitz and Anti-Racism: The Past (and racism) is Another Country', *openDemocracy*. 22 October 2018, https://www.opendemocracy.net/en/opendemocracyuk/auschwitz-and-anti-racism-past-and-racism-is-another-country/ (accessed 25 September 2020).
26. Aurelien Mondon and Aaron Winter, 'Articulations of Islamophobia: from the extreme to the mainstream?', *Ethnic and Racial Studies*, 13:40, (2017), pp. 2151–79.
27. Patrick Wintour, 'Hillary Clinton: Europe Must Curb Immigration to Stop Rightwing Populists', *Guardian*, 22 November 2018, https://www.theguardian.com/world/2018/nov/22/hillary-clinton-europe-must-curb-immigration-stop-populists-trump-brexit (accessed 15 September 2020).
28. Patrick Wintour, 'US Media Must 'Get Smarter' to Tackle Trump, Says Hillary Clinton', *Guardian*, 23 November 2018, https://www.theguardian.com/world/2018/nov/23/hillary-clinton-us-media-must-get-smarter-tackle-trump-threat (accessed 29 September 2020).
29. Paul Mason, 'Liberals Must Learn the Politics of Emotion to Beat Rightwing Populists', *Guardian*, 26 November 2018, https://www.

theguardian.com/commentisfree/2018/nov/26/liberals-politics-emotion-right-wing-populists (accessed 17 September 2020).

30. Julian Borger, 'Samantha Power: "To Fall Flat in such a Public Way and to Have No Job ... I Was a Wandering Person"', *Guardian*, 7 September 2019, https://www.theguardian.com/books/2019/sep/07/samantha-power-former-us-ambassador-un-interview (accessed 17 September 2020).
31. Martin Kettle, 'Parliament Should Use Its Power to Give the Voters Another Say on Brexit', *Guardian*, 5 December 2018, https://www.theguardian.com/commentisfree/2018/dec/05/parliament-brexit-mps-second-referendum (accessed 29 September 2020).
32. Quoted in *Belfast Telegraph*, 'Nigel Farage: I Destroyed Far-Right in British Politics', 12 August 2016, https://www.belfasttelegraph.co.uk/news/uk/nigel-farage-i-destroyed-far-right-in-british-politics-34960630.html (accessed 29 September 2020).
33. Hattenstone, '"We're Reactivating the People's Army"'.
34. Helen Lewis, 'Are You Part of the Dreaded Metropolitan Elite? Do this Quiz and Find Out', *Guardian*, 31 December 2015, https://www.theguardian.com/commentisfree/2015/dec/31/are-you-metropolitan-elite-labour-quiz (accessed 17 September 2020).
35. Luke Cartledge, 'The Left-Behind V the Metropolitan Elite? That's a Lazy, Harmful Cliche', *Guardian*, 12 April 2019, https://www.theguardian.com/commentisfree/2019/apr/12/left-behind-v-metropolitan-elite-harmful-cliche (accessed 17 September 2020).
36. Joan Williams, 'Liberal Elite, it's Time to Strike a Deal with the Working Class', *Guardian,* 23 August 2017, https://www.theguardian.com/commentisfree/2017/aug/23/liberal-elite-its-time-to-strike-a-deal-with-the-working-class (accessed 17 September 2020).
37. Kate Connolly, 'Far-right AfD Surges to Second Place in German State Election', *Guardian,* 27 October 2019, https://www.theguardian.com/world/2019/oct/27/far-right-afd-surges-to-second-place-in-german-state-elections (accessed 29 September 2020). These examples are developed at more length in Brown and Mondon, 'Populism, the Media and the Mainstreaming of the Far Right'.
38. Philip Oltermann, 'AfD Politician Threatens Journalist after Hitler Comparison', *Guardian*, 16 September 2019, www.theguardian.com/world/2019/sep/16/afd-politician-threatens-journalist-hitler-comparison-bjorn-hocke (accessed 5 February 2020).
39. Guy Chazan, 'In East Germany, History Casts a Dark Shadow over the AfD', *Financial Times*, 4 November 2019, www.ft.com/content/76c8e78c-fcbe-11e9-a354-36acbbbod9b6 (accessed 7 February 2020).
40. Arwa Mahdawi, 'When 'Hipster Fascists' Start Appearing in the Media, Something Has Gone Very Wrong', *Guardian*, 22 May 2018, https://www.theguardian.com/commentisfree/2018/may/22/when-the-media-starts-celebrating-hipster-fascists-something-has-gone-very-wrong (accessed 16 September 2020).

41. Joost de Vries, 'Meet Thierry Baudet, the Suave New Face of Dutch Rightwing Populism', *Guardian,* 3 April 2019, https://www.theguardian.com/commentisfree/2019/apr/03/thierry-baudet-dutch-rightwing-populism (accessed 16 September 2020).
42. Hattenstone, "We're Reactivating the People's Army".
43. Brown and Mondon, 'Populism, the Media and the Mainstreaming of the Far Right'.
44. Hattenstone, '"We're Reactivating the People's Army"'.
45. Halliday, J., L. Beckett, and C. Barr (2018) 'Revealed: The Hidden Global Network Behind Tommy Robinson', *The Guardian,* 7 December. https://www.theguardian.com/uk-news/2018/dec/07/tommy-robinson-global-support-brexit-march (accessed 16 September 2020).
46. Josh Halliday, Lois Beckett and Caelainn Barr, 'Tommy Robinson: From Local Loud Mouth to International Far-Right Poster Boy', *Guardian,* 7 December 2018, https://www.theguardian.com/uk-news/2018/dec/07/tommy-robinson-the-us-money-behind-the-far-right-mouthpiece (accessed 16 September 2020).
47. Gavan Titley, *Is Free Speech Racist?* (Cambridge: Polity, 2020).
48. 'A Letter on Justice and Open Debate', *Harper's Magazine,* 7 July 2020, https://harpers.org/a-letter-on-justice-and-open-debate/ (accessed 17 September 2020).
49. Nesrine Malik, Jonathan Freedland, Zoe Williams and Samuel Moyn, 'Is Free Speech Under Threat from 'Cancel Culture'? Four Writers Respond', *Guardian,* 8 July 2020, https://www.theguardian.com/commentisfree/2020/jul/08/is-free-speech-under-threat-cancel-culture-writers-respond (accessed 17 September 2020).

Contributors

Aaron Ackerley is a historian of modern Britain at the University of Sheffield. His research explores the relationship between knowledge and power, particularly the intersections between popular and elite political cultures and the media.

Mike Berry is a Senior Lecturer in Media and Public Understanding at JOMEC, Cardiff University. He has conducted research for a variety of institutions including the BBC Trust, the TUC and the UNHCR, and is the author of several books including *The Media, the Public and the Great Financial Crisis* (Palgrave-Macmillan, 2019) and *Bad News from Israel* (with Greg Philo, Pluto, 2004).

Victoria Brittain worked at the *Guardian* for more than 20 years as a foreign correspondent and then Associate Foreign Editor. She has lived and worked in Saigon, Algiers, Nairobi and reported from many countries in Africa and the Middle East for numerous media outlets in the anglophone and francophone worlds. She is the author, co-author or editor of 10 books and plays including *Love and Resistance in the Films of Mai Masri* (Palgrave-Macmillan, 2020).

Katy Brown is a final-year PhD student at the University of Bath whose research focuses on the mainstreaming of the far right in Europe. Her thesis aims to theorise mainstreaming and analyse the role of elite discourse in this process, using the Brexit referendum as a case study. She has recently had articles published in *Identities: Global Studies in Culture and Power* and (with Aurelien Mondon) in *Politics*.

Mark Curtis is editor of Declassified UK, a media organisation analysing Britain's role in the world. He is the author of five books on British foreign policy, most recently *Secret Affairs: Britain's Collusion with Radical Islam* (Serpent's Tail, 2015). www.markcurtis.info / @markcurtis30

Natalie Fenton is a Professor of Media and Communications at Goldsmiths, University of London. She has published widely on issues relating to media and democracy including the books: *New Media, Old News: Journalism and Democracy in the Digital Age* (Sage, 2010); *Misunderstanding the Internet* (with James Curran and Des Freedman, Routledge, 2012); *Digital, Political Radical* (Wiley, 2016); *The Media Manifesto* (with

Des Freedman, Justin Schlosberg and Lina Dencik, Wiley, 2020) and *Media, Democracy and Social Change: Reimagining Political Communications* (with Aeron Davis, Des Freedman and Gholam Khiabany, Sage, 2020). She was vice chair of the campaign group Hacked Off for seven years and is currently chair of the Media Reform Coalition.

Des Freedman is a Professor of Media and Communications at Goldsmiths, University of London. He is the author of several books including *The Contradictions of Media Power* (Bloomsbury, 2014) and *The Media Manifesto* (with Natalie Fenton, Justin Schlosberg and Lina Dencik, Wiley, 2020) and is one of the founding members of the Media Reform Coalition.

Hannah Hamad is Senior Lecturer in Media and Communication at Cardiff University, School of Journalism, Media and Culture. She is the author of *Postfeminism and Paternity in Contemporary US Film: Framing Fatherhood* (Routledge, 2014), and *Film, Feminism and Rape Culture in the Yorkshire Ripper Years* (Bloomsbury/BFI, forthcoming 2023).

Ghada Karmi is a Palestinian physician, academic and writer. She is a former research fellow and lecturer at the University of Exeter, and a longstanding political activist on Palestine. Amongst her best-known publications is her memoir, *In Search of Fatima*, (Verso, 2002); a political analysis of the one-state solution, *Married to Another Man: Israel's Dilemma in Palestine* (Pluto, 2007); and a second memoir, *Return* (Verso, 2015).

Jilly Boyce Kay is a Lecturer in Media and Communication at the University of Leicester. She is author of *Gender, Media and Voice: Communicative Injustice and Public Speech* (Palgrave, 2020) and has published widely on the relationship between feminism and media culture. She is founding editor of the 'Cultural Commons' short-form section in the *European Journal of Cultural Studies*.

Matt Kennard is co-founder and head of investigations at Declassified UK. He was previously director of the Centre for Investigative Journalism and a staff reporter for the *Financial Times* in the US and UK. He is the author of *Irregular Army* (Verso, 2012) and *The Racket* (ZED, 2015).

Alan MacLeod is a member of the Glasgow University Media Group. After completing his PhD in 2017 he published two books: *Bad News from Venezuela* (Routledge, 2018) and *Propaganda in the Information Age: Still Manufacturing Consent* (Routledge, 2019). He is currently senior staff writer at *MintPress News* and a contributor to Fairness and Accuracy in Reporting.

Tom Mills is Lecturer in Sociology at Aston University. He is the author of *The BBC: Myth of a Public Service* (Verso, 2016) and the vice chair of the Media Reform Coalition.

Aurelien Mondon is a Senior Lecturer in Politics at the University of Bath. He is the author of *The Mainstreaming of the Extreme Right in France and Australia: A Populist Hegemony?* (Routledge, 2013) and *Reactionary Democracy: How Racism and the Populist Far Right Became Mainstream* (with Aaron Winter, Verso, 2020).

Mareile Pfannebecker is a writer and translator living in Manchester. She is the co-author of *Work Want Work: Labour and Desire at the End of Capitalism* (with J. A. Smith, ZED, 2020).

Justin Schlosberg is Senior Lecturer in Journalism and Media at Birkbeck, University of London. He is a former Chair of the Media Reform Coalition and Edmund J. Safra Network Fellow at Harvard University. He is the author or co-author of several books about the media including *Media Ownership and Agenda Control* (Routledge, 2016) and *Bad News for Labour* (with Greg Philo, Mike Berry, Anthony Lerman and David Miller, Pluto, 2019).

Mike Wayne is a Professor of Film and Media at Brunel University. He writes widely on film, media, politics, class and Marxist cultural theory. His most recent monographs are: *Marxism Goes To The Movies* (Routledge, 2020) and *England's Discontents: Political Cultures and National Identities* (Pluto, 2018). He has co-directed several documentary feature films including (with Deirdre O'Neill) *The Acting Class* (2017).

Aaron Winter is Senior Lecturer in Criminology at the University of East London. He is co-editor of *Reflexivity in Criminological Research: Experiences with the Powerful and Powerless* (Palgrave, 2014) and *Historical Perspectives on Organised Crime and Terrorism* (Routledge, 2018) and co-author, with Aurelien Mondon, of *Reactionary Democracy: How Racism and the Populist Far Right Became Mainstream* (Verso, 2020).

Gary Younge is a Professor of Sociology at the University of Manchester, the former editor-at-large for the *Guardian*, a Type Media Fellow and an editorial board member of the *Nation* magazine. He has written five books, most recently, *Another Day in the Death of America* (Nation Books, 2016).

Index